INTERNATIONAL PRODUCTIVITY DIFFERENCES

CONTRIBUTIONS

TO

ECONOMIC ANALYSIS

233

Honorary Editor:
J. TINBERGEN†

Editors:
D. W. JORGENSON
J. -J. LAFFONT
T. PERSSON
H. K. VAN DIJK

ELSEVIER
Amsterdam – Lausanne – New York – Oxford – Shannon – Tokyo

INTERNATIONAL PRODUCTIVITY DIFFERENCES

Measurement and Explanations

Edited by

KARIN WAGNER
Wissenschaftszentrum Berlin für Sozialforschung
and
Fachhochschule für Technik und Wirtschaft Berlin
Germany

BART VAN ARK
Groningen Growth and Development Centre
University of Groningen
The Netherlands

1996

ELSEVIER
Amsterdam – Lausanne – New York – Oxford – Shannon – Tokyo

ELSEVIER SCIENCE B.V.
Sara Burgerhartstraat 25
P.O. Box 521, 1000 AM Amsterdam, The Netherlands

Library of Congress Cataloging-in-Publication Data

International productivity differences : measurement and explanations
/ edited by Karin Wagner, Bart van Ark.
      p.   cm. -- (Contributions to economic analysis ; 233)
    "Most of the papers in this volume were presented at a conference
on 'International productivity differences and their explanations'
at the Science Center Berlin in November 1993"--Ackn.
    Includes bibliographical references and index.
    ISBN 0-444-82417-0
    1. Industrial productivity--Congresses.   I. Wagner, Karin.
II. Ark, Bart van.   III. Series.
HC79.I52I62   1996
338'.06--dc20
                                                                96-10692
                                                                   CIP

ISBN: 0 444 82417 0

This book is printed on acid-free paper.

PRINTED IN THE NETHERLANDS

INTRODUCTION TO THE SERIES

This series consists of a number of hitherto unpublished studies, which are introduced by the editors in the belief that they represent fresh contributions to economic science.

The term "economic analysis" as used in the title of the series has been adopted because it covers both the activities of the theoretical economist and the research worker.

Although the analytical methods used by the various contributors are not the same, they are nevertheless conditioned by the common origin of their studies, namely theoretical problems encountered in practical research. Since for this reason, business cycle research and national accounting, research work on behalf of economic policy, and problems of planning are the main sources of the subjects dealt with, they necessarily determine the manner of approach adopted by the authors. Their methods tend to be "practical" in the sense of not being too far remote from application to actual economic conditions. In additon they are quantitative.

It is the hope of the editors that the publication of these studies will help to stimulate the exchange of scientific information and to reinforce international cooperation in the field of economics.

The Editors

Acknowledgments

Most of the papers in this volume were presented at a conference on "International Productivity Differences and their Explanations" at the Science Center Berlin in November 1993. The workshop was held at the research unit "Economic Change and Employment". We are grateful to the unit's director, David Soskice, for his support and to Ilona Köhler who assisted in organising the conference.

Many valuable comments given by discussants and participants have been processed in the final version of the papers. In this respect we wish to thank in particular Bernd Görzig, Lennart Hjalmarsson and Nick Oulton for their very detailed comments. We also benefitted from the suggestions by an anonymous referee for improving the balance between the papers in this volume.

In processing the final manuscript we received assistance from Remco Kouwenhoven and Ruppert Matzke in editing some of the graphs. We gratefully acknowledge Peter Groote for preparing the index. Last but not least we thank Agnes Cazemier, Elvira Groenewoud and Monique Tjiong, who were of great help in preparing the camera ready copy of this volume.

Berlin/Groningen, December 1995

Karin Wagner
Bart van Ark

Contents

International Productivity Differences
K. Wagner and B. van Ark (editors)
© 1996 Elsevier Science B.V. All rights reserved.

Introduction

*K. Wagner** and B. van Ark*****
* *Wissenschaftszentrum Berlin für Sozialforschung and Fachhochschule
für Technik und Wirtschaft Berlin*
** *Groningen Growth and Development Centre, University of Groningen**

1. The Importance of Productivity Studies

In the past decade productivity has received renewed attention from economists,
policy makers, business leaders and industry analysts. By the early 1970s the
"golden age" of rapid postwar productivity growth in most advanced countries
had come to an end. As table 1 shows, for five of the core countries in the
western world there has been no significant acceleration in labour productivity
growth since then. In manufacturing, Britain experienced renewed productivity
growth during the 1980s and early 1990s, but in the other countries productivity
growth in manufacturing did not accelerate either. These persistently lower
growth rates compared to the period 1950-73 have therefore become a matter of
major concern from an analytical as well as a policy point of view. The
globalisation of the world economy in terms of interdependencies between
countries in terms of trade and capital movements makes a careful study of
productivity in an international comparative perspective increasingly important.

TABLE 1
**Annual Compound Growth Rates of Value Added per Hour Worked
in Manufacturing and in the Total Economy, 1950-1994.**

	Total Economy			Manufacturing		
	1950-73	1973-87	1987-94	1950-73	1973-87	1987-94
Germany (Fed. Rep.)	6.0	2.5	3.2	6.9	2.7	2.8
France	5.0	3.1	1.7	5.7	3.5	3.4
Japan	7.7	3.0	2.6	9.4	4.8	4.1
United Kingdom	3.1	2.4	1.9	4.2	3.2	4.9
United States	2.7	1.1	1.0	2.8	2.5	2.3

Total economy from Maddison (1991, 1995); Manufacturing: see chapter by van Ark.

---

* We are grateful to Bronwyn Hall, Angus Maddison, Mary O'Mahony and Dirk Pilat
for their comments on an earlier draft.

This book represents a collection of papers which deal with the measurement and explanation of productivity in an international comparative perspective. The bulk of the papers were presented at a seminar on this topic, which was organised by the Wissenschaftszentrum Berlin für Sozialforschung (WZB) in November 1993. Following the seminar some additional papers were invited in order to produce a book which gives a broad overview of the "state of the art" in the field of international productivity studies.

International comparisons of growth performance and levels of productivity have a wide range of analytical applications. At the macro level, such estimates contribute to our understanding of differences in standards of living. Estimates of comparative per capita income can be adjusted for differences in labour force participation rates (the ratio of persons engaged to the population) and annual hours per employee across countries to obtain relative levels of labour productivity. Productivity estimates are an important ingredient of studies which aim to quantify the contribution of factor inputs, technology and other variables to differences in growth or levels of GDP across countries.[1]

Productivity level estimates are also an essential input for testing the catch-up and convergence hypothesis, which has caught much attention in recent years. In its simplest version this hypothesis suggests that a country with a low starting level of productivity compared to a country which is at the productivity frontier, is likely to show relatively rapid productivity growth in subsequent periods. The follower country can benefit from the diffusion of technological and institutional innovations from the country which has adopted the best practice.[2]

At the meso level, productivity studies focus on the comparative performance of sectors and industries. Such studies provide a major tool to analyse the strengths and weaknesses of a country's industrial structure, to assess the competitive strength of each of these industries and to explore the causal factors behind the productivity gaps between countries by industry.[3]

Even at the micro level, productivity is a measure of significant interest for individual firms and companies, in particular when comparisons can be narrowed down to a clearly specified range of similar products, so that differences in productivity are not affected by variation in product composition.[4]

The emphasis in this book is primarily on the meso level. The papers concentrate on measuring and explaining the comparative performance by sector

---

[1]   See, for example, Denison (1967) and Maddison (1987, 1991, 1995).

[2]   See Baumol, Nelson and Wolff (1994) and van Ark and Crafts (1996) for an explicit treatment of productivity issues in a catch-up and convergence framework.

[3]   See Dollar and Wolff (1993), Pilat (1994) and van Ark (1993, 1996) for studies of comparative productivity at sector and industry level.

[4]   See matched plant comparisons such as those by Daly, Hitchens and Wagner (1985), Steedman and Wagner (1989), Hitchens, Wagner and Birnie (1990, 1993) and Mason, van Ark and Wagner (1994).

(for example, agriculture or manufacturing), branch (for example, chemicals or rail transport) or industry (for example, paints or motor vehicles). Some papers also make links to the macro level (for example, Pilat and Kuroda), whereas others make a connection to the micro level (for example, Hitchens, Wagner and Birnie; and Gersbach and Baily).

Productivity is essentially a concept for analysis in the long term. In the short term, labour productivity measures can be volatile in particular at a disaggregated level, as they are strongly affected by the business cycle and shifts in product composition due to competitive pressures. Furthermore, policies to enhance productivity usually only show significant effects in the long run.[5] With the exception of two of the more micro-oriented papers (Hitchens, Wagner and Birnie; and Gersbach and Baily), the papers in this book all cover at least two decades up to half a century.

All papers in this book deal extensively with labour productivity, which is output per unit of labour input. Labour productivity is a "single factor productivity" or "partial productivity" concept. The growth rate or level can be higher in one country compared to another either because the two countries use different combinations of factor inputs, or because one country uses one or more of the factor inputs more efficiently than the other country.

A proxy for efficiency can be obtained by measuring multifactor productivity, which is real value added per composite unit of labour and capital. Such measures are used in the papers in this volume by Freudenberg and Ünal-Kesenci, Kuroda, O'Mahony and Wagner, and Pilat. Even the comparative level of multifactor productivity is not an exact indicator of differences in efficiency between two countries. Firstly, not only the quantity but also the quality of the production factors between countries needs to be taken into account. For labour one can distinguish between quality characteristics such as the level of education or the quality of the management. The quality of the capital stock, i.e. the degree of technology embodied in physical investment, can be determined by the age-distribution of the assets in the stock.

A second reason why joint factor productivity is not synonymous with efficiency is that the former still includes a variety of other factors. In growth accounting, multifactor productivity is mostly interpreted as a residual, which needs to be further decomposed into factors which influence efficiency. Examples of such factors are differences in scale advantages, the openness of the economy to international trade, the extent of structural change and institutional differences related to legal and political factors.

In micro-economic terms one can distinguish between allocative efficiency, which focuses on the allocation of scarce resources given their relative prices, and technical efficiency, which concentrates on the amount of output which is

---

[5]   See Baumol, Blackman and Wolff (1989).

achieved with a given distribution of resources. From a productivity perspective, technical efficiency is the more interesting concept as it concentrates on the distance between average and best practice. The productivity measures in this book mostly relate to the average efficiency and do not distinguish between technical and allocative. The more micro-oriented papers by Hitchens, Wagner and Birnie and by Gersbach and Baily provide additional insight into the explanations for differences in efficiency due to firm size, openness to trade, obsolete technology, work and management organisation and skills of the labour force.

Another concept which is closely related to productivity is competitiveness. Competitiveness relates not only to comparative performance in real terms, but also to the relative costs at which products are manufactured and sold. Such costs are not only determined by the prices of factor inputs, but also by those of intermediate inputs and by the exchange value of a country's currency. For example, in the short term a devaluation of the currency makes a country more competitive but not more productive. In fact devaluation may make a country less productive in the long term as pressure for further productivity gains may weaken. Competitiveness is also determined by factors such as customisation of products, after-sales services and quality aspects. These are not easily reflected in the productivity measures. The papers by van Ark, Freudenberg and Ünal-Kesenci, Kuroda, Birnie and Gersbach and Baily pay explicit attention to the relation between productivity and competitiveness.

In terms of geographical coverage the papers in this book focus mainly on the five large industrialized nations, the Federal Republic of Germany, France, Japan, United Kingdom and the United States. In addition the paper by Hitchens, Wagner and Birnie deals with former East Germany vis-à-vis West Germany and the paper by Birnie on Ireland versus the United Kingdom. The paper by van Ark also refers to productivity estimates for other countries, including Brazil, Czechoslovakia, India, Korea, the Netherlands, Portugal and Spain. A main purpose of this collection of articles is to provide the framework for and to stimulate further research along these lines for other countries in the OECD area, East European countries in transition and countries in the developing world.

In the remainder of this introduction, we will briefly assess the main approaches towards the measurement (section 2) and explanation (section 3) of productivity in an international comparative perspective. In section 4 we will summarise the main explanatory factors, and in the final section we outline some major points for a future research agenda on productivity.

2. Approaches to Productivity Measurement

This book represents a range of different approaches to productivity measurement in a comparative framework, which one may classify into three groups: (1) statistical comparisons of growth rates; (2) statistical comparisons of relative levels; and (3) productivity case studies.

The approach which has mostly been used in the past, and which can also be traced in most of the papers in this volume, concerns the comparison of productivity growth rates. However, international comparative studies of productivity are seriously deficient if they do not also include estimates of comparative levels productivity, which give an insight into the size of the productivity gaps between countries.

Therefore the second group of productivity measures in this volume concerns statistical measures of relative levels of real output and productivity. One of the major features of this volume is that almost all papers include measures of relative productivity levels. The paper by van Ark on comparisons of manufacturing productivity and competitiveness across five advanced nations (France, Germany, Japan, the UK and the USA), following this introduction, briefly describes the methodology used in studies within the framework of the International Comparisons of Output and Productivity Project (ICOP) at the University of Groningen. The subsequent papers by O'Mahony and Wagner (Germany/UK), Birnie (Ireland/UK), Freudenberg and Ünal-Kesenci (France/Germany), Pilat (Japan/USA) and Gersbach and Baily (Germany, Japan and the USA) all use ICOP-type procedures to measure relative productivity levels.

The crucial ingredient of these "industry of origin" studies is the calculation of industry-purchasing power parities, or unit value ratios, to convert the output value in different countries to the same currency. It needs to be emphasised that this approach is not without problems. Firstly, the unit value ratios are based on a limited sample of products, and rather farreaching assumptions are employed concerning their representativity for non-measured price relatives. Secondly the unit value ratios may be insufficiently adjusted for differences in product mix and product quality across countries. The paper by Gersbach and Baily includes important adjustments to the original UVRs for some industries, in particular in the investment goods sector, to catch differences in product quality between German, Japanese and US manufacturing. Gersbach and van Ark (1994) have shown that although such adjustments are necessary for comparisons at the disaggregated industry level, there were no significant systematic biases in the estimates to be observed at more aggregate levels such as major groups of branches in manufacturing or the manufacturing sector as a whole. Freudenberg and Ünal-Kesenci consider the possibility that the slight French productivity advantage over German manufacturing could be explained by higher quality of German products, but they conclude that their UVRs are mostly not biased in relation to the higher value added content of German manufacturing output. Thirdly, ideally industry of origin studies should be double deflated, which implies that separate PPPs are required for output and intermediate inputs so that value added is obtained as the difference between gross output (converted to a common currency at output PPPs) and intermediate inputs (converted to a common currency at input PPPs). Most papers in this volume employ a single deflation procedure, i.e. they use UVRs for gross output to compare value added. Only the paper by Kuroda calculates separate PPPs (though based on expenditure PPPs) for Japan vis-à-vis the USA for intermediate inputs, energy inputs and capital and labour inputs.

Table 2 shows the estimates of the ratio of value added per person employed in manufacturing in 1987 according to the "industry of origin" approach for a wide range of countries at different income levels, including all the countries dealt with in this book. "Industry of origin" comparisons of productivity are mostly of a binary nature. This raises the problem of possible intransitivity of the results between three or more countries. For example, the two binary comparisons reported by van Ark between France and the USA (71.2 per cent) and Germany and the USA (70.2 per cent) suggest a smaller productivity gap between France and Germany (1.4 per cent) than the direct comparison between the latter two countries by Freudenberg and Ünal-Kesenci (9.3 per cent). Such differences are largely caused by differences in the product sample from which the UVRs are derived. Multilateral procedures such as those used in expenditure PPP studies by OECD and EUROSTAT, which make use of the weights of all countries in a comparison, tackle this problem but are problematic to apply for industry comparisons.[6] However, an advantage of binary comparisons is that the "country characteristicy" of the samples used for each binary comparison is improved, which suggests that the best comparison for each pair of countries is a direct comparison.

An alternative approach to the ICOP method is applied by Kuroda, who makes use of multilateral expenditure PPPs which were allocated to 29 branches in the economy. He also adjusted these PPPs by, what he calls, "peeling off" indirect taxes and transport and trade margins. However, in comparison to the approach described above, the limitations of these proxy PPPs are that there are no separate PPPs for intermediate goods, and that these PPPs are not adjusted for the prices of imports (which need to be taken out) and the prices of exports (which need to be included).

Table 2 compares manufacturing productivity in terms of value added per person employed. In most papers these estimates are further adjusted for differences in annual working hours across countries. This leads to a downward adjustment of the productivity performance in the low income countries and Japan compared to the United States and an upward adjustment of productivity levels in the European countries. The most extreme cases are Korea and the Netherlands, where annual working hours in manufacturing amounted to 2,758

---

[6]   See Pilat and Prasada Rao (1991) and Pilat (1994) for experimentation with multilaterally based "industry of origin" PPPs. The major problem in multiterilising such comparisons at the most disaggregate level, i.e. the product level, is that there is not a common product sample available for each of the countries.

TABLE 2

Comparative Levels of Value Added per Person Employed in Manufacturing, 1987, as a % of the USA, West Germany and the UK

	United States = 100.0	West Germany = 100.0	United Kingdom = 100.0
India	*7.2*	10.3	13.5
East Germany	22.5	*32.0*	41.9
Czechoslovakia	23.9	*34.0*	44.6
Portugal	24.5	34.9	*45.7*
Korea	*26.3*	37.5	49.1
Brazil	*30.7*	43.7	57.3
Spain	46.4	66.2	*86.7*
United Kingdom	*53.6*	*88.7*	100.0
West Germany	*70.2*	100.0	*112.7*
France	*71.2*	*109.3*	133.0[a]
Ireland	73.4	104.6	*137.0*
Japan	*76.4*	108.9	142.7
Netherlands	*83.5*	118.7	155.6
United States	100.0	*142.5*	*186.7*

[a] derived inferentially from the France/US and UK/US binary comparisons.
Note: Countries are ranked according to their relative productivity to the USA in 1987. The estimates which are underlined are based on the actual binary comparisons and represent the geometric average of the estimate at weights of the numerator country and that at weights of the denominator country. The others are derived inferentially.
Source: Germany/UK from O'Mahony and Wagner; France/Germany from Freudenberg and Ünal-Kesenci; Ireland/UK from Birnie; other estimates are ICOP estimates: see van Ark (1993, 1996), Maddison and van Ark (1994) and Pilat (1994).

hours and 1,511 hours respectively, compared to 1,908 hours in US manufacturing in 1987.

The third approach to estimate relative productivity levels in this volume compares the productivity of plants producing similar products across countries. Complementary to the statistical approach, this approach is particularly useful when the quality and comparability of the statistical material is weak, as for example in the East-West Germany comparison by Hitchens, Wagner and Birnie. The approach makes it possible to make more exact product matches than in the statistical approach, to obtain physical productivity measures and to assess the role of quality differentials in more detail. In addition, as will be discussed in more detail below, the matched plant method contributes very significantly to the analysis of the sources of productivity differentials.

A major disadvantage of the case study approach, however, is that the sample of firms on which the analysis is based is necessarily small, that the representation of small and large firms is not always adequate, and that in exceptional circumstances no comparable plants in both countries can be obtained. The case study and the statistical approaches to productivity level comparisons therefore need to be seen as complementary. The former method, which has the advantage of greater detail and disaggregation, is counterbalanced by the more comprehensive nature of the latter method. The detailed analysis in the paper by Gersbach and Baily of the impact of quality differences on product prices is a good example of the virtues of a dual approach to obtain productivity measures at the meso level.

3. Approaches to Explain Productivity Differences

Parallel to the different approaches to measuring productivity, one can also distinguish a variety of approaches which analyse the reasons for differences in productivity. Again one can crudely distinguish, as above, between the statistical method and the case study method. Together the two approaches provide a fairly comprehensive view on the determinants of international productivity differences at the meso level.

The statistical approach largely originates from growth accounting techniques as pioneered for international comparative purposes by Denison (1967). In comparing productivity levels, the impact of differences in relative levels of physical and human capital, the relative size of firms, and the effect of differences in sectoral composition on the productivity differences is quantified.[7] This "level accounting" approach was applied in the papers by Pilat and Kuroda on Japan and the United States and by Freudenberg and Ünal-Kesenci on France and Germany. The paper by O'Mahony and Wagner on Germany and the UK measures the impact of these factors on comparative growth rates as well as levels on the basis of regression analysis.

In recent years the traditional growth accounting approach has been reconsidered in the light of new approaches to the modelling of economic growth. In the past technological progress was mainly treated as exogenous and could best be explained in terms of the diffusion of technology from productivity leaders to productivity followers. The main point of the "new growth" theorists is that technology needs to be treated at least partly as endogenous to the growth process because of learning effects to capital accumulation, in particular when one widens the concept of capital to include physical as well as human capital, i.e. education and knowledge. The argument then goes that, as the social value from accumulation of "broad" capital exceeds the private marginal product,

---

[7]   For a comprehensive overview of the technique of and problems in level accounting, see van Ark (1993, 1996).

capital may be characterised by constant or increasing scale effects instead of by diminishing returns as in the traditional growth theory.[8]

In fact many of the ideas of the "new" growth theory are not really new. Earlier growth accountants and productivity analysts had already taken many of them on board, in particular as far as the role of schooling, the impact of scale effects from firm size and markets and the effect of R&D expenditures on productivity are concerned (see, also the papers by Pilat, O'Mahony and Wagner, and Mairesse and Hall).

The real novelty of the recent contributions to growth analysis lies in its emphasis on modelling these ideas and directing the attention to the meso- and micro-level which complement the macro-approach in growth- and level accounting. However, the evidence on large increasing returns from broad capital on productivity seems not very strong in statistical studies.[9]

Despite the achievements, the statistical analysis concentrates on the quantitative relation between various factors and productivity performance. It is not so easy to explain with this approach *how* these relations arise and by what means they influence productivity. For example, with statistical methods one can measure the quantitative contribution of physical capital to productivity, but it is not possible to infer from that result whether an increase in investment affects productivity through changes in the age of the stock, a rise in embodied technology, a better utilisation of machinery, a different type of work organisation on the shopfloor, the production of better marketable products or a combination of these factors.

In their paper reporting on the results of a study by the McKinsey Global Institute of productivity in twelve manufacturing industries in Germany, Japan and the USA, Gersbach and Baily provide an assessment of some qualitative explanations behind differences in human and physical capital endowments.[10] Their explanations provide support the statistical analysis which is characteristic of many other chapters in this book (van Ark, Freudenberg and Ünal-Kesenci, Birnie, Kuroda, O'Mahony and Wagner, Pilat).

Case studies, or more specifically matched plant studies, are particularly informative when phases of transition are analysed, during which the statistical information hides much of the underlying reasons for the observed differences. While statistical analysis clearly shows that the amount of physical capital per person in East Germany is much lower than in West Germany[11], the paper by

---

[8] For an overview of recent contributions to growth theory, see special issues on this topic in *The Quarterly Journal of Economics* (May 1991 and May 1994) and *The Journal of Economic Perspectives* (vol. 8, no. 1).

[9] See, for example, the papers in van Ark and Crafts (1996).

[10] The next section deals more specifically with the most important causal factors explaining productivity differences

[11] See, for example, Görzig and Gornig (1991).

Hitchens, Wagner and Birnie tries to answer specific questions with respect to the type of technologies which have been used and the flexibility of production processes. By interviewing managers they provide an estimate of the percentage of capital stock which will still be usuable under wage parity with West Germany.

Where case studies were not available to interpret results from statistical work, additional background information has been provided in many papers to explain productivity differences in more detail and to take account of efficiency issues as described in section 1 above. Non-technical factors also receive attention in some papers. Pilat, for example, explains the surprisingly large Japanese productivity gap in the distribution sector in comparison to the US by differences in legal and social arrangements. Birnie focusses on the impact of corporate tax regulations to explain the relatively high productivity level in Irish manufacturing.

4. Causal Factors Explaining Productivity Differences

Physical capital intensity and growth

In all cross-country comparisons physical capital intensity is a major factor explaining differentials in labour productivity. Thus in the study by O'Mahony and Wagner the greater part of the productivity gap in manufacturing between Britain and Germany at the aggregate level is explained by the higher physical capital intensity in Germany. In all subperiods the growth in fixed capital intensity was positively correlated with labour productivity although the impact of differences in capital intensity on labour productivity was decreasing between 1979 and 1989. Cross section correlations of capital intensity growth in German and UK industries were largely insignificant so that the two countries have not generally experienced similar cross industry patterns of investment.

A similar result pointing at capital input as a major source of productivity growth, but again with declining importance over time, was found by Kuroda and by Pilat for the Japan/US comparison. In the France/Germany comparison, Freudenberg and Ünal-Kesenci estimate capital/labour ratios in French manufacturing to be 21 per point higher than in Germany, accounting for almost two thirds of the 9 percentage points labour productivity advantage in French manufacturing.

The case study comparisons by Gersbach and Baily and by Hitchens, Wagner and Birnie not only show differences in the amount of capital stock per worker across countries, but also examine a wide variety of related factors. Gersbach and Baily emphasise the importance of the mix of frontier and obsolete techniques in explaining productivity differentials. Although the amount of capital per unit of output can be very similar for modern and standard equipment, the resulting labour productivity and efficiency can be vastly different. An explicit example is the introduction of minimills in the steel industry in Japan and the United States, which perform at lower capital-output ratios than large steelmills but achieve a much better productivity performance.

The study of West and East German matched plants by Hitchens, Wagner and Birnie includes a detailed analysis of the quality of machine stock according to type, age, origin and technology of machinery. It suggests that the relatively low level of capital intensity in East German plants is less important in explaining lower productivity levels than the more obsolete technology embodied in equipment from East German origin. In 1991, East German managers regarded the shift to machines with western technology as the most important potential source of productivity growth. Hitchens, Wagner and Birnie also point to the huge impact of the fall in capacity utilisation on the productivity performance during the transition period.

Human capital: training and education

Although the statistical analysis suggests that human capital has a less significant impact on productivity than physical capital it nevertheless is a very important factor which is also relatively receptive for policy objectives. As in the case of physical capital, the causal relationship is not only from skills to growth but also the other way around. Growth itself usually takes place in those sectors where the demand for advanced qualifications of the labour force is relatively high.

In measuring the impact of human capital on productivity growth, the quality of labour needs to be measured. This does not only depend on the average number of years of general and vocational education, but also on the type and nature of schooling and in-company training. These vary substantially among countries and might lead to widely different quality levels of human capital.

For Britain and Germany some assessments of comparative qualifications already exist.[12] On the basis of these comparisons O'Mahony and Wagner split the vocational qualifications of the labour force into three levels: those with less than two years of formal training (unqualified), those with at least two years of formal training but without a degree (intermediate qualifications) and those with a degree or equivalent (higher qualifications). For both countries they show that the proportion of the labour force without vocational skills is negatively correlated with productivity growth between 1960 and 1989. A differentiation between intermediate skills and higher skills shows for all sub-periods a positive contribution of higher skills. Furthermore for the period between 1979 and 1989, the change in skills was measured as well. This again showed a significantly negative relation between the rise in the proportion of unskilled workers and labour productivity.

---

[12] See Prais and Wagner (1983, 1985) and Steedman, Mason and Wagner (1991).

Hitchens, Wagner and Birnie use a similar scheme of skill levels in their matched plant comparison to test the quality differences between formally equivalent qualifications in East and West Germany. Due to prevailing production methods and difficulties in getting access to West German technology in previous times, Hitchens, Wagner and Birnie find a degradation of the formal qualifications in the East relative to those in the West. On the basis of interviews the authors analyse skill deficiencies and recommend what kind of upgrading of competences is needed to bring the skills of Eastern employees up to Western training standards. Many of these results appear valid for other Eastern European nations as well (see Hitchens, Birnie, Hamar, Wagner and Zemplinerova, 1995).

Pilat uses attainment levels of the labour force in general schooling (excluding vocational training) as an indicator of the quality of human capital. With this measure the quality of the Japanese labour force was found to be similar to the US level. The strong Japanese emphasis on training in the workplace has been neglected in this method. However, as the Japanese labour force already reaches the US level of qualifications without an adjustment for on-the-job training, differences in skill levels have no direct role in explaining why the US is ahead of Japan in terms of the average productivity level.

Gersbach and Baily found relatively little impact of differences in pre-hiring skills of production workers on the productivity performance of manufacturing firms in Germany, Japan and the United States. However, this was mainly exemplified by a comparison of skills in Japanese firms and their transplants in the US. Furthermore, the sample of industries in the study by Gersbach and Baily is dominated by fairly mature industries, operating in slowly growing or stable markets, which hire relatively few new workers. For small, high-tech or rapidly growing manufacturing industries, the pool of skilled labour available may be of much greater importance. Nevertheless, Gersbach and Baily emphasise that training by the firms themselves is of great importance given the distinct impact on productivity of organisation of functions and tasks as well as multi-skilling. They also recognise strong consequences for productivity from the Japanese ability to create product designs which are easier to manufacture.

Human capital: management and work organisation

Although the organisation of functions and tasks within firms cannot be seen as entirely distinct from training and education, both case studies in this volume put much emphasis on this factor so that it deserves a separate mentioning.

Under the heading "organisation of function and tasks", Gersbach and Baily not only refer to the optimisation of time and motion in the production process (such as in just-in-time delivery systems and lean production), but also to the organisation of work and the management structure. For instance, delegation of responsibilities, such as production worker empowerment and systems where suggestions for product improvements are directly implemented, are seen as having a direct positive influence on productivity.

Work organisation also plays an essential role in the comparison of West and East German matched plants by Hitchens, Wagner and Birnie. Simple reorganisation of work by Western managers has resulted in East German productivity gains of a third of the previous level.

Human capital: knowledge

The third element of human capital, which also features prominently in recent versions of "new growth" models, concerns knowledge not directly embodied in labour. Knowledge is still measured in an imperfect manner, i.e. either by input measures such as the expenditure on research and development or by output measures such as patents of which the actual "technology content" is very difficult to determine due to different patenting practices over time and across countries.

The increased attention to technology is understandable from a policy perspective given the recognition of the much higher social than private returns on R&D. Furthermore the technology indicators suggest a significant fall in the ratio of patents to R&D expenditure since the mid 1970s.[13] This could imply that the productivity slowdown in advanced nations since the mid 1970s may be traced to a retardation in technological progress.

The impact of research and development on productivity is extremely difficult to establish. In comparing R&D data at firm level between France and the USA, Mairesse and Hall investigate a range of important methodological problems in using firm data for estimating the productivity of R&D, among which are the effects of regressing sales instead of value added on R&D and the problem of simultaneity between the accumulation of R&D capital and the output measures.

In accordance with previous studies, Mairesse and Hall find a small but positive effect of R&D on productivity growth. They measured the R&D elasticity, i.e. the percentage rise in the stock of R&D to obtain a one percentage rise in productivity, at about 0.09 per cent in France and about 0.04 per cent in the United States between 1981 and 1989. These estimates of R&D elasticity (in particular for the USA) are slightly lower than for the 1970s in both countries. Among other things this may be due to lower returns on R&D at the firm level when the growth in R&D expenditures stagnates. Mairesse and Hall also observe some huge positive effects of R&D on productivity for industries for which substantial quality adjustments have been taken into account (such as computers in the USA). These positive effects are not visible from a growth in sales value within the industry. This suggests that much of the recent effects of R&D have been very productive, but that most of the gains have gone to the consumer in

---

[13] See for an overview, Griliches (1994).

the form of lower prices.

For the Germany/UK comparison, O'Mahony and Wagner find a large variance of R&D intensity between industries in each country. Between countries a high cross-industry correlation between R&D and productivity can be shown as R&D is concentrated in a small number of industries. Pilat provides an account of differences in the institutional framework of US and Japanese research efforts. Japanese research has greatly benefitted from technology diffusion in particular from the United States. Its R&D efforts has been more focused on applied research and less on basic science. However, Pilat emphasises that technology spillovers are not instantaneous. In particular since Japan has become the productivity leader in some industries, domestic R&D efforts remain necessary to stimulate productivity growth any further.

Product quality, globalisation and competition

The papers by Gersbach and Baily and by Hitchens, Wagner and Birnie emphasise the importance of product quality in productivity studies. As discussed above, this factor is not satisfactorily captured in the statistical studies. Quality does not only include technical specifications of products (which can at least to some extent be measured) but also the effects of mix of varieties, consumer taste and after sales services. In fact the latter factors have become increasingly important in international competition.

The internationalisation of product markets has put pressure on firms to provide a wider range of varieties of products at low costs. Industries with a large range of product varieties may experience productivity shortfalls because of small production runs and a rise in machine set-ups unless they invest substantially in small-batch machinery and adopt more flexible working methods. Gersbach and Baily show that the ability of firms to create product designs that are less complex, use fewer parts and are easier to assemble (while the products remain the same from the customer's perspective), are an important source of productivity advantage for many Japanes firms.

Gersbach and Baily also identify the relationship between a competitive environment and productivity by developing a so-called globalisation index. The globalisation index for a follower industry measures the exposure to competition of the domestic operations as a weighted index of trade flows and flows of direct foreign investment between the productivity leader, the follower and third countries. Using this index, the authors find a large productivity shortfall in industries which mainly serve local markets, like the beer industry in Germany or the food processing industry in Japan. In contrast, firms which are characterised by strong exposure to global operations benefit substantially from larger scale and frontier technology.

The impact of foreign direct investment on productivity also clearly comes out of the study by Birnie on Ireland. In 1985 foreign owned plants in the

Republic of Ireland represented 40 per cent of manufacturing employment. The average labour productivity in manufacturing was 28 per cent ahead of the United Kingdom but was almost twice the UK level in the foreign owned sector. Birnie shows that part of this Irish productivity advantage in manufacturing is somewhat fictituous, as it was caused by transfer pricing which articificially raises the profits (and therefore the value added) of manufacturing firms. This effect can therefore not be considered as a genuine "real" productivity advantage but only as a nominal value added effect.

Besides the competitiveness-enhancing effects from high productivity performance, the papers by Kuroda and van Ark emphasise that competitive advantage is also a function of relative output prices and relative costs of inputs. Van Ark's comparisons of unit labour costs from 1970 to 1994 show that competitive advantages in the short run are primarily determined by the movement of exchange rates. Nevertheless the relatively high labour cost in nominal terms in German manufacturing pushed this country to a position with higher unit labour cost levels than France, Japan, the United States and even the United Kingdom in 1994. Relative price and cost levels in Germany were particularly high in investment goods industries which, as noted above, can only to a small extent be related to higher quality of German products. In contrast to Germany, van Ark's paper notes the relatively favourable cost performance of Japan up to 1990. In 1990, when the value of the Japanese yen was already extremely high, relative manufacturing price levels exceeded those of the US by only 7 per cent, although there was a big variation between extremes such as food products (Japanese price levels which were 40 per cent higher than in the USA) and investment goods (15 per cent lower than in the USA). However, the relative unit labour cost position of Japan vis-á-vis the United States deteriorated strongly during the early 1990s, partly because of the continuous increase in US dollar-based labour costs, but also because of the slowdown in Japanese productivity growth.

Using a slightly different procedure, Kuroda who covers the period 1960 to 1985, confirms the observations by van Ark on the relatively low labour costs and the relatively good unit labour cost performance of investment goods industries in Japan. Kuroda also emphasises the exceptionally high cost of capital goods in Japan between 1960 and 1985.

As far as the nature of Japan's competitive advantage is concerned, Kuroda emphasises that before 1973 Japan primarily benefitted from its lower wage costs despite its lower productivity performance in all industries. However, since 1973 Japan's competitive advantage had to be sought primarily in productivity advances which were unequally divided over the economy. These differences in productivity performance across industries contributed to the dualistic nature of the Japanese economy which is also observed by Pilat, and which may be seen as one of the main causes of the present "trade frictions" between Japan and the United States.

5. Conclusions: Where Do We Go from Here?

The main purpose of this book is to provide an overview of what we know about the quantitative and qualitative aspects of international productivity differentials at industry level. Below we briefly summarise our knowledge to date, and what the main items on our future research agenda ought to be.

Catch-Up and Convergence

The productivity estimates at the meso level which are provided in the various papers in this volume provide important information on the explanatory factors behind the catch-up and convergence process which is usually primarily studied at the macro level. In order to fully understand the mechanisms behind catch-up and convergence it is important to look at sectoral and industry estimates of productivity, changes in industry composition, differences in working hours and labour force participation rates.

At the sectoral level, the estimates of manufacturing productivity performance during the postwar period confirm the picture of catch-up as exemplified for the economy as a whole: countries with lower productivity levels at the beginning of the period show more rapid productivity growth since. This in itself may be an explanation for the productivity slowdown since 1973. As follower countries have moved closer to the productivity frontier (represented by the USA) the potential for catch-up has declined. However, this does not explain why growth at the productivity frontier (the United States) itself slowed down as well.

At the industry level we also find catch-up taking place for most countries and during most subperiods, but the degree to which this led to the elimination of productivity gaps differs substantially. Van Ark shows that presently the US productivity advantage is biggest in typically light industries, such as food, beverages and tobacco, textiles, wearing apparel and leather products, etc.. Pilat and Kuroda confirm this view by emphasising the rapid catch-up in Japanese investment goods industries, whereas the productivity performance of light industries in Japan stayed way behind that of the USA. This has led to the present situation of shared leadership in manufacturing mainly between Japan and the United States. For European countries we also mostly find a better performance compared to the USA in investment good industries than in light industries.

As far as comparisons among the West European countries themselves are concerned, there have been phases of divergence as well as convergence such as between Germany and the UK (O'Mahony and Wagner) and between France and Germany (Freudenberg and Ünal-Kesenci). The most significant divergence episodes were Germany/UK during the period 1973-79 and France/Germany performance during the 1980s. However, for the period as a whole the dispersion of relative productivity levels, as measured by the coefficients of variation, between France and Germany and between Germany and the UK have decreased significantly. Estimates of the productivity performance at the industry level for other European countries need to be awaited before more definitive conclusions can be derived on the nature and extent of industry convergence in Europe.

In any case there are also two cases of extreme divergence between European countries represented in this book. The study by Birnie puts emphasis on the role of foreign investment in Ireland explaining the widening of the productivity gap between Ireland and the UK during the 1980s. Hitchens, Wagner and Birnie look at factors which have led to the dismal productivity performance of East Germany compared to West Germany, and the potential sources for acceleration of growth in former East Germany. Both cases, though very different in nature, point our attention towards the role of institutional factors in the catch-up and convergence process, which include among other things the functioning of labour and capital markets and institutional arrangements surrounding technological progress.

It is also important to note that the performance of output and inputs underlying the productivity convergence process, can differ substantially across industries, countries and subperiods. For example, the rapid convergence of UK and German productivity during the 1980s is more the result of a shake-out of the most unproductive factors in UK manufacturing than an improvement in the efficiency of the remaining stock of human and physical capital.[14] Thus the skill level in British and German manufacturing is now more similar not because of an increase in skills in the UK but by laying off a larger share of unskilled employees.

Capital, Production Techniques and Innovation

Most studies in this volume have emphasised the role of physical capital in explaining productivity performance across countries. However, it is also clear that absolute differences in capital intensity among advanced nations are gradually becoming less important. To understand productivity performance one needs to shift attention to differences in the provision of "broad" capital, which includes education and knowledge.

Again studies of sectoral and industry performance are essential in analysing the impact of human capital and technology on productivity. To this end more micro-oriented plant-based studies are required to obtain better knowledge of the mix of labour and "broad" capital in the production techniques in use for each industry. Gersbach and Baily point to important differences in productivity performance in some industries (for example in steel) due to different vintages

---

[14] A similar process is observed in the paper by Freudenberg and Ünal-Kesenci for France during the 1980s.

of equipment across countries. Production techniques are also determined by the product mix. For example, Gersbach and Baily show that the production of powdered detergents in Germany requires a more complex production process than that for producing liquid detergents, and thus lower labour productivity.

Production techniques and the composition of the capital stock are not independent of the types of products and available labour skills. Some examples of this are quoted in the paper by O'Mahony and Wagner referring to case studies in the German and British kitchen furniture and women's outerwear industry.[15] In Germany a move to small batch production of customised products had taken place in both industries. To operate these processes efficiently skilled people as well as flexible machinery are essential. Highly computerised and linked equipment, controlled and handled by skilled workers, was therefore implemented in the kitchen industry. This kind of machinery can easily and quickly be adapted to almost continuously changing dimensions. However, flexible machinery is not necessarily computerised. In contrast to the kitchen industry, it would not be functional in the women's outerwear industry because of the pliant material used. Thus German companies in the latter industry have reintroduced conventional machinery and skilled machinists who can handle rapid changeovers to different types of garments.

In the corresponding British industries a different mix of skills, products and machinery was found. British products were highly standardised and produced in large batches requiring rather low skills of the labour force. In contrast to the German kitchen industry, traditional woodworking machinery specifically dedicated to one or only a few products was used by semi-skilled workers. However, in the British clothing industry modern and automated machinery was implemented. This seemed to be a worthwhile investment as unskilled workers could process large batches extremely fast.

These sample studies show that the type of products, production process and the quality of the labour force affect the composition and utilisation of the capital stock in very diverse ways across industries and countries. Much more industry-focused research is required to fully understand the processes which take place at the macro level.

Apart from focusing on the impact of production techniques on productivity, there is a need for further research into a possible slowdown in the creation of new technology, i.e. in invention and innovation. The paper by Mairesse and Hall on France and the USA shows that the contribution of R&D to productivity growth is fairly small and has even shown a somewhat declining trend during the 1980s.

---

[15] See Steedman and Wagner (1987, 1989) for the original studies.

Product Quality

In the past decades products have become more customised and more specialised. This has complicated statistical comparisons of matched products. The unit value ratios, which are used as conversion factors in a range of papers in this volume, may become even more difficult to construct with increased specialisation of products.

The study by Gersbach and Baily briefly describes the procedure by which census unit value ratios can be adjusted for quality differences.[16] UVRs were adjusted only when these were recognised by consumers in such a way that they were willing to pay a price premium, and when they were the result of differences in the products and production process, and not of advertising or taste. The remaining notions of quality were treated as differences in consumer preferences which may *explain* differences in productivity and which can improve the competitive situation of companies and industries, but which are not used in adjusting the productivity measure itself. This method to adjust census UVRs for studies at the industry level needs to be further extended in future work.

Mairesse and Hall point at the possibility that recent benefits of new technology accumulation have been largely appropriated by consumers through a fall in product prices, which demands further research into the question how quality improvements can be incorporated in the productivity measures.

Freudenberg and Ünal-Kesenci looked at the quality of French and German products by comparing the export unit values of identical products. They found that French export prices were slightly lower than German export prices, but it is not clear from such a comparison whether this reflects lower production costs of French products or higher quality of German products.

Hitchens, Wagner and Birnie show a substantial quality difference between East and West German goods which they measure as the disparity between physical and value added productivity, but also this method is rough as different cost and price structures could not be taken into account. To improve the reliability of productivity comparisons more research on product quality issues is required.

Productivity in Service Industries

Most papers in this book deal exclusively with the productivity performance of commodity sectors, and primarily with manufacturing. Only the two papers on Japan by Pilat and Kuroda include measures of the performance of service industries. Although one would expect smaller productivity gaps in service sectors, where capital and technology have traditionally been of less importance,

---

[16]   See Gersbach and van Ark (1994) for more details.

the actual estimates do not confirm this view. In particular, the gaps are large for modern service sectors, such as business services and transport and communication.

The extension of comparative productivity studies to services, which represent an increasing share in output and employment of the economies of advanced nations, should now be a top priority on the productivity research agenda. Despite the difficulties in finding appropriate and comprehensive output indicators for comparison-resistant service industries, such as retailing, the financial sector and government, even imperfect measures are helpful. It will be important to assess to what extent productivity differentials across countries in the service sector vary with those for commodity sectors, and how much slower their productivity growth actually is.[17]

Institutional Environment

Even with the best measures available the causal contribution of a range of institutional factors and their effects on productivity remain difficult to quantify. Growth accountants have made a distinction between proximate and ultimate causes affecting productivity. Proximate causes relate to the quantities and quality of factor inputs. These are measurable and can be directly related to the output growth in a production function framework. Ultimate causes are factors which Abramovitz (1986) has summarised under the umbrella of the "social capability" of a country to catch up. Social capability is a somewhat vague and broad concept, which partly refers to personal attributes and culture, but also to the infrastructure of political and economic institutions, which include rules and regulations concerning product markets, labour and capital markets.

It would go beyond the brief nature of this introduction to go deeply into all these factors, but we emphasise two institutional factors which come out clearly from various papers in this volume. Firstly, the effect of human capital on productivity is largely determined by the education system and the organisation of innovation systems. For example, the extensive vocational training system in Germany can only be afforded given the relatively low compensation for trainees over a period as long as three years. Trainees will only accept such a loss in present income if their expected future earnings are high enough and their career prospects widen. This requires a complex system of labour relations with clear and extensive responsibilities taken by trade unions, chambers of industry, the Federal Institute of Vocational Training, companies, in-company trainers and the government itself.

Secondly, the papers by Birnie and by Gersbach and Baily emphasise the

---

[17] See the paper by Pilat, but also for example Smith and Hitchens (1985), McKinsey Global Institute (1992) and Baily (1993).

importance of competitive forces and globalisation trends in explaining productivity. The case of Ireland may be somewhat extreme, but the tendency towards the "one world-one factory" model, makes it possible that huge productivity differences can arise because of differences in legislation on taxing corporate profits and import of foreign capital. At the same time, Gersbach and Baily show that taking part in a globalised world economy can create substantial real productivity benefits, as international competition and foreign direct investment are prime vehicles in technology diffusion and invention.

References

Abramovitz, M. (1986), "Catching up, forging ahead, and falling behind", *Journal of Economic History*, vol. 46, no. 2, pp. 385-406.

Ark, B. van (1993), *International Comparisons of Output and Productivity*, Monograph Series No. 1, Groningen Growth and Development Centre, Groningen.

Ark, B. van (1996), *The Economics of Convergence, A Comparative Analysis of Industrial Productivity Since 1950*, Edward Elgar Publishers, forthcoming.

Ark, B. van and N.F.R. Crafts, eds. (1996), *Quantitative Aspects of Europe's Postwar Growth*, CEPR, Cambridge University Press, forthcoming.

Baily, M.N. (1993), "Competition, Regulation and Efficiency in Service Industries", *Brookings Papers on Economic Activity: Microeconomics 2*, December, pp. 71-159.

Baumol, W.J., S.A.B. Blackman and E.N. Wolff (1989), *Productivity and American Leadership, The Long View*, MIT Press, Cambridge Mass.

---, R.R. Nelson and E.N. Wolff (1994), *Convergence of Productivity*, Oxford University Press.

Daly, A., D.M.W.N. Hitchens and K. Wagner (1985), "Productivity, Machinery and Skills in a Sample of Manufacturing Plants", *National Institute Economic Review*, February, London, pp. 48-61.

Denison, E.F. (1967), *Why Growth Rates Differ*, The Brookings Institution, Washington D.C.

Dollar, D. and E.N. Wolff (1993), *Competitiveness, Convergence and International Specialization*, MIT Press, Cambridge Mass.

Gersbach, H. and B. van Ark (1994), "Micro Foundations for International Productivity Comparisons", *Research Memorandum GD-11*, Groningen Growth and Development Centre.

Görzig, B. and M. Gornig (1991), *Produktivität und Wettbewerbsfähigkeit der Wirtschaft der DDR*, DIW, Heft 121, Berlin.

Griliches, Z. (1994), "Productivity, R&D, and the Data Constraint", *The American Economic Review*, vol. 84, pp. 1-23.

Hitchens, D.M.W.N., K. Wagner and J.E. Birnie (1990), *Closing the Productivity*, Avebury, Aldershot.

---, --- and --- (1993), *East German Productivity and the Transition to the Market Economy*, Avebury, Aldershot.

Hitchens, D.M.W.N., Birnie, J.E., Hamar, J., Wagner, K., and Zemplinerova, A. (1995), *The competitiveness of industry in the Czech Republic and Hungary*, Avebury, Aldershot.

Maddison, A. (1987), "Growth and Slowdown in Advanced Capitalist Countries: Techniques of Quantitative Assessment", *Journal of Economic Literature*, vol. 25, no. 2, June.

--- (1991), *Dynamic Forces in Capitalist Development*, Oxford University Press.

--- (1995), *Monitoring the World Economy 1820-1992*, OECD Development Centre, Paris.

Mason, G., B. van Ark and K. Wagner (1994), "Productivity, Product Quality and Workforce Skills: Food Processing in Four European Countries", *National Institute Economic Review*, January, London.

McKinsey Global Institute (1992), *Service Sector Productivity*, Washington D.C.

McKinsey Global Institute (1993), *Manufacturing Productivity*, Washington D.C.

Pilat (1994), *The Economics of Rapid Growth. The Experience of Japan and Korea*, Edward Elgar, Aldershot.

Prais, S.J. and K. Wagner (1983), "Practical Aspects of Human Capital Investment: Training Standards in Five Occupations in Britain and Germany", *National Institute Economic Review,* No. 105, London, pp. 46-65.

--- and --- (1985), "Schoolings Standards in England and Germany: Some Summary Comparisons Bearing on Economic Efficiency", *National Institute Economic Review*, No. 112, London.

Smith, A.D. and D.M.W.N. Hitchens (1985), *Productivity in the Distributive Trades - A Comparison of Britain, Germany and America*, Cambridge University Press, Cambridge.

Steedman, H., G. Mason and K. Wagner (1991), "Intermediate Technical Skills: Britain, France and West Germany", *National Institute Economic Review*, No. 136, London, pp. 60-76.

--- and K. Wagner (1987), "A Second Look at Productivity, Machinery and Skills in Britain and Germany", *National Institute Economic Review*, November, London, pp. 84-95.

--- and --- (1989), "Productivity, Machinery and Skills: Clothing Manufacture in Britain and Germany", *National Institute Economic Review*, No. 128, London, pp. 40-57.

International Productivity Differences
K. Wagner and B. van Ark (editors)
© 1996 Elsevier Science B.V. All rights reserved.

Productivity and Competitiveness in Manufacturing: A Comparison of Europe, Japan and the United States

*B. van Ark**
Groningen Growth and Development Centre, University of Groningen

1. Introduction

Over the past decade, there have been significant changes in the competitive performance of the world's main industrial nations. Following a massive restructuring, manufacturing industries in the United States have shown a strong recovery from the slowdown in output and productivity growth during the 1970s. For manufacturing as a whole, the United States has clearly maintained its position as a leader in terms of the level of productivity during the 1980s and early 1990s. Since the mid 1980s, the export volume of manufactured products from the United States has increased rapidly and the US current account position has improved.

During the 1970s and 1980s the Japanese share in world output increased sharply in several industries. Productivity levels in Japan rose rapidly, especially in investment goods industries. However, the Japanese economy currently faces a need for major restructuring, following a slowdown in domestic demand and a continuous appreciation of the yen. At the same time, the Japanese domestic market continues to be strongly protected against the potential exports of other nations.

The competitive performance of European countries has been rather diverse. For example, there are signs that during the 1980s Germany[1] lost its competitive edge in several manufacturing industries. Compared to Germany, France and the United Kingdom experienced a faster rise in productivity and a slower increase

---

* **Acknowledgement**
  This paper is a follow up to an earlier article by Dirk Pilat and Bart van Ark, "Competitiveness in Manufacturing: A Comparison of Germany, Japan and the United States", *Banca Nazionale del Lavoro Quarterly Review* (June 1994). This contribution extends the former one by adding detailed comparisons for two other European countries, i.e. France and the United Kingdom. I am grateful to Dirk Pilat for sharing the ideas on the earlier article, letting me use it as the starting point for the present paper, and for his comments on an earlier draft. I would also like to acknowledge Peter Hooper, Angus Maddison, Arthur Neef and Karin Wagner for helpful comments.
[1]   Throughout this paper "Germany" refers to the former Federal Republic of Germany.

in labour cost. German manufactured exports have also grown more slowly than those of France and the United Kingdom since the mid 1980s.

In addition to changes in competitiveness among themselves, all advanced industrial nations have experienced increasing competitive pressure from traditionally low income countries, in particular from countries in East and South East Asia, which have made substantial progress in raising productivity levels over the past two decades.

Despite such pieces of evidence, competitiveness remains a somewhat vague and popularised concept which deserves further precision. One cannot really speak of a "competitive economy", as it is always necessary to differentiate between industries with and without comparative advantages. Changes in the competitiveness structure are important determinants of the structural transformation of economies. Competitiveness at an aggregate level is therefore only an indication of whether, compared to other nations, a country has relatively more or less industries with rising shares in world exports, relatively low price levels, high productivity or low labour cost performance.

The summary measure of competitiveness in this paper concerns the relative level of unit labour cost for six major branches in manufacturing in France, Germany, Japan, the United Kingdom and the United States from 1970 to 1994.[2] In US dollars, unit labour cost of any country X can be expressed as the ratio of labour cost per hour and labour productivity:

$$ULC^X = \frac{(LCH^{X(X)})/ER^{XU}}{(OH^{X(X)})/UVR^{XU}} \qquad (1)$$

where ER^{XU} is the exchange rate between country X and U, UVR^{XU} is the UVR between country X and U, $LCH^{X(X)}$ are the labour cost per hour in country X in prices of X and $OH^{X(X)}$ is output (value added) per hour in country X in prices of country X.

According to this equation, labour cost are converted into US dollars on the basis of the exchange rate, whereas productivity is based on unit value ratios. The latter represent ratios of producers' sales values per unit of output of each country compared to the USA.[3] The use of unit value ratios is important because in practice prices of goods and services are not the same across countries, so that the use of exchange rates would bias the results. In fact equation (1) can be

---

[2] The major branches are food products and beverages; textiles, wearing apparel and leather products; chemical products, petroleum refining and rubber and plastic products; basic metals and metal products; electrical and non-electrical machinery and transport equipment; and other manufacturing, including paper and paper products, wood products and furniture and non-metallic mineral products.

[3] In other studies such measures have often been called "purchasing power parities", but unit value ratios more clearly indicate the nature of the price information used.

rewritten to decompose our summary measure of the difference in unit labour cost between country X and country U into three components, i.e. the difference in labour cost, the difference in nominal labour productivity (that is unadjusted for differences in price levels) and differences in relative price levels:

$$\log(ULC^{X(U)} - ULC^U) = \log(\frac{LCH^X}{ER^{XU}} - LCH^U) -$$

$$\log(\frac{OH^X}{ER^{XU}} - OH^U) - \log(ER^{XU} - UVR^{XU}) \qquad (2)$$

Below these three measures will be analysed in more detail. Section 2 deals with relative price levels, which are defined as the ratio of the average unit value ratio and the exchange rate. These estimates have been obtained within the framework of the International Comparisons of Output and Productivity (ICOP) project at Groningen University, which makes use of product information derived from national production censuses and industrial surveys. As the ICOP method of estimating UVRs has also been applied in other papers in this volume, including those of Freudenberg and Ünal-Kesenci, Pilat, Birnie and O'Mahony and Wagner, section 2 of this paper deals extensively with various methodological aspects of the ICOP procedure to obtain UVRs. These unit value ratios have been used to derive the comparative productivity levels in section 3 of this paper. Section 4 deals with the relative levels of labour cost and unit labour costs. In the final section I will draw some conclusions concerning the relevance of unit labour cost as an indicator of competitiveness in relation to other measures.

2. Relative Price Levels of Manufacturing Products

One of the most straightforward measures of cost competitiveness is the difference in price levels between countries. For this purpose it is especially useful to compare relative levels of ex-factory prices, such as the ICOP estimates of unit value ratios for manufacturing products between each country and the United States.[4]

---

[4] Most studies of the International Comparisons of Output and Productivity (ICOP) project so far dealt with the manufacturing sector, which now cover 20 countries. These countries are Argentina, Australia, Brazil, China, Czechoslovakia, Ecuador, France, Germany (FRG and GDR), India, Indonesia, Korea, Japan, Mexico, the Netherlands, Portugal, the former Soviet Union, Spain, the United Kingdom and the United States. Below I will give a brief description of the ICOP procedure which has also been used (in a more or less adjusted form) in some of the other papers in this volume, including Birnie, Freudenberg and Ünal-Kesenci, O'Mahony and Wagner and Pilat. A more extensive description of ICOP studies for manufacturing will appear in van Ark (1996). Substantial progress has also been made in ICOP studies

The ICOP Methodology to Estimate Unit Value Ratios

Unit values are obtained from each country's production census or survey for a recent benchmark year (in this paper, 1987) by dividing producers' sales values by the corresponding quantities of sales. Matches are then made between each pair of countries for as many products as possible.[5] However, in practice only a proportion of manufacturing products could be matched to calculate the unit value ratios. For many products, values are reported but not quantities. In addition, for some products, there is no counterpart in the other country, for other products the information is not disclosed for confidentiality reasons, and some products could not be compared because they represent a different mix of product varieties for each country or because there are large quality differences.

For the benchmark comparison between Germany and the United States, 271 unit value ratios were derived, which represented 24.4 percent of German manufacturing shipments and 24.8 percent of US manufacturing shipments (see table 1). Coverage was lowest for the France/US comparison, which comprised 109 product matches covering 12.5 to 15.1 of shipments in France and the United States respectively.

As it appeared impossible to match all products between countries, a method was required to fill the holes for the 75 to 85 per cent of output which could not covered by unit value ratios. This method basically involves a stage-wise aggregation of the UVRs. Firstly the manufacturing sector was divided up in 16 branches, which roughly correspond to the International Standard Industry Classification (ISIC) of the United Nations. For each binary comparison, a maximum number of industries within each branch was distinguished as producing the same products in each country. Matches were then made for as many products as possible within each industry. The average unit value ratio for

---

for other sectors of the economy, including agriculture and services. See Maddison and Van Ooststroom (1993) for a comparison of agricultural output and productivity for 13 countries. See Pilat (1994) for a total economy comparison based on sectoral estimates. See Mulder and Maddison (1993) for a detailed account of comparative productivity performance in distribution. For an up-to-date description and presentation of the ICOP project, see Maddison and van Ark (1994).

[5]   Industry of origin UVRs are usually based on binary comparisons, in contrast to expenditure PPPs (which are discussed below) which are usually based on index numbers of a multilateral nature. See Pilat and Prasada Rao (1991) for experimentation with multilateral weights in industry studies. In general the differences between PPPs at binary and multilateral weights are not very big for a small sample of countries with comparable price structures. However, the results depend on the choice of the numéraire country, which in this case is the United States. This implies that comparisons of three countries based on binary UVRs, are not transitive. For example, a direct comparison between Germany and the United Kingdom does not yield an identical result to an implicit comparison between these countries based on UVRs for Germany/USA and UK/USA.

the industry was obtained by weighting the unit values by the corresponding quantity weights for one of the two countries:

$$UVR_j^{XU(X)} = (\sum_{i=1}^{s} P_{ij}^X * Q_{ij}^X) / (\sum_{i=1}^{s} P_{ij}^U * Q_{ij}^X) \qquad (3a)$$

at quantity weights of country X, and:

$$UVR_j^{XU(U)} = (\sum_{i=1}^{s} P_{ij}^X * Q_{ij}^U) / (\sum_{i=1}^{s} P_{ij}^U * Q_{ij}^U) \qquad (3b)$$

at quantity weights of country U (i.e. the USA) ($i=1...s$ is the sample of matched items in matched industry j).

The second stage of aggregation from industry to branch level was constructed by weighting the unit value ratios for gross output (UVR_{go}) as derived above by the value added of each industry in country X or country U, i.e.:

$$UVR_k^{XU(U)} = \frac{\sum_{j=1}^{r} [UVR_{j(go)}^{XU(U)} * VA_j^U]}{VA_k^U} \qquad (4a)$$

for the UVR of branch k at quantity weights of country U, and:

$$UVR_k^{XU(X)} = \frac{VA_k^X}{\sum_{j=1}^{r} [VA_j^X / UVR_{j(go)}^{XU(X)}]} \qquad (4b)$$

for the UVR of branch k at country X's quantity weights ($j=1...r$ are the industries j in branch k).

The second step described above has usually been applied only to so-called "matched" industries, for which at least 25 per cent of output in both countries could be matched. For industries within each branch with lower coverage percentages, equations (3a) and (3b) customarily were used for all items within a branch, which therefore resulted in the same UVR across all non-matched industries in the branch.[6]

---

[6]   Other studies, including some in this volume have used slightly different criteria for matching, but the essentials of the procedure are similar. See the chapters by Birnie, Freudenberg and Ünal-Kesenci and O'Mahony and Wagner.

In the final stage, branch UVRs were weighted at value added to obtain unit value ratios for major groups of branches (such as in table 1) and for total manufacturing. The stage-wise aggregation using either quantities (in the first stage from product to industry level) or value added (in the following stages) has the advantage that the original product UVRs are successively reweighted according to their relative importance in the aggregate. As a result the aggregate unit value ratios are less sensitive to outlier UVRs.

Table 1 shows the manufacturing UVRs at the level of six major branches in manufacturing. There appears some variation in UVRs across the major branches. In all binary comparisons UVRs for machinery and equipment are among the lowest and closest to the market exchange rate. This suggests smaller differences in price levels than in other major branches in manufacturing. The variation in UVRs was greatest for Japan, with food, beverages and tobacco having the highest UVR at 320.2 Yen/US$, and machinery and equipment the lowest UVR at 131.2 Yen/US$. This indicates the dual nature of Japanese manufacturing. Some branches (in particular electronics and cars) are very competitive on the export market, whereas other branches (in particular food) are almost entirely protected from the world market.[7]

TABLE 1

Number of Unit Value Ratios, Coverage Percentages and Unit Value Ratios at Own Country and US Weights by Major Manufacturing Branch, 1987

	Number of UVRs	Matched Sales as as % of Total Sales		Unit Value Ratios (national currency/US$)		
		Own Country	USA	Own Country Quantity Weights	USA Quantity Weights	Geometric Average
France/USA	(unit)	(%)	(%)	(FF/US$)		
Food, Beverages & Tobacco	13	30.9	34.1	7.30	8.02	7.65
Textiles, Apparel & Leather	25	21.4	17.4	7.76	8.72	8.23
Chemicals & Allied Products	13	6.3	7.3	6.93	8.51	7.68
Basic & Fabr. Metal Products	6	11.4	6.5	7.44	7.61	7.52
Machinery & Equipment	35	13.1	13.6	6.47	7.11	6.78
Other Manufacturing	17	13.4	5.4	6.82	7.81	7.00
Total Manufacturing	109	15.1	12.5	6.87	7.59	7.22

(table continued on the next page)

---

[7]   See also the paper by Pilat on Japan in this volume.

TABLE 1 (continued)

	Number of UVRs	Matched Sales as as % of Total Sales		Unit Value Ratios (national currency/US$)		
		Own Country	USA	Own Country Quantity Weights	USA Quantity Weights	Geometric Average
Germany/USA	(unit)	(%)	(%)	(DM/US$)		
Food, Beverages & Tobacco	55	47.9	39.0	1.94	2.00	1.97
Textiles, Apparel & Leather	59	48.5	49.8	2.66	2.82	2.74
Chemicals & Allied Products	26	13.6	30.5	2.40	2.51	2.45
Basic & Fabr. Metal Products	31	46.5	23.9	2.16	2.25	2.20
Machinery & Equipment	61	24.9	18.7	2.08	2.04	2.06
Other Manufacturing	39	19.8	17.0	2.16	2.35	2.25
Total Manufacturing	271	24.4	24.8	2.16	2.25	2.21
Japan/USA	(unit)	(%)	(%)	(Yen/US$)		
Food, Beverages & Tobacco	20	19.0	17.9	332.6	308.3	320.2
adjusted for double deflation[a]	-	-	-	251.0	234.9	242.8
Textiles, Apparel & Leather	27	25.1	34.2	181.9	184.7	183.3
Chemicals & Allied Products	43	20.7	31.9	173.8	217.6	194.4
Basic & Fabr. Metal Products	34	24.9	22.9	164.4	193.7	178.4
Machinery & Equipment	45	17.1	16.1	108.7	158.4	131.2
Other Manufacturing	21	15.9	11.3	196.4	237.4	215.9
Total Manufacturing	190	19.1	19.9	150.7	212.2	178.8
with double deflation for food[a]	-	-	-	148.5	202.9	173.6
United Kingdom/USA	(unit)	(%)	(%) (pound/US$)			
Food, Beverages & Tobacco	31	24.4	21.3	0.679	0.771	0.723
Textiles, Apparel & Leather	54	40.2	50.3	0.670	0.677	0.673
Chemicals & Allied Products	41	22.5	29.2	0.587	0.641	0.613
Basic & Fabr. Metal Products	8	21.4	12.4	0.661	0.677	0.669
Machinery & Equipment	20	9.3	13.6	0.642	0.649	0.646
Other Manufacturing	22	11.5	7.5	0.809	0.956	0.880
Total Manufacturing	176	17.6	18.1	0.670	0.748	0.708

[a] Double deflation for food products was calculated by applying a UVR for agricultural inputs for 1985 from Prasada Rao (1993), extrapolated to 1987.
Note: See original sources for details at level of fourteen to sixteen branches.
Sources: see Annex A. See also van Ark and Kouwenhoven (1994) for France/USA; van Ark and Pilat (1993) for Germany and Japan; van Ark (1992) for UK.

B. van Ark

TABLE 2

Comparisons of Unit Value Ratios for Manufacturing, ICP Purchasing Power Parities and Exchange Rates, 1987

	Unit Value Ratio (national currency/ US$)	Exchange Rate		GDP PPP (1987)	
		national currency/ US$	relative price level	1985 base	1990 base
France/USA	7.22	6.01	120	7.68	6.78
Germany/USA	2.21	1.80	123	2.57	2.15
Japan/USA	173.6	144.64	120	235.71	213.83
UK/USA	0.708	0.612	116	0.604	0.567

Notes: UVRs and GDP-based PPPs are geometric averages of UVRs and PPPs weighted at national and US weights.
Source: UVRs see table 1. PPPs for 1985 and 1990 were provided by Eurostat and extrapolated to 1987 with GDP deflators from OECD (1993).

Table 2 shows the manufacturing unit value ratios for 1987 along with market exchange rates. In the case of all four country pairings, the manufacturing UVRs were substantially above the exchange rates in 1987, which implies that the price level of manufactured products was higher in each of the countries than in the United States. Because of the low exchange value of the US dollar in 1987, none of the countries was able to compete on favourable terms with the United States on the basis of relative prices in 1987, although in this respect the UK was in a slightly better position than the Germany.

The last two columns of table 2 show expenditure purchasing power parities for total gross domestic product (GDP) from the International Comparisons Project. The latter are based on relative market prices of consumer goods and investment goods. Expenditure PPPs are nowadays provided on a regular basis by international organisations such as EUROSTAT, OECD and the United Nations. Some analysts have used these PPPs for comparisons of relative prices at industry level.[8] This obviously creates biases if relative prices at the industry level differ from those at the level of total GDP. Table 2 shows two variants of the GDP PPPs, namely from the 1985 and 1990 benchmark studies by the International Comparisons Project. Both estimates have been extrapolated to 1987 with national GDP deflators.

---

[8]   See, for example, Dollar and Wolff (1993).

The two variants show surprisingly large differences.[9] With respect to the base-1985 variant, the relative price levels in manufacturing are lower than the expenditure price levels vis-à-vis the USA for France, Germany and Japan, but not for the United Kingdom. However, a comparison of the manufacturing UVRs with the base-1990 variant of the GDP PPPs suggests that France and Germany also have lower expenditure price levels than manufacturing price levels compared to the USA. This last observation could imply that in the European countries price levels in manufacturing are relatively high compared to services, whereas in Japan they are relatively low. Alternatively, it could also be that distribution or transport margins (which are included in the GDP PPP and not in the manufacturing UVR) are lower in European countries than in the USA and Japan, or that European prices of intermediate goods (which are included in the manufacturing UVR and not in the GDP PPP) are relatively high.

Other authors constructed so-called "proxy PPPs" by selecting PPPs for certain expenditure items which were then allocated to industries.[10] Here the problem remains that cross-country differences in transport and distribution margins and net indirect taxes may affect the estimates, and that the prices of imported products are reflected in the expenditure PPPs whereas the prices of exported products are excluded. Kuroda's paper in this volume, following Jorgenson, Nishimizu and Kuroda (1987) comes a step closer to measuring relative prices by industry by "peeling off" indirect taxes and trade and transportation margins from the expenditure PPPs.[11] All these adjustments seem an improvement over the use of unadjusted expenditure PPPs, but they also make the PPPs increasingly sensitive to the procedures used and the quality of the data. However, the most fundamental problem of using ICP PPPs for the purpose of industry comparisons is that those PPPs exclude price measures for intermediate products (iron and steel, cement, pulp and paper and most kinds of semi-manufactured goods), which account for a substantial part of manufacturing output.

Therefore, neither expenditure PPPs for total GDP nor proxy PPPs are a good alternative over the UVRs used in the ICOP studies. What is most needed are more detailed and comparable data on quantities and prices of products to refine the UVRs, and which take account of cross-country differences in product

---

[9]   See Maddison (1995), Appendix C, for a more detailed account of differences in PPPs and per capita income estimates from various ICP rounds. For the countries in the present paper, Maddison's estimates suggest that the PPP estimates from ICP IV (for 1980) and ICP VI (for 1990) are more consistent with each other than with the ICP V estimates (for 1985). As the UVRs presented here are of a binary nature, they are compared with the unpublished Fisher variant of the GDP PPPs instead of the published multilateral variants.

[10]   See, for example, Hooper and Larin (1989).

[11]   See also a more recent paper by Hooper and Vrankovich (1995).

mix and product quality. The importance of this problem was investigated in a recent study by the McKinsey Global Institute (1993), which looked in detail at several of the ICOP UVRs for the Germany/USA and Japan/USA comparisons. In some cases (in particular in the machinery and equipment sector) substantial adjustments were made at the product level to correct for different product mixes or qualities among the countries. However, no systematic bias in the original ICOP estimates was found, so that at the aggregate level of the six major manufacturing branches at which the estimates are presented in the present paper, these adjustments led to changes of the results in the order of only 3 to 5 per cent.[12]

Relative Price Levels from 1970 to 1992

As a next step the UVRs for 1987 have been extrapolated to other years through the use of price deflators derived from each country's national accounts. Graph 1 shows the relation between the manufacturing UVR and the exchange rate for the period 1970 to 1992. If a country's manufacturing UVR is below the prevailing exchange rate, its relative price level in manufacturing is lower than that of the United States, implying that it can compete on favourable terms with the United States on the world market.

Graph 1 shows that, following the collapse of the Bretton Woods system with fixed exchange rates in 1971, the French franc, the German mark and the Japanese yen all appreciated against the dollar, with the result that the relatively low price levels compared to the USA were largely eroded by 1975. In 1980, only Japan still enjoyed lower price levels than the United States. Between 1975 and 1980 the UK showed a strong rise in relative price levels. The high dollar period from 1980 to 1985, led to a short-lived return to low price levels in Germany and Japan, but since 1985 their price levels have again risen rapidly and the competitiveness of the United States, as far as relative prices are concerned, has increased substantially.

Graph 1 also shows PPPs for total GDP which have been obtained on the basis of the expenditure approach. Here the geometric average is shown of the PPP of each country at its own weights and at the weights of the USA (the Fisher variant) for 1990, extrapolated at GDP deflators. It appears that the PPP for France, Germany and Japan has been substantially above the manufacturing UVR throughout the period, although the gap was somewhat reduced in recent years. In contrast, the ICP PPP and the manufacturing UVR for the UK vis-à-vis the USA were relatively close until the early 1980s. The manufacturing UVR has exceeded the ICP PPP since then.

---

[12] See Gersbach and Van Ark (1994) and the paper by Gersbach and Baily in this volume. See also the paper by Freudenberg and Ünal-Kesenci in this volume for their own evaluation of the effect of quality differences on the UVRs.

GRAPH 1
Manufacturing UVRs, the Exchange Rate and Expenditure PPPs

(a) France/USA, FF/US$

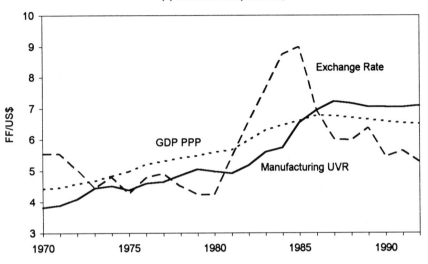

(b) Germany/USA, DM/US$

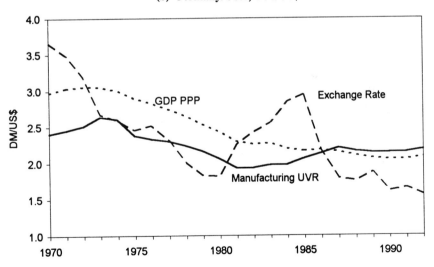

B. van Ark

GRAPH 1 (continued)
Manufacturing UVRs, the Exchange Rate and Expenditure PPPs

(c) Japan/USA, Yen/US$

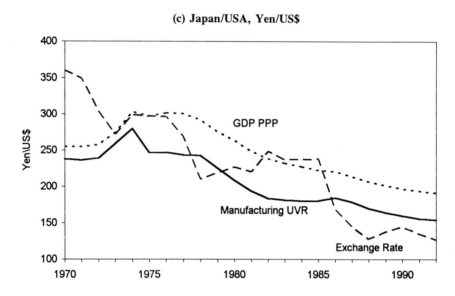

(d) United Kingdom/USA, pound/US$

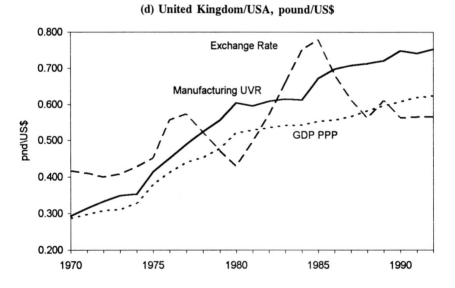

Sources: Manufacturing UVR for 1987 see table 1, extrapolated with national accounts deflators for manufacturing (see Annex A). GDP PPPs for 1990 (Fisher type) provided by EUROSTAT and extrapolated on the basis of GDP deflators from OECD (1993).

TABLE 3
Manufacturing Price Levels by Major Manufacturing Branch,
1970-1992, USA=100

	1970	1975	1980	1985	1990	1992
France/USA						
Food, Beverages & Tobacco	70.4	106.7	159.2	86.8	127.2	
Textiles, Apparel & Leather	60.0	107.6	140.1	82.0	148.2	
Chemicals & Allied Products	70.6	97.1	114.1	73.4	114.5	
Basic & Fabr. Metal Products	94.7	112.1	119.0	76.2	128.7	
Machinery & Equipment	59.0	92.6	101.8	67.6	136.4	
Other Manufacturing	73.3	119.1	126.8	70.2	128.7	
Total Manufacturing	68.8	102.3	117.8	72.8	129.5	133.9
Germany/USA						
Food, Beverages & Tobacco	60.4	86.9	118.0	63.2	116.7	
Textiles, Apparel & Leather	77.1	122.2	150.9	86.8	168.3	
Chemicals & Allied Products	70.4	104.8	120.5	77.8	131.3	
Basic & Fabr. Metal Products	83.0	98.0	110.3	68.9	125.1	
Machinery & Equipment	50.2	81.9	95.3	64.1	132.7	
Other Manufacturing	78.2	115.1	130.4	74.0	137.9	
Total Manufacturing	65.7	96.8	113.2	70.1	132.8	140.0
Japan/USA						
Food, Beverages & Tobacco	62.6	81.0	135.5	124.3	184.6	
Textiles, Apparel & Leather	51.5	73.5	89.8	76.1	128.7	
Chemicals & Allied Products	67.5	70.7	90.9	72.3	110.4	
Basic & Fabr. Metal Products	86.7	89.0	96.4	74.7	114.5	
Machinery & Equipment	65.8	84.9	72.3	60.6	84.8	
Other Manufacturing	73.5	113.5	118.3	90.5	138.2	
Total Manufacturing	66.1	83.2	91.9	75.7	110.3	121.6
United Kingdom/USA						
Food, Beverages & Tobacco			168.5	91.1	132.5	
Textiles, Apparel & Leather			139.7	80.2	137.0	
Chemicals & Allied Products			112.1	72.7	97.0	
Basic & Fabr. Metal Products			139.2	79.2	118.6	
Machinery & Equipment			119.2	77.9	130.8	
Other Manufacturing			185.2	111.8	163.7	
Total Manufacturing	70.3	91.6	140.5	86.2	132.9	132.9

Source: Based on 1987 benchmark UVRs from table 1, extrapolated with national accounts deflators for manufacturing (see Annex A). Exchange rate from OECD (1993).

Table 3 shows the relative price levels for the six major manufacturing branches.[13] The appreciation of the French franc, the D-Mark and the Yen during the early 1970s led to a rise in manufacturing price levels in all major branches in France, Germany and Japan compared to the United States. In France and Germany, the rise in relative prices was rather rapid in food, beverages and tobacco products and in textiles, wearing apparel and leather goods but slower in basic metals and metal products.

By 1980, France and the United Kingdom had lost their price advantage to the USA in all major branches, and Germany still enjoyed a small advantage in only one branch, machinery and equipment.[14] In the UK relative price levels in 1980 were very high in food, beverages and tobacco and "other manufacturing".

In 1980, only Japan still had lower price levels than the USA especially in machinery and equipment. That branch even showed a slight decline in price level between 1975 and 1980 despite the appreciation of the yen. In contrast, relative prices of food, beverages and tobacco products increased rapidly between 1970 and 1980. After 1980, there was even more diversity in Japanese price levels. In 1990, the Japanese price level of food products, beverages and tobacco was about 85 per cent above the US level, whereas that for machinery and equipment was 15 percentage points below the US level.

Diversity in relative price levels in France and Germany was much less than in Japan. In 1990, all manufacturing branches had relatively high price levels at 15 to 35 percent above the US level, with the exception of the textiles, wearing apparel and leather products branch which showed even higher relative price levels. In the UK, relative price levels in 1990 were high in "other manufacturing" (which includes wood and paper products and non-metallic mineral products), but rather low in basic and fabricated metal products and even slightly below the US level in chemicals.

It may be concluded that in terms of price competitiveness, the US has improved its performance over the past two decades, especially in light industries such as food, beverages and tobacco products and textiles, wearing apparel and leather products. However, this US price advantage is to a large extent due to the depreciation of the US dollar during the 1970s and second half of the 1980s, and not simply to a more moderate rise in costs in terms of national prices. Against the tide of an appreciating currency, only Japan has been able to keep its price levels, in particular in machinery and equipment, relatively low into the late 1980s.

---

[13] Unfortunately, appropriate deflators to extrapolate the relative price levels for the UK by major branch to the period before 1978 could not be constructed for the UK.

[14] Clearly there may have been industries with lower relative price levels in other branches. The fairly aggregate analysis in this paper locates only those areas of manufacturing in which countries enjoy an overall competitive advantage.

3. Comparative Productivity Levels

Productivity is one of the most important determinants of competitiveness. Productivity (especially labour productivity) improvements are a necessary prerequisite for producing high quality products at a reasonable cost without losing the competitive edge to other countries. Productivity growth indicates how a company, an industry or a country manages to raise output with a minimum increase in inputs, or to prevent output from falling more rapidly than inputs. Comparisons of productivity levels show how much the average practice within an industry, within a sector or for the economy as a whole differ between countries. If the "numéraire" country is the world productivity leader, such comparisons indicate how much each country differs from best practice.

The ICOP Methodology to Compare Productivity Levels

An adequate comparison of productivity levels between countries depends on two components, namely reliable and comparable indicators of output and labour input for each country, and a conversion factor to translate output values to a common currency unit. The exchange rate is not suitable for the latter purpose, since it is heavily influenced by capital flows and speculation and in general does not indicate real price differences between countries. Therefore use was made of the unit value ratios discussed in the previous section to obtain comparative levels of output and labour productivity.

The basic data for the comparisons of manufacturing productivity are derived from the manufacturing censuses of each of the countries. Accordingly, estimates of output and labour input are derived from one and the same survey of manufacturing establishments, which implies the use of a relatively consistent data framework. Although production censuses and surveys are not as well harmonised across countries as, for example, national accounts, the detail in these sources is such that one can adjust the data to the same concepts of employment and value added and the same classification scheme of industries across the countries.

It has been suggested that the use of value added as the output concept in combination with unit value ratios based on gross output complicates the connection between productivity and competitiveness.[15] Indeed at industry level there are important theoretical advantages to measuring productivity with gross output and treating intermediate inputs symmetrically with capital and labour inputs.

At the relatively aggregate level of analysis in this paper, value added is a

---

[15] See, for example, Jorgenson (1993, pp. 45-56) commenting on van Ark and Pilat (1993).

more useful measure because it avoids double counting of the value of intermediate inputs. If the estimates were derived from gross output by industry, aggregation would require separate deflation of gross output and intermediate inputs. In practice this procedure easily leads to volatile results because of important measurement problems.[16] In particular when intermediate inputs make up a large part of gross output, small measurement errors tend to become magnified in the double deflated value added measures. The ICOP measures are therefore based on the adjusted single deflation method: value added at national prices is converted to a common currency with unit value ratios based on gross output. This approach provides more robust results than the double deflation method.[17]

Trends in Comparative Productivity Performance from 1970 to 1994

The relative productivity estimates were benchmarked on 1987, and extrapolated using national time series of output and labour input which were mainly derived from national accounts for the whole period 1970 to 1994. Table 4 shows the productivity estimates for the six manufacturing branches in selected years relative to the United States.

Between 1970 and 1980 France, Germany and Japan strongly converged towards US productivity levels, which in fact was a continuation of a process that had begun during the 1950s.[18] By 1980 France and Germany had higher productivity than the USA in the manufacture of machinery and equipment, and Germany was also ahead in chemicals and allied products. During the 1970s almost no convergence took place in the UK, and in some major branches (par-

---

[16] Firstly, double deflated estimates are very sensitive to the weights used in the index. This may be overcome by the use of translogarithmic indexes, which are based on average value shares of the two countries in each binary comparison (see, for example, the contribution of Kuroda to this volume). However, the latter method still requires meticulous measurement of the value and prices of output and material inputs. In particular in the case of material inputs, the coverage of measured prices needs to be quite substantial. Furthermore it is necessary to have an integrated framework of intersectoral accounts, the production census and the national product accounts. These conditions are difficult to meet in practice. Comparable price measures for intermediate inputs are hardly available, and as mentioned above, by definition they cannot be obtained from ICP expenditure PPPs.

[17] See Pilat (1994) and van Ark (1993; 1996) for a description of estimates using double deflation techniques. An exception to adjusted single deflation was made in the case of the food products branch in Japan, for which the double deflated UVR from table 1 was used. As intermediate inputs were excessively highly priced in Japan, it was felt necessary to derive a specific value added UVR for this extreme case.

[18] For example, in 1950 value added per hour worked in manufacturing in France and the UK was 38 per cent of that of the USA; in Germany it was 39 per cent, whereas in Japan it was only 12 per cent of the US level. See van Ark (1996).

TABLE 4
Value Added per Hour Worked in Manufacturing,
by Major Manufacturing Branch, 1970-1994, USA=100

	1970	1975	1980	1985	1990	1994[a]
France/USA						
Food, Beverages & Tobacco	72.3	72.2	66.7	66.9	78.8	
Textiles, Apparel & Leather	78.2	85.2	83.2	93.7	89.0	
Chemicals & Allied Products	81.1	81.6	92.4	83.3	84.4	
Basic & Fabr. Metal Products	53.7	58.1	73.2	80.9	93.2	
Machinery & Equipment	81.8	91.6	108.8	101.0	98.0	
Other Manufacturing	67.9	72.0	86.6	93.3	90.1	
Total Manufacturing	73.3	78.5	89.8	89.8	91.3	90.5
Germany/USA						
Food, Beverages & Tobacco	76.5	74.4	73.3	71.6	75.8	
Textiles, Apparel & Leather	82.9	88.0	84.5	89.0	88.2	
Chemicals & Allied Products	86.7	92.8	105.6	84.9	76.7	
Basic & Fabr. Metal Products	67.7	82.9	86.9	92.0	98.8	
Machinery & Equipment	89.9	99.6	110.8	99.7	87.6	
Other Manufacturing	66.0	71.5	80.3	79.9	79.3	
Total Manufacturing	78.7	87.3	95.2	90.5	85.9	85.0
Japan/USA						
Food, Beverages & Tobacco	37.4	44.2	38.5	33.5	37.0	
Textiles, Apparel & Leather	52.6	65.1	61.9	58.1	48.0	
Chemicals & Allied Products	58.0	71.9	83.1	84.4	83.8	
Basic & Fabr. Metal Products	47.2	62.5	81.1	85.6	95.6	
Machinery & Equipment	46.8	59.2	90.0	96.2	114.4	
Other Manufacturing	31.3	33.0	41.3	50.6	54.9	
Total Manufacturing	44.5	54.1	66.2	69.9	77.9	76.2
United Kingdom/USA						
Food, Beverages & Tobacco	40.0	40.1	39.2	44.2	53.8	
Textiles, Apparel & Leather	61.7	62.7	56.0	66.7	64.8	
Chemicals & Allied Products	63.8	67.5	71.3	73.7	86.1	
Basic & Fabr. Metal Products	44.5	44.9	40.9	64.0	79.9	
Machinery & Equipment	55.3	61.4	58.6	60.8	65.8	
Other Manufacturing	47.4	43.8	46.6	50.5	60.4	
Total Manufacturing	51.3	53.0	52.3	58.3	66.0	69.3

[a] provisional
Source: See Annex A, and sources quoted under table 1.

ticularly textiles, basic metals and metal products, and machinery and equipment)
quite some divergence occurred.

During the first half of the 1980s, the trend by which France was "catching
up" with the US productivity level stagnated, and manufacturing productivity
levels in Germany and the United States even began to diverge. These
development were related in part to the acceleration of productivity growth in the
USA during this period; in addition Germany suffered a substantial slowdown
in productivity growth during the 1980s.[19] Germany's deterioration in
comparative terms was especially strong in chemicals and allied products and in
machinery and equipment. By 1990, German productivity levels relative to the
US in these two major branches were below those of 1970. In comparison to
France, Germany had substantially lower productivity levels in 1990 in
chemicals, machinery and equipment and "other manufacturing" branches,
whereas it was more or less at par with France in food, beverages and tobacco
products and in textiles, wearing apparel and leather products.[20]

Japan continued to catch up with US productivity levels during the 1980s,
although at a rate slower than during the 1970s. As a result Japan was much
closer to German and French productivity levels in 1990 than in 1980. However,
there is a wide spread in productivity levels by manufacturing branch in Japan.
In machinery and equipment, Japan surpassed US productivity performance
during the late 1980s, and in basic metals and metal products Japan stood
roughly at par with the United States. The performance in food, beverages and
tobacco, and in textiles, apparel and leather has been especially poor compared
to that in machinery and equipment. The performance of the food sector seems
related in part to the small scale of its firms, but probably also reflects a lack of
competition in this area (McKinsey Global Institute, 1993).

In contrast to its performance during the 1970s, the UK showed remarkable
improvement in productivity during the 1980s. In comparison to the USA,
productivity levels rose especially rapidly in food, beverages and tobacco
products and chemical and allied products (particularly during the second half of
the 1980s) and in textiles, wearing apparel and leather products and basic metals
and metal products (particularly during the first half of the 1980s). By 1990 the
UK productivity performance in chemicals and allied products was even better
than in France, Germany and Japan, though for the manufacturing sector as a
whole it still lagged substantially behind that of the other three countries.[21]

---

[19]   The annual compound growth rates of value added per hour worked in manufacturing
       between 1979 and 1990 were 3.1 per cent for France, 1.8 per cent for Germany, 4.9
       per cent for Japan, 4.8 per cent for the UK and 2.8 per cent for the USA.

[20]   Compare also with the article by Freudenberg and Ünal-Kesenci in this volume which
       reports on the results of a direct comparison between France and Germany.

[21]   See the paper by O'Mahony and Wagner in this volume for details on the
       Germany/UK comparison.

In summary, in terms of productivity performance, the United States has been the best performer throughout the period, although it faced increasing challenges from France and Germany before 1980 and from Japan thereafter. Presently leadership in manufacturing is shared between Japan and the United States, a situation that is likely to last for some time given the large differences in the comparative productivity performance among the major manufacturing branches, and the widening of the US-Japanese productivity gap in recent years. Although France and Germany are closer to the US productivity level than is Japan, there are no manufacturing branches in which they clearly lead, although the French performance in machinery and equipment and the German performance in basic and fabricated metal products was relatively good in 1990.

4. Labour Compensation and Unit Labour Costs

The estimates of manufacturing UVRs and productivity levels in sections 2 and 3 make it possible to construct the summary indicator of competitiveness in this paper, namely unit labour costs. Because labour costs account for the largest share of value added in advanced countries, unit labour costs serve as an important indicator of competitive performance. The US Bureau of Labor Statistics and the OECD regularly publish trend estimates of manufacturing unit labour costs.[22]

For the calculations of comparative levels of unit labour costs, ratios of labour costs per hour derived from each country's national accounts were combined with the relative estimates of value added per hour presented above. Labour costs refer to total compensation: they include wages and salaries before tax, employer's social security contributions, contributions to pension, insurance and health plans, and other expenses related to employment. These figures are more comprehensive than the labour cost estimates shown in the manufacturing censuses, which often exclude at least part of employer's contributions to compensation of labour.

Table 5 shows labour costs per hour worked of all employees by major branch in manufacturing. The figures are converted from national currency values to a common currency using the average exchange rate for each year. The trends in comparative labour costs are therefore not only determined by changes in labour costs in national currency values, but also by exchange rate fluctuations.[23]

Between 1970 and 1980, labour costs per hour worked more than doubled relative to those of the USA for all four competitor countries. In 1980 relative

---

[22] See, for example, Neef and Kask (1991), Greiner, Kask and Sparks (1995), and OECD, *Economic Outlook*, various issues, Paris.

[23] Compare, for example, the estimates on changes in labour cost on a national currency basis and on a US dollar basis in the BLS *Monthly Labor Review*.

B. van Ark

TABLE 5
Labour Costs per Hour by Major Branch, 1970-1994, USA=100

	1970	1975	1980	1985	1990	1994[a]
France/USA						
Food, Beverages & Tobacco	56.6	105.3	126.0	76.0	121.1[c]	
Textiles, Apparel & Leather	53.3	105.1	134.8	85.7	125.9[c]	
Chemicals & Allied Products	55.8	94.1	113.0	71.1	100.9[c]	
Basic & Fabr. Metal Products	44.1	73.8	89.8	60.1	87.7[c]	
Machinery & Equipment	44.2	79.8	104.5	65.2	97.2[c]	
Other Manufacturing	47.8	89.0	120.2	76.8	106.9[c]	
Total Manufacturing	48.4	86.9	110.5	69.9	101.8[c]	116.5
Germany/USA						
Food, Beverages & Tobacco	43.9	70.1	83.9	47.7	91.9	
Textiles, Apparel & Leather	55.0	99.0	127.7	75.6	143.2	
Chemicals & Allied Products	51.7	89.5	112.9	68.1	122.8	
Basic & Fabr. Metal Products	46.3	77.9	98.3	61.3	119.8	
Machinery & Equipment	42.8	79.2	104.2	60.6	118.8	
Other Manufacturing	46.0	80.0	104.5	60.8	110.7	
Total Manufacturing	47.0	83.2	106.8	63.4	121.6	132.8
Japan/USA						
Food, Beverages & Tobacco	20.4	38.6	46.5	41.1	79.1	
Textiles, Apparel & Leather	23.3	45.8	62.0	46.5	66.5	
Chemicals & Allied Products	30.2	55.7	72.3	68.9	119.4	
Basic & Fabr. Metal Products	22.2	43.4	50.5	47.4	78.0	
Machinery & Equipment	19.6	41.5	48.9	42.8	72.8	
Other Manufacturing	20.6	42.1	52.7	46.1	75.6	
Total Manufacturing	21.4	43.0	52.1	45.8	77.5	112.5
United Kingdom/USA						
Food, Beverages & Tobacco			80.5	55.7	100.5	
Textiles, Apparel & Leather			135.0	61.3	102.4	
Chemicals & Allied Products			82.1	53.4	95.9	
Basic & Fabr. Metal Products			66.7	48.1	91.5	
Machinery & Equipment			70.9	46.7	82.8	
Other Manufacturing			81.2	55.0	93.3	
Total Manufacturing	38.0[b]	52.9	76.4	51.1	90.4	91.9

[a] provisional
[b] 1971; [c] 1989
Sources: Labour costs and employment see annex A.

labour cost in French and German manufacturing were approximately 10 per cent above the US level; in the UK they were about three quarters of the US level; and in Japan about half. Following the appreciation of the dollar during the early 1980s, relative labour costs in all four countries were significantly reduced, although much more so in the European countries than in Japan. During the second half of the 1980s, the relative labour cost level rose most rapidly in Germany, driven by the rapid appreciation of the D-mark. Subsequently Germany had the highest relative labour cost of all countries by 1990, followed by France, the United States, the United Kingdom and Japan.

There is some variation in hourly labour costs across the manufacturing branches, but it is significantly less than the spread in the productivity ratios presented in table 4. In all of the European countries, labour cost levels in textiles, wearing apparel and leather products were relatively high compared to those of the USA. France and the UK had relatively low labour cost levels in basic and fabricated metal products and in machinery and equipment, whereas Germany had lower labour cost levels than France and the UK in food, beverages and tobacco products. In Japan labour cost levels were relatively high in chemicals but otherwise were lower than in any of the other countries.

The trends in labour cost are basically the same across the major branches. This is, of course, to be expected in countries where wage settlements are relatively centralised. Only in the UK there were fairly substantial differences in the trends in relative labour cost levels across the branches during the 1980s.

As exemplified in equation (1) at the beginning of this paper, unit labour costs can be directly derived by dividing the estimates in table 5 by those in table 4. For each of the four countries, graph 2 shows the labour costs per hour worked, the value added per hour worked and the unit labour costs for total manufacturing relative to the United States.

Although relative productivity levels in France and Germany improved significantly during the 1970s, that trend was slower than the relative increases in labour costs so that the unit labour cost position of these countries relative to that of the USA deteriorated. In 1975, because of France's lower productivity level in comparison to Germany, it was the first country to post unit labour cost in manufacturing that were higher than those of the USA, France was followed by Germany and the UK in 1978. The "high dollar" period from 1980 to 1985 led to a short-lived return to lower unit labour cost levels, but the slowdown in comparative productivity performance and the rise in labour compensation levels after 1985 caused another increase in unit labour costs in France and Germany. By 1990 the unit labour cost level in Germany was more than 40 per cent above the US level; by 1994, it was almost 60 per cent higher.

Because of the substantially lower levels of productivity in UK manufacturing, the relative level of unit labour cost around 1980 was higher than in any of the other countries. Similarly, despite the somewhat slower rise in the labour compensation in the UK during the second half of the 1980s, unit labour cost

44   *B. van Ark*

GRAPH 2
Relative Labour Costs, Labour Productivity and Unit Labour Costs

(a) France (USA=100)

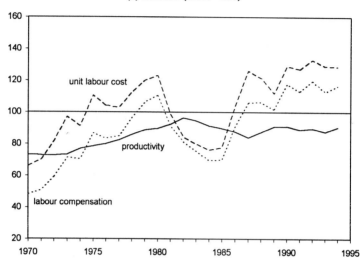

(b) Germany (USA=100)

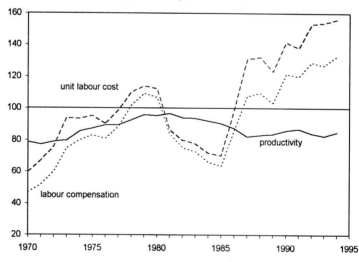

GRAPH 2 (continued)
Relative Labour Costs, Labour Productivity and Unit Labour Costs

(c) Japan (USA = 100)

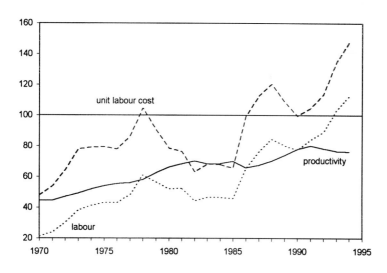

(d) United Kingdom (USA = 100)

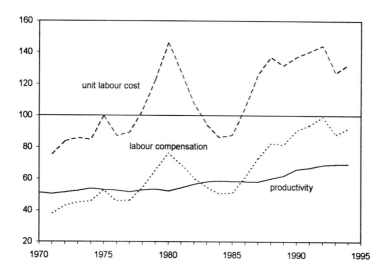

Sources: See tables 4 and 5.

B. van Ark

TABLE 6
Unit Labour Cost Levels by Major Branch, 1970-1994, USA=100

	1970	1975	1980	1985	1990	1994[a]
France/USA						
Food, Beverages & Tobacco	78.2	145.9	189.0	113.6	151.3[c]	
Textiles, Apparel & Leather	68.1	123.4	162.0	91.5	145.8[c]	
Chemicals & Allied Products	68.8	115.3	122.2	85.3	129.3[c]	
Basic & Fabr. Metal Products	82.1	127.0	122.7	74.3	91.8[c]	
Machinery & Equipment	54.0	87.2	96.0	64.5	97.7[c]	
Other Manufacturing	70.3	123.6	138.8	82.3	115.8[c]	
Total Manufacturing	66.0	110.6	123.1	77.8	111.8[c]	128.7
Germany/USA						
Food, Beverages & Tobacco	57.4	94.2	114.5	66.6	121.2	
Textiles, Apparel & Leather	67.0	112.4	151.1	84.9	162.4	
Chemicals & Allied Products	59.6	96.4	106.9	80.2	160.0	
Basic & Fabr. Metal Products	68.4	94.0	113.1	66.6	121.3	
Machinery & Equipment	47.9	79.6	94.1	60.8	135.6	
Other Manufacturing	69.8	112.0	130.2	76.1	139.7	
Total Manufacturing	59.7	95.2	112.3	70.1	141.6	156.1
Japan/USA						
Food, Beverages & Tobacco	54.5	87.3	121.0	122.8	213.5	
Textiles, Apparel & Leather	44.2	70.4	100.2	80.1	138.5	
Chemicals & Allied Products	52.1	77.4	87.1	81.6	142.5	
Basic & Fabr. Metal Products	47.0	69.5	62.2	55.4	81.5	
Machinery & Equipment	41.8	70.1	54.3	44.4	63.7	
Other Manufacturing	65.8	127.7	127.6	91.1	137.8	
Total Manufacturing	48.1	79.5	78.6	65.5	99.5	147.7
United Kingdom/USA						
Food, Beverages & Tobacco			205.5	126.1	186.8	
Textiles, Apparel & Leather			241.2	92.0	157.9	
Chemicals & Allied Products			115.3	72.4	111.4	
Basic & Fabr. Metal Products			163.2	75.2	114.6	
Machinery & Equipment			121.0	76.8	125.9	
Other Manufacturing			174.3	108.8	154.6	
Total Manufacturing	75.3[b]	99.8	146.1	87.6	137.1	132.5

[a] provisional
[b] 1971; [c] 1989
Sources: Labour costs from table 5. Relative value added per hour worked from table 4.

levels were much higher than in the US during this period. However, table 6 and graph 2 show that the unit labour cost position of the UK improved during the early 1990s.

Except in 1978, relative labour costs in Japan stayed below relative productivity up to 1985. Although Japan's labour cost position deteriorated during the second half of the 1980s, its unit labour cost level for total manufacturing more or less equalled that of the USA in 1990. However, unit labour costs in Japanese manufacturing rose dramatically between 1990 and 1994, which may be partly ascribed to the appreciation of the yen, but also to the decline in comparative productivity performance.

Table 6 shows the differences in unit labour cost levels for the major manufacturing branches. It is clear that France experienced relatively high unit labour cost levels during the 1970s in all branches except in machinery and equipment. Unit labour costs in the latter branch were also relatively low in Germany during the 1970s. Following the fall in unit labour cost levels during the early 1980s, another rise occurred during the second half of the past decade. In 1990 unit labour cost levels in textiles, wearing apparel and leather products proved very high in France and Germany. France also had high unit labour costs in food products and Germany in chemicals and allied products.

In the United Kingdom, unit labour cost levels in 1980 were exceptionally high in food products, beverages and tobacco and in textiles, wearing apparel and leather products, and this was still the case in 1990. However, unit labour cost levels in the UK were substantially below those of Germany in chemicals, basic metals and metal products and in machinery and equipment.

The Japanese experience shows a larger diversity in levels among branches as well as in changes over time. In 1970 Japan had lower unit labour cost levels than Germany in all major branches, but the differences were only substantial for textiles, wearing apparel and leather products and for basic metals and metal products. After 1970 the diversity between the branches further increased. Food products as well as chemicals and textiles, showed increasingly high unit labour cost levels over time, whereas in basic metals and metal products and in machinery and equipment relatively low unit labour costs were maintained despite the rising Yen/US$ exchange rate. In 1990, Japan enjoyed a very substantial unit labour cost advantage over the USA in machinery and equipment.

In summary, in terms of unit labour costs, France and Germany had already lost most of their competitive advantage in manufacturing to the USA by the early 1980s, and since then have competed only on the basis of the appreciation of the US dollar during the first half of the 1980s. During the second half of the decade, a sharp deterioration of French and German competitiveness took place which continued into the 1990s due to slow productivity growth, above average wage rises and currency appreciation.

During the 1970s Japan greatly benefitted from relatively low wage levels. However, during the 1980s, Japan's performance varied widely by major branch.

Several manufacturing branches were not able to respond to the appreciation of the yen by way of increasing productivity and cutting cost and therefore posted very high levels of unit labour costs. However, particularly in metals and in machinery and equipment, Japanese companies appeared able to achieve high productivity levels and remained competitive against US producers. Between 1990 and 1994, however, Japan's unit labor cost position deteriorated strongly to a level higher than that of France and the United Kingdom.

5. Concluding Remarks on Competitiveness Indicators

The estimates of relative prices, productivity and labour cost levels (together summarised in the unit labour cost measure) presented in this paper bear out some important aspects of changes in the competitive performance of the manufacturing sectors of France, Germany, Japan, the United Kingdom and the United States over the past 25 years. In this concluding section, a brief overview is given of the nature of these measures of cost competitiveness in relation to other competitiveness indicators. First it might be useful to broaden the country coverage somewhat, and compare the productivity and unit labour cost performance of these five major industrialised nations with that of some other countries.

Firstly there has been great concern about competitive pressures generated by low wage economies, such as South Korea and Taiwan. A recent study by Pilat (1994) showed that relative levels of unit labour costs in Korea were much lower than those in the United States during the 1970s and 1980s. However, as for the Japan/US comparison, the variation in unit labour cost levels between Korea and the USA was quite large among the major branches. In 1989, Korean unit labour cost levels were higher than in the USA in food products, beverages and tobacco and in chemicals and allied products, but only half the US level in basic metals and metal products and in machinery and equipment. Pilat emphasises that in comparison with low income countries, one needs also to take account of other costs, such as those of capital, which account for a larger share of value added than in high income countries. Given the low value of the US dollar, average price levels in Korean manufacturing were in fact 11 per cent above the US level in 1990.[24]

Secondly, the countries discussed in this paper are all relatively large in terms of their share in world manufacturing output. There are a substantial number of smaller industrialized nations which have much bigger export-output ratios than the countries considered in this paper, a typical example being the Netherlands. A recent ICOP study has shown that Dutch manufacturing labour productivity was approximately 5 per cent higher than the US level in 1993. This high

---

[24]   See Pilat (1994), pp. 193-204.

productivity level was partly associated with a relatively large share of capital intensive industries, especially basic chemicals and textile industries, in Dutch manufacturing. Because of a fairly strong wage moderation during the 1980s, labour compensation in Dutch manufacturing was even slightly lower than in the USA in 1993, so that its unit labour cost level was only 94 per cent of the US level.[25]

As mentioned above the indicators presented in this paper are all primarily measures of cost competitiveness, focussing on the efficiency of the productivity process in terms of lowering the cost per unit of output. In recent years and under the influence of authors such as Porter, the literature has made an increasingly strict distinction between competitiveness related to efficiency and competitiveness related to differentiation.[26] In Porter's view, differentiation refers to the creation of additional value added per unit of output through the improvement of product quality, customisation or improved after-sales services. Both efficiency and differentiation help to improve productivity, but the mechanism through which it is achieved is different. Although Porter acknowledges that both types of competitive advantage are important, he points out that any successful competitiveness strategy needs to focus on only one of the two factors. For the advanced industrial nations this usually implies a strategy based on differentiation.

However, such a strict distinction between efficiency and differentiation is not helpful in adequately understanding the development path of the most competitive nations. In the long term these are the countries which have simultaneously operated at relatively low cost levels and that have improved their productivity performance. There are at least two reasons why high income countries should not only concentrate on differentiation. Firstly, in an increasingly "globalised" world economy, more and more countries have got access to the same technology and the same product markets. As a result productivity gaps among these countries narrow in the long term, so that a reduction of costs and prices may be more effective in maintaining a competitive edge than differentiation.[27] Secondly, improving the competitive advantage of nations involves a continuous process of structural change within manufacturing (and within the economy as a whole) from high cost and low productivity industries to low cost and high

---

[25] See van Ark (1994, updated; 1996).

[26] See, for example, Porter (1990), pp. 37-38.

[27] According to McKinsey (1993) factors such as product quality, product variety, the quality of after-sales services currently play a relatively small role in explaining the differences in comparative productivity performance between Germany, Japan and the United States, as all three countries have adopted such strategies in the past decades. More important is the role of "design for manufacturing" and the "organisation of function and tasks" in manufacturing operations. See also the paper by Gersbach and Baily in this volume.

productivity sectors. In the long term such a competitive advantage cannot primarily be achieved by devaluation of the currency, as it takes away the pressure on firms to cut cost and increase productivity as described above. In contrast, cost competitiveness which is based on cutting of domestic costs not only improves the comparative cost position of countries, but also increases the room for manoeuvre to introduce and strengthen aspects of competitiveness based on differentiation strategies.

Annex A - Statistical Sources

Unit value ratios (table 1) for 1987 are derived from the following production sources. For France from SESSI/Organisation professionnels/SCEES, *Enquêtes de Branches 1987*, Paris. For Germany from Statistisches Bundesamt, *Produktion im Produzierenden Gewerbe 1987*, Wiesbaden. For Japan from MITI, *Census of Manufactures 1987, Report by Commodities*, Tokyo. For the UK from BSO, *Business Monitor, Quarterly Sales Inquiries*, various issues. For the USA from Bureau of the Census, *1987 Census of Manufactures, Industry Series*, Washington D.C.
Value added and employment for productivity calculations for 1987 are derived from the following sources. For France from INSEE, *La situation de l'industrie en 1987. Résultats définitifs de l'enquête annuelles d'entreprise 1987*, Paris. For Germany from Statistisches Bundesamt, *Kostenstruktur der Unternehmen 1987*, Wiesbaden. For Japan from MITI, *Census of Manufactures 1987, Report by Industries*, Tokyo. For the UK from CSO, *Business Monitor, Report on the Census of Production*, various issues. For the USA from Bureau of the Census, *1987 Census of Manufactures, Industry Series*, Washington D.C.
The series on value added, employment and deflators up to 1990 are derived from the following national accounts sources. For France from INSEE, *20 ans de comptes de la nation*, Paris, 1992, and INSEE, *Rapport sur les comptes de la nation*, Paris, 1993. For Germany from Statistisches Bundesamt, *Volkswirtschaftliche Gesamtrechnungen, Revidierte Ergebnisse 1950-1990*, Wiesbaden, 1991, and Statistisches Bundesamt, *Volkswirtschaftliche Gesamtrechnungen, Konten und Standardtabellen 1991*, Wiesbaden, 1992. For Japan from Economic Planning Agency, *Report on National Accounts from 1955 to 1989*, Tokyo, 1991, and Economic Planning Agency (1993), *Annual Report on National Accounts 1993*, Tokyo, 1993. For the United Kingdom from CSO (Central Statistical Office), *United Kingdom National Accounts*, various issues. UK employment from Dept. of Employment, *Employment Gazette* and additional series supplied by the Dept. of Employment. For the United States from Bureau of Economic Analysis (1986), *The National Income and Product Accounts of the United States, 1929-1982*, Washington D.C., and *Survey of Current Business* (April 1991, May 1993), Washington D.C..
For the calculations of hours see the detailed explanations in van Ark and

Kouwenhoven (1994) for France, van Ark and Pilat (1993) for Germany, Japan and the USA and van Ark (1992) for the UK, though the time series of the latter have been revised on the basis of more up-to-date information kindly provided by Mary O'Mahony.

Labour compensation and employment for labour cost calculations are derived from the following sources. For France (1977-89) from OECD, *National Accounts Volume II*, Paris, 1993, and for France (1970-77) from INSEE, *Les Comptes de l'industrie en 1987*, Les collections de l'INSEE, no. C150, 1988. For Germany, Japan and USA as for national accounts sources (see above). See also Pilat and van Ark (1994). For the UK (1983-90) from national accounts sources as described above, for UK (1975-83) from OECD, *National Accounts Volume II, 1975-87*, Paris, and for UK (1971-75) from OECD, *National Accounts Volume II, 1971-83*, Paris.

All time series from 1990 onwards are derived from Bureau of Labor Statistics (1995), "International Comparisons of Manufacturing Productivity and Unit Labor Cost Trends", USDL: 95-342, Washington D.C.

References

Ark, B. van (1992), "Comparative Productivity in British and American Manufacturing', *National Institute Economic Review*, No. 142, November.

--- (1993), *International Comparisons of Output and Productivity*, Monograph Series No. 1, Groningen Growth and Development Centre, Groningen.

--- (1994), "Arbeidsproduktiviteit, arbeidskosten en internationale concurrentie", *Economische en Statistische Berichten*, 23 november, pp. 1066-1069.

--- (1996), *The Economics of Convergence, A Comparative Analysis of Industrial Productivity Since 1950*, Edward Elgar Publishers, forthcoming.

--- and D. Pilat (1993), "Productivity Levels in Germany, Japan, and the United States: Differences and Causes", *Brookings Papers on Economic Activity: Microeconomics 2*, December, pp. 1-48.

--- and R.D.J. Kouwenhoven (1994), "Productivity in French Manufacturing: An International Comparative Perspective", *Research Memorandum GD-10*, Groningen Growth and Development Centre.

Dollar, D. and E.N. Wolff (1993), *Competitiveness, Convergence and International Specialization*, MIT Press, Cambridge Mass.

Gersbach, H. and B. van Ark (1994), "Micro Foundations for International Productivity Comparisons", *Research Memorandum GD-11*, Groningen Growth and Development Centre.

Greiner, M., C. Kask and C. Sparks (1995), "Comparative Manufacturing Productivity and Unit Labor Costs", *Monthly Labor Review*, February, pp. 26-38.

Hooper, P. and K.A. Larin (1989), "International Comparisons of Labor Costs in Manufacturing, *The Review of Income and Wealth*, December, Vol. 35, pp. 335-356.

Hooper, P. and E. Vrankovich (1995), "International Comparisons of the Levels of Unit Labor Costs in Manufacturing", *International Finance Discussion Papers No. 527*, Board of Governors of the Federal Reserve System, October, Washington D.C..

Jorgenson, Dale W. (1993), "Comments and Discussion" of Bart van Ark and Dirk Pilat, "Productivity Levels in Germany, Japan and the United States: Differences and Causes", in *Brookings Papers on Economic Activity, Microeconomics 2*, Brookings Institute, Washington D.C., pp. 49-56.

---, Mieko Nishimizu and Masahiro Kuroda (1987),"Japan-US Industry-Level Productivity Comparisons, 1960-1979", *Journal of the Japanese and International Economies*, Vol. 1, No. 1, March, pp. 1-30.

Maddison, A. (1995), *Monitoring the World Economy 1820-1992*, OECD Development Centre, Paris.

Maddison, A. and H. van Ooststroom (1993), "The International Comparison of Value Added, Productivity and Purchasing Power Parities in Agriculture", *Research Memorandum GD-1*, Groningen Growth and Development Centre.

--- and B. van Ark (1994), "Comparisons of Real Output and Productivity", *Research Memorandum GD-6*, Groningen Growth and Development Centre.

McKinsey Global Institute (1993), *Manufacturing Productivity*, Washington DC.

Mulder, N. and A. Maddison (1993), "The International Comparison of Performance in Distribution: Value Added, Labour Productivity and PPPs in Mexican and US Wholesale and Retail Trade 1975/7", *Research Memorandum GD-2*, Groningen Growth and Development Centre.

Neef, A., and C. Kask (1991), "Manufacturing Productivity and Labor Costs in 14 Economies", *Monthly Labor Review*, December, Vol. 114, pp. 24-37.

OECD (1993), *National Accounts 1960-1991, Main Aggregates, Volume I*, Paris.

Pilat, D. (1994), *The Economics of Rapid Growth: The Experience of Japan and Korea*, Edward Elgar Publishers, Aldershot.

--- and D.S. Prasada Rao (1991), "A Multilateral Approach to International Comparisons of Real Output, Productivity and Purchasing Power Parities in Manufacturing", *Research Memorandum, no. 440*, Institute of Economic Research, Groningen.

--- and B. van Ark (1994), "Competitiveness in Manufacturing: A Comparison of Germany, Japan and the United States", *Banca Nazionale del Lavoro Quarterly Review*, June.

Porter, M. (1990), *The Competitive Advantage of Nations*, The Free Press, New York.

Prasada Rao, D.S (1993), "International Comparisons of Agricultural Output and Productivity", *FAO Economic and Social Development Paper No. 112*, Rome.

International Productivity Differences
K. Wagner and B. van Ark (editors)
© 1996 Elsevier Science B.V. All rights reserved.

French and German Productivity Levels in Manufacturing

*Michael Freudenberg and Deniz Ünal-Kesenci**
Centre d'études prospectives et d'informations internationales (CEPII)

1. Introduction

This paper presents the main results of a comparison of levels of producer prices, inputs, output and productivity in France and West Germany for total manufacturing, as well as for eight major branches.[1]

When it comes to European integration, "convergence" is surely one of the most frequently used notions in the economic literature of the 1990s. Convergence has often been referred to in a macroeconomic sense, especially since the Delors report in 1989. For example, the convergence criteria defined in the Maastricht Treaty which EU members must meet to join the Economic and Monetary Union (EMU) are clearly all macroeconomic indicators relating to inflation rates, budget deficits, the public debt, long term interest rates and exchange rate stability. However, the question of convergence in productive structures at a more micro- or meso-economic level among member states cannot be put aside, and this is true not only between the more and the less advanced EU members, but even between "core" countries. This paper analyses the situation of the two major European economies, France and West Germany.

As Kravis states, "since economics is in its very essence concerned with the organisation of inputs (scarce means) to produce outputs (satisfy human wants), comparisons of productivity go to the heart of the assessment of economic

---

* We thank Bart van Ark for technical advice and fruitful discussions. Further thanks go to Michel Fouquin, Remco Kouwenhoven, Gérard Lafay, Jean Pisani-Ferry, the participants in the workshops "International Productivity Differences and their Explanations" (Wissenschaftszentrum Berlin, 26-27 November 1993) and "International Comparisons of Price and Productivity Levels" (CEPII, 25 February 1994) for comments and advice, and to Guillaume Gaulier for research assistance. Thanks to the Conseil national de l'information statistique, the SESSI kindly provided us with confidential information for some industries, which helped to increase the number of product matches.

[1] For a detailed presentation of the results of the French-German comparison, including product matches and tables of correspondence between different classifications, see Freudenberg and Ünal-Kesenci (1994a and 1994b).

M. Freudenberg and D. Ünal-Kesenci

performance".[2] Our comparison is based on the "industry-of-origin" approach, in which producer price ratios are used as conversion factors for value added. The use of these so-called "unit value ratios" (UVRs), which are based on ex-factory unit values derived from production censuses, is the major advantage of the industry-of-origin approach, but may at the same time be a stumbling block, as the results stand or fall with the calculated UVRs.[3] It was not possible in this paper to overcome completely the problem of product quality differences that lead to price differences, though particular attention was paid to presumable outliers in the product matches.

The relative level of producer prices suggests that France has benefitted from a competitive price advantage of about 10 per cent compared to Germany, since about 1987. However, this price gap may be necessary to compensate for German non-price competitiveness which is often evoked in international trade comparisons. Despite the remaining absolute price gap for total manufacturing, we found a remarkable convergence in relative price levels among major branches. This is most probably due to the increasing openness of the economies and the resulting stronger competition among enterprises.

During the time period considered (1970-1992), the relative levels of joint factor productivity were very close in both countries, whereas a breakdown of labour productivity and capital productivity shows a clear divergence. At about the same level until the early 1980s, French labour productivity increased strongly (to a level about 10 per cent higher than Germany's) while capital productivity declined substantially when compared to Germany's (to a level of some 90 per cent).

However, a study which concentrates solely on comparisons of productivity levels over time, risks missing out other important issues. The similarity of total factor productivity in manufacturing between two countries does not imply a similarity in underlying industrial performance indicators. For example, a country may well catch-up in terms of productivity levels (i.e. the level of output per unit of input increases), but at the same time fall behind in terms of inputs, or both inputs and output. In other words, one reason for a catch-up in productivity levels may well be a shrinkage in activity by "shaking out" the most inefficient operations. The present study shows this very phenomenon for France when compared to Germany. Whereas France caught up with Germany in terms of a rise of the volume of output and the factors of production until the end of the 1970s, the 1980s reversed most of these relative gains. At the beginning of the 1990s, the relative size of French manufacturing was again at almost the same level as 20 years before, that is at about half of German manufacturing.

---

[2]   Kravis (1976, p. 1).
[3]   See the chapter by van Ark in this volume. See also Maddison and van Ark (1988) and van Ark (1993) for an overview of the industry-of-origin approach.

This process of deindustrialization may have put France on a more productive, but smaller industrial base compared to Germany.[4]

The symmetric evolution of relative labour and capital productivity is closely linked to the much stronger substitution of labour by capital in France than in Germany. French capital intensity in manufacturing has risen increasingly above that of Germany, despite lower labour costs and higher real interest rates. This paradox might be a major reason for the high French unemployment rate, despite relatively high growth rates in the late 1980s.

The paper is organised as follows. The second section shows the core results of the study. Several factors are then analysed to explain labour productivity differences between the two countries (section 3). In section 4, the focus will be on the problem of quality differences in international comparisons. Lastly, in section 5, the benchmark results are extrapolated backwards to 1970 and forwards to 1992.

2. Results of the French-German Comparison for Manufacturing in 1987

Producer Prices

The levels of output and productivity were compared on the basis of the "industry-of-origin" approach, in which producer price ratios are used as conversion factors for value added. These so-called "unit value ratios" (UVRs) are based on ex-factory unit values derived from production censuses. This methodology is explained in detail in the chapter by van Ark in this volume.

Here we concentrate on the core results from our France/Germany comparison. Table 1 shows the number of product matches, the coverage ratio and the final UVRs as well as the relative French-German price level in 1987. In total, 237 products could be matched, which correspond to some 18 per cent of total manufacturing sales in both countries.[5]

The Fisher geometric average for value added weighted UVRs for total manufacturing is 3.06 FF/DM. UVRs are highest in basic metals and metal products, chemicals, rubber and plastic products and wearing apparel, textiles and leather (3.18 to 3.20 FF/DM), indicating relatively high French unit values. They are lowest in transport equipment and machinery.[6]

---

[4] See Freudenberg and Ünal-Kesenci (1994b).

[5] Not a single match could be made for food and beverages as there are two, different and incompatible French censuses for data on quantities and values. See Freudenberg and Ünal-Kesenci (1994a) for full details and tables of correspondence. Note that oil refining and tobacco are excluded from the comparison.

[6] We applied a step-wise aggregation of the product UVRs in order not to overestimate the importance of matched products compared to non-matched products. See the chapter by van Ark in this volume for further details.

TABLE 1
Results of Product Matches by Major Branches, France and Germany, 1987

	Matches (Number)	Coverage Ratios		Final Fisher UVRs[a] (FF/DM)	Relative Price Levels (Germany=100)
		Germany (%)	France (%)		
Food and Beverages	0	0.0	0.0	3.04	91.1
Wearing Apparel, Textiles and Leather	30	22.3	19.8	3.18	95.3
Wood, Paper and other Industries	25	27.4	25.3	3.11	93.0
Chemicals, Rubber and Plastic Products	68	20.3	25.5	3.18	95.4
Basic Metals and Metal Products	38	26.0	24.2	3.19	95.9
Machinery	42	6.6	9.1	2.94	88.1
Transport Equipment	8	37.1	34.3	2.84	84.9
Electric and Electronic Products	26	7.0	4.5	3.05	91.5
Total Manufacturing	237	18.2	18.0	3.06	91.7
Exchange Rate				3.35	

[a] Geometric average of UVRs at German and French prices.
Sources: For product information, SESSI, *Enquêtes de branches 1987*, Statistisches Bundesamt, *Produktion im produzierenden Gewerbe des In- und Auslands 1987* and United Nations (1988), *Annual Bulletin of Steel Statistics for Europe*. Industry information is from SESSI and SCEES, *Enquête annuelle d'entreprise 1987*, and Statis-tisches Bundesamt, *Kostenstruktur der Unternehmen 1987*. The exchange rate is from CEPII, database "CHELEM".

To estimate relative French-German price levels, the UVRs are divided by the average exchange rate of 3.35 FF/DM in 1987. The relative price level is 92 per cent for the manufacturing sector. If we interpret UVRs as a conversion factor for average production costs in the other country's prices, relatively low UVRs as compared to the exchange rate indicate more, price-competitive French products. This is true not only for total manufacturing but also for each major branch as relative price levels are all below 100.

Value Added

Table 2 presents three indicators concerning gross value added at factor cost in 1987. For each country, the share of value added in the total sales value, the distribution of value added among major branches and the French-German ratio of value added is shown.

In total manufacturing, as for most major branches, the share of value added in sales is a little higher in Germany than in France. For example, in machinery the ratio is 42 per cent for Germany and 36 per cent for France. This suggests slightly stronger vertical integration in Germany.[7]

The distribution of value added by major branch (in international prices) shows that among the most important major branches, three have a similar weight in both countries: chemicals, rubber and plastic products with about 20 per cent, followed by electric and electronic products and transport equipment. Machinery

TABLE 2
Gross Value Added at Factor Cost in Manufacturing
France and Germany, 1987

	Value Ratio Added to Sales		Distribution of Value Added		Relative Level of Value Added (Germany = 100)
	Germany	France	Germany	France	
	(%, national prices)		(%)	(%)	
Food and beverages	20.0	19.5	6.3	11.1	101.2
Wearing apparel, textiles and leather	33.4	34.5	4.8	7.7	92.5
Wood, paper and other industries	37.7	35.1	7.9	9.8	71.5
Chemicals, rubber and plastic products	36.1	32.4	20.7	20.5	57.5
Basic metals and metal products	37.6	32.8	13.1	11.2	49.5
Machinery	42.3	36.0	15.7	9.2	34.1
Transport equipment	34.1	29.2	14.4	15.2	61.6
Electric and electronic products	42.7	40.2	17.0	15.4	52.4
Total Manufacturing	35.9	31.2	100.0	100.0	58.0

Sources: For Fisher UVRs used to convert value added, see table 1. Industry information is from SESSI and SCEES, *Enquête annuelle d'entreprise 1987*, and Statistisches Bundesamt, *Kostenstruktur der Unternehmen 1987*.

---

[7] From these figures, it is not clear at which level vertical integration is higher in Germany. It could be (1) at the enterprise level, where German firms produce more of their own intermediate consumption; or (2) at the branch level, where outsourcing in Germany is done to a larger extent within the branch, i.e. compared to France, a higher share of intermediate inputs is produced by other firms in the same major branch. However, there are also two other possibilities at the aggregate level of total manufacturing, namely that manufacturing inputs in Germany are produced to a greater extent by other German enterprises in the manufacturing sector, whereas outsourcing in France concerns relatively more enterprises in services; or that France outsources abroad and imports relatively more intermediate products than Germany.

is much more important in Germany, whereas the weight of food and beverages in France is almost twice that in Germany.

The last colum of table 2 shows that French manufacturing value added represents about 58 per cent of the German level.[8] While for food and beverages, France produces more value added even in absolute terms than Germany, French output in machinery represents only a third of the German level.

Productivity

Since value added for both countries is expressed in FF and in DM, it can be compared to relative levels of different inputs (employees, hours worked, capital stock) to estimate French-German productivity levels. Calculating French and German value added per employee is the most straightforward way of comparing levels of labour productivity, as figures for both value added and employees are from the same sources. In our study self-employed persons are excluded.[9] The figures for labour input in 1987 are indicated in the top part of table 3. French employment of 3.6 million employees in manufacturing represents 54 per cent of the German level. These census employment figures (in enterprises with 20 persons or more) represent about 81 per cent of the total employment in both countries when compared to those in national accounts.

In manufacturing, France produces about 58 per cent of German value added with relatively fewer employees (54 per cent). The relative French-German level of value added per employee is therefore 108.4 per cent (bottom part of table 3). This higher French labour productivity for total manufacturing has been suggested by other studies as well.[10] The French advantage persists in almost all major branches.[11]

In order to take into account differences in working time, we calculated rela-

---

[8] The relative importance of German value added in manufacturing is not only due to the larger size of its economy, but also to its sectoral composition, since the share of manufacturing in German GDP is more important than in France.

[9] The concept of employees refers to "effectif employé" in France (*Enquête annuelle d'entreprise*, Table I) and to "beschäftigte Arbeitnehmer" in Germany (*Kostenstruktur der Unternehmen*, Table 7).

[10] See van Ark and Kouwenhoven (1994) whose implicit French-German level through their own France-USA and Germany-USA comparisons is very close to our result. See also the paper by van Ark in this volume. Different studies by the OECD are based on PPPs and data from national accounts, but yield similar results for total manufacturing. See also Guinchard (1984), who suggested that France overtook Germany at the end of the 1970s.

[11] As already noted, the estimate for the UVR in food and beverages is rather crude. However, even if we had excluded this major branch from the comparison, French labour productivity in manufacturing would still be about 7% higher than in Germany.

TABLE 3
Labour Input and Productivity in Manufacturing, France and Germany, 1987

	Employees		Annual Hours Worked	
	Germany (1,000)	France (1,000)	Germany	France
Food and Beverages	451.2	370.8	1,814	1,609
Wearing Apparel, Textiles and Leather	446.6	417.6	1,571	1,607
Wood, Paper and Other Industries	562.2	385.1	1,671	1,623
Chemicals, Rubber and Plastic Products	1,146.0	609.4	1,665	1,602
Basic Metals and Metal Products	934.4	441.9	1,630	1,624
Machinery	1,124.4	352.5	1,632	1,644
Transport Equipment	895.9	498.8	1,557	1,608
Electric and Electronic Products	1,111.3	496.5	1,561	1,599
Census Manufacturing	6,671.9	3,572.5	1,627	1,614
National Accounts Manufacturing	8,203.0	4,377.6		
Census/National Accounts (%)	81.3	81.6		

	Value Added per Employee (Germany = 100)	Value Added per Hour (Germany = 100)
Food and Beverages	123.2	138.9
Wearing Apparel, Textiles and Leather	99.0	96.7
Wood, Paper and Other Industries	104.3	107.4
Chemicals, Rubber and Plastic Products	108.1	112.3
Basic Metals and Metal Products	104.7	105.1
Machinery	108.8	108.0
Transport Equipment	110.7	107.2
Electric and Electronic Products	117.2	114.4
Census Manufacturing	108.4	109.3

Sources: Information on employees is from SESSI and SCEES, *Enquête annuelle d'entreprise 1987*, and Statistisches Bundesamt, *Kostenstruktur der Unternehmen 1987*, Hours worked are from INSEE, database "NOUBA" and H. Kohler and L. Reyher, *Arbeitszeit und Arbeitvolumen in der Bundesrepublik Deutschland: 1960-1990*, Institut für Arbeitsmarkt und Berufsforschung (IAB). For Fisher UVRs used to convert value added, see table 1.

tive levels of value added per hour worked. Annual hours effectively worked take into account differences in holidays, working days lost due to sickness or strikes, as well as differences in parttime workers. For this, however, we have to rely on different sources (see table 3). In 1987 average annual hours worked in the French manufacturing sector (1,614 hours) are only slightly lower than in

Germany (1,627 hours). The French hourly productivity advantage in manufacturing is about 9 per cent over Germany. Again, France has a higher productivity in virtually all major branches.

Comparisons of capital productivity are much more problematic than those for labour productivity. As with labour input, capital as a production factor must be considered in terms of a stock. Production censuses do not provide information on capital stocks, but such data can be found in national accounts. Therefore, one possibility to estimate a capital stock comparable to census employment figures is to assume that capital intensity according to national accounts is identical to that in the production censuses.

In many countries capital stock is estimated by the so-called "perpetual inventory method" (PIM). Annual investment is cumulated and asset scrapping and depreciation are deducted.[12] However, assumptions regarding the average life time and the mortality function of capital can differ between two countries.[13] Van Ark (1993) applied the perpetual inventory method using the same assumptions for all countries, and found on that basis that German manufacturing capital stock is underestimated when compared to France, but compared to other countries the difference is rather small.[14] We would have preferred to apply the perpetual inventory method at a major branch level ourselves, but were unable to do so as data on investment at that level do not stretch back far enough. Therefore, we used figures from national accounts and assumed an identical capital intensity in national accounts and production censuses to estimate "census capital stock".[15]

As we estimated UVRs to convert value added into the other country's

---

[12] See for example Kessler (1979) and O'Mahony (1993) for an overview of the different methods.

[13] While differences in mortality functions have only a small effect on the outcome of capital stock estimates, differences in the average life time can substantially alter the results, see Maddison (1993) and O'Mahony (1993). The average life in the 1980s for equipment was 17 years in France and 15 in Germany, and 37 and 41 years, respectively, for buildings and structures (O'Mahony, 1993, pp. 7-8). In contrast to France where the life time of service lives is considered constant, German national accounts assume that they have been declining over time.

[14] Van Ark (1993) applied the average life time for OECD countries. While French official figures for manufacturing capital stock in 1987 are only 4 per cent lower when compared to his standardised method, the difference for Germany is about 15 per cent.

[15] Gross fixed capital stock is in 1980 prices for France, but in 1985 prices for Germany. The French series was adjusted to "1985" prices on the basis of current prices. Since French current prices and constant 1980 prices are not identical for 1980, we had to make an additional adjustment. In both countries, the nomenclature in national accounts is more aggregated than in the census and, therefore, not exactly compatible (see Freudenberg and Ünal-Kesenci, 1994, for the table of correspondence). The major problem arises in basic metals and metal products, which includes certain extraction industries in France but not in Germany.

currency, we had to find a suitable conversion factor to compare French and German capital stock as well. We used purchasing power parities (PPPs) for gross fixed capital formation from World Bank (1993), which came at 3.23 FF/DM at German and 3.26 FF/DM at French weights in 1985 prices. As we did not have more detailed information, we used these PPPs both for total manufacturing as well as for the capital stock of each major branch.

Capital stock in French manufacturing represents 64 per cent of the German level in 1987 (table 4). Given the relative level of labour input (53 per cent), French capital intensity in manufacturing is about 21 per cent above that of Germany. The capital intensity is higher for almost all major branches. Especially

TABLE 4
Relative Levels of Capital Stock, Capital Intensity and Capital
Productivity in Manufacturing, France and Germany, 1987

	Capital Intensity (manufacturing = 100)		France as a percentage of Germany			
	Germany	France	Relative Capital Stock	Relative Capital Intensity	Relative Capital Productivity	Relative Capital Productivity (national prices)
Food and Beverages	115.7	130.4	99.6	136.6	101.7	95.3
Wearing Apparel, Textiles and Leather	84.9	62.9	85.8	89.7	107.8	105.7
Wood, Paper and Other Industries	92.2	74.9	65.5	98.5	109.1	104.4
Chemicals, Rubber and Plastic Products	140.8	123.7	54.5	106.4	105.6	103.6
Basic Metals and Metal Products	109.1	168.5	88.1	187.0	56.2	55.5
Machinery	66.0	64.5	37.4	118.4	91.2	82.7
Transport Equipment	109.4	91.8	58.5	101.7	105.3	92.1
Electric and Electronic Products	78.4	71.7	50.7	110.9	103.2	97.2
Total Manufacturing	100.0	100.0	64.4	121.2	90.2	85.2

Note: Capital intensity is measured in terms of capital stock per hour worked.
Sources: Information on employment and capital stock in national accounts is from INSEE, database "NOUBA" and Statistisches Bundesamt, *Volkswirtschaftliche Gesamtrechnungen, Revidierte Ergebnisse, 1950 bis 1990.* The resulting capital intensity is applied to census employment figures from same source as table 3. For UVRs used to convert value added, see table 1. PPPs for gross fixed capital formation are for industrial buildings and some producer durables (machinery & non-electrical equipment and electrical machinery & appliances) from World Bank (1993). The PPPs in OECD dollars (table 23) are weighted by per capita GDP expenditure in national currencies (table 24).

in basic metals and metal products, French capital intensity is extremely high, both when compared to Germany as well as to the French manufacturing average. The configuration is quite different from that of labour productivity. Given the relative abundance of French capital stock, it was about 10 per cent less productive than German capital in 1987. As for capital intensity, basic metals and metal products are a clear outlier, since French productivity is just half of the German level.

Even though the assumptions concerning capital stock estimates are rather crude, the high capital intensity in French manufacturing is compatible with other studies which pointed out the strong substitution of labour by capital and the decline in capital productivity in France.[16] A rough cross-check is to calculate capital productivity in national prices, where UVRs and PPPs do not intervene (last column in table 4).[17] For manufacturing, relative capital productivity based on national prices is even lower (85 per cent) than the one based on international prices (90 per cent), and the two are virtually identical in basic metals and metal products.

Calculating labour or capital productivity separately leads to attributing all value added to a single production factor. To estimate the combined effect of labour and capital on output, we have to assume a relationship between these factors. In the literature, joint factor productivity is often estimated via a Cobb-Douglas production function, where α corresponds to the partial elasticity of output with respect to labour:

$$Y = AL^{\alpha} K^{1-\alpha} \qquad (1)$$

The factor share of labour is the geometric average of the share of labour compensation in gross domestic product.[18] We interpret the term A as the joint factor productivity. Equation (1) can be rewritten to calculate relative levels of total factor productivity, in France vis-à-vis Germany:

$$\ln\left[\frac{A^F}{A^G}\right] = \ln\left[\frac{Y^F/L^F}{Y^G/L^G}\right] - (1 - \alpha) \ln\left[\frac{K^F/L^F}{K^G/L^G}\right] \qquad (2)$$

Table 5 shows that overall joint factor productivity is very close in the two

---

[16] See for example Fleurbaey and Joly (1990).

[17] Since both value added and capital stock are in FF for France and in DM for Germany, the ratio VA/K eliminates the monetary unit for each country. While this method easily permits calculation of relative levels of capital productivity, it does not take into account differences in relative prices for value added and capital. Neither can the level of capital stock and capital intensity be compared between two countries.

[18] The share of labour compensation is from the OECD (1984b, 1988, 1992). For each country, the share of labour compensation in gross domestic product in manufacturing minus indirect taxes plus subsidies was calculated for the years for which there are data available. Alpha is the geometric average for the two countries. The OECD data cover the years 1970 to 1990 for Germany, but only 1977 to 1988 for France. The

countries, but nevertheless there is a slight French advantage (about 3 per cent in 1987). France is more productive in food and beverages, electric and electronic products and chemicals, rubber and plastic products, whereas Germany has an advantage only for basic metals and metal products. The difference between relative labour and capital productivity is substantial for some major branches.

TABLE 5

**Relative Labour, Capital and Joint Factor Productivity
in Manufacturing, France as a percentage of Germany (Germany = 100), 1987**

	Hourly Labour Productivity	Capital Productivity	Joint Factor Productivity with Factor Shares
Food and Beverages	138.9	101.7	127.2
Wearing Apparel, Textiles and Leather	96.7	107.8	99.7
Wood, Paper and Other Industries	107.4	109.1	107.9
Chemicals, Rubber and Plastic Products	112.3	105.6	110.4
Basic Metals and Metal Products	105.1	56.2	88.1
Machinery	108.0	91.2	102.9
Transport Equipment	107.2	105.3	106.7
Electric and Electronic Products	114.4	103.2	111.1
Total Manufacturing	109.3	90.2	103.5

Sources: See tables 3 and 4. The average share of labour compensation in gross domestic product in manufacturing minus indirect taxes plus subsidies is from OECD (1984b, 1988, 1992).

The similarity between France and Germany in terms of joint factor productivity levels breaks down once the two components are analysed separately. France has a substantial advantage in labour productivity, while Germany has a better performance in capital productivity.

3. Explaining Labour Productivity Differences

The hourly labour productivity gap between France and Germany in 1987 may have several causes. In this paper we analyse three explanatory factors: the effect of the employment structure, firm size and capital intensity. The basic procedure

average share of labour compensation in GDP in both countries was 71.8 per cent. See also Fleurbaey and Joly (1990, p. 37).

in estimating the effect of each of these factors is to calculate a "corrected" labour productivity by assuming same conditions in the two countries. For example, to check if the high overall French labour productivity is due to a concentration of labour input in better performing branches, one country's input structure is used to reestimate hourly labour productivity in the other country. The difference between the "initial" and the "corrected" relative productivity is then interpreted as being due to this factor.

The structural effect is rather small but positive. Table 6 shows that French-German relative hourly labour productivity adjusted for structural differences is 111 per cent, i.e. about one and a half percentage points higher than the original one estimate. The effect of structural differences therefore does not explain the productivity gap. On the contrary, the adjustment suggests an even higher relative French performance if the industrial composition were the same in the two countries.

We used five categories of firm size to estimate the effect of firm size on relative productivity performance: 20-49, 50-99, 100-199, 200-499 and 500 or more employees. On average German firms are larger than French companies,

TABLE 6
Explaining Hourly Labour Productivity Differences in Manufacturing between France and Germany (Germany=100), 1987

	Labour Productivity	Adjusted for the Effect of			Adjusted Labour Productivity
		Structure	Firm Size	Capital Intensity	
Food and Beverages	138.9		142.4	127.2	130.3
Wearing Apparel, Textiles and Leather	96.7		97.1	99.7	100.1
Wood, Paper and Other Industries	107.4		108.7	107.9	109.2
Chemicals, Rubber and Plastic Products	112.3		114.8	110.4	112.6
Basic Metals and Metal Products	105.1		107.6	88.1	89.8
Machinery	108.0		111.7	102.9	106.5
Transport Equipment	107.2		108.5	106.7	108.0
Electric and Electronic Products	114.4		116.7	111.1	113.3
Total Manufacturing	109.3	111.0	113.0	103.5	108.8
Additive effect		+1.6	+3.6	-5.8	-0.5

Sources: See tables 3 to 5.

in total manufacturing as well as for each major branch.[19] The overall effect of firm size is positive. French-German relative manufacturing hourly labour productivity rises from 109.3 to 113 per cent when adjusted for firm size differences (table 6). As with structural differences, firm size differences do not explain the productivity gap, but on the contrary increase the relative French performance by more than three percentage points.

As already noted, calculating labour or capital productivity separately means attributing all value added to a single production factor. Since value added is the combined effect of labour and capital, high French labour productivity might be due to the relative abundance of capital compared to labour. To take into account the effect of capital intensity, we assume the same capital intensity in the two countries. Equation (2) can be used to reestimate labour productivity, i.e.:

$$\ln\frac{(Y^F/L^F)^{corr}}{(Y^G/L^G)^{corr}} = \ln\frac{A^F}{A^G} \tag{3}$$

when $(1-a)\ln\left[\dfrac{K^F/L^F}{K^G/L^G}\right] = 0$

Relative labour productivity adjusted for differences in capital intensity thus equals the relative joint factor productivity, i.e. 103.5 per cent in terms of hours worked. This represents a drop of some 6 points compared to the initial relative labour productivity, and partly explains the productivity difference between the two countries.

Table 6 shows that the labour productivity gap in favour of France remains largely unexplained by the differences in the effect of structure, firm size and capital intensity; the "adjusted" labour productivity is still 9 per cent higher in France than in Germany. In this study we have not yet examined the role of another important explanatory factor, that is the quality of the labour force. Other studies showed that the share of employees with intermediate or higher vocational qualifications is more important in Germany than in France.[20] Therefore, if we had included this factor the productivity gap would have increased even more.

---

[19] According to our calculations from census data (excluding firms with less than 20 employees), the German average firm size in 1987 in total manufacturing was 211 employees as compared to 141 for France, while the median size was 782 and 501 employees respectively. In both countries productivity increases with firm size suggesting economies of scale, which are more pronounced in France. However, a more detailed analysis shows that this phenomenon does not exist for all major branches (see Freudenberg and Ünal-Kesenci, 1994a and 1994b).

[20] See, for example, Prais (1995), table 2.5.

4. The Product Quality Problem

The results so far indicate a rather low French price level and a labour productivity advantage in manufacturing compared to Germany. This is true not only for the manufacturing total but for virtually all major branches. At the same time, the unexplained productivity difference remains rather important. In this section another factor is investigated in more detail, namely the extent to which differences in product quality may influence the results.[21]

There are two main sources for the differences in UVRs which were used for converting value added to a common currency. These are differences in production cost and in product quality which can be, but do not necessarily have to be, closely intertwined. Though one has been aware of the problem of product quality, it has been assumed that there is no quality difference when the UVRs were estimated, and differences in UVRs were entirely attributed to differences in production costs. However, in reality relatively low UVRs do not tell us if production costs or product quality (or both) are higher in Germany than in France. In the first case the industry-of-origin approach might correctly indicate lower German productivity, whereas in the second case this result is misleading.

If there were no systematic quality differences between countries, errors due to mismatches might cancel out for the total manufacturing sector.[22] However, they might persist at a more detailed level and therefore impede a meaningful analysis by industry or branch. Germany's productivity estimates might be biased downwards for some branches because of relatively high prices due to high quality, a phenomenon which may not have been picked up by the product matches. In general, researchers who themselves do the product matches using production censuses, have little information to verify the validity of their results.

In a study on German and French trade specialisation, Freudenberg and Müller (1992) put forward exactly the opposite hypothesis compared to the industry-of-origin approach. Differences in unit values between products were interpreted as reflecting differences in quality and not in production costs.[23] The analysis was made at a very detailed level (looking at exports and imports for some 9,500 products with 20 geographic regions, yielding some 400,000 basic observations for each country). Unit values of each elementary trade flow were compared to a European norm, to establish product price/quality ranges: up-market products (with unit values exceeding the European norm by at least 15 per cent), down-market products (more than 15 per cent below the norm), and middle-market products. As exports and imports were analysed separately, flows for the same

---

[21] For a discussion of quality problems, see van Ark (1990a, p. 81 and 1990c, p. 347) and Maddison and van Ark (1988, p. 35). For possible product-mix and quality adjustments, see van Ark (1990b, p. 73).
[22] See for example, Gersbach and van Ark (1994).
[23] This was an extension of an approach initially proposed by Abd-El-Rahman (1986).

TABLE 7

Product Quality Ranges in German and French Foreign Trade, 1989

Product Price/ Quality Ranges	Exports (%)		Imports (%)		Export-Import Ratio (%)		Comparative Advantage[a]	
	Germany	France	Germany	France	Germany	France	Germany	France
Up-Market	51.6	40.2	32.1	30.8	201.7	120.0	48.2	19.4
Middle-Market	37.3	40.7	44.5	45.6	105.4	82.0	-17.7	-10.2
Down-Market	10.6	18.1	22.0	22.7	60.6	73.5	-28.2	-9.4
Total	100.0	100.0	100.0	100.0	125.6	92.0	0.0	0.0

[a] See footnote 22.
Note: The sum over the three quality ranges is slightly less than 100 per cent, as "residual" trade flows were not taken into account.
Source: Freudenberg and Müller (1992).

product with a given trade partner can exist in different ranges.

Table 7 shows that while the two countries have a similar import structure, Germany exports more up-market products than France. In 1989, 52 per cent of German exports concerned up-market products, compared to 40 per cent for France. Both countries had a "revealed comparative advantage" in up-market products and comparative disadvantages in the other two ranges, but this phenomenon was much more pronounced in Germany than in France.[24]

Graph 1 shows comparative advantages for price/quality ranges by industry. For France, the most important comparative advantage is in up-market products in machinery, whereas the two following comparative advantages concern middle-market products in food (including agriculture) and transport (mostly cars). Germany has quite a different configuration. It appears to be characterised by some sort of "quality hierarchy", in the sense that it does not "dominate" certain industries over all price/quality ranges, but often exhibits comparative advantages in up-market products, which are accompanied by disadvantages for

---

[24] This indicator was developed by Lafay (1987, 1990). If there were no comparative advantage or disadvantage for any industry k (in a given country), then total trade surplus or deficit should be distributed across all industries according to their share in total trade. The "contribution to the trade balance" is the difference between the actual and the theoretical balance. Expressed in thousandths of GDP, that is:

$$\left(\frac{1000}{Y}\right)\left(\left(X_k - M_k\right) - \left(X - M\right)\left(\frac{X_k + M_k}{X + M}\right)\right)$$

By definition, the sum over all industries is zero. Another important feature is that the values can be aggregated to any given level without biasing the results. For example, summing up over the three price/quality ranges for an industry yields the total comparative advantage for this industry.

GRAPH 1
Revealed Comparative Advantage by Branch and Price/Quality Range
France and Germany, 1989

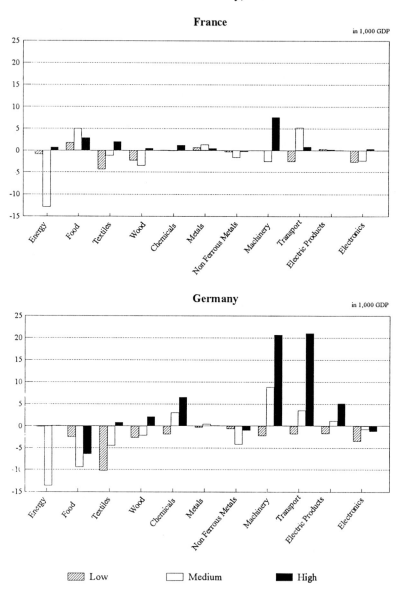

Source: Freudenberg and Müller (1992).

down-market products. This phenomenon is particularly manifest in its key industries like machinery, transport, chemicals and electric products. Overall, however, Germany does best for more expensive goods. Of course, these results from international trade data cannot be directly compared to the present study. They show that Germany exports relatively *more* high priced products than France. However, it does not tell us if German export unit values are on average *higher* than French ones.

The relative price levels based on "producer price" UVRs from this study were therefore directly compared with the price levels derived from export unit value ratios.[25] We calculated French and German unit values for manufacturing exports (fob) to the rest of the world at the most detailed level of the Harmonised System (about 7,300 products). Table 8 shows that relative French-German producer price and export price levels in 1987 were strikingly similar, namely at a level of about 92 per cent.

Also for most major branches, the two relative price levels were quite close. There were two major exceptions. Wearing apparel, textiles and leather products was the only major branch where French export prices were clearly higher than

TABLE 8
Relative French-German Producer and Export Price Levels
in Manufacturing (Germany=100), 1987

	Producer Price Levels	Export Price Levels	Export/ Producer Prices
Food and Beverages	91.1	93.2	102.4
Wearing Apparel, Textiles and Leather	95.3	117.2	123.0
Wood, Paper and other Industries	93.0	99.3	106.8
Chemicals, Rubber and Plastic Products	95.4	101.8	106.8
Basic Metals and Metal Products	95.9	92.6	96.5
Machinery	88.1	87.6	99.4
Transport Equipment	84.9	79.1	93.1
Electric and Electronic Products	91.5	89.7	98.1
Manufacturing	91.7	92.0	100.3

Sources: For producer price ratios, see table 1. Export unit values from Eurostat, database "Comext".

[25] A potential problem is that relative prices of goods produced locally and exported can differ considerably, as market deficiencies, differences in consumer tastes and income levels etc. can be exploited by exporting firms.

Germany's (about 17 per cent). Also French relative export prices were notably higher (23 per cent) than relative producer prices. For transport equipment, the situation was the opposite. In this case, France's export prices were much lower than Germany's (79 per cent), and its relative export prices were also lower than its relative producer prices (93 per cent).

One interpretation of the generally lower French export prices is that the French price advantage in manufacturing costs is translated into a competitive advantage in export prices. Another is that these price differences were justified by presumed or actual quality differences. The validity of these alternative explanations could not be tested for this study.

Recently, the McKinsey Global Institute (1993) compared productivity in the United States, Germany and Japan with the assistance of members of the ICOP project. The study did not cover the whole manufacturing sector, but provided some case studies. While based to a large extent on the industry-of-origin approach, sectoral experts were able to carry out a more in-depth analysis. In contrast to our study, some matched products were adjusted for quality differences. "We compare like products to like products. (...) We decided to assume quality was the same across countries unless there are differences that meet the following two-part test. The differences in quality are: 1) recognized by consumers and such that they are willing to pay a price premium; and 2) are a result of differences in the production process, and not of advertising, tradition, nationalism, differences in information, etc. We adjust our comparable products for quality only if the product differences meet these two condi-tions...".[26]

The McKinsey study basically made the same assumptions as we do to estimate total output from the covered part of matched products. "The second step in accounting for quality differences across countries arises with products that are not comparable. We argue that, provided the PPP has been correctly estimated for the standard products in that industry, there is no further adjustment necessary to take account of specialty products that are either higher or lower in quality than standard products. The basis for this is that specialty products will command a higher or lower price in the market than the standard industry products, and will consequently add more or less to value added per unit than the standard industry products. The price system in market economies automatically provides a quality adjustment because it reflects value as perceived by customers."[27]

It is assumed that differences in prices and value added of non-standard products compared to standard products move in the same direction. As

---

[26] McKinsey Global Institute (1993); box after page 8 on "productivity and the measurement of quality". See also Gersbach and van Ark (1994).
[27] Ibid.

mentioned above, the relatively low productivity in Germany might be "penalised" by the industry of origin approach because of relatively high prices partly due to higher quality product, a phenomenon which may not have been picked up by the product matches. If this assumption is correct, and our product matches are "representative", relatively high German unit values should go along with relatively high value added (corrected for labour input).

One may therefore consider the relationship between value added per employee and UVRs. The observed, relative French-German productivity level (here in FF) is:

$$\left[\frac{VA^{F(FF)}}{L^F} \right] \Big/ \left[\frac{VA^{G(DM)}\ UVR_{observed}}{L^G} \right] \qquad (4)$$

The UVRs used here are derived from the product matches. We therefore call them "observed UVRs". Yet, from the industry information, one can calculate a "theoretical UVR" for each industry, which assumes the same productivity in the two countries. The theoretical relative productivity in FF is then:

$$\left[\frac{VA^{F(FF)}}{L^F} \right] \Big/ \left[\frac{VA^{G(DM)}\ UVR_{theoretical}}{L^G} \right] = 1 \qquad (5)$$

Equations (4) and (5) give the relationship between relative French-German labour productivity and observed and theoretical UVRs:

$$\frac{UVR_{theoretical}}{UVR_{observed}} \qquad (6)$$

There appears to be an inverse relation between observed unit value ratios and relative labour productivity levels. If the observed UVR is lower than the theoretical one (we multiply German value added by less than we would if its productivity were the same as in France), German labour productivity is lower than French productivity. For total manufacturing, the theoretical UVR (3.32 FF/DM) is almost identical to the exchange rate of 3.35 FF/DM in 1987, but 8.4 per cent higher than the observed UVR of 3.06 FF/DM. In fact, these 8.4 percentage points correspond to the French advantage in labour productivity.

Graph 2 shows both theoretical and observed UVRs for all industries (sorted in descending order of relative labour productivity). Here, we are not so much interested in the magnitude of the differences between theoretical and observed UVRs,[28] but whether the two UVRs for a given industry deviate roughly in the same direction when compared to their average. For example, the cement industry shows very high observed UVRs (4.16 FF/DM, due to high French prices), but even higher theoretical ones (5.13 FF/DM, due to relatively higher French value added), yielding a labour productivity advantage for France. For

---

[28] In fact outliers of theoretical UVRs might indicate an incorrect industry match, while outliers of observed UVRs might indicate a product mismatch.

72   *M. Freudenberg and D. Ünal-Kesenci*

GRAPH 2
Observed Versus Theoretical UVRs, France and Germany, 1987

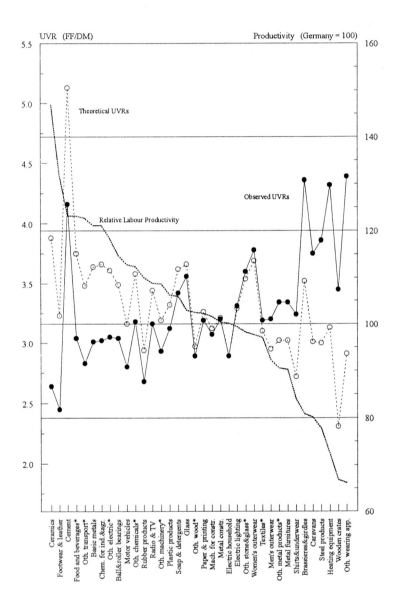

Sources: See table 3.

brassieres and girdles, the observed UVR is very close to that of cement, but as the theoretical UVR is much lower, it is Germany that has a productivity advantage. There are some industries which fit less nicely in the framework observed/theoretical UVRs, like for example ceramics or wooden crates. While all product matches were checked several times, particular emphasis was put on presumable "outlier" UVRs. Overall, one can put quite some confidence in the validity of UVRs and productivity levels.

5. Extrapolating the Benchmark Year Results

The results presented in the previous sections refer to 1987. Using national time series, we extrapolated the benchmark results for UVRs and input, output as well as productivity levels backwards to 1970 and forwards to 1992. Below the evolution for total manufacturing and for major branches is presented. The data refer to former West Germany only, even for the period after the German unification.

Evolution of UVRs

The 1987 value added weighted UVR is extrapolated to other years by applying the ratio of French and German price indices for value added in national currencies.[29] Graph 3 shows the evolution of (value added weighted) UVRs for total manufacturing, market exchange rates, as well as purchasing power parities for Gross Domestic Product. During the time period considered, the French franc regularly depreciated compared to the German mark, from about 1.50 FF/DM in 1970 to 3.35 FF/DM in 1987, entering a period of relative stability thereafter.[30] While nominal exchange rates may be erratic in the short run and influenced by trade balance or capital movements for example, the depreciation of the French franc in the long run seems justified by the evolution of manufacturing UVRs as well as by the purchasing power parities. Until the mid 1980s, the nominal exchange rate converged systematically on these two indicators, which themselves are strikingly similar and (by nature) more inert than market exchange rates.

After 1987 the pivoting rates for exchange rates were frozen within the European Monetary System. UVRs as well as PPPs also levelled off, but at different levels, creating a stable but significant gap between exchange rates and these two indicators. This gap suggests that the French franc is slightly undervalued when compared to the German mark, and that France benefits from a competitive price advantage over Germany. This price gap may be necessary

---

[29] See van Ark (1993, pp. 68-69).
[30] Until the speculations against the franc in September 1992 and the summer of 1993.

GRAPH 3
Evolution of Manufacturing UVR, PPP for GDP and the Exchange Rate,
France-Germany (FF/DM)

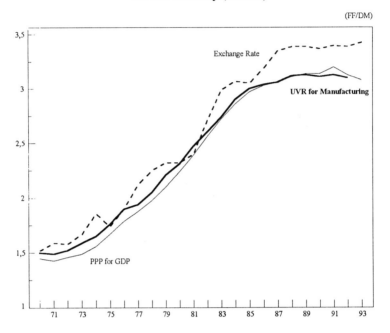

Sources: For the UVR in 1987, see table 1. Extrapolations are based on series from INSEE, database "NOUBA" and Statistisches Bundesamt, *Volkswirtschaftliche Gesamtrechnungen, Revidierte Ergebnisse, 1950 bis 1990* (with updates to 1992 kindly provided by N. Räth). Exchange rates and PPPs in 1990 prices are from CEPII, database "CHELEM".

to compensate for the often evoked German non-price competitiveness.

The upper part of graph 4 shows the relative French-German price level in major branches, which is obtained by dividing UVRs by the exchange rate. While the exchange rate and the manufacturing UVR move closely together (see also graph 3), the relative French price level for manufacturing is slightly below the German level for most years. At the beginning of the time period, the dispersion among major branches was high and more or less evenly distributed above and below the level of 100. After the mid 1980s, the relative price level of all major branches converged strongly to a level of about 90 per cent.

The coefficient of variation (lower part of graph 4) among the eight major branches dropped substantially after the first oil shock until 1986. After this date the dispersion of relative prices among major branches slightly increased again.[31] Despite the remaining price gap of some 10 per cent for total manufacturing, there was a clear convergence in relative producer prices among major branches.

GRAPH 4
Relative French Price Levels in Major Branches (Germany=100)

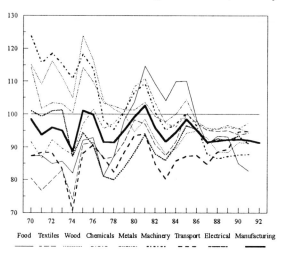

Food   Textiles   Wood   Chemicals   Metals   Machinery   Transport   Electrical   Manufacturing

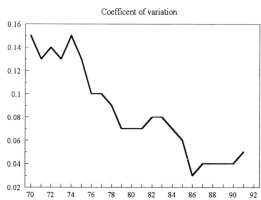

Sources: See graph 3.

---

[31] This increase is mainly due to the relative price level of food and beverages, which has continued to decline.

Evolution of Input, Output and Productivity in Manufacturing

In order better to apprehend the evolution of relative French-German levels of manufacturing inputs, outputs and productivity, first several indices from national accounts for total manufacturing are presented.[32]

Graph 5 shows that during the 1970s (with the exception of the period after the first oil shock) both countries experienced sustained growth in manufacturing value added, with France by far outpacing Germany. In contrast, the volume of hours worked fell in both countries. While before 1974 labour input rose in France and declined in Germany, the first oil shock reversed the trend in France and sharply accelerated the fall in labour input in Germany. During the decade labour productivity growth was similar in the two countries, as higher French growth in value added was counterbalanced by a stronger reduction in inputs in Germany. Capital stock rose faster than output in both countries. In contrast to labour productivity, capital productivity actually declined.

Graph 6 shows relative French-German levels of manufacturing inputs, output and productivity. The upper part of the graph shows that at the beginning of the 1970s, French value added, hours worked and capital stock represented about 54 per cent of the German level. Productivity was almost identical in the two countries (lower part of graph 6). During the 1970s, as growth in value added and capital stock in France was higher and the decline in labour input less pronounced than in Germany (graph 5), France caught up with Germany, both in terms of output and of production factors to a level of 61-62 per cent, while productivity in the two countries remained very close, despite minor fluctuations.

The second oil shock and the recession of the early 1980s had stronger negative effects on economic growth and labour input in France than the first oil shock (graph 5). However, from the mid 1980s onwards, the oil counter-shock as well as the preparation for the Single Market and German unification were positive factors for economic growth. Nevertheless, while the 1970s were a decade of catching up for France, the 1980s reversed most of these relative gains. In the beginning of the 1990s the relative size of French manufacturing (as indicated by value added) was again at almost the same percentage as 20 years before, i.e. at about 55 per cent of German manufacturing (graph 6), whereas French labour input dropped to an even lower level than in 1970. If measured in terms of employees only, the relative French decline is even more pronounced. Only the relative French capital stock continued to increase to some 65 per cent of the German level.

---

[32] The base year is 1970, except for indicators of capital stock where it is 1971. We used data from 1970 onwards, but while German national accounts indicate figures for the beginning of the year, French national accounts provide end year figures. We adjusted both series to obtain mid year figures.

GRAPH 5
Indices on Data from National Accounts for Manufacturing,
France and Germany

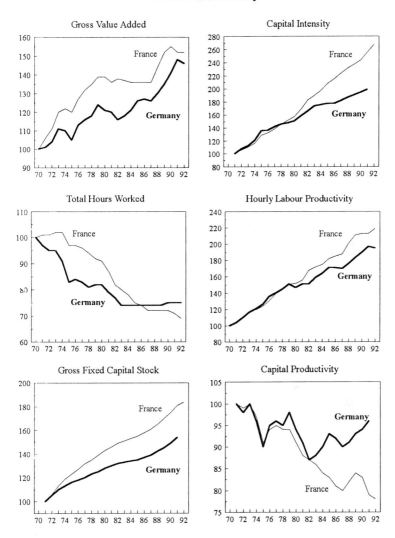

Sources: Extrapolations are based on series from INSEE, database "NOUBA" and Statistisches Bundesamt, *Volkswirtschaftliche Gesamtrechnungen, Revidierte Ergebnisse, 1950 bis 1990*, with updates to 1992 kindly provided by N. Räth. Hours worked for Germany are from H. Kohler and L. Reyher, *Arbeitszeit und Arbeitvolumen in der Bundesrepublik Deutschland: 1960-1990*, Institut für Arbeitsmarkt und Berufsforschung (IAB), with updates to 1992 kindly provided by H. Kohler.

GRAPH 6
Relative French Levels of Inputs, Outputs and Productivity in
Manufacturing (Germany = 100)

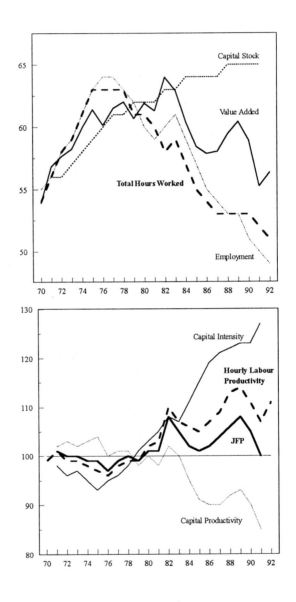

Sources: See tables 1, 2, 3 and 4 as well as graph 5.

Therefore while joint factor productivity remained very close in the two countries until the end of the period, its components show a radically different evolution. Relative French labour productivity improved considerably. The French labour productivity advantage would have been even higher if we had included former East Germany with West Germany after 1990.[33] In contrast relative French capital productivity fell from about the same level as Germany, to about 85 per cent. These two phenomena are closely related to relative capital intensity (lower part of graph 6), which has increased in France from less than 100 per cent to more than 125 per cent of the German level. Gains in labour productivity and losses in capital productivity in France are basically due to the substitution of labour by capital, which was much stronger than in Germany. Nevertheless, since the early 1980s this link has almost disappeared and the stronger substitution in France does not translate anymore in relative French labour productivity gains.

GRAPH 7
Decomposition of Total Hours Worked, France and Germany

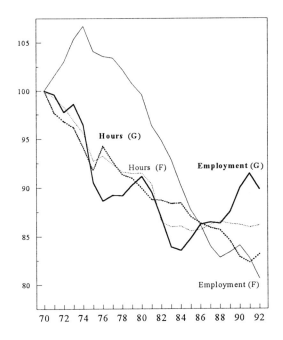

Sources: See graph 5.

---

[33] Beintema and van Ark (1993) estimate the value added per hour worked in manufacturing in East Germany at about 28 per cent of the West German level in 1987.

GRAPH 8
**Levels and Dispersion of Relative French-German Productivity
in Major Branches (Germany=100)**

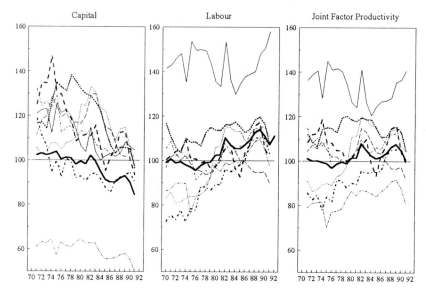

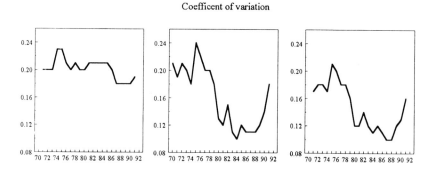

Coefficent of variation

Sources: See tables 3, 4, 5 and 6 as well as graph 5.

Apart from the much stronger substitution of labour by capital in France compared to Germany, an interesting pattern was found when analysing the evolution of labour input in both countries seperately. In graph 7 labour input is decomposed into employment and annual hours worked per employee. The evolution of employment in Germany is sensitive to business cycles, while French employment declines regularly even in periods of growth. After around

1984 Germany experienced a decline in annual hours per employee to go along with a rise in the number of employees, whereas in France annual hours were almost constant while employment was further adjusted downwards.

Despite these differences, there was a convergence in the relative levels of labour, capital and joint factor productivity as was also the case for relative prices among the eight major branches. Graph 8 shows relative French-German productivity levels in major branches and the coefficient of variation. At the beginning of the 1970s, relative French-German labour productivity levels among major branches were more or less evenly distributed, above and below the level of 100. While relative French labour productivity increased in general, it was mainly France's least productive branches which improved most from the mid-1970s to mid-1980s. The resulting convergence can be seen by the coefficient of variation which dropped strongly during this period. Thereafter the dispersion increased again, and has been due mostly to food and beverages which have become even more productive in France, and textiles which have continued to decline in relative terms. Thus despite the remaining labour productivity gap for total manufacturing, there is a convergence in relative productivity for most major branches.

The coefficient of variation for capital productivity remains rather stable. This is mostly due to basic metals and metal products, which stayed at an exceptionally low level, while the other major branches converged in relative terms. Joint factor productivity also shows a clear convergence among major branches. Due to the high share of labour compensation in GDP, the evolution of the coefficient of variation is quite close to that of labour productivity.

6. Concluding Remarks

Applying the industry-of-origin approach to France and West Germany, unit value ratios (UVRs) were calculated for about 240 products, which correspond to some 18 per cent of manufacturing sales (i.e. manufacturing enterprises with 20 employees or more). These UVRs were used to convert value added in national prices into the currency of the other country. This allowed the estimation of relative price, output and productivity levels of the two countries.

Since around 1987 French price levels in manufacturing have been about 10 per cent lower than in West Germany. One possible interpretation of the price gap is that French enterprises may have benefitted from a certain price advantage which may have partly compensated the supposedly stronger non-price competitiveness in Germany. However, the problem of product quality differences translating into price differences could not be completely set aside. Despite the remaining absolute price gap for total manufacturing, there is a remarkable convergence in relative price levels among major branches. This is most probably due to the increasing openness of the economies, and the resulting stronger competition among enterprises.

In terms of output and factors of production, the 1970s were a decade during which France caught up with Germany, whereas the 1980s reversed most of these relative gains. French and German labour, capital and joint factor productivity were very close during most of the 1970s. However, the picture has changed radically since the end of the 1970s. Whereas joint factor productivity in the two countries remained rather close, its two components have shown a clear divergence. Relative French labour productivity has improved considerably while its relative capital productivity has declined substantially.

The factors examined in this paper explain only partly the French advantage in labour productivity over Germany. Structural differences like the concentration of employment and firm size do not explain the differences. On the contrary, they suggest even higher French labour productivity. However, capital intensity explains some of the productivity gap. France's capital intensity in manufacturing has become increasingly higher than Germany's. Despite lower labour costs and higher real interest rates than in Germany, the substitution of labour by capital was much stronger in France during the 1980s. This substitution might be a major reason for the rise in the French unemployment rate despite relatively high growth rates in the late 1980s.

Statistical Sources

CEPII, database "CHELEM"

EUROSTAT, database "COMEXT"

INSEE, database "NOUBA".

INSEE, *Bulletins mensuels de statistique*, December 1987 and May 1988.

INSEE, *Annuaire statistique de la France, résultats 1988.*

INSEE (1990), *20 ans de comptes nationaux, 1970-1989*, Economie générale no. 27-28, résultats no. 104-105

Kohler H. and L. Reyher (1991), *Arbeitszeit und Arbeitvolumen in der Bundesrepublik Deutschland: 1960-1990*, Institut für Arbeitsmarkt und Berufsforschung (IAB), Nürnberg. Updates to 1992 kindly provided by H. Kohler.

OECD (1984a), *Produit brut réel et parités de pouvoir d'achat dans les pays de l'OCDE*, Working Paper No. 17, December.

OECD (1984b, 1988, 1992), *National Accounts, Detailed Tables, Volume II*, 1970-1982, 1974-1986, 1979-1991.

SCEES (Service central des enquêtes et des études statistiques), *Enquête annuelle d'entreprise 1987*, Industries agricoles et alimentaires (IAA)

SESSI (Service des statistiques industrielles), *Enquête annuelle d'entreprise 1987.*

SESSI, *Enquêtes de branches 1987.*

SESSI, *Annuaire de statistique industrielle 1990-91.*

Statistisches Bundesamt, *Kostenstruktur der Unternehmen 1987,* Produzierendes Gewerbe, Fachserie 4, Reihe 4.3.1 - 4.3.3.

Statistisches Bundesamt, *Produktion im produzierenden Gewerbe des In- und Auslands 1987,* Produzierendes Gewerbe, Fachserie 4, Reihe 3.1.

Statistisches Bundesamt, *Volkswirtschaftliche Gesamtrechnungen, Revidierte Ergebnisse, 1950 bis 1990,* Fachserie 18, Reihe S. 15. Updates to 1992 kindly provided by N. Räth.

United Nations (1988), *Annual Bulletin of Steel Statistics for Europe,* Vol. XVI.

World Bank (1993), *Purchasing Power of Currencies : Comparing National Incomes Using ICP Data,* International Economics Department.

References

Abd-El-Rahman, K. (1986), "Réexamen de la définition et de la mesure des échanges croisés de produits similaires entre les nations", *Revue économique,* Vol. 37, No. 1.

Ark, B. van (1990a), "Comparative Levels of Labour Productivity in Dutch and British Manufacturing", *National Institute Economic Review,* February.

--- (1990b), "Manufacturing Productivity Levels in France and the United Kingdom", *National Institute Economic Review,* August.

--- (1990c), "Comparative Levels of Manufacturing Productivity in Postwar Europe: Measurement and Comparisons", *Oxford Bulletin of Economics and Statistics,* November.

--- (1993), *International Comparisons of Output and Productivity: Manufacturing Productivity Performance of Ten Countries Since 1950,* Monograph Series No. 1, Groningen Growth and Development Centre.

--- and R.D.J. Kouwenhoven (1994), "Productivity in French Manufacturing: An International Comparative Perspective", *Research Memorandum No. 571 (GD-10),* Groningen Growth and Development Centre.

Beintema, N. and B. van Ark (1993), "Comparative Productivity in East and West German Manufacturing before Reunification", *Research Memorandum No. 550 (GD-5),* Groningen Growth and Development Centre.

Fleurbaey, M. and P. Joly (1990), "La reprise de la productivité à la fin des années quatre-vingt n'est-elle qu'apparente ?", *Economie et Statistique,* No. 237-238, November-December.

Freudenberg, M. and F. Müller (1992), "France et Allemagne: quelles spécialisations commerciales?", *Economie prospective internationale,* No. 52, 4e trimestre.

--- and D. Ünal-Kesenci (1994a), "French and German Productivity Levels in Manufacturing: A Comparison Based on the Industry-of-Origin Method", *CEPII Working Paper* 94-10.

--- and --- (1994b), "France-Allemagne: prix et productivité dans le secteur manufacturier", *Economie Internationale,* no. 60, CEPII, pp. 33-70.

Gersbach, H. and B. van Ark (1994), "Micro Foundations for International Productivity Comparisons", *Research Memorandum GD-11*, Groningen Growth and Development Centre.

Guinchard, P. (1984), "Productivité et compétitivité des grands pays industriels", *Economie et Statistique,* January.

Kessler, V. (1979), "La mesure du capital", *Document de travail du CEPII*, October.

Kravis, I.B. (1976), "A Survey of International Comparisons of Productivity", *The Economic Journal,* No. 86, March.

--- and R. Lipsey (1990), "The International Comparison Program: Current Status and Problems", *NBER Working Paper Series*, No. 3304.

---, A. Heston and R. Summers (1982), *World Product and Income: International Comparisons of Real Gross Output*, Johns Hopkins University Press, Baltimore and London.

Lafay, G. (1987), "Avantage comparatif et compétitivité", *Economie prospective internationale*, No. 29, 1er trimestre.

--- (1990), "La mesure des avantages comparatifs révélés", *Economie prospective internationale*, No. 41, 1er trimestre.

--- and C. Herzog with L. Stemitsiotis and D. Ünal (1989), *Commerce international: la fin des avantages acquis*, Economica, Paris.

Maddison, A. (1993), "Standardised Estimates of Fixed Capital Stock: A Six Country Comparison", *Innovazione E Materie Prime*, April.

--- and B van Ark (1988), "Comparisons of Real Output in Manufacturing", *Working Papers WPS5*, World Bank, Washington D.C.

McKinsey Global Institute (1993), *Manufacturing Productivity,* October, Washington D.C.

O'Mahony, M. (1993), "International Measures of Fixed Capital Stocks: A Five-Country Study", *NIESR Discussion Paper Series*, No. 51, September.

Prais, S.J. (1995), *Productivity, Education and Training. An International Perspective*. National Institute of Economic and Social Research, Cambridge University Press.

Smith, A.D., D.M.W.N. Hitchens and S.W. Davies (1982), *International Industrial Productivity: A Comparison of Britain, America and Germany,* National Institute of Economic and Social Research, Cambridge University Press.

Szirmai, A. and D. Pilat (1990), "The International Comparison of Real Output and Labour Productivity in Manufacturing: A Study for Japan, South Korea and the USA for 1975", *Research Memorandum No. 354*, Institute of Economic Research.

International Productivity Differences
K. Wagner and B. van Ark (editors)

Productivity in a Dual Economy - The Case of Japan

*Dirk Pilat**
Groningen Growth and Development Centre, University of Groningen

1. Introduction

Japan is currently considered to be the main challenger to the US leadership position in the world economy (van Ark and Pilat, 1993). It has experienced extremely rapid growth in the postwar period and has become one of the major industrial powers. Japan was among a large group of industrialised countries which showed rapid growth (Maddison, 1991). However, it performed better than most others, and was therefore catching up with countries which initially had much higher income levels than itself. By 1990, Japan's income level was still slightly below that in the United States, but it had surpassed several countries in Western Europe (OECD, 1992a).

How far has Japan really progressed in the postwar period and how does its performance vary between different sectors of the economy? To answer these questions it is necessary to compare its achievement with that of other countries. Such a comparison can be made in a number of ways. The usual method is the comparison of growth rates. Another is the comparison of levels of achievement, such as income and productivity levels. The latter method is an important complement to the comparison of growth rates, since countries may be able to achieve high growth rates if they start from a lower level. At lower levels of productivity there is a much larger stock of internationally available technology for the country to be adopted, then if the country is already close to the levels achieved by the world productivity leader, i.e. the United States. This "catch up" factor is currently regarded as an important factor underlying the fast growth of European and other industrialising countries in the postwar period, compared to the much slower growth in the United States (Baumol, 1986; Abramovitz, 1989; Nelson and Wright, 1992). In addition, level comparisons give insight in a country's position compared to best practice and compared to its main competitors.

This paper analyses the productive performance of Japan in a comparison with the United States. It first looks at relative productivity growth from 1953 onwards, for the main sectors of the economy. Next, it estimates relative

---

*   I am grateful for comments received from Bart van Ark, Karin Wagner, an anonymous referee and participants of the Berlin conference.

productivity levels, in order to assess how far Japan has progressed in the postwar period and how its achievement varies between sectors of the economy. Finally, some explanatory factors for the remaining productivity gap between Japan and the United States are considered.

2. Relative Productivity Growth

Japan's catch up is the result of its productivity growth within sectors and the sectoral reallocation of production factors from sectors with low absolute productivity levels to those with high absolute levels of productivity. Most of Japan's catch up with the United States is due to its faster productivity growth within sectors of the economy (Dollar and Wolff, 1993; Pilat, 1993).

Table 1 shows the productivity growth rates for the nine main sectors of the economy for three periods, 1953-73, 1973-90 and 1953-90. The figures refer to GDP per hour worked and are primarily based on the national accounts series in both countries, supplemented with detailed series on hours worked by sector. The 1953 to 1973 period corresponds to the high growth period for most of the world economy. The second period, 1973-90, corresponds to the period of slower growth.

Japanese productivity growth was particularly fast in the period 1953-73. High growth rates were achieved in mining, manufacturing, utilities and wholesale and retail trade. After 1973, productivity growth slowed down. The highest growth rate was achieved in manufacturing, but growth rates in most sectors were only half of those achieved over the previous period. Productivity growth rates in the United States were much lower than Japan's in both periods. In the second period, some sectors in the United States experienced negative or zero productivity growth.

In both periods and in all sectors except agriculture, Japan was catching up with the United States. However, the differences between sectors are substantial. The fastest rates of catch up were achieved in mining, manufacturing and wholesale and retail trade. Little progress was made in agriculture and services, although in the latter sector the productivity series are very rough for both countries.

A problem with table 1 are the underlying time series of real output and labour input. A recent debate in the United States concerns the substantial problems involved in several of the sectoral GNP series. In some sectors, the official GNP series show no productivity growth at all. For instance, the US output series for government is still primarily based on extrapolation of value added in the base year with employment. This implies that over time, the US series show no labour productivity change in government. Recently Kendrick (1990) has presented estimates of government output based on much better indicators. The Japanese series are based on the deflation of current value added (mainly compensation of employees; see OECD, 1987), that are likely to show

TABLE 1
Growth Rates of GDP per Hour Worked, 1953-1990
(annual average compound growth rates)

	Japan			United States		
	1953- 1973	1973- 1990	1953- 1990	1953- 1973	1973- 1990	1953- 1990
Agriculture, Forestry & Fisheries	5.87	2.94	4.51	4.15	3.48	3.84
Mining	13.73	4.30	9.29	3.66	-1.81	1.11
Manufacturing	8.82	5.18	7.13	2.82	2.24	2.55
Electricity, Gas & Water	8.94	3.56	6.44	5.22	0.68	3.11
Construction	4.52	1.79	3.26	0.23	-1.46	-0.55
Transport & Communication	7.91	2.59	5.43	3.21	2.32	2.80
Wholesale & Retail Trade	10.38	4.19	7.49	2.63	1.76	2.23
Finance, Insurance & Real Estate	3.24	2.16	2.74	1.81	0.02	0.98
Services & Government	2.02	1.27	1.68	0.81	0.00	0.44
Total Economy	6.26	3.29	4.88	2.13	0.81	1.52

Source: GDP and employment Japan from Economic Planning Agency, *Report on National Accounts from 1953 to 1989*, Tokyo, 1991, EPA, *Annual Report on National Accounts 1993*, Tokyo, 1993 and from K. Ohkawa and H. Rosovsky, *Japanese Economic Growth*, Stanford University Press, Stanford; Hours worked based on Ministry of Labour, *Monthly Labour Force Survey*, Tokyo, various issues and Statistics Bureau, Management and Coordination Agency, *Labour Force Survey*, Tokyo, various issues; United States based on Bureau of Economic Analysis (BEA), *National Income and Product Accounts of the United States, 1929-1982*, Washington DC, 1986, BEA, *National Income and Product Accounts of the United States, Vol. 2, 1959-1988*, Washington DC, 1992, and BEA, *Survey of Current Business*, Washington DC, various issues.

some productivity change over time. Others, in particular the US construction sector, have had negative productivity growth since the middle of the 1960s.

The differences between Japan and the United States are related to the methods used in constructing their national accounts (OECD, 1987; Gordon and Baily, 1991). Japan is among those countries which annually construct input-output tables. It uses double deflation in almost all sectors of the economy. Until recently the United States made fairly little use of double deflation, with the exception of its manufacturing series. The recent revisions by BEA use double deflation to a much larger extent. Another difference between the two countries concerns the use of a hedonic price index in the United States for the computer industry. This hedonic price index (Sinclair and Catron, 1990) takes account of quality changes to a much greater extent than a conventional price index. The US computer industry therefore is likely to show much faster growth than its counterparts in other countries.

All this implies that the time series of productivity growth have to be interpreted with care and that more work needs to be done to reconcile the time series between different countries. Some work in this area has recently been done for the manufacturing sector (Gordon and Baily, 1991), but in other sectors of the economy the problems may be just as large.

3. Comparing Productivity Levels

Measurement Issues

The sectoral approach to international comparisons is in its essence quite simple. To convert sectoral value added, representative price ratios, based on the ex-factory prices of products produced in that sector, must be derived.[1] Ex-factory prices, and their corresponding quantity weights, are not available for all sectors and the direct pricing approach is mainly applicable to comparisons of output and prices in sectors producing commodities, such as agriculture, mining and manufacturing. For other sectors, indirect methods can be used. If suitable quantity indicators for sectoral output are available, which is for instance the case for the sectors transport, communication and public utilities, these quantity indicators can be used to derive implicit price relatives.

For some sectors, especially those producing non-market services (education, health, government), statistical information on prices or quantities is almost completely lacking. The ICP project faced similar problems with these sectors and termed them "comparison resistant" (Kravis, Heston and Summers, 1982). Since these services are usually not traded in the market, no price can be observed for them. An indicator of output for these services is also quite difficult to define. ICP used some price information and further based its comparison on input indicators. It is difficult to do much more from a sectoral perspective. In this paper, an output indicator for education was used, but for the other non-market services ICP PPPs were used as a proxy. For services, the use of "proxy" PPPs may sometimes be a second-best alternative to the use of proper industry of origin PPPs. However, this is only the case if there is little trade in that particular sector, if there are no trade and transport margins, if the sector has no or few intermediate components, and if taxes and subsidies have little influence on the prices observed. Typically, this is more likely to be the case in

---

[1]   See the paper by van Ark in this volume for a more formal description of the industry-of-origin approach.

service sectors than in sectors such as agriculture or manufacturing.

The PPPs derived according to these methods are based mainly on output prices and output information, not on gross domestic product by industry. Theoretically, PPPs for GDP must be derived by double deflation. This implies that separate PPPs for sectoral output and input must be derived. The main problem here is that information on prices and quantities of inputs is even more difficult to derive than information on output prices and quantities. For the agricultural sector some detailed double deflated estimates have been made (van der Meer and Yamada, 1990). For other sectors, only rough attempts have been made using input-output tables, which often led to implausible or highly unstable estimates (Szirmai and Pilat, 1990; van Ark, 1993). Especially if the ratio of value added to output is small, or if the price ratios for inputs are only rough approximations, double deflation can give highly unreliable results. In the current literature, most authors prefer to use the adjusted single deflation method (Paige and Bombach, 1959; van Ark, 1993) instead. In this approach, output price ratios are applied to sectoral gross domestic product and weighted at that level to derive a PPP for the whole of GDP. David (1966) suggested that single deflation may not be such a bad alternative for double deflation. Double deflation of value added over time, or between countries, may lead to a substantial index number problem, since the relation between output and input at a specific date or place may not be appropriate given production possibilities at another time or place. David's suggestion was therefore to use single deflation.

International comparisons of productivity are time-consuming. Statistical sources have to be consulted and translated, and products, industries and classification systems have to be matched. Some sources are not available on an annual basis. For these reasons international comparisons are usually made for a limited number of benchmark years, and the results are updated for intermediate years. Data availability and the results from the ICP investigation suggested 1985 as the benchmark year for the current paper. The data and measurement issues underlying the productivity estimates for each sector are not further discussed in this paper. More detail is available in Pilat (1994).

PPPs and Productivity in 1985

To derive indicators of real output and productivity, the estimated PPPs have to be applied to the basic GDP and labour input information. The results of this procedure are shown in table 2. Productivity and price levels[2] in Japan show extreme variations between sectors. On the one hand, sectors such as agriculture, electricity, gas and water, and real estate had extremely high PPPs and price levels, and correspondingly low productivity levels. On the other hand, finance,

---

[2]   The relative price level is the purchasing power parity divided by the exchange rate.

insurance, education and health had relatively low price levels and correspondingly high productivity levels.

The PPP for total GDP is quite close to the exchange rate (238.5 Yen/US$) in 1985, indicating that the overall price level in Japan in that year was close to that in the United States. The PPP for total GDP is somewhat lower than that derived by the expenditure approach for the same year (Eurostat, 1991), which

TABLE 2
Comparative Productivity and Price Levels
Japan and the United States, 1985

	Purchasing Power Parity (Yen/US$)	GDP per Person Engaged Japan (USA=100)	GDP per Hour Worked Japan (USA=100)	Relative Price Level Japan (USA=100)
Agriculture, Forestry & Fisheries	745.5	7.0	8.8	312.4
Mining	268.2	27.6	25.8	112.4
Manufacturing	175.3	85.7	76.0	73.5
Electricity, Gas and Water	409.7	53.2	50.7	171.7
Construction	301.1	50.5	45.3	126.2
Transport and Communication				
- Transport and Storage	298.0	48.5	40.7	124.9
- Communication	231.1	52.3	43.6	96.8
Wholesale and Retail Trade				
- Wholesale Trade	257.1	56.1	50.4	107.7
- Retail Trade	251.9	66.9	47.3	105.6
Finance, Insurance & Real Estate				
- Finance	236.8	106.0	95.7	99.2
- Insurance	173.7	128.5	116.3	72.8
- Real Estate	539.0	50.1	45.3	225.9
Services and Government				
- Education	109.2	254.3	188.3	45.8
- Health	111.4	181.5	137.9	46.7
- Other Services	234.8	73.9	58.4	98.4
- Government	173.4	169.3	125.6	72.7
Total Economy	241.6	64.5	53.3	101.2

Source: Basic GDP and employment data from sources quoted in table 1, with additional breakdown Japan from MITI, *1975-1980-1985 Link Input-Output Tables*, Tokyo, 1985 and EPA worksheets; hours worked Japan from sources quoted in table 1; in United States from Bureau of Labor Statistics, *Monthly Labor Review*, Washington DC, various issues, adjusted to actual hours worked based on BLS worksheets.

was 262.3 Yen to the US$ (Fisher PPP), implying that my PPPs give higher estimates of relative productivity than the expenditure PPPs. Based on the industry of origin PPPs, GDP per person engaged in Japan was only 64.5 percent of that in the United States, and GDP per hour worked only 53.3 percent.

Japan has very low productivity levels in agriculture and mining. Japanese agriculture is characterised by a very small scale, and therefore has only limited benefits from economies of scale. In addition, a considerable share of farmers consists of part-timers, who due to high price levels can still attain a reasonable income from inefficient holdings. The high degree of protection has led to excessive input use, which would be irrational at lower price levels. Furthermore, a general effect of protection has been that farmers are not open to competition from the world market and therefore do not rationalise production (van der Meer and Yamada, 1990).

In mining, productivity was also relatively low, partly because the output structure of mining is quite different between Japan and the United States. In Japan, production consists mainly of coal mining and quarrying of gravel and stone, which are activities where value added per person is quite low. In the United States, oil and gas extraction are much more important. These are much more capital intensive activities, where labour productivity is much higher.

For manufacturing, only the productivity results for the total sector are shown in table 2. GDP per hour worked was 76 percent of the US level in 1985. The variation within manufacturing was quite large, however. Productivity in machinery, transport equipment, metal products and electrical equipment was close to the US level, but in food products, wearing apparel and wood products productivity was far below US levels. More detailed results are discussed elsewhere (van Ark and Pilat, 1993).

In electricity, gas and water, construction, and transport and communication Japan was still considerably behind US productivity levels in 1985. Productivity in utilities was only 51 percent of the US level, in construction it was only 45 percent, in transport 41 percent, and in communication only 44 percent.

Japanese distribution is also a laggard in terms of its productivity level. Establishments are, on average, smaller than in the United States, partly due to regulations which have constrained the growth of large scale establishments (McKinsey, 1992; 1994). Distribution is usually regarded as a safety net, in which the least qualified workers have to make a living. Productivity in wholesale trade was only 50 percent of the US level, and in retail trade the level was only 47 percent of that in the United States. Ito and Maruyama (1991) have recently argued that productivity in Japanese distribution is not that different from the United States. They measured productivity as sales per worker, converted with OECD PPPs for GDP. The main problem with their estimates is that they use sales as their indicator of output. An important characteristic of the Japanese distribution system is the large number of layers (OECD, 1992c).

Products may move from the manufacturer through several wholesalers before reaching the retailer. It is even possible that the product may move between retailers. Use of sales as the output concept for the distribution sector leads to double counting and therefore to an overstatement of relative output and productivity levels in this sector. This is especially the case in a comparison between Japan and the United States, since the GDP/sales ratio in the United States is much lower than in Japan. In wholesale trade the difference between sales based productivity measures and GDP based productivity measures is quite large in relative terms.

In finance, insurance and real estate the spread in productivity was also considerable. Japanese banks have grown to be the largest in the world, handling enormous amounts of assets. In this respect the output of the financial sector is very large indeed. On the other hand, transactions in Japanese banks are often slow and there is a high level of inefficiency involved in simple withdrawals. A confrontation of the transactions approach used here and the liquidity approach might provide additional insights (see Smith, 1989). Productivity in finance was estimated to be slightly below the US level, at 99 percent. In insurance, productivity was also quite high, at 73 percent of the United States. In real estate, productivity was much lower. Prices of dwellings in Japan are extremely high and the quality of housing is often much less than in the United States. The high price level partly reflects the extreme land scarcity in Japan, a situation which is aggravated by a restrictive land policy (OECD, 1994).

In other services and government, productivity varies considerably as well, although output measurement in these sectors is faced with great uncertainties. Price levels in education and health were quite low, leading to very high productivity levels, of 188 percent of the US level in education and 138 percent of the United States in health. Other services consists of many activities, with an average productivity level of 58 percent of the US level. In government, Japanese productivity was somewhat above the United States.

Productivity Levels, 1953-1990

By combining data on productivity growth in table 1 with the estimates of productivity levels in table 2, an intertemporal perspective of relative productivity levels can be derived. Graph 1 shows the comparative performance of Japan versus the United States since 1953. The graph consists of three components. The first one shows comparative productivity in agriculture, mining, manufacturing and the total economy. It is clear that Japanese agriculture has made no progress against the United States at all in the postwar period. Its productivity level has stagnated slightly below 10 percent of the US level. This low productivity level of Japanese agriculture is a continuation of the situation before the war (Pilat, 1993).

GRAPH 1
Sectoral GDP per Hour Worked
Japan/USA, 1953-1990, USA=100

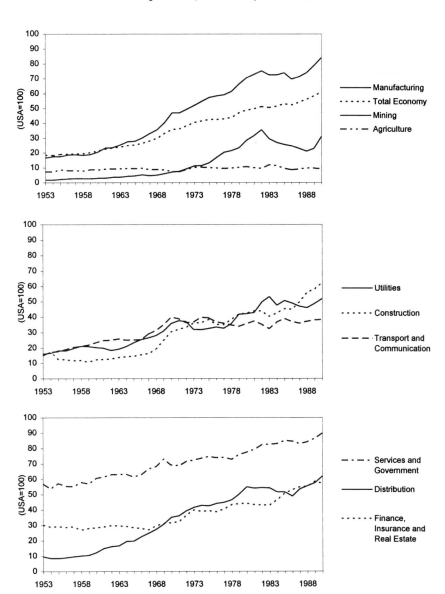

Source: Based on 1985 results from table 2 and time series underlying table 1.

Progress in mining has been much faster. Fast productivity growth in Japan as well as poor performance in US mining from the early 1970s to early 1980s caused a very fast increase in relative productivity levels. During the 1980s the situation reversed and the Japanese productivity declined from some 75 percent of that in the United States in 1982 to only 50 percent in the late 1980s.

Much of the dynamism of Japan lies in the productivity growth of its manufacturing sector. Starting from a productivity level slightly above 20 percent, Japan had reached more than 90 percent of the US level by 1990. The breakdown in catch up in the 1980s corresponds to much higher productivity growth rates in the United States in this period. The series for the economy as a whole show a steady upward trend from 20 percent of the United States in 1953 to almost 65 percent in 1990.

The second panel of graph 1 shows productivity performance in utilities, transport and communication and construction. Construction has made rapid progress in terms of productivity, but in utilities and transport and communication productivity has stagnated at relatively low levels (40 percent of the US level).

The final panel of graph 1 shows the service sectors. In finance, insurance and real estate postwar productivity levels were relatively high in 1953. In both countries productivity increases in this sector were small, but after 1973 productivity growth in this sector in the United States declined, whereas growth rates in Japan remained fairly high. Services and government started at a substantially higher productivity level than other sectors, but still succeeded in making progress against the United States.

Surprising is the fast rate of catch up in distribution, not usually regarded as a dynamic sector. The breakdown of catch up in this sector in the late 1970s corresponds to the introduction of the Large-Scale Retail Store Law in Japan in 1979 (Saxonhouse, 1987; Ito and Maruyama, 1991), which restricted the expansion of stores and the emergence of new and large outlets.

4. Explaining Productivity Levels

Differences in labour productivity levels across countries can be decomposed in differences in the use of other factor inputs in the production process, structural factors and a residual factor, which can be regarded a rough measure of efficiency differences. Van Ark and Pilat (1993) and van Ark (1993) have recently made a detailed decomposition of productivity differentials in manufacturing, by looking at differences in capital intensity, labour quality and economic structure. This section looks at these factors and also makes some remarks about the role of research and development (R&D).

The Role of Capital

Apart from labour, the most important production factor is capital. The greater use of capital in the production process in the United States was long regarded as the main factor underlying the US productivity advantage.

Quantification of the role of capital depends on reliable and comparable estimates of capital stock across countries. The US Dept. of Commerce publishes detailed estimates of capital stock by industry (BEA, 1993). However, the Japanese official estimates (EPA, 1991) are less elaborate. They refer only to private enterprises and therefore exclude a large share of the total capital stock. Their sectoral breakdown is also more limited than in the United States.

I have used standardised estimates of capital stock for the whole economy from Maddison (1993). In Japan as well as in the United States, capital stock estimates are primarily based on the Perpetual Inventory Method (PIM). The PIM method cumulates annual investment and deducts the annual scrapping of assets. Countries use very different assumptions on the life of assets and their scrapping pattern, often based on very weak empirical evidence (Maddison, 1993; van Ark, 1993).[3] The standardised estimates quoted above use the same life time and scrapping pattern for Japan and the United States.

Graph 2 shows two measures for relative capital intensity, namely the total gross stock of capital, and the gross stock of capital equipment, per person engaged. Equipment is only part of the total non-residential capital stock, which also consists of capital structures, but is currently regarded as the most important part of capital stock in terms of its productive capacity (De Long and Summers, 1991, 1992). In 1950, equipment per person in Japan for the whole economy was only 33 percent of the US level. Total non-residential capital per person was even lower, as the Japanese stock was more concentrated in equipment than the US stock. From 1950 to 1960 Japan's capital intensity fell compared to the United States. In this period, employment increased rapidly and investment in equipment did not keep up. Between 1960 and 1973 there was a tremendous growth in capital intensity. Since 1973, growth of capital intensity has slowed down. In 1990, equipment per person was more than 103 percent of that in the United States.

Capital equipment per person has therefore become almost the same in Japan and the United States. Total capital stock per person was 100 percent of the US level in 1990. These figures imply that differences in capital intensity between Japan and the United States have become relatively unimportant in explaining the labour productivity gap, at least for the economy as a whole. Between the different sectors of the economy and for manufacturing branches (see van Ark and Pilat, 1993) there still exist considerable differences. For instance, compa-

---

[3]   See Blades (1993) for a critical assessment of standardisation.

GRAPH 2
Capital Stock and Equipment per Person Engaged
Japan/USA, 1950-1990, USA=100

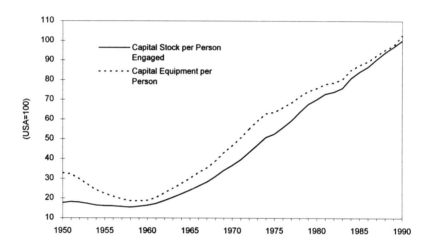

Source: Based on investment series from Maddison (1993), converted with Fisher PPPs for 1985 from EUROSTAT (1991); persons engaged based on series quoted in table 1.

rison of official estimates of capital stock per person for 1985 (EPA, 1991; BEA, 1993) suggest that relative capital intensity in Japanese agriculture was only 40 percent of the United States, in mining only 13 percent and in wholesale trade 37 percent. In these sectors of the economy, capital still plays a significant role in explaining labour productivity differences. However, at the aggregate level capital intensity has ceased to play an important role.

It is possible to formalise the role of capital by combining capital and labour in one indicator of joint factor productivity (van Ark, 1993). I use a simple Cobb-Douglas production function, with constant returns to scale and where the factor inputs are paid according to their marginal product. The relative level of joint factor productivity in country X compared to country U (A^X/A^U) is then (in logs):

$$\ln\frac{A^X}{A^U} = \ln\frac{Y^X}{Y^U} - \alpha * \ln\frac{L^X}{L^U} - (1-\alpha) * \ln\frac{K^X}{K^U} \qquad (1)$$

This can be reformulated as:

$$\ln\frac{A^{X}}{A^{U}} = \ln\frac{Y^{X}/L^{X}}{Y^{U}/L^{U}} - (1-\alpha) * \ln\frac{K^{X}/L^{X}}{K^{U}/L^{U}} \qquad (2)$$

where Y is output, L labour input and K capital input, α is the share of labour in value added, and X and U represent countries X and U respectively.

Relative output (Y^{X}/Y^{U}) is based on the benchmark comparison for 1985 and is extrapolated backwards and forwards with GDP series quoted in table 1. Relative labour input is also derived from these series. Relative capital stock is derived from Maddison (1993). The factor shares are based on the average labour share in Japan and the United States, and are derived from the national accounts of both countries.

TABLE 3
Labour Productivity, Capital Intensity and Joint Factor Productivity
Whole Economy, Japan/USA, 1950-1990, USA=100

	1950	1960	1965	1973	1979	1990
GDP per Person Engaged	16.4	24.7	28.7	47.5	56.0	73.0
GDP per Hour Worked	16.2	21.5	25.4	40.6	47.2	61.3
Capital Stock per Person	17.7	16.5	24.2	47.1	67.8	100.1
Capital Stock per Hour Worked	17.7	14.4	21.5	40.4	57.5	84.6
Equipment per Person	32.9	18.9	30.2	59.2	74.4	102.8
Equipment per Hour Worked	32.8	16.6	26.9	50.8	63.1	86.9
Capital Productivity	91.3	148.2	117.5	99.8	81.6	72.0
Joint Factor Productivity (a)	31.3	45.2	46.1	56.0	56.9	65.4
JFP-LP (a)	15.0	23.6	20.7	15.5	9.8	4.1

Note: (a) With hours worked as the basis for labour input.
Source: GDP per person engaged and per hour based on 1985 benchmark, updated with time series underlying graph 1, capital stock based on investment series from Maddison (1992), but converted to 1985 US$ with 1985 Fisher PPPs supplied by Eurostat, instead of Paasche PPPs used by Maddison.

Table 3 shows labour productivity, capital intensity, capital productivity and joint factor productivity. In 1950, the joint factor productivity level was almost double the labour productivity level. Up to 1960, joint factor productivity increased faster than labour productivity, as the relative capital intensity of Japan fell compared to the United States and capital productivity in Japan increased to levels substantially higher than in the United States. Since 1960, the difference

D. Pilat

between labour productivity and joint factor productivity has fallen rapidly as
relative levels of capital intensity between the two countries converged and
capital productivity in Japan fell to levels similar to the United States. In 1990,
the difference between the two estimates was only 4 percent. This implies firstly
that the role of capital in explaining the labour productivity gap has now become
rather limited, and secondly that labour productivity is currently a close
approximation of joint factor productivity.

Assessments of the role of capital in explaining productivity differences
between countries depend on the estimates of capital stock used. I have used
estimates of gross capital stock with rectangular scrapping and rather long life
times of assets. Recent other studies (De Long and Summers, 1992) have used
estimates of net stock based on rapid depreciation and short life times of assets
(Summers and Heston, 1991). These studies suggest that Japan is now
considerably ahead of the United States in terms of capital per person employed.
Such estimates imply that capital productivity in Japan is now substantially below
US levels and that joint factor productivity is also lower than suggested in table
3. These capital stock estimates therefore imply an even smaller proportion of
the productivity gap between the two countries which can be explained by
differences in capital intensity, and therefore leave a larger share of the gap
unexplained.

The Quality of Labour Input

In accounting for the role of education in economic growth, most studies have
tended to look at the average years of schooling of the population. However, in
accounting for productivity differences across countries it is of greater use to

TABLE 4

**Distribution of Employment According to Highest Level of General Education
Manufacturing and Whole Economy, Japan and the USA, 1987**

	Elementary or Junior High School	Senior High School	Junior College	Senior College & University
Japan				
Manufacturing	32.2	50.8	5.3	11.8
Whole Economy	30.1	47.4	8.2	14.4
United States				
Manufacturing	20.8	45.0	16.5	17.7
Whole Economy	16.6	40.0	20.5	22.9

Source: Japan from Statistics Bureau, Management and Coordination Agency, *1987
Employment Status Survey*, Tokyo, 1989; United States from BLS, *Current Population
Survey 1987*, Washington DC, 1991.

look at the level of schooling of the work force only, distinguishing between types of education. Table 4 shows the composition of the labour force in manufacturing and in the economy as a whole for 1987 on the basis of the highest level of qualification received.

The composition of the work force in manufacturing and the economy as a whole is rather similar within the countries, but differs between the countries. In Japan a significantly larger share of the work force did not have a senior high school qualification, compared to the situation in the United States. These workers are mostly older. For instance, in the age group from 50-54 years old, more than 44 percent did not have a senior high school degree. This compares to only 12.3 percent in the age group from 30-34 years old. The share of senior high school graduates in Japan is slightly higher than in the United States. In the United States more students continue their education after graduating from high school for a college or university degree. The share of both junior college degrees and senior college and university degrees in the US work force is larger than in Japan.

Van Ark and Pilat (1993) and van Ark (1993) have calculated a quality index for the work force in both countries, using the composition shown in table 4. Each component was weighted with its relative wage level. The arithmetic average of the wage differentials in both countries was taken, but was reduced by 40 percent to exclude the effect of other factors on wage differentials, such as social background (van Ark, 1993). For manufacturing the quality of the Japanese work force was estimated to be 97.4 percent of that in the United States. For the whole work force the quality was estimated to be 95.6 percent of the US level.

The difference in the quality of the labour force between Japan and the United States, at least where general levels of education are concerned, had become fairly small in 1987. Its contribution in explaining the labour productivity gap is therefore negligible. One might even argue that if account is taken of the quality of education, and of training of workers outside the general education system, the Japanese labour force probably has a higher quality than that in the United States. The estimates of educational achievement levels used earlier in this chapter suggested that the relative achievement of Japanese students was some 20 percent above that in the United States. In addition, Japanese firms are known to spend much more time and effort on training in the workplace than US firms. Taking account of these factors implies that the quality of labour input has no direct role in explaining why the United States is still ahead in labour productivity.

Structural Factors

Across countries, differences in the composition of the economy over different sectors can have a large effect on comparative productivity. If relative productivity levels between two countries were the same in all sectors of the economy, but one economy is more engaged in activities with a high absolute level of productivity than the other, the former economy would still have a higher level of relative productivity for the economy as a whole (Smith, Hitchens and Davies, 1982).

The structural element can be captured by reweighting sectoral productivity, at prices of either country, by a unique set of labour input, or value added weights. The reweighted result will differ from the original productivity outcome and the gap between the two can be interpreted as the effect of structural differences.

For 1985, the sectoral breakdown in table 2 was used to reweight the productivity ratios by labour input and value added weights. At labour input weights, Japan's productivity level rose from 53.3 percent to 61.5 percent, a difference of more than 8 percentage points. At value added weights, the effect was substantially smaller and the adjusted productivity level was only 56.4 percent of the US level. It is preferable to calculate the effect at a low level of detail. Unfortunately, the detail of table 2 is insufficient to capture the structural differences within sectors. For instance, the productivity level of the Japanese mining sector is to a large extent the effect of compositional differences within the mining sector between Japan and the United States.

The Role of Technology and Research and Development

A fourth factor which may help explain productivity differences between countries relates to the role of technology and research and development (R&D). If Japan would be less technologically advanced than the United States, its productivity level would likely be lower. Some recent work (Lichtenberg, 1992) has suggested a substantial role for R&D in explaining productivity differences between countries. Technology can be either the result of domestic R&D efforts or from its acquisition from abroad.

The Japanese growth process, as that of most "follower" countries (Abramovitz, 1989; Nelson and Wright, 1992), has until the past few decades primarily relied upon acquisition from abroad. It was early realised in the country that technology was the primary means through which Japan would be able to catch up with the West. Even during the late Tokugawa period Dutch technology acquired through contacts at the port of Deshima was an important source of learning. During the Meiji period and before the Second World War the search for Western technology intensified.

The Second World War increased the technological gap between Japan and the leader country, the United States. After the war, Japanese companies were extremely active in the search for new technology abroad, especially in the early postwar period. Technology imports were regulated by MITI, and priority was given to targeted industries. During the early postwar period, government controls were strictly enforced and only certain technologies were allowed. The government controls were not due to balance of payments problems, but seemed mainly influenced by a desire to achieve an industrial structure which offered high growth prospects in the long term (Peck and Tamura, 1976).

As countries catch up in technology with the leader, indigenous technology becomes more important. Japan's performance in this respect has been somewhat different from that of other countries. First, its research had an almost totally civilian character. In contrast to US R&D outlays, very little has been spent on defence research in Japan (Okimoto and Saxonhouse, 1987). In general, defence research has a different character from civilian research. It is often aimed at high performance, but usually at high cost. Commercial applications are only secondary. In addition, defence research has often led to great waste and misdirected spending. Furthermore, the best engineers and researchers were not diverted to defence research, as was the case in the United States, but could work on civilian applications (Okimoto and Saxonhouse, 1987).

Partly related to this first aspect is that in the Japanese system of R&D government's role is much smaller than in most other industrialised countries. Most research is done in private companies, and government procurement, for instance for defence purposes, plays a limited role. Government's role is less direct. Especially in the early high growth period government played an important role in technology imports. Furthermore, government's long-term projections play an important role in the evolution of the Japanese economy and help to focus research on high growth areas.

In general, Japanese research is more aimed at commercial application than in the United States. A large share of total research is aimed at modification and adaptation of technology (Mansfield, 1988), often with small improvements in terms of quality, cost and manufacturability. In Japanese companies, R&D are integrated within the production process, and there is considerable interaction between researchers and producers. Much more than in the United States, product designs have been aimed at simplicity and manufacturability (Dertouzos, Lester and Solow, 1989).

Japan has shown itself to be apt mainly in making technological progress in areas where the technology is predictable and incremental (Okimoto and Saxonhouse, 1987), for instance semiconductors. Japan is much less advanced in making progress in areas with technological uncertainties, such as software. These issues relate to the fact that Japanese research has been focused mainly on applied research and much less on basic research. As Japan has reached the edge of world technology in several areas, this has become a matter of great concern for Japanese companies. A number of problems are generally mentioned with regards to basic R&D in Japan. First, the Japanese educational system, and especially its universities, has not aimed at producing innovative and creative researchers. It has aimed at providing a large number of highly educated people with general skills. Second, the mobility of researchers between large enterprises is still extremely limited, partly due to the lifetime employment system, thus leading to a slow spread of research findings between companies. A third problem is the reluctance of large companies to spend much on basic research, which has much less predictable results.

In 1953, Japan spent less than 0.5 percent of its GDP on R&D. Since 1953 the trend has been steadily upwards, with only a short interruption of the trend after the first oil crisis and the following recession. In 1990 Japan spent more than 3 percent of GDP on research and development (OECD, 1992b), slightly more than Germany and the United States (both 2.8 percent in 1990). In relative terms, Japan therefore appears not to spend less than the United States, in particular since its R&D efforts seem much more aimed at commercial application.

It is therefore difficult to derive strong statements on the role of R&D in explaining productivity differences. Industry-studies (McKinsey, 1993) have sometimes suggested that technology between the major industrialised countries diffuses rapidly and is, in principle, available to firms in both Japan and the United States. More macro-economic studies (Lichtenberg, 1992) suggest that international R&D spillovers are not instantaneous and that R&D does have a big impact on productivity performance. More research in this area seems appropriate. Several hypotheses could be considered, for instance:
- Does the relatively large US expenditure on basic R&D translate into positive spillovers to the rest of the economy, which are relatively larger than the Japanese expenditure on applied research?
- Does the longer US history of domestic R&D perhaps translate into the broader diffusion of technology, beyond a number of R&D-intensive industries?

5. Concluding Remarks

This paper has presented a comparison of productivity growth and levels between Japan and the United States since 1953. It appears that Japan's catch up with the United States varies substantially between sectors. Some sectors, notably manufacturing and non-market services, are now close to US productivity levels, others, for instance mining, construction, distribution and finance, insurance and real estate, are slowly catching up, but are still quite far from US levels, whereas a few sectors have stagnated at low levels of productivity. This is primarily the case in agriculture, utilities and transport and communication.

Differences in capital intensity and quality of the work force between Japan and the United States do not help much in explaining the labour productivity gap between the two countries. Japanese workers have as much capital equipment at their disposal as US workers and it may be newer as that in the United States as well. The Japanese work force is also at least as well educated as its US counterparts. Structural effects appear to play a considerable role, but can not explain more than 25 percent of the productivity gap. R&D may play a role, but this effect is difficult to quantify and requires further research.

The explanation for the considerable difference in productivity levels between the two countries, and the dual nature of the economy at the sectoral level, may also be related to some specific factors. For instance, the US advantage may still be partly related to its abundancy in natural resources. This is most obvious in agriculture, where the productivity gap is much larger than for the economy as a whole. Low agricultural productivity is partly the result of protectionist policies (van der Meer and Yamada, 1990), but there is also an effect of land scarcity. The natural resource advantage of the United States is partly related to its much larger land surface. The latter factor may also have an effect on productivity performance in transport, since terminal services in Japan compose a much larger share of total cost than in the United States.

Another related specific factor which helps to explain the labour productivity gap between the two countries is the cost of land. The enormous scarcity of land in Japan, together with restrictive land policies, have led to a very high price for land. In combination with restrictions through the Large-Scale Retail Store Law, this has made it difficult for retailers to reap economies of scale through large scale outlets. An additional effect is that large infrastructural projects, like roads and airports, have been very costly and have therefore developed only slowly.

Overall, the estimates suggest a considerable duality in the Japanese economy, even within broad sectors of the economy. Within manufacturing, the most productive industries are those that export on the world market, whereas more domestically oriented manufacturing branches tend to have much lower productivity levels (van Ark and Pilat, 1993).

This dual character of the Japanese economy, particularly within manufacturing, seems also related to protection (McKinsey, 1992; 1993) and high degrees of regulation (OECD, 1992c). In agriculture and distribution, regulations and protection have reduced the degree of (international) competition that producers are faced with. Interestingly the breakdown of the catch up process of the distribution sector corresponds with the introduction of the Large-Scale Retail Law in 1979. Even in manufacturing, some sectors, and notably food products, have been strongly protected from international competition, contributing to lagging productivity performance (McKinsey, 1993).

References

Abramovitz, M. (1989), *Thinking About Growth*, Cambridge University Press, Cambridge.

Ark, B. van (1993), *International Comparisons of Output and Productivity*, Monograph Series No. 1, Groningen Growth and Development Centre, Groningen.

Ark, B. van, and D. Pilat (1993), "Cross Country Productivity Levels: Differences and Causes", *Brookings Papers on Economic Activity (Microeconomics)*, No. 2, pp. 1-69.

Baily, M.N. (1993), "Competition, Regulation, and Efficiency in Service Industries", *Brookings Papers on Economic Activity (Microeconomics)*, No. 2, pp. 71-159.

Baumol, W.J. (1986), "Productivity, Convergence and Welfare: What the Long-Run Data Show", *American Economic Review*, Vol. 76, December, pp. 1072-1085.

Blades, D. (1993), "Comparing Capital Stocks", in: A. Szirmai, B. van Ark and D. Pilat, eds., *Explaining Economic Growth - Essays in Honour of Angus Maddison*, North Holland, Amsterdam, pp. 399-409.

Bureau of Economic Analysis (1993), *Fixed Reproducible Tangible Wealth in the United States, 1925-1989*, Washington DC.

David, P.A. (1966), "Measuring Real Net Output: A Proposed Index", *Review of Economics and Statistics*, Vol. 48, pp. 419-425.

De Long, J.B. and L.H. Summers (1991), "Equipment Investment and Economic Growth", *Quarterly Journal of Economics*, Vol. 106, May, pp. 445-502.

De Long, J.B. and L.H. Summers (1992), "Equipment Investment and Economic Growth: How Strong is the Nexus", *Brookings Papers on Economic Activity*, No. 2, pp. 157-211.

Dertouzos, M.L., R.K. Lester and R. Solow (1989), *Made in America - Regaining the Productive Edge*, HarperCollins, New York.

Diewert, W.E. (1992), "Fisher Ideal Output, Input, and Productivity Indexes Revisited", *Journal of Productivity Analysis*, Vol. 3, September, pp. 211-248.

Dollar, D. and E.N. Wolff (1993), *Competitiveness, Convergence, and International Specialization*, MIT Press, Cambridge.

Economic Planning Agency (1991), *Gross Capital Stock of Private Enterprises, 1965-1989*, Tokyo.

Eurostat (1991), "Binary PPPs for 1985", Luxembourg, processed.

Gordon, R.J. and M.N. Baily (1991), "Measurement Issues and the Productivity Slowdown in Five Major Industrial Countries", in OECD, *Technology and Productivity: the Challenge for Economic Policy*, Paris.

Ito, T. and M. Maruyama (1991), "Is the Japanese Distribution System Really Inefficient", in: P. Krugman, ed., *Trade with Japan - Has the Door Opened Wider?*, University of Chicago Press, Chicago, pp. 149-173.

Kendrick, J.W. (1990), "Appraising the U.S. Output and Productivity Estimates for Government - Where do we go from here?", *Review of Income and Wealth*, Vol. 37, No. 2, June, pp. 149-158.

Kravis, I.B., A. Heston and R. Summers (1982), *World Product and Income*, Johns Hopkins University Press, Baltimore.

Lichtenberg, F.R. (1992), "R&D Investment and International Productivity Differences", *NBER Working Paper No. 4161*, NBER, Cambridge, MA.

Maddison, A. (1991), *Dynamic Forces in Capitalist Development*, Oxford University Press, London.

Maddison, A. (1992), "Standardised Estimates of Fixed Investment and Capital Stock at Constant Prices: A Long Run Survey for 6 Countries", paper presented at 22nd General Conference of IARIW, Flims.

Maddison, A. (1993), "Standardised Estimates of Fixed Capital Stock: A Six Country Comparison", *Innovazione e Materie Prime*, Vol. 1, May, pp. 20-47.

Maddison, A. and B. van Ark (1988), "Comparisons of Real Output in Manufacturing", *Policy, Planning and Research Working Papers WPS5*, World Bank, Washington DC.

Mansfield, E. (1988), "Industrial R&D in Japan and the United States: A Comparative Study", *American Economic Review*, Vol. 78, May, pp. 223-228.

McKinsey (1992), *Service Sector Productivity*, McKinsey Global Institute, October, Washington D.C.

McKinsey (1993), *Manufacturing Productivity*, McKinsey Global Institute, October, Washington D.C.

McKinsey (1994), *Employment Performance*, McKinsey Global Institute, Washington D.C.

Meer, C.L.J. van der, and S. Yamada (1990), *Japanese Agriculture, A Comparative Economic Analysis*, Routledge, London.

Mulder, N. (1991), "A Comparison of Output and Labour Productivity in Transport: France, the UK and the USA", Groningen, processed.

Nelson, R. and G. Wright (1992), "The Rise and Fall of American Technological Leadership", *Journal of Economic Literature*, Vol. 30, December, pp. 1931-1964.

OECD (1987), *Measurement of Value Added at Constant Prices in Service Activities*, Paris.

OECD (1992a), *National Accounts - Main Aggregates 1960-1990*, Paris.

OECD (1992b), *Science and Technology Indicators*, Paris.

OECD (1992c), *OECD Economic Surveys - Japan*, Paris.

OECD (1994), *OECD Economic Surveys - Japan*, Paris.

Ohkawa, K., and H. Rosovsky (1973), *Japanese Economic Growth*, Stanford University Press, Stanford.

Okimoto, D.I. and G.R. Saxonhouse (1987), "Technology and the Future of the Economy", in: K. Yamamura and Y. Yasuba (eds) (1987), *The Political Economy of Japan - Vol. 1: The Domestic Transformation*, Stanford University Press, Stanford.

Paige, D. and G. Bombach (1959), *A Comparison of National Output and Productivity*, OECC, Paris.

Peck, M. and S. Tamura (1976), "Technology", in: H. Patrick and H. Rosovsky (eds.), *Asia's New Giant - How the Japanese Economy Works*, Brookings Institution, Washington DC.

Pilat, D. (1993), "The Sectoral Productivity Performance of Japan and the United States, 1885-1990", *Review of Income and Wealth*, Vol. 39, No. 4, December, pp. 357-375.

Pilat, D. (1994), *The Economics of Rapid Growth - The Experience of Japan and Korea*, Edward Elgar, Aldershot.

Saxonhouse, G.R. (1987), "Comparative Advantage, Structural Adaptation, and Japanese Performance", in: T. Inoguchi and D.I. Okimoto, eds., *The Political Economy of Japan - Vol. 2: The Changing International Context*, Stanford University Press, Stanford, pp. 225-248.

Sinclair, J. and B. Catron (1990), "An Experimental Price Index for the Computer Industry", *Monthly Labor Review*, Vol. 113, October, pp. 16-24.

Smith, A.D. (1989), "New Measures of British Service Outputs", *National Institute Economic Review*, May, pp. 75-88.

Smith, A.D., D.M.W.N. Hitchens and S.W. Davies (1982), *International Industrial Productivity*, Cambridge University Press, Cambridge.

Summers, R. and A. Heston (1991), "The Penn World Table (Mark 5); An Expanded Set of International Comparisons, 1950-1988", *Quarterly Journal of Economics*, Vol. 106, No. 2, May, pp. 327-368.

Szirmai, A. and D. Pilat (1990), "Comparisons of Purchasing Power, Real Output and Labour Productivity in Manufacturing in Japan, South Korea and the USA, 1975-1985", *Review of Income and Wealth*, Vol. 36, No. 1, March, pp. 1-31.

International Productivity Differences
K. Wagner and B. van Ark (editors)
© 1996 Elsevier Science B.V. All rights reserved.

International Competitiveness and Japanese Industries, 1960-1985

*M. Kuroda**
Keio University, Japan

1. Introduction

The purpose of this paper is to provide an international comparison of the level of differences in technology between industries in the United States and Japan during the period 1960-1985. Comparisons of the aggregate economic growth between these two countries found that this period was one of substantial economic growth in the USA and of extremely rapid growth in Japan. Almost all of the narrowing of the gap between the levels of output of the two economies during this period was due to (1) the increase in the level of technology in Japan relative to the USA and (2) the rapid growth of capital accumulation in Japan. These changes are closely related to fluctuations in the relative prices of factor inputs. In the 1970s, especially after the first oil crisis, the economies of the USA and Japan experienced a strong decline in economic growth, which one might expect to have had an enormous impact on the relative prices as well.

In this paper we focus on a disaggregated analysis of the differences in the pattern of production at the industry level. This will facilitate a better understanding of the anatomy of our findings at the macro level. During the period of rapid economic growth a dramatic structural change of the Japanese economy occurred which led to important shifts in output, labour and capital stock from low productivity to high productivity industries, as exemplified in the paper by Pilat in this volume.

In addition there were important changes in the Japanese economy in its relationship to the foreign sector. The ratio of Japanese export to total world trade was only 3.6 per cent in 1960 and increased to 10.1 per cent in 1985. Bilateral trade between Japan and the USA was balanced until the first oil crisis in 1973. Since then the foreign trade balance of the Japanese economy has

---

* **Acknowledgments**
  This paper is the result of joint work in the Keio-Harvard Project. Of course, any remaining errors are solely my own.

fluctuated between deficit and surplus during the last half of 1970s and the surplus was gradually extended during the 1980s. On the other hand, the US trade deficit increased rapidly after 1975.

Recently the political relationship between Japan and the United States has become increasingly preoccupied with "trade frictions". These disputes over trade issues have accompanied the massive expansion of Japanese exports to the United States. Explanations for the resulting trade imbalance must include variations in the yen-dollar exchange rate, changes in the relative prices of capital and labour in the two countries, and the relative growth of productivity in Japanese and US industries. In this paper, we analyse the role of each of these factors in explaining the rise in competitiveness of Japanese industries relative to their US counterparts.

Our measure of competitiveness is the price of an industry's output in Japan relative to the price in the USA. Japanese exports are generated by US purchases from Japanese industries, while US exports result from Japanese purchases from US industries. The relative price of an industry's output enters the decisions of purchasers in both countries and the rest of the world. In order to explain changes in international competitiveness we must account for changes in the determinants of this relative price.

The starting point for our analysis of the competitiveness of Japanese and US industries is the yen-dollar exchange rate. This is simply the number of yen required to purchase one US dollar in the market for foreign exchange. Variations in the yen-dollar exchange rate are easy to document and are often used to characterize movements in relative prices in the two countries. However, movements in relative prices of goods and services do not coincide with variations in the exchange rate. To account for changes in international competitiveness a measure of the relative prices of specific goods and services is required.

Relative prices between Japanese and US industries can be summarized by means of purchasing power parities. The purchasing power parity for a specific industry's output is the number of yen required to purchase an amount of the industry's output in Japan costing one dollar in the USA. The dimensions of purchasing power parities are the same as the yen-dollar exchange rate, namely, yen per dollar. However, the purchasing power parities reflect the relative prices of the goods and services rather than currencies.

The most familiar application of the notion of purchasing power parity is to construct the relative prices of same aggregates as the gross domestic product. This application has been the focus of the landmark studies of Kravis, Heston and Summers (1978). As a consequence of their research, it is now possible to compare the relative prices of gross domestic product for a wide range of countries, including Japan and the USA. Kravis, Heston and Summers have based their purchasing power parities for gross domestic product on relative prices for 153 commodity groups.

In this study we estimate purchasing power parities for twenty-nine industries in Japan and the USA for the period 1960-1985 based on the original estimates of Kravis, Heston and Summers.[1] These are relative prices of the outputs of each industry in the two countries in terms of yen per dollar. We divide the relative price of each industry's output by the yen-dollar exchange rate to translate purchasing power parities into relative prices in terms of dollars. We find it convenient to employ relative prices in dollars as measures of international competitiveness. Variations in the exchange rate are reflected in the relative prices of outputs for all twenty-nine industries. Our results are shown in section 3.

To account for changes in international competitiveness between Japanese and US industries, we have compiled purchasing power parities for the inputs into each industry, which are also presented in section 3. The purchasing power parities for inputs are based on the relative prices of the goods and services that make up the inputs of each industry. We have disaggregated inputs among capital and labour services, which are primary factors of production, and energy and other intermediate goods, which are produced by one industry and consumed by other industries. We can translate purchasing power parities for inputs into relative prices in dollars by dividing by the yen-dollar exchange rate.

Our final step in accounting for international competitiveness between Japanese and US industries is to measure the relative levels of productivity for all twenty-nine industries. For this purpose we employ a model of production for each industry. This model enables us to express the price of output in each country as a function of the prices of inputs and the level of productivity in that country. We can account for the relative prices of output between Japan and the USA by allowing input prices and levels of productivity to differ between countries. We have compiled data on relative productivity levels in Japan and the USA for the period 1960-1985.

We present comparisons of productivity levels between the USA and Japan by industry in section 4. Finally, we employ changes in relative productivity levels and relative prices of inputs in accounting for changes in international competitiveness between Japanese and US industries over the period 1960-1985.

The methodology for our study was originated by Jorgenson and Nishimizu (1978). They provided a theoretical framework for productivity comparisons based on a bilateral production function at the aggregate level. They employed this framework in comparing aggregate output, input, and productivity for Japan and the USA. This methodology was extended to the industry level by Jorgenson and Nishimizu (1981) and employed in international comparisons between Japanese and US industries. The industry-level methodology used models of production for individual industries based on bilateral production functions for

---

1 The industry classification is shown in table A.1 at the end of this paper.

each industry. We will summarise our method briefly in section 2.

2. Theoretical Framework

Our methodology is based on the economic theory of production, which departs from the concept of an aggregate production function as identified in the work of Paul H. Douglas and his associates and that of Jan Tinbergen. Their theoretical work was integrated with that of pioneers of economic measurement such as Abramovitz, Fabricant and Kendrick in the work of Robert Solow and associates.[2] Our point of departure is a production function for each industry giving output as a function of inputs, a dummy variable equal to zero for the United States and one for Japan, and time. We consider production under constant returns to scale, so that a proportional change in all inputs results in a proportional change in output. In analyzing differences in each industry's production patterns between the two countries, we combine the production function with necessary conditions for producer equilibrium. We express these conditions as equalities between shares of each input in the value of output of each industry and the elasticity of output with respect to that input in the industry. The elasticities depend on input levels, the dummy variable for each country, and time. Under constant returns to scale the sum of the elasticities with respect to all inputs is equal to unity, so that the value shares also sum to unity. We begin with a model of production that gives the analytical framework to international comparison of differences in outputs, inputs, and levels of technology. Our methodology is based on a specific form of production function giving output as a function of inputs, a country dummy variable and time for each industry.

To represent our bilateral models of production we require the following notation:

q^j	: price of the output of the j-th industry,
$p^j_K, p^j_L, p^j_E, p^j_M$	: prices of capital, labour, energy, and other intermediate inputs in the j-th industry,
$v^j_K, v^j_L, v^j_E, v^j_M$	: value shares of capital, labour, energy and other intermediate inputs in the j-th industry,
v^j	: the vector of value shares of input in the j-th industry,
$\ln p^j$	: the vector of logarithms of input prices of the j-th industry,
T	: a state variable as an index of technology,

---

2 For a more extensive discussion of the relation between the theory and measurement of productivity and economic growth in the framework of the methodology applied in this paper, see Jorgenson (1990).

D   : a dummy variable D, equal to one for Japan
                             and zero for the USA to represent differences
                             in technology between the two countries.

Under competitive conditions we can represent technology by a price function that is dual to the production function relating each industry's output to the corresponding inputs, the level of technology, and differences in technology between the two countries:

$$\ln q^j = \ln p^{j'} \alpha^j + \alpha^j_t T + \alpha^j_d D + \frac{1}{2} \ln p^{j'} B^j \ln p^j + \ln p^{j'} \beta^j_t T +$$

$$\ln p^{j'} \beta^j_d D + \frac{1}{2} \beta^j_{tt} T^2 + \beta^j_{td} TD + \frac{1}{2} \beta^j_{dd} D^2, \quad (j = 1, 2, \ldots, J). \quad (1)$$

For each industry the price of output is a transcendental or, more specifically, an exponential function of the logarithms of the input prices. In this translog representation the scalars, α_t^j, α_d^j, β_{tt}^j, β_{dd}^j, the vectors, α^j, β_t^j, β_d^i, and the matrices, B^j, are constant parameters that differ among industries. These parameters reflect differences in technology among industries. Within each industry differences in technology among time periods are represented by time as an index of technology. Differences in technology between Japan and the USA are represented by a dummy variable, equal to one for Japan and zero for the USA.

In analysing differences in each industry's production patterns between Japan and the USA, we combine the price function with demand functions for inputs. We can express these functions as equalities between shares of each input in the value of the output of the industry and the elasticity of the output price with respect to the price of that input. These elasticities depend on input prices, dummy variables for each country, and time as an index of technology. The sum of the elasticities with respect to all inputs is equal to unity, so that the value shares also sum to unity.

For each industry the value shares are equal to the logarithmic derivatives of the price function with respect to logarithms of the input prices:

$$v^j = \alpha^j + B^j \ln p^j + \beta^j_t T + \beta^j_d D, \quad (j = 1, 2, \ldots, J). \quad (2)$$

We can define rates of productivity growth, v^j_T, as the negative of rates of growth of the price of output with respect to time, holding the input prices constant:

$$-v^j_T = \alpha^j_t + \beta^{j'}_t \ln p^j + \beta^j_{tt} T + \beta^j_{td} D, \quad (j = 1, 2, \ldots, J). \quad (3)$$

Similarly, we can define differences in technology between Japan and the

USA, $v^j{}_D$, as the negative of rates of growth of the price of output with respect to the dummy variable, holding the input prices constant:

$$-v_D^j = \alpha_d^j + \beta_d^{j'}\ln p^j + \beta_{td}^j T + \beta_{dd}^j D, \quad (j = 1, 2, \ldots, J). \tag{4}$$

The price of output, the prices of inputs, and the value shares for all four inputs are observable for each industry in the period 1960-1985 in both countries. The rates of productivity growth are not directly observable, but average rates of productivity growth between two points of time, t and $t - 1$, can be expressed as the difference between a weighted average of growth rates of input prices and the growth rates of the price of output for each industry:

$$-\bar{v}_T^j = \ln q^j(t) - \ln q^j(t-1) - \bar{v}^{j'}[\ln p^j(t) - \ln p^j(t-1)], \quad (j = 1,2,..,J), \tag{5}$$

where the average rates of technical change are:

$$\bar{v}_T^j = \frac{1}{2}[v_T^j(t) + v_T^j(t-1)], \tag{6}$$

and the weights are given by the average value shares:

$$\bar{v}^j = \frac{1}{2}[v^j(t) + v^j(t-1)]. \tag{7}$$

We refer to the index numbers (5) as translog price indices of the rates of productivity growth.

Similarly, differences in productivity v_D^j are not directly observable. However, the average of these differences for Japan and the USA can be expressed as a weighted average of differences between the logarithms of the input prices, less the difference between logarithms of the output price:

$$-\bar{v}_D^j = \ln q^j(JAPAN) - \ln q^j(U.S.) - \bar{v}^{j'}[\ln p^j(JAPAN) - \ln p^j(US)], \quad (j = 1, 2, \ldots, J), \tag{8}$$

where the average differences in productivity are:

$$\bar{v}_D^j = \frac{1}{2}[v_D^j(JAPAN) + v_D^j(US)], \tag{9}$$

and the weights are given by the average value shares:

$$\bar{v}^j = \frac{1}{2}[v^j(JAPAN) + v^j(US)]. \tag{10}$$

We refer to the index numbers (8) as translog price indices of differences in productivity.

In our bilateral models of production the capital, labour, energy and other intermediate input prices are aggregates that depend on the prices of individual capital inputs, labour inputs, energy inputs and other intermediate inputs in Japan and the USA. The product of price and quantity indices must equal the value of all the components of each aggregate. We define quantity indices corresponding to each aggregate as ratios of the value of the components of the aggregate to the corresponding price index. In international comparisons the price indices represent purchasing power parities between the yen and the dollar. For example, the price index for labour input represents the Japanese price in yen for labour input costing one dollar in the United States.

Our methodology for estimating purchasing power parities is based on linking time series data sets on prices in Japan and the USA. Suppose that we observe the price of the output of the j-th industry in Japan and the USA, say q^j (JAPAN,0) and q^j (US,0), in the base period, where these prices are evaluated in terms of yen and dollars, respectively. We can define the purchasing power parity for the output of the j-th industry, say $PPP^j(0)$, as follows:

$$PPP^j(0) = \frac{q^j(JAPAN,0)}{q^j(US,0)}, \quad (j = 1, 2, ..., J).$$ (11)

The purchasing power parity gives the number of yen required in Japan to purchase an amount of the output of the j-th industry costing one dollar in the USA in the base period.

To estimate purchasing power parities for outputs of all industries in Japan and the USA we first construct a time series of prices for the output of each industry in both countries in domestic currency. To obtain price indices for industry outputs in the USA, we normalise the price index for each industry, that is $q^j(US,t)$, at unity in the base period. We normalise the corresponding price index for Japan, $q^j(JAPAN,t)$, at the purchasing power parity in the base period. We obtain estimates of purchasing power parities for all years, $PPP^j(t)$, from these price indices and the purchasing power parity for the base period from the equation:

$$PPP^j(t) = PPP^j(0)\frac{q^j(JAPAN,T)}{q^j(JAPAN,0)} \frac{q^j(US,0)}{q^j(US,T)}, \quad (j=1,2,..,J).$$ (12)

where $PPP^j(0)$ is the purchasing power parity in the base period and q^j(JAPAN, 0) and q^j(US,0) are the prices of outputs of the j-th industry in Japan and the USA in the base period.

Finally, we define the relative price of the output of the j-th industry in Japan and the US in dollars, say p^j(JAPAN,US,t), as the ratio of the purchasing power parity for that industry to the yen-dollar exchange rate, say E(t):

$$p^j(JAPAN, US, t) = \frac{PPP^j(t)}{E(t)}, \quad (j = 1, 2, ..., J). \tag{13}$$

The relative price of the output of the j-th industry in Japan and the USA is the ratio of the number of dollars required in Japan to purchase an amount of the industry's output costing one dollar in the United States. This index is our measure of international competitiveness between the Japanese industry and its US counterpart.

3. Purchasing Power Parities for Outputs and Inputs

In order to construct purchasing power parities and the corresponding relative prices for each industry between Japanese and US industries in the base period, we have developed purchasing power parities based on the results of Kravis, Heston, and Summers (1978).[3] They have provided purchasing power parities between the yen and the dollar for 153 commodity groups for the year 1970. These commodity groups are components of the gross domestic product of each country, corresponding to deliveries to final demand at purchasers' prices.

We begin with the construction of purchasing power parities for industry outputs, energy inputs, and other intermediate inputs by mapping the 153 commodity groups employed by Kravis, Heston, and Summers (1978) into our industry classification. Unfortunately, a complete correspondence between the two classifications is impossible, since not all intermediate goods delivered by the different industrial sectors are included among the 153 commodity groups delivered to final demand. We have eliminated the gap between the two classifications by utilising the purchasing power parities of close substitutes for the missing commodity groups. Furthermore, we have to adjust the price indices for commodity groups in Japan and the USA by "peeling off" the indirect taxes paid and trade and transportation margins for each industry. We estimate these margins from the inter-industry transactions table for 1970 for each country. Finally, we try to aggregate the results for commodity groups to the industry, using as weights the relative shares of each commodity in the value of industry output from the 1970 inter-industry transactions tables. As concerns purchasing power parities for components of intermediate and energy inputs in each industry

---

3 In this respect (and others) our methodology differs from that applied in other papers in this volume, including those by van Ark, Freudenberg and Ünal-Kesenci, Pilat, Birnie, and O'Mahony and Wagner. Their estimates of purchasing power parities are mostly "unit value ratios" based on producer unit values of samples of matched products. Furthermore their approach looks primarily at value added and not at gross output. For a comment on the industry of origin approach, see Jorgenson (1993).

at 1970, we aggregate purchasing power parities for goods and services delivered by that industry to other industries. We employ relative shares in the value of deliveries of intermediate and energy inputs from other industries from the 1970 inter-industry transactions tables as weights.

Next we turn to estimate purchasing power parities for capital and labour input. Capital stock in each industrial sector is measured in seven types of depreciable assets and two types of nondepreciable assets for each industry in both Japan and the USA. These assets are further subdivided among legal forms of organization. We employ the equality between the price of an asset in each type and the discounted flow of future capital services to derive service prices for capital input under the assumption of the same rate of returns on capital stock among various types in a given industry. Although we estimate the decline in efficiency of capital goods for each component of capital input separately for Japan and the USA, we assume that the relative efficiency of new capital goods in a given industry is the same in both countries. The appropriate purchasing power parity for capital service input in the industry is composed of the purchasing power parity for the corresponding component of investment goods output and the differences of the rate of returns on capital stock, economic rate of replacement and tax structure on capital assets between the USA and Japan. Then, in order to obtain the purchasing power parity for capital input, we multiply the purchasing power parity for investment goods by the ratio of the price of capital services to the price of capital goods for Japan relative to the United States in 1970. The resulting price index represents the purchasing power parity for capital service input. On the other hand, purchasing power parity of labour input can be estimated rather directly. In both Japan and the US labour inputs are cross-classified by employment status, sex, age, education and occupation. Given the detailed classification of labour input for each industry in our data base, we construct purchasing power parities for labour input as an index on the basis of relative wage levels for each component of labour input in each industry. Purchasing power parities for industry output, capital, labour, energy, and other intermediate inputs in 1970 are shown in table 1.

Jorgenson, Kuroda, and Nishimizu (1987) have reported relative productivity levels for two countries for the period 1960-1979. In order to compare our new results with the previous ones, we must note a number of revisions on our methodology and data base. First, we have revised US intermediate input measures by constructing a time series of inter-industry transactions tables for the period 1947-1985. The methodology is consistent with the approach used for constructing a time series of Japanese inter-industry transactions tables for the period 1960-1985. Second, the purchasing parity index for capital input has been revised by taking account of the differences of the level of rate of returns on capital between both countries. Third, we were able to obtain more detailed information on wage differentials between full time employees and other employees in Japan. We used this information to improve our estimates of labour

M. Kuroda

TABLE 1
Purchasing Parity Index by Industry in 1970 (US(1970) = 1.0)

Industry	Output Price	Capital Price	Labour Price	Energy Price	Material Price
1.agric.	1.02130	3.99477	.21352	1.43274	.92199
2.mining	.77340	2.99340	.21263	1.27503	.80039
3.construct.	1.03500	1.65628	.18607	1.46919	.74848
4.foods	1.03556	2.16218	.21894	1.19129	.92087
5.textile	.78162	1.15814	.24099	1.12298	.80014
6.fab.text.	.77450	.56882	.18975	1.17723	.77532
7.lumber	.79181	1.04757	.22805	1.22808	.82623
8.furniture	.68521	2.20712	.22952	1.15917	.77358
9.paper	.59360	1.21441	.22170	1.15790	.67570
10.printing	.79861	1.41038	.21251	1.11898	.70020
11.chemicals	.67776	1.05366	.25039	1.20974	.73766
12.pet.coal.	1.31966	2.42765	.21846	1.32853	.75575
13.rubber	1.06956	2.17054	.24042	1.15030	.76700
14.leather	.72520	.89584	.23569	1.21048	.81117
15.stone clay	.71897	1.38720	.23083	1.18335	.71407
16.Prim.metal	.82050	2.47340	.25200	1.19381	.78255
17.fab.metal	.80856	2.08015	.21072	1.20457	.78825
18.machinery	.62605	1.48772	.22564	1.23078	.72933
19.elec.mach.	.68389	2.64950	.22308	1.17283	.74152
20.mot.veh.	.82326	7.41474	.18581	1.14751	.77536
21.trsp.equip.	.91280	1.00718	.21944	1.19919	.78679
22.prec.inst.	.71999	1.58136	.23150	1.19002	.75154
23.misc.mfg.	.70809	2.27222	.22549	1.23099	.74950
24.trsp.comm.	.49445	1.56940	.22713	1.41891	.72007
25.utilities	.99224	1.46405	.26605	1.27060	.80149
26.trade	.75287	1.35016	.26889	1.23466	.81936
27.finance	1.04497	.45178	.30796	1.14891	.89099
28.Services	.86168	.97985	.30796	1.18945	.80000
29.gov.servic.	.31934	1.00000	.19482	1.28298	.79952

compensation for temporary employees, day labourers, and unpaid family workers in Japan. Our earlier estimates of purchasing power parities for labour input were based on relative wage levels for full time workers in Japan and the USA. In the agricultural sector in Japan, however, there is a substantial number of irregular and part-time workers, especially unpaid family workers. Taking the labour compensation of these workers into account, we found that we had overestimated the purchasing power parity of labour input in the agricultural sector in our earlier work. According to our purchasing power parities for industry output in 1970, prices in Japan were higher than those in USA in only six sectors, agriculture, forestry and fisheries, construction, food and kindred products, petroleum refinery and coal products, rubber products, and finance, insurance and real estate. The purchasing power parities for labour input in 1970 show substantially lower costs of labour input in Japan relative to the USA. In that year hourly wages in Japan were 30 percent or less of US hourly wages. By contrast the cost of capital in Japan were on average 30 percent higher than that in the USA in 1970. Especially, in agriculture, forestry and fisheries and motor vehicles the Japanese cost of capital input were much higher than those in the USA. The purchasing power parities for intermediate inputs are estimated as a weighted average of the purchasing power parities of industry outputs. The cost of intermediate inputs in Japan, other than energy, is between 60-90 percent of the cost in the USA in 1970. On the other hand, the purchasing power parities for energy inputs in 1970 are greater than unity, implying that the cost of energy was higher in Japan.

Table 2 presents time series estimate for price indices of value added and capital and labour inputs for the period 1960-1985 in Japan. The second and third columns represent price indices of value added for Japan and the USA. The second column is the Japanese price index with base equal to the purchasing power parity in 1970, divided by an index of the yen - dollar exchange rate equal to one in 1970. The third column gives the corresponding price index in the USA with base equal to one in 1970. Similarly the fourth and fifth columns provide price indices for labour inputs in Japan and the USA in terms of dollars and the sixth and seventh columns represent price indices for capital inputs.

According to the results presented in table 2, the price deflator for aggregate value added in Japan was 0.52806 in 1960, while that in the USA was 0.78658 in that year. This implies that the Japanese aggregate price index in 1960 was only 67 percent of that in the USA. Under the fixed yen - dollar exchange rate of 360 yen to the dollar that prevailed until 1970, the Japanese price index rose to 82 percent of the US price index in 1970. The price index in Japan, denominated in dollars, exceeded the corresponding US price index after the collapse of the fixed exchange rate regime in 1970 and the beginning of the energy crisis in 1973. This was a consequence of more rapid inflation in Japan and a substantial appreciation of the yen through 1973. The competitiveness of US industries relative to their Japanese counterparts reached a temporary peak in 1979, reflecting the severe impact of the second oil crisis on the Japanese economy in that year. After 1979 the US inflation rate remained relatively high, while Japan underwent a severe deflation, accompanied by depreciation of the yen. This situation continued until 1985 as inflation in the USA stayed high. During the 1980s US prices came gradually closer to the level of Japanese prices in dollars due to the rapid appreciation of the US dollar relative to the Japanese yen. By 1984 the Japanese price level in dollars was only 110 percent of the US price, which implies that Japanese industries had regained their substantial com-

M. Kuroda

TABLE 2
Denominated Price by Purchasing Power Parity Index
Japan and United States During 1960-1985

Year	Aggregate Pv		Aggregate P_L		Aggregate P_K	
	Japan	USA	Japan	USA	Japan	USA
1960	.528058	.786578	.072932	.608330	.830322	.816640
1961	.568492	.796636	.082009	.643138	.920746	.813070
1962	.590994	.805579	.093238	.655190	.871798	.880437
1963	.618792	.810572	.103964	.670786	.921335	.926329
1964	.640153	.819958	.112652	.694631	.962464	.974993
1965	.665867	.834661	.130191	.714306	.946835	1.058653
1966	.696917	.865277	.144270	.756451	1.010095	1.087785
1967	.726698	.883920	.159460	.797704	1.126424	1.056667
1968	.750210	.912276	.185906	.860579	1.149478	1.075485
1969	.779443	.955919	.209934	.915133	1.212468	1.085649
1970	.818180	1.000000	.242890	1.000000	1.311050	1.000000
1971	.867358	1.045649	.287003	1.075368	1.208758	1.075693
1972	1.042812	1.093679	.372083	1.149949	1.480999	1.172096
1973	1.324395	1.170864	.529019	1.234038	1.779527	1.252209
1974	1.505756	1.296034	.608927	1.357641	1.686070	1.206110
1975	1.571936	1.427681	.708139	1.482192	1.522120	1.356638
1976	1.677587	1.503407	.768754	1.610017	1.770463	1.497214
1977	1.935963	1.608306	.924936	1.715731	1.997131	1.707900
1978	2.701635	1.734743	1.241712	1.835993	2.780000	1.876374
1979	2.637814	1.887843	1.237434	1.994157	2.801112	1.948161
1980	2.687678	2.067245	1.278604	2.211318	2.772001	1.969454
1981	2.865282	2.249397	1.390593	2.391880	2.828508	2.231036
1982	2.597304	2.393829	1.288131	2.545560	2.496833	2.232436
1983	2.783590	2.480873	1.350639	2.659729	2.596986	2.422641
1984	2.825835	2.567638	1.377496	2.756791	2.649348	2.690583
1985	2.845722	2.631761	1.438161	2.880045	2.670997	2.674274

petitive advantage relative to their US counterparts.

According to the international comparison of capital input prices shown in table 2, the cost of capital in Japan was almost 101 percent of that in the USA in 1960 and gradually rose to within 131 percent of the US level by 1970. After the energy crisis in 1973 the cost of capital in Japan increased relative to the USA, exceeding the US level by almost fifty percent in 1980. The appreciation of the US dollar reversed this trend. By 1984 the relative cost of capital in Japan had fallen to only 98 percent of the US level, which is below the level prevailing almost a quarter century earlier in 1960. The rise in the cost of capital in Japan relative to that in the USA after the energy crisis was a consequence of the appreciation of the yen. The fall of this relative price during the 1980s resulted from the appreciation of the dollar.

Finally, a comparison of labour input prices in table 2 shows that the Japanese wage rate in 1960 was only 12 percent of the US wage rate. By 1970 the Japanese wage rate had reached 24 percent of the US level. Rapid wage increases in Japan during the 1970s and the sharp appreciation of the yen raised wage rates in Japan to 59 percent of the US level in 1980. The subsequent appreciation of the dollar and rapid wage increases in the USA resulted in a decline in Japanese wage rates relative to the USA. The relative price of labour input in Japan was only 50 percent of the US level in 1985.

Our international comparisons of relative prices of aggregate output and inputs show, first, that the Japanese economy has been more competitive than the USA economy throughout the period 1960-1972. Japan's competitiveness deteriorated substantially after 1973 and recovered gradually due to the appreciation of the dollar in the 1980s. Second, lower wage rates have contributed to Japan's international competitiveness throughout the period, especially before the energy crisis in 1973. Lower costs of capital in the USA have contributed to the US competitiveness position for most of the period with important exceptions in 1960, 1962-1966 and 1984.

4. Relative Productivity Levels

In this section we estimate relative levels of productivity in Japan and the USA for each of the twenty-nine industries included in our study. By using (8), we can estimate the proportional gap of technology between Japan and the United States. Here we will define the proportional gap of technology in the year t as follows:

$$D(t)^j = \bar{v}_D^t(t) = \ln T^j(Japan, t) - \ln T^j(US, t), \qquad (14)$$

where T^j (Japan, t) and T^j (USA, t) represent the states of technology of the j-th industry in Japan and the USA in year t respectively. A negative (positive) value of D^j (t) implies that the Japanese technology of the j-th industry in year t is behind (ahead) of the US technology. We can define the index of technology level in Japan compared to that in the USA as follows:

$$Index_{tech}(Japan, t) = T^j(Japan, t)/T^j(US, t) = Exp(D(t)^j) \qquad (15)$$

Table 3 represents the index of technology by industry in Japan for each year since 1960. An index of more than unity implies that the technology level in Japan is higher than in the USA. According to our results in table 3, there were large differences of technology between Japan and the USA in 1960. The US

M. Kuroda

technology had absolute advantages in almost all industries except agriculture, forestry and fisheries, transportation and communication, and government services. During the period 1960-1970, technical progress in Japanese industries was remarkably higher than in US industries. Although technical progress in some Japanese industries slowed down during the 1970s, the US industries experienced an even greater stagnation in the technology growth rate for most industries. Consequently six industries in Japan, including mining, chemicals, electric machinery, motor vehicle, miscellaneous manufacturing and utilities, had caught up in terms of their technology level with their US counterparts by the

TABLE 3
Relative Technology Level by Industry in Japan (US level=1.0)

Industry	1960	1965	1970	1975	1980	1985
1.agric.	1.14232	1.04516	.92224	.88631	.74061	.58190
2.mining	.89665	1.20582	1.26705	1.49539	2.35948	2.47129
3.construct.	.58185	.48605	.53869	.54167	.55946	.52311
4.foods	.84590	.78367	.82546	.82463	.84551	.78506
5.textile	.91700	.85370	.85354	.95499	.92383	.91231
6.fab.text.	.66224	.67043	.70075	.75243	.76782	.75448
7.lumber	.66058	.71181	.78786	.79870	.84680	.92059
8.furniture	.79980	.80555	.89591	.81100	.80903	.84427
9.paper	.92073	.92994	1.00303	.97695	.95203	.97657
10.printing	.54005	.55228	.64699	.49087	.49953	.51856
11.chemicals	.79353	.82012	.99650	1.01679	1.19132	1.22087
12.pet.coal	.83742	.75936	.68266	.48733	.51934	.40512
13.rubber	.61814	.64483	.55582	.57955	.56382	.60793
14.leather	.75545	.75699	.81481	.81044	.81376	.85877
15.stone clay	.72327	.70786	.82593	.73151	.74907	.65131
16.Prim.metal	.87422	.83487	.92903	.94637	.97709	.92602
17.fab.metal	.60810	.62905	.74400	.71681	.74161	.71994
18.machinery	.84973	.77442	.94722	.89980	.89209	.74485
19.elec.mach.	.77406	.74893	.93030	.99194	1.08165	1.19078
20.mot.veh.	.86832	.78615	.99983	1.04154	1.09548	.97496
21.trsp.equip.	.39016	.45642	.59806	.52905	.66222	.55854
22.prec.inst,	.70657	.67427	.79777	.78044	.98487	.86153
23.misc.mfg.	.95955	1.00302	.91447	1.08118	1.47747	1.64576
24.trsp.comm.	1.00964	1.02949	1.08015	1.06982	.77534	.79902
25.utilities	.76718	.86817	.92791	.91159	1.07592	1.28086
26.trade	.70700	.65841	.78667	.76686	.84722	.83920
27.finance	.31139	.37921	.46694	.46210	.51171	.58544
28.Services	.63472	.65657	.68915	.64919	.57453	.56316
29.Gov.services	1.07580	1.02312	1.05555	.94591	.83651	.80124

end of the 1970s. During the 1980s, technological progress began to restore again in both Japan and the United States. In five of the six industries, mentioned above, excluding motor vehicles, the technological progress in Japan continued to be more rapid than in the USA.[4]

On the other hand, in 1985 there were also some industries in which the USA had increased its advantage in technology. These include agriculture, forestry and fisheries, petroleum refinery and coal products, construction and foods and kindred products. For these industries productivity gaps between Japan and the USA are expected to persist into the future. There were also some industries in which the USA still had an advantage in the 1985 technology although the differences of technology between both countries had become smaller since 1960. These industries include textile, fabricated textile, furniture, printing, rubber, stone and clay, fabricated metal, machinery, transportation and communication, services, and government services. There were also some industries in which the technology gap is expected to close in the near future in spite of the US advantages in 1985. This group on industries include lumber, paper, leather, primary metal, transportation equipment except motor, precision instruments, trade and finance, insurance and real estate. Next we turn to international competitiveness in terms of output prices between Japan and the USA. We can account for movements in the relative prices of industry outputs in the two countries by changes in relative input prices and changes in relative productivity levels. Table 4 represents the proportional gap of prices of industrial outputs, inputs and technology between Japan and the USA in 1960, 1965, 1979, 1975, 1980 and 1985. A negative difference in the proportional gap in prices implies that the US prices are higher than the Japanese, while a positive difference implies the Japanese price is higher than the USA. Similarly, a negative difference in the proportional gap in technology implies that the technology level in Japan has an advantage relatively to the US level and it contributes to the advantage in the output price. Values in parenthesis from columns 3 to 7 represent the percental contributions of input prices and technology to difference in output price.

In the 1960s, output prices in all industries except petroleum refinery and coal products and other transportation equipment (except motor) were relatively low in Japan. This was primarily due to lower labour costs and in spite of Japan's disadvantages in technology. Although lower relative wage rates in Japan helped to reduce relative prices of output during the 1970s, this advantage was almost completely offset by the lower levels of productivity in Japan.

Japan's competitiveness in terms of output prices gradually disappeared at the

---

4   It might have been better to exclude mining industry from our comparison. The commodities produced in the Japanese mining industry are completely different from those of the US industry. More than 60 percent of the products in Japanese mining is "stone & gravel" which are not genuine mining products.

beginning of 1970s with a few exceptions such as mining, chemicals, electric machinery, motor vehicle, miscellaneous manufacturing, transportation and communication, and utilities, where their technology levels have caught up to the US levels. There is the industry such as petroleum refinery and coal products where the advantage in terms of output price in Japan has never been taken since 1960 in spite of their lower cost of labour. The output prices of other transportation equipment except motor and finance sector in Japan, where the US industries still have an advantage in their technology level, did not have competitiveness, although the differences of the technology between two countries are gradually closing since 1960.

Below we try to point out the sources of international competitiveness in terms of output price by industry.

1. Agriculture, forestry and fisheries. In the beginning of the 1960s, Japanese agriculture had a slight advantage in its technology level. This contributed to maintain the competitiveness of the Japanese industry with lower wage cost. Japanese agriculture has completely lost the technology advantage since 1970 and the proportional technology gap has continued to expand. The relatively high capital cost was one of the main sources of incompetiveness in this industry.

2. Mining. Mining in Japan has remained competitive because of the lower wage cost and higher technology level since 1960. As mentioned in footnote 3, however, this statement has to be treated carefully, because of differences in product composition in the mining industry in Japan and the USA.

3. Construction. During the 1960s the Japanese construction industry was competitive in terms of output prices because of the lower cost of labour and materials in spite of the disadvantages of the technology level. However, the competitive position to the USA has been lost since 1970, because of increases in material cost and the increase in the technology disadvantage.

4. Foods and kindred products. In this industry Japanese technology level has not caught up since 1960. Although international competitiveness in terms of the output price in 1960 was mainly maintained by the lower cost of labour and materials, the advantage in material costs has been lost since 1975 and the advantage of lower labour cost has been offset by the expansion of the proportional gap in technology.

5. Textile mill products. The Japanese technology level has not caught up since 1960 and the proportional gap has even widened since 1975. However, price competitiveness still has been maintained since 1960 because of the lower labour cost.

6. Apparel and other fabricated textiles. The Japanese technology level has not caught up significantly since 1960 and the proportional gap has even widened slightly since 1980. Price competitiveness during the 1960s has been maintained by the lower cost of labour and material despite the

disadvantages in the technology level. The advantage in materials cost was lost in 1975 and the advantage in labour cost has been offset by the increase in the proportional gap in technology.

7. Lumber and wood products except furniture. Japanese price competitiveness in output has been maintained for the whole period except the beginning of the 1980s. This is mainly due to the lower cost of labour and capital in spite of the disadvantage of the technology. Especially, the lower cost of capital has contributed to Japan's competitiveness. The proportional gap in technology has also been gradually reduced.

8. Furniture and fixtures. Japanese price competitiveness in output has been maintained for the whole period except the beginning of the 1980s. The sources of competitiveness were mainly the lower cost of labour and material in spite of the increasing trend of the proportional gap in technology.

9. Paper and allied products. Japanese price competitiveness in output has been maintained for the whole period except the beginning of the 1980s. Although the US industry has a slight advantage in technology, it has been completely offset by the lower cost of labour, capital and material in Japan.

10. Printing, publishing and allied products. The US industry has maintained a large advantage in technology since 1960. However, until 1970 this was offset by the lower cost of labour and material in Japan compared to the USA.

11. Chemical and allied products. The Japanese price competitiveness has been maintained continuously during the whole period. Although one of the sources of the competitiveness is the lower cost of labour, technological progress in Japan also greatly contributed to the competitiveness of this industry.

12. Petroleum refinery and coal products. The US price competitiveness has been continuously maintained during the whole period since 1960. The main source of the USA advantage comes is the technology level. The proportional gap between both countries has been expanding gradually. The lower cost of labour, capital and material in Japan could not offset the technology disadvantage.

13. Rubber and allied products. The technology level in the USA has been advantageous during the whole period since 1960 and the proportional gap between Japan and the USA has expanded. Although the output price in Japan was lower than in the USA during the 1960s (because of the lower labour cost in spite of the technological disadvantage), Japanese competitiveness in this industry was lost along with the rise in labour cost and the widening of the technology gap.

14. Leather and leather products. Price competitiveness in Japan has been lost since 1970 because of the widening of the technology gap. Although the lower cost of labour in Japan has been maintained until 1985, it did not

have enough impact on the output price to offset the technology disadvantage.

15. Stone, clay and glass products. The trend in price competitiveness in this sector is similar to that of leather and related products. The United States still has a technological advantage and the gap between the USA and Japan has been continuously rising.

16. Primary metal products. Japan has experienced price competitiveness for the whole period since 1960 (except the beginning) of 1980s in spite of the technological disadvantage. The sources of competitiveness came from the lower cost of labour and material. Although the technological gap has been gradually reduced, higher cost of capital in Japan became another source which affected the Japanese competitiveness in terms of output price.

17. Fabricated metal products. The technology gap between Japan and the USA has been widened continuously. Japan lost price competitiveness since the end of the 1970s in spite of the lower cost of labour.

18. Machinery. The trend in the price competitiveness in this sector is similar to that in fabricated metal products. The technological gap between the two countries has widened, and was the main source to push down Japanese competitiveness in spite of the lower cost of labour.

19. Electric machinery. This is one of the industries in which Japan has maintained price competitiveness for the whole period since 1960. Japan has a technological advantage and the proportional gap with the USA has expanded. The lower lost of labour and materials also contributed to the Japanese price competitiveness.

20. Motor vehicles and equipment. The Japanese price competitiveness has been maintained during the whole period except for the beginning of the 1980s. The main sources of competitiveness are the lower cost of labour and materials, while the higher cost of capital in Japan partly offset the advantage. Although the proportional technology gap gradually reduced at the end of the 1970s, it expanded again during the 1980s.

21. Transportation equipment except motor. With the exception of the beginning of the 1970s, Japan did not have a price competitiveness advantage over the USA. This was mainly caused by the technology disadvantage in spite of the lower cost of labour in Japan.

22. Precision instruments. This is one of the industries in which Japan has been characterised by a continuous price competitiveness advantage. This is caused by the lower cost of labour, capital and materials in spite of the technological disadvantage.

23. Transportation and communication. Price competitiveness in Japan for the period 1960-1975 has been lost since the end of the 1970s. This is primarily caused by the more rapid technical progress in the USA and the higher increase in capital cost in Japan.

24. Electric utilities and gas supply. The Japanese price competitiveness

advantage was lost at the end of the 1970s, but recovered again during the 1980s because of the acceleration in technical progress in Japan. The lower cost of labour in Japan remained one of the sources of the Japanese price competitiveness advantage.

25. Wholesale and retail trade. The USA has continuously maintained a technological advantage during the whole period. Japan's price competitiveness position was negatively affected by the increasing labour cost.

26. Finance, insurance and real estate. The US price competitiveness advantage has been maintained during the whole period except for 1960. The USA has taken advantage of higher technical progress and the proportional gap between the USA and Japan has been expanding gradually.

27. Other service. The Japanese price competitiveness advantage was lost during the middle of the 1970s. The lower cost of labour and capital could not offset the disadvantage in technology in Japan. The proportional gap in technology has been expanding to the advantage of the United States.

TABLE 4
Decomposition of Sources of Proportional Gaps of Prices

Industry/ Year	Output	Capital	Labour	Energy	Material	Technology
1. agric.						
1960	-.41623	.43742	-.59520	.00701	-.13240	-.13306
	(-31.89)	(33.52)	(-45.61)	(.54)	(-10.15)	(-10.20)
1965	.14583	.64481	-.42923	.00260	-.02819	-.04417
	(12.69)	(56.12)	(-37.36)	(.23)	(-2.45)	(-3.84)
1970	.37203	.69482	-.38623	.00216	-.01967	.08095
	(31.43)	(58.69)	(-32.63)	(.18)	(-1.66)	(6.84)
1975	.41877	.64890	-.39043	.00471	.03491	.12069
	(34.91)	(54.09)	(-32.55)	(.39)	(2.91)	(10.06)
1980	.63925	.54583	-.29638	.00532	.08420	.30028
	(51.89)	(44.30)	(-24.06)	(.43)	(6.83)	(24.37)
1985	.57233	.21585	-.26476	.00433	.07544	.54146
	(51.94)	(19.59)	(-24.03)	(.39)	(6.85)	(49.14)
2.mining						
1960	-.84648	-.05071	-.82414	.00803	-.08875	.10909
	(-78.33)	(-4.69)	(-76.26)	(.74)	(-8.21)	(10.09)
1965	-.79071	.07759	-.60386	.00618	-.08346	-.18716
	(-82.52)	(8.10)	(-63.02)	(.64)	(-8.71)	(-19.53)
1970	-.64193	.22453	-.53828	.00425	-.09575	-.23669
	(-58.38)	(20.42)	(-48.96)	(.39)	(-8.71)	(-21.53)
1975	-.79510	.03588	-.42128	.01270	-.02001	-.40239
	(-89.11)	(4.02)	(-47.21)	(1.42)	(-2.24)	(-45.10)
1980	-1.09590	.052463	-.32873	.01677	.01987	-.85844
	(-85.72)	(4.27)	(-25.71)	(1.31)	(1.55)	(-67.15)
1985	-1.39225	-.04741	-.40654	.00788	-.04143	-.90474
	(-98.88)	(-3.37)	(-28.87)	(.56)	(-2.94)	(-64.26)
3.construct.						
1960	-.23371	.05034	-.64153	.00780	-.19187	.54155
	(-16.31)	(3.51)	(-44.77)	(.54)	(-13.39)	(37.79)
1965	-.42918	-.03782	-1.03565	.00964	-.08680	.72145
	(-22.69)	(-2.00)	(-54.76)	(.51)	(-4.59)	(38.14)
1970	-.35272	.06135	-.95523	.00712	-.08456	.61861
	(-20.43)	(3.55)	(-55.32)	(.41)	(-4.90)	(35.82)
1975	.08752	.08517	-.61045	.01427	-.01457	.61310
	(6.54)	(6.37)	(-45.64)	(1.07)	(-1.09)	(45.84)
1980	.28900	.08066	-.43175	.02256	.03675	.58078
	(25.08)	(7.00)	(-37.46)	(1.96)	(3.19)	(50.39)
1985	.15550	-.02928	-.47872	.02485	-.00931	.64796
	(13.07)	(-2.46)	(-40.22)	(2.09)	(-.78)	(54.44)

TABLE 4 (Continued)

Industry/ Year	Output	Capital	Labour	Energy	Material	Technology
4.foods						
1960	-.10731	.18880	-.25258	.00170	-.21260	.16736
	(-13.04)	(22.94)	(-30.69)	(.21)	(-25.83)	(20.33)
1965	.05526	.13428	-.23018	.00209	-.09470	.24377
	(.84)	(19.05)	(-32.65)	(.30)	(-13.43)	(34.58)
1970	.02402	.10020	-.21021	.00173	-.05950	.19181
	(4.26)	(17.78)	(-37.31)	(.31)	(-10.56)	(34.04)
1975	.30783	.06740	-.09550	.00480	.13832	.19282
	(61.71)	(13.51)	(-19.14)	(.96)	(27.73)	(38.65)
1980	.50158	.10328	-.09037	.00708	.31378	.16782
	(73.51)	(15.14)	(-13.24)	(1.04)	(45.99)	(24.59)
1985	.41745	.00274	-.11717	.00112	.28876	.241996
	(64.05)	(.42)	(-17.98)	(.17)	(44.30)	(37.13)
5.textile						
1960	-.44298	.02514	-.35427	.00086	-.20137	.08665
	(-66.28)	(3.76)	(-53.01)	(.13)	(-30.13)	(12.97)
1965	-.33442	-.02351	-.29768	.00207	-.17345	.15817
	(-51.07)	(-3.59)	(-45.46)	(.32)	(-26.49)	(24.15)
1970	-.24696	.01558	-.26855	.00167	-.15401	.15836
	(-41.28)	(2.60)	(-44.90)	(.28)	(-25.75)	(26.47)
1975	-.10283	-.00365	-.13883	.00568	-.01208	.04605
	(-49.85)	(-1.77)	(-67.30)	(2.75)	(-5.85)	(22.32)
1980	.09471	-.02385	-.11280	.00914	.14298	.07923
	(25.74)	(-6.48)	(-30.65)	(2.48)	(38.85)	(21.53)
1985	-.03932	-.03251	-.14052	-.00130	.04325	.09177
	(-12.71)	(-10.51)	(-45.42)	(-.42)	(13.98)	(29.67)
6.fab.text.						
1960	-.52951	-.03616	-.63544	.00076	-.27080	.41212
	(-39.07)	(-2.67)	(-46.89)	(.06)	(-19.98)	(30.41)
1965	-.33158	-.03888	-.47840	.00107	-.21521	.39984
	(-29.26)	(-3.43)	(-42.21)	(.09)	(-18.99)	(35.28)
1970	-.25641	-.02740	-.40839	.00131	-.17754	.35561
	(-26.43)	(-2.82)	(-42.09)	(.14)	(-18.30)	(36.65)
1975	-.04293	-.03205	-.31357	.00410	.01413	.28445
	(-6.62)	(-4.94)	(-48.37)	(.63)	(2.18)	(43.88)
1980	.23843	.00302	-.18817	.00414	.15524	.26420
	(38.78)	(.49)	(-30.61)	(.67)	(25.25)	(42.98)
1985	.08826	.01277	-.26030	.00094	.05311	.28173
	(14.50)	(2.10)	(-42.75)	(.16)	(8.72)	(46.27)

TABLE 4 (Continued)

Industry/ Year	Output	Capital	Labour	Energy	Material	Technology
7.lumber						
1960	-.33756	-.05331	-.51193	.00221	-.18917	.41463
	(-28.82)	(-4.55)	(-43.71)	(.19)	(-16.15)	(35.40)
1965	-.29208	-.09431	-.42005	.00366	-.12131	.33994
	(-29.83)	(-9.63)	(-42.89)	(.37)	(-12.39)	(34.71)
1970	-.23433	.00492	-.35981	.00327	-.12116	.23844
	(-32.21)	(.68)	(-49.45)	(.45)	(-16.65)	(32.77)
1975	-.16299	-.33024	-.17855	.00557	.11545	.22477
	(-19.07)	(-38.64)	(-20.89)	(.65)	(13.51)	(26.30)
1980	.13264	-.19130	-.16114	.00609	.31268	.16629
	(15.84)	(-22.84)	(-19.24)	(.73)	(37.34)	(19.86)
1985	-.27621	-.34818	-.20324	.00147	.19099	.08274
	(-33.41)	(-42.12)	(-24.59)	(.18)	(23.10)	(10.01)
8.furniture						
1960	-.64169	.01132	-.69460	.00072	-.18252	.22339
	(-57.68)	(1.02)	(-62.43)	(.06)	(-16.41)	(20.08)
1965	-.41446	.02598	-.50828	.00193	-.15032	.21623
	(-45.91)	(2.88)	(-56.30)	(.21)	(-16.65)	(23.95)
1970	-.37883	.08546	-.42322	.00153	-.15252	.10992
	(-49.03)	(11.06)	(-54.77)	(.20)	(-19.74)	(14.23)
1975	-.01242	.03341	-.24544	.00427	-.01415	.20949
	(-2.45)	(6.569)	(-48.43)	(.84)	(-2.79)	(41.34)
1980	.21623	.05315	-.17673	.00469	.12321	.21192
	(37.96)	(9.33)	(31.02)	(.82)	(21.63)	(37.20)
1985	-.02389	.01833	-.20973	.00013	-.00190	.16928
	(-5.98)	(4.59)	(-52.51)	(.03)	(-.48)	(42.39)
9.paper						
1960	-.67119	-.01498	-.42518	.00246	-.31609	.08259
	(-79.78)	(-1.78)	(-50.54)	(.29)	(-37.57)	(9.82)
1965	-.57426	-.03017	-.36526	.00633	-.25779	.07263
	(-78.43)	(-4.12)	(-49.89)	(.86)	(-35.21)	(9.92)
1970	-.52234	.02542	-.30050	.00497	-.24921	-.00303
	(-89.58)	(4.36)	(-51.53)	(.85)	(-42.74)	(-.52)
1975	-.15954	-.00656	-.14622	.01228	-.04236	.02332
	(-69.15)	(-2.84)	(-63.37)	(5.32)	(-18.36)	(10.11)
1980	.03431	.00315	-.13344	.01724	.09820	.04916
	(11.39)	(1.05)	(-44.30)	(5.72)	(32.60)	(16.32)
1985	-.24273	-.03812	-.17588	.00032	-.05276	.02371
	(-83.47)	(-13.11)	(-60.48)	(.161)	(-18.14)	(8.15)

TABLE 4 (Continued)

Industry/ Year	Output	Capital	Labour	Energy	Material	Technology
10.printing						
1960	-.37191	-.03490	-.73528	-.00010	-.21773	.61610
	(-23.18)	(-2.18)	(-45.84)	(-.01)	(-13.57)	(38.41)
1965	-.17744	.00352	-.60519	.00096	-.17043	.59370
	(-12.92)	(.26)	(-44.05)	(.07)	(-12.41)	(43.22)
1970	-.22586	.04604	-.52208	.00079	-.18603	.43543
	(-18.97)	(3.87)	(-43.86)	(.07)	(-15.63)	(36.58)
1975	.43426	-.03128	-.27757	.00245	.02908	.71157
	(41.28)	(-2.97)	(-26.39)	(.23)	(2.76)	(67.64)
1980	.65994	.00340	-.19479	.00270	.5456	.69408
	(62.88)	(.32)	(-18.56)	(.26)	(14.73)	(66.13)
1985	.37547	-.06935	-.22875	-.00074	.01761	.65670
	(38.58)	(-7.13)	(-23.51)	(-.08)	(1.81)	(67.48)
11.chemicals						
1960	-.31282	-.05671	-.34290	.00868	-.15316	.23126
	(-39.46)	(-7.15)	(-43.26)	(1.09)	(-19.32)	(29.17)
1965	-.27641	-.07919	-.26797	.01146	-.13904	.19831
	(-39.72)	(-11.38)	(-38.50)	(1.65)	(-19.98)	(28.49)
1970	-.38965	.01041	-.23689	.00960	-.17628	.00351
	(-89.23)	(2.38)	(-54.25)	(2.20)	(-40.37)	(.80)
1975	-.27745	-.13008	-.11074	.03405	-.05403	-.01665
	(-80.29)	(-37.65)	(-32.05)	(9.85)	(-15.64)	(-4.82)
1980	-.11198	.04491	-.08383	.04266	.05934	-.17506
	(-27.60)	(11.07)	(-20.66)	(10.51)	(14.62)	(-43.14)
1985	-.35934	.02553	-.12605	.01210	-.07137	-.19956
	(-82.68)	(5.88)	(-29.00)	(2.78)	(-16.42)	(-45.92)
12.pet.coal						
1960	.41251	.25274	-.14840	.02016	.11058	.17743
	(58.16)	(35.63)	(-20.92)	(2.684)	(15.59)	(25.01)
1965	.32662	.21537	-.11035	.02342	-.07709	.27528
	(46.56)	(30.70)	(-15.73)	(3.34)	(-10.99)	(39.24)
1970	.26978	.15287	-.09015	.02038	-.19509	.38176
	(32.11)	(18.19)	(-10.73)	(2.43)	(-23.22)	(45.43)
1975	.58835	-.07233	-.03622	.03433	-.05623	.71881
	(64.10)	(-7.88)	(-3.95)	(3.74)	(-6.13)	(78.31)
1980	.61596	-.05284	-.02372	.03437	.00295	.65520
	(80.09)	(-6.87)	(-3.08)	(4.47)	(.38)	(85.19)
1985	.69417	-.00236	-.03709	.02673	-.19668	.90357
	(59.51)	(-.20)	(-3.18)	(2.29)	(-16.86)	(77.47)

TABLE 4 (Continued)

Industry/ Year	Output	Capital	Labour	Energy	Material	Technology
13.rubber						
1960	-.11950	.11754	-.63983	.00285	-6.08109	.48104
	(-9.04)	(8.89)	(-48.39)	(.22)	(-6.13)	(36.38)
1965	-.09795	.09964	-.49458	.00364	-.14542	.43877
	(-8.294)	(8.43)	(-41.84)	(.31)	(-12.30)	(37.12)
1970	.05815	.05602	-.42675	.00285	-.16128	.58731
	(4.71)	(4.54)	(-34.58)	(.23)	(-13.07)	(47.59)
1975	.31967	.00746	-.21596	.01050	-.02784	.54551
	(39.60)	(.92)	(-26.75)	(1.30)	(-3.45)	(67.57)
1980	.56678	.02164	-.13974	.01278	.09908	.576302
	(66.97)	(2.56)	(-16.51)	(1.51)	(11.71)	(67.71)
1985	.32178	.00380	-.17148	.00226	-.01049	.49769
	(46.93)	(.55)	(-25.01)	(.33)	(-1.53)	(72.58)
14.leather						
1960	-.48159	-.01164	-.54120	.00159	-.21079	.28044
	(-46.06)	(-1.11)	(-51.76)	(.15)	(-20.16)	(26.82)
1965	-.35910	-.04099	-.44737	.00155	-.15070	.27841
	(-39.07)	(-4.46)	(-48.68)	(.17)	(-16.40)	(30.29)
1970	-.32204	-.00679	-.38342	.00201	-.13864	.20480
	(-43.78)	(-.92)	(-52.12)	(.27)	(-18.85)	(27.84)
1975	.08632	.01956	-.18437	.00427	.03668	.21018
	(18.97)	(4.30)	(-40.52)	(.94)	(8.06)	(46.19)
1980	.20346	-.01380	-.13043	.00504	.13656	.20609
	(41.36)	(-2.81)	(-26.51)	(1.02)	(27.76)	(41.90)
1985	.05093	.04568	-.20264	.00082	.05481	.15225
	(11.16)	(10.01)	(-44.42)	(.18)	(12.02)	(33.37)
15.stone clay						
1960	-.48343	.01435	-.61703	.01049	-.21521	.32397
	(-40.93)	(1.21)	(-52.24)	(.89)	(-18.22)	(27.43)
1965	-.32731	-.00917	-.50724	.01356	-.16997	.34551
	(-31.31)	(-.88)	(-48.52)	(1.30)	(-16.26)	(33.05)
1970	-.33079	.04820	-.40185	.00883	-.17721	.19125
	(-39.98)	(5.83)	(-48.57)	(1.07)	(-21.42)	(23.12)
1975	.06407	-.02920	-.23170	.03333	-.02099	.31264
	(10.20)	(-4.65)	(-36.90)	(5.31)	(-3.34)	(49.79)
1980	.19807	-.01123	-.19217	.04075	.07180	.28892
	(32.75)	(-1.86)	(-31.77)	(6.74)	(11.87)	(47.77)
1985	.01104	-.16090	-.22768	.00577	-.03491	.42877
	(1.29)	(-18.75)	(-26.54)	(.67)	(-4.07)	(49.97)

TABLE 4 (Continued)

Industry/ Year	Output	Capital	Labour	Energy	Material	Technology
16.Prim.metal						
1960	-.17163	.12208	-.35797	.00703	-.07718	.13442
	(-24.56)	(17.47)	(-51.24)	(1.01)	(-11.05)	(19.24)
1965	-.19479	.02246	-.27240	.00940	-.13474	.18048
	(-31.44)	(3.63)	(-43.97)	(1.52)	(-21.75)	(29.13)
1970	-.19828	.10445	-.21757	.00815	-.16693	.07361
	(-34.74)	(18.3	(-38.12)	(1.43)	(-29.25)	(12.90)
1975	-.06154	.06402	-.12175	.03600	-.09493	.05512
	(-16.55)	(17.22)	(-32.74)	(9.68)	(-25.53)	(14.82)
1980	.07313	.12689	-.11843	.03660	.00489	.02318
	(23.59)	(40.93)	(-38.20)	(11.81)	(1.58)	(7.48)
1985	-.08970	.10947	-.16984	.00680	-.11299	.07686
	(-18.85)	(23.00)	(-35.68)	(1.43)	(-23.74)	(16.15)
17.fab.metal						
1960	-.23855	.10510	-.73639	.00219	-.10687	.49741
	(-16.48)	(7.26)	(-50.86)	(.15)	(-7.38)	(34.35)
1965	-.23656	.02110	-.61490	.00345	-.10975	.46355
	(-19.51)	(1.74)	(-50.70)	(.28)	(-9.05)	(38.22)
1970	-.21363	.08604	-.46313	.00306	-.13531	.29571
	(-21.73)	(8.75)	(-47.10)	(.31)	(-13.76)	(30.07)
1975	-.05451	-.05622	-.29430	.01134	-.04827	.33294
	(-7.34)	(-7.57)	(-39.61)	(1.53)	(-6.50)	(44.81)
1980	.11448	-.01371	-.24757	.01182	.06501	.29893
	(17.97)	(-2.15)	(-38.86)	(1.86)	(10.20)	(46.92)
1985	.00212	-.01498	-.29075	.00171	-.02247	.32859
	(.32)	(-2.27)	(-44.15)	(.26)	(-3.41)	(49.90)
18.machinery						
1960	-.45673	.13498	-.61475	.00196	-.14175	.16284
	(-43.24)	(12.78)	(-58.20)	(.19)	(-13.42)	(15.42)
1965	-.45346	-.03259	-.53880	.00303	-.14074	.25564
	(-46.71)	(-3.36)	(-55.50)	(.31)	(-14.50)	(26.33)
1970	-.46919	.05698	-.40131	.00245	-.18155	.05422
	(-67.36)	(8.18)	(-57.62)	(.35)	(-26.07)	(7.79)
1975	-.22763	-.01772	-.23928	.00577	-.08198	.10558
	(-50.55)	(-3.93)	(-53.13)	(1.28)	(-18.21)	(23.44)
1980	.02240	.05846	-.18984	.00669	.03290	.11419
	(5.57)	(14.54)	(-47.21)	(1.66)	(8.18)	(28.40)
1985	.10418	.06545	-.24500	.00179	-.01264	.29457
	(16.82)	(10.57)	(-39.55)	(.29)	(-2.04)	(47.55)

TABLE 4 (Continued)

Industry/ Year	Output	Capital	Labour	Energy	Material	Technology
19.elec.mach.						
1960	-.49915	.04749	-.65467	.00164	-.14971	.25611
	(-44.98)	(4.28)	(-59.00)	(.15)	(-13.49)	(23.08)
1965	-.36723	-.02137	-.49114	.00228	-.14613	.28911
	(-38.66)	(-2.25)	(-51.70)	(.24)	(-15.38)	(30.43)
1970	-.38072	.12872	-.40823	.00164	-.17509	.07225
	(-48.44)	(16.38)	(-51.94)	(.21)	(-22.28)	(9.19)
1975	-.29635	.05099	-.26488	.00580	-.09635	.00809
	(-69.55)	(11.97)	(-62.16)	(1.36)	(-22.61)	(1.90)
1980	-.18621	.07863	-.18652	.00690	-.00672	-.07849
	(-52.12)	(22.01)	(-52.21)	(1.93)	(-1.88)	(-21.97)
1985	-.48907	.04196	-.22075	.00047	-.13614	-.17461
	(-85.21)	(7.31)	(-38.46)	(.08)	(-23.72)	(-30.42)
20.mot.veh.						
1960	-.22891	.13400	-.32318	.00058	-.18150	.14120
	(-29.33)	(17.17)	(-41.41)	(.07)	(-23.26)	(18.09)
1965	-.04332	.15557	-.31773	.00137	-.12313	.24061
	(-5.17)	(18.56)	(-37.90)	(.16)	(-14.69)	(28.70)
1970	-.20431	.27367	-.30826	.00112	-.17101	.00017
	(-27.09)	(36.29)	(-40.87)	(.15)	(-22.67)	(.02)
1975	-.12820	.19405	-.20927	.00297	-.07524	-.04070
	(-24.55)	(37.16)	(-40.07)	(.57)	(-14.41)	(-7.79)
1980	.03839	.27402	-.19178	.00388	.04347	-.09119
	(6.35)	(45.34)	(-31.73)	(.64)	(7.19)	(-15.09)
1985	-.05954	.13863	-.18185	-.00093	-.04075	.02536
	(-15.36)	(35.77)	(-46.93)	(-.24)	(-10.51)	(6.54)
21.trsp.equip.						
1960	.22487	.13367	-.77796	.00185	-.07388	.94119
	(11.66)	(6.93)	(-40.34)	(.10)	(-3.83)	(48.80)
1965	.12720	.02446	-.59456	.00264	-.08969	.78435
	(8.50)	(1.64)	(-39.75)	(.18)	(-6.00)	(52.44)
1970	-.09076	.00058	-.46236	.00179	-.14482	.51406
	(-8.08)	(.05)	(-41.15)	(.16)	(-12.89)	(45.75)
1975	.39485	.01223	-.24112	.00459	-.01753	.63667
	(43.29)	(1.34)	(-26.43)	(.50)	(-1.92)	(69.80)
1980	.34340	.07864	-.23744	.00566	.08439	.41216
	(41.97)	(9.61)	(-29.02)	(.69)	(10.31)	(50.37)
1985	.46101	.07975	-.22302	.00153	.02032	.58243
	(50.83)	(8.79)	(-24.59)	(.17)	(2.24)	(64.21)

TABLE 4 (Continued)

Industry/ Year	Output	Capital	Labour	Energy	Material	Technology
22.prec.inst.						
1960	-.30418	.17471	-.68905	.00144	-.13862	.34734
	(-22.51)	(12.93)	(-51.00)	(.11)	(-10.26)	(25.71)
1965	-.30178	.02586	-.60465	.00219	-.11930	.39412
	(-26.33)	(2.26)	(-52.76)	(.19)	(-10.41)	(34.39)
1970	-.32938	.06617	-.47416	.00170	-.14903	.22594
	(-35.92)	(7.22)	(-51.71)	(.19)	(-16.25)	(24.64)
1975	-.12277	-.04595	-.28644	.00551	-.04380	.24790
	(-19.50)	(-7.30)	(-45.50)	(.87)	(-6.96)	(39.37)
1980	-.09527	.03838	-.21089	.00674	.05527	.01525
	(-29.18)	(11.75)	(-64.59)	(2.06)	(16.93)	(4.67)
1985	-.27432	-.11233	-.27832	.00113	-.03384	.14904
	(-47.74)	(-19.55)	(-48.43)	(.20)	(-5.89)	(25.94)
23.misc.mfg.						
1960	-.60383	.07763	-.57661	.00233	-.14848	.04129
	(-71.35)	(9.17)	(-68.13)	(.28)	(-17.54)	(4.88)
1965	-.55015	.05828	-.46812.	.00311	-.14040	-.003026
	(-81.75)	(8.66)	(-69.56)	(.46)	(-20.86)	(-.45)
1970	-.34628	.10281	-.36426	.00313	-.17737	.08941
	(-46.99)	(13.95)	(-49.43)	(.42)	(-24.07)	(12.13)
1975	-.31164	.02685	-.21909	.00817	-.04952	-.07805
	(-81.65)	(7.03)	(-57.40)	(2.14)	(-12.97)	(-20.45)
1980	-.43282	.04472	-.15173	.00782	.05670	-.39033
	(-66.45)	(6.87)	(-23.30)	(1.20)	(8.71)	(-59.93)
1985	-.80122	-.01357	-.22366	.00238	-.06817	-.49820
	(-99.41)	(-1.68)	(-27.75)	(.30)	(-8.46)	(-61.81)
24.trsp.comm.						
1960	-.89231	.06412	-.86051	.02132	-.10766	-.00959
	(-83.93)	(6.03)	(-80.94)	(2.01)	(-10.13)	(-.90)
1965	-.76398	.09389	-.76429	.01815	-.08266	-.02906
	(-77.32)	(9.50)	(-77.35)	(1.84)	(-8.37)	(-2.94)
1970	-.71246	.09878	-.64839	.01394	-.09969	-.07710
	(-75.96)	(10.53)	(-69.13)	(1.49)	(-10.63)	(-8.22)
1975	-.38904	.10295	-.45512	.02824	.00239	-.06749
	(-59.29)	(15.69)	(-69.36)	(4.30)	(.36)	(-10.29)
1980	.27656	.20177	-.33248	.03639	.11643	.25445
	(29.37)	(21.43)	(-35.31)	(3.86)	(12.37)	(27.03)
1985	.04023	.16447	-.43153	.02692	.05601	.22437
	(4.45)	(18.21)	(-47.77)	(2.98)	(6.20)	(24.84)

TABLE 4 (Continued)

Industry/ Year	Output	Capital	Labour	Energy	Material	Technology
25.utilities						
1960	-.19888	-.11575	-.32493	.05492	-.07815	.26504
	(-23.71)	(-13.80)	(-38.74)	(6.55)	(-9.32)	(31.60)
1965	.00631	.10179	-.22802	.05022	-.05906	.14137
	(41.09)	(17.54)	(-39.28)	(8.65)	(-10.17)	(24.35)
1970	-.00861	.13307	-.21378	05487	-.05761	.07482
	(-1.61)	(24.91)	(-40.02)	(10.27)	(-10.78)	(14.01)
1975	.08847	-.06824	-.10016	.18925	-.02495	.09257
	(18.62)	(-14.36)	(-21.08)	(39.83)	(-5.25)	(19.48)
1980	.09767	-.00589	-.05194	.22258	.00610	-.07318
	(27.15)	(-1.64)	(-14.44)	(61.88)	(1.70)	(-20.34)
1985	-.39690	-.07393	-.07458	.06759	-.06846	-.24753
	(-74.59)	(-13.89)	(-14.02)	(12.70)	(-12.87)	(-46.52)
26.trade						
1960	-.59005	.00150	-.84409	.00624	-.10044	.34673
	(-45.42)	(.12)	(-64.98)	(.48)	(-7.73)	(26.69)
1965	-.38608	-.07028	-.68345	.00697	-.05725	.41793
	(-31.24)	(-5.69)	(-55.30)	(.56)	(-4.63)	(33.82)
1970	-.33111	.06281	-.57367	.00531	-.06551	.23995
	(-34.95)	(6.63)	(-60.56)	(.56)	(-6.92)	(25.33)
1975	.05198	.00137	-.26961	.01210	.04267	.26545
	(8.79)	(.23)	(-45.60)	(2.05)	(7.22)	(44.90)
1980	.18893	.06485	-.19881	.01455	.14255	.16579
	(32.21)	(11.06)	(-33.89)	(2.48)	(24.30)	(28.27)
1985	.00954	-.02156	-.22387	.00494	.07470	.17531
	(1.91)	(-4.31)	(-44.74)	(.99)	(14.93)	(35.04)
27.finance						
1960	-.05055	-.71096	-.44211	.00044	-.06462	1.16670
	(-2.12)	(-29.81)	(-18.54)	(.02)	(-2.71)	(48.92)
1965	.02150	-.62362	-.29725	.00093	-.02823	.96967
	(1.12)	(-32.49)	(-15.48)	(.05)	(-1.47)	(50.51)
1970	.03555	-.38229	-.31648	.00089	-.02813	.76156
	(2.39)	(-25.67)	(-21.25)	(.06)	(-1.89)	(51.13)
1975	.52486	-.18793	-.13614	.00235	.07460	.77197
	(44.75)	(-16.02)	(-11.61)	(.20)	(6.36)	(65.81)
1980	.71080	-.06225	-.03371	.00243	.13434	.66999
	(78.74)	(-6.90)	(-3.73)	(.27)	(14.88)	(74.22)
1985	.45360	-.09945	-.06343	-.00091	.08200	.53539
	(58.07)	(-12.73)	(-8.12)	(-.12)	(10.50)	(68.54)

TABLE 4 (Continued)

Industry/ Year	Output	Capital	Labour	Energy	Material	Technology
28.Services						
1960	-.28140	-.09383	-.50569	.00313	-.13957	.45457
	(-23.51)	(-7.84)	(-42.25)	(.26)	(-11.66)	(37.98)
1965	-.14795	-.05340	-.42857	.00439	-.09108	.42072
	(-14.82)	(-5.35)	(-42.94)	(.44)	(-9.12)	(42.15)
1970	-.15598	-.00381	-.43181	.00300	-.09566	.37229
	(-17.21)	(-.42)	(-47.63)	(.33)	(-10.55)	(41.07)
1975	.31375	-.01170	-.17691	.00921	.06111	.43203
	(45.41)	(-1.69)	(-25.60)	(1.33)	(8.84)	(62.53)
1980	.59421	-.01766	-.10636	.00978	.15425	.55420
	(70.55)	(-2.10)	(-12.63)	(1.16)	(18.31)	(65.80)
1985	.36368	-.06503	-.21163	.00130	.06484	.57420
	(39.66)	(-7.09)	(-23.08)	(.14)	(7.07)	(62.62)

5. Conclusions

As we mentioned earlier, the period 1960-1970 was characterised by a substantial economic growth in the USA and very rapid economic growth in Japan. Capital input was by far the most important source of growth in both countries, accounting for about forty percent of US economic growth and sixty percent of Japanese growth. The period 1973-1979 was dominated by the energy crisis, which began with drastic increases in petroleum prices in 1973. Growth in the USA slowed down significantly and declined dramatically in Japan during this period. The growth of capital input remained the most important source of economic growth in both countries, but productivity growth at the sectoral level essentially disappeared.

During the period 1960-1973 productivity growth in Japan exceeded that in the USA for almost all industries. After the energy crisis in 1973, there were very few significant differences between growth rates of productivity in Japanese and US industries. An important focus in our work has been the assessment of longer term trends in productivity growth by industry. In particular, we are interested in evaluating whether or not the slowdown in productivity growth in Japan and the USA after the energy crisis has become permanent.

To resolve the issue of the stagnation of growth since 1973 we can consider average productivity growth rates in Japanese and US industries over the period 1960-1985 (table 5). We conclude that productivity growth in Japan and the USA has been revived slightly since 1980. However, the growth rates for the period 1980-1985 are well below those for the period 1960-1973, especially in Japan.

M. Kuroda

TABLE 5
Annual Compound Growth Rates of Productivity in Japanese
and US Industries, 1960-85

	Japan	USA
1960-1965	4.214	2.701
1965-1970	3.718	0.005
1970-1973	4.918	2.033
1973-1975	4.867	-2.123
1975-1980	1.532	0.004
1980-1985	2.258	0.008

The second issue we have considered is the trend of industry-level productivity differences between the two countries. Almost every Japanese industry had a lower level of productivity compared to its US counterpart in 1960. By the end of 1970s, there were six industries in which productivity gaps between the two countries had closed. These industries were primarily concentrated in producers goods manufacturing and were represented export-oriented industries. In the remaining 23 industries productivity gaps between Japan and the USA still remained in 1985.

A third issue is whether productivity levels in Japan and the USA have tended to converge. While the mean of relative productivity levels between Japan and the USA has been stable since 1980, the variance has expanded rapidly. This implies that convergence of Japanese and US levels of productivity during the 1960s has given way to sharply divergent trends in relative productivity by industry during the 1970s and, especially, during the 1980s. The competitiveness of US industries has been declining since 1980, due to more rapid growth of input prices in the USA and the appreciation of the dollar relative to the yen. While the USA retains an overall advantage in relative productivity levels, there is a substantial number of industries where Japan has gained an advantage and seems likely to increase it. Perhaps equally important, the increase in the variance of relative productivity levels among industries has created opportunities for both countries to benefit from the great expansion in Japan-US trade that has already taken place. However, this increase is also an important source of "trade frictions".

TABLE A1
Industry Classification for International Comparisons

No.	Industry	Abbreviation
1.	Agriculture - forestry - fisheries	Agric.
2.	Mining	Mining
3.	Construction	Construct.
4.	Food and kindred products	Foods
5.	Textile mill products	Textiles
6.	Apparel and other fabricated textile	Apparels
7.	Lumber & wood products excp. furniture	Lumber
8.	Furniture and fixtures	Furniture
9.	Paper and allied products	Paper
10.	Printing, publishing & allied products	Printing
11.	Chemical and allied products	Chemical
12.	Petroleum refinery & coal products	Petroleum
13.	Rubber & allied products	Rubber
14.	Leather and leather products	Leather
15.	Stone, clay and glass products	Stone
16.	Primary metal products	Prim.Metal
17.	Fabricated metal products	Fab.Metal
18.	Machinery	Machinery
19.	Electric machinery	Elec.Mach.
20.	Motor vehicles and equipment	Mot.Veh.
21.	Transportation equipment excp. motor	Trsp.Eqpt.
22.	Precision instruments	Prec.Inst.
23.	Miscellaneous manufacturing	Mfg.Misc.
24.	Transportation and communication	Trsp.Comm.
25.	Electric utility and gas supply	Utilities
26.	Wholesale and retail trade	Trade
27.	Finance, insurance and real estate	Finance
28.	Other service	Service
29.	Government services	Gov.Service

References

Berndt, Ernst R., and Dale W. Jorgenson (1973), "Production Structure", in Dale W. Jorgenson and Hendrik S. Houthakker, eds., *US Energy Resources and Economic Growth*, Washington, Energy Policy Project.
--- and Melvyn Fuss (1986), "Editor's Introduction", *Journal of Econometrics*, Vol. 33, Nos. 1/2, October/November, pp. 1-5.
Christensen, Laurits R. and Dale W. Jorgenson (1973a), "Measuring the Performance of the Private Sector of the US Economy, 1929-1969," in Milton Moss, ed., *Measuring Economic and Social Performance*, New York, National Bureau of Economic Research, pp. 233-238.
--- and --- (1973b), "US Income, Saving, and Wealth, 1929-1969", *Review of Income and Wealth*, Series 19, No. 4, December, pp. 329-362.
---, --- and Lawrence J. Lau (1971), "Conjugate Duality and the Transcendental Logarithmic Production Function", *Econometrica*, Vol. 39, No. 4, July, pp. 255-256.
---, --- and --- (1973), "Transcendental Logarithmic Production Frontiers", *Review of Economics and Statistics*, Vol. 55, No. 1, February, pp. 28-45.
Conrad, Klaus (1985), *Produktivitätslucken nach Wirtschaftszweigen in internationalen Vergleich*, Berlin, Springer-Verlag.
--- and Dale W. Jorgenson (1975), *Measuring Performance in the Private Economy of the Federal Republic of Germany, 1950-1973*, Tübingen, J.C.B. Mohr.
--- and --- (1977), "Tests of a Model of Production for the Federal Republic of Germany, 1950-1973", *European Economic Review*, Vol. 10, No. 1, October, pp. 51-75.
--- and --- (1978), "The Structure of Technology: Nonjointness and Commodity Augmentation, Federal Republic of Germany, 1950-1973", *Empirical Economics*, Vol. 3, Issue 2, pp. 91-113.
--- and --- (1985), "Sectoral Productivity Gaps between the United States, Japan, and Germany, 1960-1979", in Herbert Giersch, ed., *Probleme und Perspektiven der weltwirtschaftlichen Entwicklung*, Berlin, Duncker and Humblot, pp. 335-347.
Denison, Edward F. (1957), "Theoretical Aspects of Quality Change, Capital Consumption, and Net Capital Formation", in Conference on Research in Income and Wealth, *Problems of Capital Formation*, Princeton, Princeton University Press, pp. 215-261.
--- (1961), "Measurement of Labour Input: Some Questions of Definition and the Adequacy of Data", in Conference on Research in Income and Wealth, *Output, Input, and Productivity Measurement*, Princeton, Princeton University Press, pp. 347-372.

--- (1962a),"How to Raise the High-Employment Growth Rate by One Percentage Point", *American Economic Review*, Vol. 52, No. 2, May, pp. 67-75.

--- (1962b), *Sources of Economic Growth in the United States and the Alternatives Before Us*, New York, Committee for Economic Development.

--- (1964a), "Capital Theory and the Rate of Return (A Review Article)", *American Economic Review*, Vol. 54, No. 5, September, pp. 721-725.

--- (1964b),"The Unimportance of the Embodied Question", *American Economic Review*, Vol. 54, No. 5, September, pp. 721-725.

--- (1966), "Discussion", *American Economic Review*, Vol. 66, No. 2, May, pp. 76-78.

--- (1967), *Why Growth Rates Differ*, Washington, The Brookings Institution.

--- (1969), "Some Major Issues in Productivity Analysis: An Examination of Estimates by Jorgenson and Griliches", *Survey of Current Business*, Vol. 49, No. 5, Part 2, May, pp. 1-27.

--- (1972), "Final Comments", *Survey of Current Business*, Vol. 52, No. 5, Part 2, May, pp. 95-110.

--- (1974), *Accounting for United States Economic Growth, 1929 to 1969*, Washington, The Brookings Institution.

Denny, Michael, and Melvyn Fuss (1977),"The Use of Approximation Analysis to Test for Separability and the Existence of Consistent Aggregates", *American Economic Review*, Vol. 67, No. 3, June, pp. 404-418.

--- and --- (1983),"A General Approach to Intertemporal and Interspatial Productivity Comparisons", *Journal of Econometrics*, Vol. 23, No. 3, December, pp. 315-330.

--- , --- and Leonard Waverman (1981a), "The Measurement and Interpretation of Total Factor Productivity in Regulated Industries, with an Application to Canadian Telecommunications", Thomas G. Cowing and Rodney E. Stevenson, eds., *Productivity Measurement in Regulated Industries*, New York, Academic Press, pp. 179-218.

---, --- and --- (1981b),"The Substitution Possibilities for Energy: Evidence from US and Canadian Manufacturing Industries", in Ernst R. Berndt and Barry C. Field, eds., *Modelling and Measuring Natural Resource Substitution*, Cambridge, M.I.T. Press, pp. 230-258.

Fisher, Irving (1922), *The Making of Index Numbers*, Boston, Houghton-Mifflin.

Gollop, Frank M., and Dale W. Jorgenson (1980),"US Productivity Growth by Industry, 1947-1973", in John W. Kendrick and Beatrice Vaccara, eds., *New Developments in Productivity Measurement*, Chicago, University of Chicago Press, pp. 17-136.

--- and --- (1983),"Sectoral Measures of Labour Cost for the United States, 1948-1978", in Jack E. Triplett, ed., *The Measurement of Labour Cost*, Chicago, University of Chicago Press, pp. 185-235, 503-520.

Griliches, Zvi (1961a), "Discussion", *American Economic Review*, Vol. 51, No. 2, May, pp. 127-130.

--- (1961b), "Hedonic Price Indexes for Automobiles: An Econometric Analysis of Quality Change", in *The Price Statistics of the Federal Government*, New York, National Bureau of Economic Research, pp. 137-196.

--- (1964), "Notes on the Measurement of Price and Quality Changes", in Conference on Research in Income and Wealth, *Models of Income Determination*, Princeton, Princeton University Press, pp. 301-404.

--- and Dale W. Jorgenson (1966),"Sources of Measured Productivity Change: Capital Input", *American Economic Review*, Vol. 56, No. 2, May, pp. 50-61.

Hulten, Charles R. (1973), "Divisia Index Numbers", *Econometrica*, Vol. 41, No. 6, November, pp. 1017-1026.

--- (1978), "Growth Accounting with Intermediate Inputs", *Review of Economic Studies*, Vol. 45 (3), No. 141, October, pp. 511-518.

--- and Frank C. Wykoff (1981a), "Economic Depreciation and the Taxation of Structures in United States Manufacturing Industries: An Empirical Analysis", in Dan Usher, ed., *The Measurement of Capital*, Chicago, University of Chicago Press, pp. 83-120.

--- (1981b), "The Estimation of Economic Depreciation Using Vintage Asset Prices: An Application of the Box-Cox Power Transformation", *Journal of Econometrics*, Vol. 15, No. 3, April, pp. 367-396.

--- (1981c), "The Measurement of Economic Depreciation", in Charles R.Hulten, ed., *Depreciation, Inflation, and the Taxation of Income from Capital*, Washington, The Urban Institute Press, pp. 81-125.

---, --- and James W. Robertson (1989),"Energy, Obsolescence, and the Productivity Slowdown", in Dale W. Jorgenson and Ralph Landau, eds., *Technology and Capital Formation*, Cambridge, MIT Press, pp. 225-258.

Jorgenson, Dale W. (1988a),"Productivity and Economic Growth in Japan and the USA", *American Economic Review*, Vol. 78, No. 2, May, pp. 217-222.

--- (1988b), "Productivity and Postwar US Economic Growth", *Journal of Economic Perspectives*, Vol. 2, No. 4, Fall, pp. 23-41.

--- (1989), "Capital as a Factor of Production", in Dale W. Jorgenson and Ralph Landau, eds., *Technology and Capital Formation*, Cambridge, MIT Press, pp. 1-36.

--- (1990), "Productivity and Economic Growth", in Ernst R. Berndt and Jack E. Triplett, eds., *Fifty Years of Economic Measurement*, NBER, The University of Chicago Press, pp. 19-118.

--- (1993), "Comments and Discussion" of Bart van Ark and Dirk Pilat, "Productivity Levels in Germany, Japan and the United States: Differences and Causes", in *Brookings Papers on Economic Activity, Microeconomics 2*, Brookings Institute, Washington D.C., pp. 49-56.

--- and Zvi Griliches (1967), "The Explanation of Productivity Change", *Review of Economic Studies*, Vol. 34 (3), No. 99, July, pp. 249-283.

--- and Mieko Nishimizu (1978), "US and Japanese Economic Growth, 1952-1974: An International Comparison", *Economic Journal*, Vol. 88, No. 352, December, pp. 707-726.

---, --- and Masahiro Kuroda (1987),"Japan-US Industry-Level Productivity Comparisons, 1960-1979", *Journal of the Japanese and International Economies*, Vol. 1, No. 1, March, pp. 1-30.

Kendrick, John W. (1983a), *Interindustry Differences in Productivity Growth*, Washington, American Enterprise Institute.

--- (1983b), "International Comparisons of Recent Productivity Trends", in Sam H. Schurr, Sidney Sonenblum and David O. Wood, eds., *Energy, Productivity and Economic Growth*, Cambridge, Oelgeschlager, Gunn and Hain, pp. 71-120.

--- (1984), "International Comparisons of Productivity Trends", in Japan Productivity Centre, *Measuring Productivity*, New York, UNIPUB, pp. 95-140.

Kravis, Irving B., Alan Heston and Robert Summers (1978), *International Comparisons of Real Product and Purchasing Power*, United Nations International Comparison Project Phase II, The Statistical Office of the United Nations and the World Bank, World Bank.

Kuroda, Masahiro, Kanji Yoshioka, and Dale W. Jorgenson (1984), "Relative Price Changes and Biases of Technical Change in Japan", *Economic Studies Quarterly*, Vol. 35, No. 2, August, pp. 116-138.

Kuznets, Simon (1961), *Capital in the American Economy*, Princeton, Princeton University Press.

--- (1971), *Economic Growth of Nations*, Cambridge, Harvard University Press.

Nishimizu, Mieko, and Charles R. Hulten (1978), "The Sources of Japanese Economic Growth: 1955-1971", *Review of Economics and Statistics*, Vol. 60, No. 3, August, pp. 351-361.

Ohkawa, Kazushi, and Henry Rosovsky (1973), *Japanese Economic Growth*, Stanford, Stanford University Press.

Tornquist, Leo (1936), "The Bank of Finland's Consumption Price Index", *Bank of Finland Monthly Bulletin*, No. 10, pp. 1-8.

International Productivity Differences
K. Wagner and B. van Ark (editors)

Anglo German Productivity Performance: 1960-1989

Mary O'Mahony* and Karin Wagner** with Marcel Paulssen
* National Institute of Economic and Social Research, London
** Wissenschaftszentrum für Sozialforschung, Berlin*

1. Introduction

Productivity performance in manufacturing is an important indicator of a country's well being. In gauging this performance economists traditionally considered the productivity record in each country in isolation and focused entirely on growth rates. More recently research has emphasised the need to relate each country's performance to that of other similar nations, in particular to take account of trends towards catch-up and convergence of productivity in industrial nations. Thus the focus has switched to considering relative productivity levels. This study looks at the relative performance of two industrial nations, the United Kingdom and Germany.[1] It builds on previous research which presented measures of relative manufacturing productivity levels in these two countries in the late 1980s (O'Mahony, 1992a) and attempted to explain these by differences in various forms of capital (O'Mahony, 1992b). This paper returns to the traditional focus on productivity growth rates by examining the productivity performance over the three decades 1960 to 1989 for a number of industries within manufacturing. However it utilises the results of the earlier work by relating productivity growth rates to levels.

This study is concerned with the variation in productivity performance across industries but it is useful first to examine the productivity trends in total manufacturing. This is illustrated in graph 1. In aggregate manufacturing the growth of labour productivity in Germany out performed that in Britain over the three decades 1960 to 1989. Up to 1973 annual productivity growth rates in

---

* Acknowledgement
This research was financed by a grant from the Anglo-German Foundation to whom we owe thanks. We are grateful to Jorn Mallok and Amanda Davies for research assistance. Earlier versions were presented at conferences in Berlin, November 1993, and at NIESR in February 1994. We are grateful to participants at these conferences, in particular, Jacques Mairesse for helpful comments. Also we would like to acknowledge comments from our colleagues at NIESR and WZB and from Steve Broadberry, Bart van Ark and Peter Hart.
[1] This paper is concerned only with the productivity record of the Federal Republic of Germany as it existed prior to unification.

German manufacturing were on average about one percentage point higher than in Britain. This was followed by a surge in the German advantage from 1973 to 1979 but much of this deficit was made up by Britain in the following decade. The graphs for the individual countries show clearly that in Germany there was a serious decline in productivity in the early 1980s whereas in Britain the 1970s was the period of slowest growth and this was followed by a revival of productivity growth in the eighties.

These trends in aggregate manufacturing, however, mask considerable differences in the relative fortunes of individual industries. In fact dividing manufacturing into thirty sub-branches we find that in about half of the industries productivity growth was higher in Britain over the three decades 1960 to 1989 and this is true also for the sub-periods 1960 to 1973 and 1973 to 1989. In this paper we will be concerned to see if the time trends we observe for total manufacturing also hold for the majority of industries.

The paper begins with an examination of the cross industry pattern of productivity growth in the two countries. By relating productivity growth to productivity levels we consider the question of whether there has been any trend towards convergence of productivity levels in the two countries over time. We then ask if productivity growth is correlated with the growth of output or labour input and examine the relationship with average plant size.

Recent contributions to the theory of economic growth, for example Lucas (1988), Romer (1990b) emphasise the importance of the accumulation of various forms of capital in explaining cross country patterns of productivity growth. Section three presents data on the relative amounts of three forms of capital accumulation in the two countries ie. fixed capital (equipment and structures), labour force skills and research and development expenditure and considers the relationship between capital accumulation and productivity growth. A further analysis which uses growth accounting methods is available in O'Mahony, Wagner and Paulssen (1994).

2. Productivity Growth, Productivity Levels and Convergence

Labour Productivity Growth: the Cross Industry Pattern.

This section examines the labour productivity record of manufacturing industries in Germany and Britain over the period 1960 to 1989. It first considers the cross industry pattern of labour productivity growth and then looks at the link between growth rates and relative productivity levels in the two countries. Growth rates of gross value added per worker hour are shown in table 1 for selected time periods and table 2 shows summary statistics. The growth rates are shown for thirty industries within manufacturing; this division was dictated by the availability of continuous time series for output and employment for these industries in Germany. For purposes of comparability real gross value added in both countries is measured using single deflation. A discussion of single versus double deflation together with data sources and methods is given in Appendix A. Details of the industrial classification are available in O'Mahony, Wagner and Paulssen (1994).

TABLE 1a
Growth Rates of Labour Productivity: Germany
(% per annum)

	1960-89	1960-73	1973-89	1973-79	1979-89
Chemicals	5.65	8.94	2.97	3.00	2.96
Mineral Oil Refining	5.51	9.55	2.22	4.35	0.94
Plastic Products	4.96	8.27	2.27	2.32	2.24
Rubber Products	3.39	5.80	1.43	1.26	1.54
Mineral Products	4.24	6.41	2.48	3.11	2.11
Ceramic Goods	3.02	4.91	1.49	1.85	1.27
Glass	4.50	5.48	3.70	4.85	3.02
Iron & Steel	4.44	5.68	3.43	3.76	3.24
Non Ferrous Metals	3.50	4.01	3.09	4.90	2.00
Plant & Steelwork	3.72	6.08	1.81	2.68	1.28
Mechanical Engineering	2.92	4.11	1.96	2.69	1.52
Office Machinery	8.02	9.59	6.74	11.25	4.04
Motor Vehicles	3.46	4.66	2.49	4.42	1.33
Shipbuilding	3.97	6.60	1.83	0.76	2.46
Aerospace	3.98	6.59	1.87	1.75	1.94
Electrical Engineering	5.53	6.65	4.63	6.29	3.63
Instrument Engineering	3.73	5.81	2.05	2.56	1.74
Finished Metal Products	3.81	5.49	2.45	2.70	2.29
Toys, Musical & Sports Goods	3.17	3.61	2.81	3.43	2.43
Timber & Board	4.69	7.33	2.55	1.78	3.02
Wood Products	3.81	7.70	0.65	1.34	0.23
Paper & Pulp	5.32	7.06	3.90	5.96	2.67
Paper Products	2.79	4.23	1.63	1.92	1.45
Printing & Publishing	3.22	4.61	2.10	3.27	1.39
Leather & Footwear	2.50	2.10	2.82	2.26	3.16
Textiles	4.55	4.86	4.30	6.29	3.10
Clothing	3.55	3.96	3.21	3.59	2.99
Food	3.59	4.38	2.94	3.12	2.83
Drink	5.47	7.86	3.54	2.51	4.15
Tobacco	6.36	7.24	5.65	7.90	4.30
Total Manufacturing	4.23	6.10	2.71	3.37	2.30

Sources: see Appendix A.

The first striking feature of tables 1 and 2 is the similarity of the cross industry pattern of labour productivity growth in the two countries over the entire period 1960 to 1989. Thus in both countries higher than average labour productivity growth rates were recorded in office machinery, chemicals, mineral oil refining and plastic products and lower than average growth rates were recorded

TABLE 1b
Growth Rates of Labour Productivity: United Kingdom
(% per annum)

	1960-89	1960-73	1973-89	1973-79	1979-89
Chemicals	5.08	7.61	3.02	-0.52	5.15
Mineral Oil Refining	5.04	10.03	0.97	-1.12	2.23
Plastic Products	5.65	9.28	2.69	1.07	3.66
Rubber Products	4.08	5.92	2.59	-0.74	4.58
Mineral Products	3.11	4.48	2.00	-0.81	3.69
Ceramic Goods	2.67	3.74	1.79	1.96	1.69
Glass	4.12	5.89	2.68	0.52	3.97
Iron & Steel	4.55	3.31	5.55	-8.69	14.10
Non Ferrous Metals	2.49	4.34	0.99	-1.74	2.62
Plant & Steelwork	3.89	6.53	1.74	2.50	1.29
Mechanical Engineering	2.97	4.09	2.07	0.70	2.89
Office Machinery	8.09	8.59	7.69	10.15	6.21
Motor Vehicles	3.71	3.80	3.63	0.68	5.41
Shipbuilding	4.44	5.22	3.81	0.86	5.57
Aerospace	4.62	5.99	3.51	-5.31	8.81
Electrical Engineering	3.99	4.40	3.65	2.97	4.06
Instrument Engineering	5.28	7.49	3.48	3.40	3.53
Finished Metal Products	2.57	2.54	2.59	2.43	2.68
Toys, Musical & Sports Goods	3.56	5.43	2.04	1.21	2.54
Timber & Board	3.25	4.87	1.94	-0.74	3.55
Wood Products	2.70	3.98	1.66	1.15	1.96
Paper & Pulp	3.60	3.84	3.40	-0.28	5.62
Paper Products	3.05	5.00	1.47	0.98	1.76
Printing & Publishing	3.20	3.89	2.64	0.31	4.04
Leather & Footwear	3.32	4.81	2.10	3.84	1.06
Textiles	4.37	5.46	3.48	2.49	4.07
Clothing	4.23	4.94	3.66	4.88	2.93
Food	3.55	5.13	2.28	-0.37	3.87
Drink	3.37	5.73	1.44	2.52	0.80
Tobacco	3.55	3.62	3.49	-0.26	5.74
Total Manufacturing	3.83	5.03	2.86	0.72	4.15

Sources: see Appendix A.

TABLE 2
Summary Statistics of Labour Productivity Growth

	1960-89	1960-73	1973-89	1973-79	1979-89
Germany					
mean	4.25	5.99	2.83	3.60	2.38
std	1.18	1.80	1.26	2.18	0.99
max	8.02	9.59	6.74	11.25	4.30
min	2.50	2.10	0.65	0.76	0.23
United Kingdom					
mean	3.94	5.33	2.80	0.80	4.00
std	1.12	1.75	1.34	3.10	2.55
max	8.09	10.03	7.69	10.15	14.10
min	2.49	2.54	0.97	-8.69	0.80
corr[a]	0.65	0.56	0.62	0.36	0.27
N (> mean)[b]	8	7	8	3	3
N (< mean)[c]	13	11	14	8	11
N (G > U)[d]	16	17	15	24	3

[a] correlation between labour productivity growth in Germany and the UK;
[b] number of industries with below average productivity growth in both countries;
[c] number of industries with above average productivity growth in both countries;
[d] number of industries where productivity growth in Germany was greater than in the UK.

in ceramic goods, mechanical engineering and paper products. The cross section correlation between productivity growth in Germany and Britain was high at 0.65 and the majority of industries showed simultaneously either above or below average productivity growth rates in both countries. In the long run countries at similar stages of industrial development are likely to imitate each others technological changes so that the high correlation of productivity growth rates in the two countries is not unexpected. Examination of the two sub-periods 1960-73 and 1973-89 also shows high correlations in the cross industry pattern of productivity growth.

In both countries productivity growth rates were generally higher in the earlier period - 29 industries in Germany experienced higher average annual growth rates from 1960 to 1973 than in the later period and the corresponding figure for the UK was 28 industries. Also the ratio of the standard deviation to the mean, was much higher in the period 1973 to 1989 indicating a greater variability in the fortunes of industries from 1973 onwards.

We might ask if the industries which experienced high productivity growth in the period 1960-73 were also those with high productivity growth in the later years 1973-89. In the case of Germany the correlation between productivity growth in the two periods was positive but insignificant at 0.24, in the UK the correlation was even smaller at 0.08. Thus industries whose productivity growth record was favourable in the earlier period were not in general those which performed well in the later period, ie. there was no evidence of serial correlation in productivity growth over long time periods.

From 1960 to 1989 aggregate manufacturing labour productivity growth in Germany was a little less than half a percentage point higher per annum than in Britain. This was due to a much greater growth rate in Germany in the period 1960 to 1973 which outweighed the slightly superior British performance in the period 1973 to 1989. Comparing the growth rates in the two countries by industry, however, shows that in all three time periods nearly half the industries showed superior German growth performance whereas the remaining industries experienced greater productivity growth in the UK. Therefore, if we just look at the number of industries neither country had a significant advantage.

If we look more closely at the relative productivity performance in the two countries we see that the manufacturing industries where Germany achieved higher productivity growth than in the UK in the years 1960-73 were not in general those industries for which Germany had a superior productivity growth record in the later period 1973-89. Thus only six industries showed a superior German performance in both periods - these were mineral products, electrical engineering, timber, paper and board, drink and tobacco. The cross section correlation between relative (German minus UK) productivity growth in the two time periods was negative and insignificant at -0.01.

Large differences in the productivity record in the two countries only emerge when the later period is further sub-divided into the years 1973-79 and 1979-89. In general productivity growth in British manufacturing was historically low in the period 1973-79 which is notorious as a time when British industry experienced severe difficulties - 11 of the 30 industries experienced negative productivity growth. Only office machinery showed higher annual average productivity growth in the years 1973-79 over that achieved in 1960-73. German annual productivity growth rates in 1973-79 showed some slowdown from those achieved over the period 1960-73 but by a considerably lesser extent than was the case for the UK. In Germany productivity growth rates remained positive in all industries and four industries achieved higher productivity growth than in 1960 to 1973.

In the decade from 1979 to 1989 British manufacturing industry showed a remarkable turn around in terms of labour productivity performance. Only five of the thirty industries had lower productivity than for 1973-79 and eight industries showed growth rates which were higher than the 'golden age' 1960-73. The increase was most marked in iron and steel which showed a pronounced reduction in its labour force of 63 per cent between 1979 and 1989. The important motor vehicles sector also showed a pronounced improvement where there was also evidence of a reduction in overmanning, of a little under half the

1979 workforce. This may also be due in part to Japanese transplants which implemented new methods of production such as total quality control and job flexibility.

The experience in Germany during this period was very different. In general annual productivity growth rates slowed considerably from those experienced in 1960-73 - none of the thirty industries had higher productivity growth than in 1960-73 - and were lower even than in 1973-79, whence only six industries showed higher productivity growth than in the period 1973 to 1979. Productivity growth was very low in this decade in traditional areas of German strength such as mechanical engineering and vehicles. The problems encountered by these industries are currently the subject of much press coverage in Germany.

The above discussion relates to productivity growth over a number of years. But in the course of this work we collected annual data on labour productivity growth rates from 1961 to 1989. These data can be used to test if they suggest structural breaks in trend productivity after 1973 or 1979. We regressed labour productivity growth in aggregate manufacturing and in each industry on two dummy variables, the first taking the value one for the years 1974 to 1979 and the second taking the value one in the years 1980 to 1989. In Germany the post 1979 dummy is negative and significant for total manufacturing. This coefficient is negative for all industries but only significant in twelve. The dummy for 1974-79 is negative and significant for only four industries. In the UK the dummy for 1974-79 is negative and significant in total manufacturing but is significant for only six individual industries although this coefficient is again invariably negative. Only one industry showed a significant structural break in the UK in the period after 1979. These results suggest that the reduced productivity growth rates in the UK in the period 1973-79 and Germany after 1979 apparent in table 1 were, in the majority of industries, more the result of particularly poor performance in a few years rather than evidence of structural breaks over the long period.

Productivity Levels and Convergence

The correlation between relative (German minus UK) productivity growth in the two periods 1973 to 1979 and 1979 to 1989 was significantly negative at -0.68 so that, on average, industries where the British performance was relatively poor in the earlier period made up the deficit in the later period. From 1973 to 1979 twenty four industries in Germany had higher productivity growth than in Britain but in the following decade only three German industries performed better.

The low or negative correlation between relative labour productivity growth in adjacent time periods may reflect, among other things, a catch-up process whereby industries with a pronounced productivity level disadvantage in 1960 experienced faster relative productivity growth in subsequent decades as firms imitated technological improvements in the leading country. There is a considerable literature on the process of catch-up and convergence among industrial economies which concludes that, for the aggregate economy, these countries levels of labour productivity have converged in the post war period (see Baumol, 1986; Maddison, 1991). The evidence for convergence in manufacturing, however, is not as strong although there appears to be some local convergence among European countries (see Broadberry, 1993). Convergence at the aggregate (or sectoral) level is predicted by the neoclassical theory of economic growth which assumes constant returns in the production function. Recent contributions to growth theory (for example, Lucas, 1988; Romer, 1986, 1990a) emphasise external benefits of capital accumulation which give rise to increasing returns at the aggregate level. In these models it is possible for one country to achieve a permanent productivity level advantage.

At the industry level the scope for increasing returns from learning by doing may be more pronounced than at the sectoral or aggregate economy level due to country's abilities to exploit their comparative advantage in certain product areas. Thus, one country achieving an initial productivity advantage in an industry, say because of a new technological process which is protected by patent, could lead in the short run, to diverging productivity levels if the industry grew rapidly in that country and there were significant productivity gains from learning by doing. There could even be a permanent effect if the industry in the laggard country was wiped out by competition. An example is the manufacturing of sewing machines in Britain where the last manufacturer closed its doors in 1979.

It is interesting, therefore, to see if the observed sectoral or aggregate convergence of productivity levels across countries is replicated at the industry level. This requires estimates of relative levels of output per worker hour. O'Mahony (1992a) presents relative productivity levels for fourteen branch industries within manufacturing for 1987. In that study estimates of industries' relative producer prices were used to convert output to a common currency. This was deemed to give a more accurate picture of relative productivity levels than those using the official exchange rate since the latter is influenced by short-term capital movements and so, at any one point in time, is a poor indicator of differences in relative producer prices. The estimates of relative prices were based either on unit values of products (values divided by quantities) or on purchasing power parities collected by the OECD. These price estimates were constructed for a large number of products and so enabled the calculation of relative productivity for the more detailed thirty industries considered in this paper (see van Ark (1993) for a discussion of methodological issues in constructing price estimates).

The productivity levels for 1987 were based on data from each countries' censuses of production rather than the national accounts data, used to construct productivity growth rates. The censuses report output and employment from the same firms whereas it is not clear if output and employment levels in the national accounts are consistent with each other, in particular in Britain where these data are collected by two different statistical offices. The time series data on productivity growth in table 1 were used to yield estimates of relative productivity levels back to 1960 and forward to 1989.

Table 3 shows the productivity level estimates for selected years. In 1960 German aggregate manufacturing had a slight productivity level advantage which increased steadily up to 1973 and showed a dramatic increase between 1973 and 1979. The reversal of the productivity trends in the following decade led to a productivity gap in 1989 which was lower than in the early seventies. In 1960, seventeen of the thirty industries showed levels of labour productivity in Germany greater than in Britain, by 1973 this had risen to 20 and to 27 in 1979 but fell back to 23 by 1989.

In half of the industries, Germany had a productivity level advantage throughout the entire three decades. These were mostly in the engineering sector but also included plastics, rubber, paper products, printing and publishing, toys, sports equipment and musical instruments and clothing. The UK had a productivity levels advantage in each period in only two industries, drink and tobacco, but performed relatively well also in chemicals, mineral products, office machinery, electrical engineering, leather and footwear and textiles.

The estimates in table 3 show clearly the contrasting patterns of relative productivity between the period from 1973 to 1979 and the following decade. In the earlier period Britain's relative position showed a marked deterioration even in traditional areas of British strength such as food, textiles and chemicals. In the decade 1979 to 1989 in some industries, most notably iron and steel, aerospace and motor vehicles the British turnaround was remarkable, but Britain improved her relative position in almost all sectors. The only significant deterioration was in leather and footwear and drink and there was a small increase in Germany's advantage in clothing.

The productivity level estimates in table 3 were based on calculations for 1987. However we also have access to a previous study (Smith, Hitchens and Davies, 1982) which compared productivity levels in the two countries in 1968. Comparison of our estimates with that study presents serious difficulties for the following reasons. First the SHD study presented results using only UK quantity weights on relative prices whereas this study uses a geometric average of both countries weights. Secondly the definition of output is not comparable in the two studies with SHD using net output and this study using gross value added. Also the German census overestimates net output by including part of industrial services, ie. payments for repair and maintenance but the UK 1968 census underestimated net output by excluding payments for transport which are part of non-industrial services. Thirdly the UK census in 1968 covered all firms whereas the German census excluded firms employing less than 10 workers. Finally, the 1987 study uses the UK 1980 Standard Industrial Classification which is very different from the 1968 SIC used in SHD.

A crude adjustment was made to the SHD estimates to take account of the first

TABLE 3
Relative Labour Productivity levels, Germany/UK
(UK=100)

	1960	1973	1979	1989
Chemicals	86.9	103.3	127.6	102.5
Mineral Oil Refining	93.9	88.2	122.5	107.7
Plastic Products	133.7	117.3	126.4	109.7
Rubber Products	126.4	124.5	140.3	103.5
Mineral Products	65.5	84.1	106.4	90.9
Ceramic Goods	112.9	131.5	130.6	125.2
Glass	105.4	99.9	129.5	117.7
Iron & Steel	91.7	124.8	263.4	88.9
Non Ferrous Metals	84.1	80.5	119.9	112.7
Plant & Steelwork	131.1	123.7	125.0	124.9
Mechanical Engineering	125.5	125.9	141.9	123.7
Office Machinery	88.5	100.7	107.6	86.6
Motor Vehicles	132.9	148.5	186.0	123.7
Shipbuilding	120.9	144.6	143.7	105.3
Aerospace	121.5	131.2	200.4	100.9
Electrical Engineering	62.3	83.5	101.9	97.6
Instrument Engineering	224.6	180.5	171.6	143.6
Finished Metal Products	88.6	130.0	132.1	127.1
Toys, Musical & Sports Goods	146.2	115.4	131.8	130.4
Timber & Board	69.2	95.3	110.9	105.1
Wood Products	108.7	176.4	178.4	150.1
Paper & Pulp	97.4	147.9	215.1	160.2
Paper Products	182.3	164.9	174.4	169.1
Printing & Publishing	144.5	158.5	189.3	145.3
Leather & Footwear	132.8	93.3	84.9	104.8
Textiles	95.5	88.3	110.8	100.6
Clothing	151.5	133.5	123.5	124.2
Food	111.8	101.5	125.3	112.9
Drink	45.0	59.3	59.3	83.0
Tobacco	26.3	42.1	68.7	59.5
Total Manufacturing	104.0	119.4	140.0	116.5

Sources: see Appendix A.

three differences but accounting for the reclassification change would have involved detailed calculations which are beyond the scope of this paper. Where the reclassification problems were major we aggregated two industries - this was carried out for textiles and clothing and office machinery and instrument engineering. Also the SHD did not distinguish paper and pulp from paper products. Thus we had twenty seven industries where we could compare our estimates of relative levels of output per worker with those produced by SHD for 1968.

With adjustments the correspondence between the two studies was found to be reasonable for the majority of industries. Thus relative productivity levels in sixteen of the twenty six industries were found to be within ten percentage points in the two studies. In chemicals, food and mechanical engineering the two studies gave virtually identical results but the estimates were also very close for vehicles and electrical engineering. The two estimates of productivity levels were very far apart in a number of industries notably iron and steel and non-ferrous metals, both of which were significantly affected by the 1980 reclassification, and drink and tobacco, which may have been affected by differences in the treatment of excise taxes in the two studies. There were also large differences in non-metallic mineral products, timber and board and printing and publishing. In the case of the first two the number and type of products matched was greater in the 1987 study. In Germany publishing is classified to non-manufacturing so that productivity level estimates for that industry are particularly uncertain.

Given the estimates of productivity growth rates and levels in tables 1 and 3, we are now in a position to consider the question of whether there has been convergence of productivity levels over time. We first look at the relationship between productivity growth and initial levels of productivity by regressing the former on the latter - the results are given in table 4. The first column shows that relative productivity growth over the entire period 1960 to 1989 is significantly negatively related to relative productivity levels in 1960. Thus those industries which showed a high Germany productivity level advantage in 1960 experienced lower rates of productivity growth in the following three decades enabling some catch up of British productivity levels to those in Germany. The

TABLE 4
Regression Results: Convergence

	Relative	Productivity (Germany/UK)	Levels
	1960	1973	1979
1960-1989	-0.021 (14.50)	-	-
1960-1973	-0.027 (8.12)	-	-
1973-1989	-	-0.028 (7.57)	-
1973-1979	-	-0.030 (1.85)	-
1979-1989	-	-	-0.059 (3.60)

Notes: Dependent variable is the growth of labour productivity in Germany relative to the growth in labour productivity in the UK. Independent variable for each year is the log of the ratio of German to UK productivity, absolute values of t-ratios in parentheses, standard errors are heteroscedastic consistent estimates.

TABLE 5
Summary Statistics of Relative Productivity Levels

	1960	1973	1979	1989
Mean	110.3	116.6	138.3	114.6
Standard Deviation	39.0	32.4	42.7	23.3
Coefficient of Variation	0.35	0.28	0.31	0.20

coefficients are all negative, implying trends towards convergence in all time periods, but the coefficient for the period 1973 to 1979 is not significant at the 95 per cent level.

An alternative way of looking at convergence is to ask if the variation across industries in relative productivity has decreased over time. Barro and Sala-i-Martin (1991) suggest a distinction between b-convergence (a negative correlation between productivity growth rates and productivity levels) and σ-convergence (a reduction over time in the coefficient of variation of relative productivity levels) and argue that neither one type of convergence necessarily implies the other. Thus in an analysis of industry data we may see on average b-convergence but in a small number of industries we could also observe either country having a sustained increasing productivity advantage so that the variation across industries increases over time. Table 5 shows that in general the coefficient of variation has decreased over time so that this measure also shows that productivity levels have become closer in the two countries over time. Again the subperiod 1973 to 1979 was exceptional when there was a (temporary) divergence of productivity levels in the two countries.

The Growth of Output and Labour Input

We next examine briefly the growth of output and labour input. Table 6 shows summary statistics of growth in output, employment and annual hours worked in both countries; detailed tables for selected years are shown in Appendix tables B.1 to B.3. In Germany mean output growth was positive for each of the time periods but was considerably more variable after 1973 as shown both by the higher ratio of the standard deviation to the mean and the much larger number of industries with negative output growth. Mean output growth in British manufacturing was lower in all periods than in Germany and was negative for the period 1973 to 1989.

This was due to strong negative output growth over the period 1973 to 1979 - mean output growth became positive again in the period 1979 to 1989. In general more industries experienced negative output growth in the UK than in Germany. In 1979 twenty three industries in Britain had lower output levels than in 1973 whereas the comparable figure for Germany was fifteen. In eighteen industries in the UK and thirteen in Germany output in 1989 was lower than in 1973.

In both countries mean labour input was reduced in all time periods. The rate of reduction was greatest in the UK over the entire period 1960 to 1989 but was higher in Germany up to 1973. This was due primarily to a greater reduction in the number of hours per worker per year in Germany rather than a larger reduction in employment. The number of workers in German manufacturing was reduced by 800,000 or 9 per cent from 1960 to 1989 whereas in the same period average annual hours worked declined by 23 per cent. In 1960 annual average hours per worker were in fact about 3 per cent higher in Germany than in Britain but by 1989 the ranking was reversed so that average hours per worker were about 7 per cent higher in Britain. This may be attributed to a strong union movement in Germany to reduce weekly working time rather than working places. An example of this is the shortening of the working week in Volkswagen plants to a four day week in 1993. It may also reflect the greater importance of overtime in Britain since the scope for workers to do overtime in Germany is restricted. Labour input was reduced at a considerably greater rate in the UK post 1979, due to a very large reduction in employment. Manufacturing employment in Britain declined by nearly three million from 7.7 million workers in 1960 to 4.9 million in 1989 with two million lost in the decade 1979 to 1989.

There has also been some change in the industrial structure in the two countries in the past three decades as can be seen from table B.3. In 1960 the share of total employment of the combined engineering sector[2] was somewhat smaller in Germany, 38 per cent as against 42 per cent in the UK. By 1989 this sectors share had risen to 51 per cent in Germany but remained at 42 per cent in Britain. The engineering industries saw an increase of employment of about 800,000 or 22 per cent in Germany whereas employment was reduced by 1.1 million or 35 per cent in Britain. In both countries the share of chemicals increased but again this represented an increase in absolute numbers in Germany and a reduction in the UK. Some German industries experienced a significant reduction in employment share from 1960 to 1989 - this occurred to a considerable extent in mineral products, shipbuilding and iron and steel but in the latter the reduction in total numbers was about half as great in Germany as in Britain. In both countries the share of leather and footwear, textiles and clothing was considerably reduced, reflecting the increasing importance of competition from newly developing countries, but the decline was much greater in Germany.

Salter (1966) found a positive significant correlation between labour productivity growth and output growth for a cross section of British industries for the period 1924 to 1950. Oulton and O'Mahony (1994) found a similar cor-

---

[2] Industrial plant & steelwork, mechanical, electrical and instrument engineering, transport equipment and finished metal products.

M. O'Mahony and K. Wagner

TABLE 6
Growth of Output and Labour Input
(% per annum)

	1960-1989	1960-1973	1973-1989	1973-1979	1979-1989
Germany					
Output					
Mean	2.56	4.95	0.61	0.30	0.80
Standard deviation	2.47	3.50	2.05	2.49	2.03
N < 0	2.00	1.00	12.00	14.00	11.00
Hours					
Mean	-1.69	-1.04	-2.22	-3.29	-1.58
Standard deviation	2.13	2.61	1.92	2.30	2.08
N < 0	26.00	20.00	28.00	27.00	26.00
Correlation					
(dPG,dQG)	0.53	0.71	0.41	0.39	0.07
Correlation					
(dPG,dLG)	0.06	0.27	-0.20	-0.37	-0.25
United Kingdom					
Output					
Mean	1.77	4.50	-0.45	-1.86	0.39
Standard deviation	2.01	2.41	2.19	3.37	3.01
N < 0	6.00	0.00	18.00	23.00	15.00
Hours					
Mean	-2.17	-0.84	-3.25	-2.65	-3.61
Standard deviation	1.45	1.35	1.87	1.56	2.67
N < 0	29.00	23.00	29.00	29.00	28.00
Correlation					
(dPU,dQU)	0.71	0.83	0.52	0.89	0.55
Correlation					
(dPU,dLU)	0.20	0.17	-0.12	-0.11	-0.35
Correlation					
(dQG,dQU)	0.75	0.72	0.67	0.01	0.71
Correlation					
(dLG,dLU)	0.62	0.43	0.58	0.48	0.54

Notes: dPG,dPU = labour productivity growth, dQG,dQU = output growth, dLG, dLU = annual hours growth, N < 0 = number of industries with negative growth rates.

relation for a cross section of British industries both for the period 1954-86 and the subperiods 1954-73 and 1973-86. Table 6 shows that these results are replicated for both countries in all time periods although the correlation between output growth and labour productivity growth is very low in Germany in the period 1979 to 1989. Productivity growth in general is not significantly related to labour input growth over long time periods which was also the result found by Salter and Oulton and O'Mahony. However there is a significant negative correlation in Germany for the period 1973 to 1979 and in the UK for the period 1979 to 1989. We get a similar result in both cases when we correlate labour productivity growth with the change in employment so that these results are consistent with reductions in overmanning.

The last two rows of table 6 show that the cross section pattern of output growth, and to a lesser extent the reduction in labour input is similar in the two countries. Thus, on average, industries with high growth in output tend to have high labour productivity growth and these are likely to be the same industries in both countries. The exception was the period 1973 to 1979 where the correlation in output growth across the two countries was not significantly different from zero.

TABLE 7
Median Plant Size, 1987

	Germany	UK
Chemicals	1,666	503
Mineral Oil Refining	533	1,335
Plastic Products	162	131
Rubber Products	1,701	430
Mineral Products	61	106
Ceramic Goods	158	390
Glass	440	377
Iron & Steel	2,116	715
Non Ferrous Metals	543	208
Plant & Steelwork	326	225
Mechanical Engineering	373	159
Office Machinery	1,705	536
Motor Vehicles	2,446	1,432
Shipbuilding	1,221	1,961
Aerospace	2,397	2,337
Electrical Engineering	707	502
Instrument Engineering	60	184
Finished Metal Products	180	113
Toys, Musical & Sports Goods	60	48
Timber & Board	40	50
Wood Products	36	69
Paper & Pulp	596	367
Paper Products	177	176
Printing & Publishing	69	115
Leather & Footwear	109	157
Textiles	232	178
Clothing	63	122
Food	20	345
Drink	124	309
Tobacco	659	1,506
Total Manufacturing	358	261

Sources: see Appendix A.

Finally in this section we consider the influence of differences in the average size of plants in industries in the two countries. Table 7 shows the median plant size in 1987 for the thirty industries. The median plant size is measured as the plant size for which 50 per cent of the workforce are employed in plants with more than that number of employees. It is preferable to the mean plant size since it is less sensitive to the lower tail of the employment distribution.

The median plant size was larger in Germany in aggregate manufacturing but it was not true that Germany operated at a larger scale in all industries. In fact in thirteen industries the median plant size was larger in the UK. The cross section correlation of median plant size was 0.68 indicating a similar distribution of plant scale across industries in the two countries.

Davies and Caves (1987) show that the median plant size can be interpreted as a measure of economies of scale. With this interpretation we should generally observe a positive correlation between labour productivity growth and median plant size. But in some circumstances there may be significant diseconomies, e.g. Prais (1981) suggested that poor industrial relations in large plants gave rise to a negative correlation between median plant size and labour productivity in the UK. Table 8 shows that these correlations are positive for all time periods in Germany and mostly positive for the UK. The one exception is the period 1973-79 in Britain when the correlation is significantly negative. The correlation is positive and highly significant in the UK in the following decade. Thus the results in table 8 confirm Prais's result for the seventies but show that this adverse effect of plant size on productivity was not a constraint in the eighties.

TABLE 8
Correlation Between Labour Productivity Growth
and Median Plant Size

	1960-1989	1960-1973	1973-1989	1973-1979	1979-1989
Germany	0.26	0.25	0.15	0.18	0.08
United Kingdom	0.26	0.10	0.28	-0.35	0.49

The use of median plant size as a measure of scale economies may be misleading in practice since the optimal plant size varies across industries. For example in electrical engineering a plant employing 300 workers is small but this would be considered large in the clothing industry. Given this it may make more sense to correlate productivity growth in each country with the relative median plant size across the two countries. We find that the only significant relationship is for the UK in the period 1979 to 1989 and this correlation coefficient is negative. Thus in the 1980s British manufacturing growth rates were higher in industries where they had a size disadvantage with Germany. At first sight this result seems counter intuitive. But there was a considerable reduction in median plant size in Britain in the 1980s as compared to the 1970s which could be interpreted as an increase in competition (see the discussion in O'Mahony, 1992a). Lansbury and Mayes (1994), however, do not find a strong relationship between firm turnover and productivity growth.

3. Explanatory Factors: Fixed Capital, Human Capital and R&D

This section examines the contribution of investment in various forms of capital to explaining labour productivity growth in the two countries. We will examine in turn the influence of fixed capital (plant and machinery, vehicles and structures), labour force skills and research and development expenditure. We examine the trends in these explanatory factors and some simple correlations between these and labour productivity growth. Finally we present some multiple regression results which combine the results for the influence of capital with the results on convergence and plant size discussed above.

Fixed Capital

Estimates of fixed capital stocks were calculated for all years from 1960 to 1989; details of the estimation methods and data sources are given in Appendix A. Table 9 shows summary statistics on the levels of fixed capital per unit of labour input - Appendix table B.4 gives the industry estimates of gross capital stocks per hour for selected years. In aggregate manufacturing fixed capital intensity in

TABLE 9
Gross Capital Stocks per Hour Worked
(1985 £ per 1000 hour worked)

	1960	1973	1979	1989
Germany				
Total Manufacturing	6,470	16,363	21,774	27,828
Mean	6,621	19,009	28,665	37,418
Standard deviation	4,583	16,442	31,732	37,004
United Kingdom				
Total Manufacturing	5,610	10,698	14,009	21,866
Mean	6,903	14,143	17,940	30,517
Standard deviation	9,270	19,847	22,136	38,106
N (G >	19	28	29	28
Correlation (KG,KU)	0.74	0.94	0.98	0.96

Notes: KG, KU are gross capital stocks per hour worked in Germany and the UK, respectively.

Germany was about 15 per cent per cent higher than in Britain and this had risen to a German capital advantage of over 50 per cent in the seventies before falling back to less than 30 per cent in the late 1980s. Germany had a fixed capital advantage in almost all industries from the nineteen seventies. The cross industry pattern of capital intensity was remarkably similar in the two countries.

In both countries the growth in the aggregate manufacturing capital labour ratio, as shown in table 10, was higher in the period 1960 to 1973 than in the later period 1973 to 1989, but the difference was only marginal in the UK. In Germany there appears to have been a considerable reduction in capital intensity growth in the period after 1973 which was most pronounced in the decade 1979 to 1989. In Germany none of the thirty industries experienced higher growth in capital intensity after 1973 than in the earlier period whereas in the UK the growth rates increased post 1973 in fifteen industries.

TABLE 10
Growth of Gross Fixed Capital Stocks per Hour Worked

	1960-1989	1960-1973	1973-1989	1973-1979	1979-1989
Germany					
Total Manufacturing	5.03	7.14	3.32	4.76	2.45
Mean	5.94	8.14	4.16	5.98	3.06
Standard deviation	1.50	1.95	1.44	2.40	1.58
correlation (dPG,dKG)	0.24	0.31	0.30	0.42	0.18
United Kingdom					
Total Manufacturing	4.69	4.97	4.47	4.49	4.45
Mean	4.98	5.16	4.83	4.66	4.93
Standard deviation	1.03	1.38	1.36	1.77	1.78
correlation (dPU,dKU)	0.32	0.34	0.45	0.29	0.38
correlation (dKG,dKU)	0.17	0.05	0.36	0.20	0.26
correlation (dPG,KG)	0.41	0.50	0.11	0.17	-0.03
correlation (dPU,KU)	0.18	0.45	-0.17	-0.27	0.08

Notes: dPG, dPU = labour productivity growth, dKG, dKU = growth in gross capital stocks per unit of labour input; all growth rates are in per cent per annum.

In general the growth in fixed capital intensity was positively correlated with labour productivity growth in all time periods but the correlations were small in some cases, in particular, in Germany during the period 1979 to 1989. In contrast to labour productivity growth, the cross section correlations between capital intensity growth in Germany and the UK were largely insignificant so that the two counties have not generally experienced similar cross industry patterns of investment.

The final correlation we examine is between the level of capital intensity and the growth rate of labour productivity. A positive correlation could occur if technical progress is embodied in capital goods leading to greater productivity growth in more capital intensive industries. Also, as suggested by David (1975) it may be easier to improve capital intensive technologies, ie. local technical progress which involves small improvements to production techniques may occur more readily the more machinery intensive is the production process.

The final two rows of table 10 show the cross section correlations between labour productivity growth and the levels of capital intensity, the latter measured by the average of the capital labour ratios for the end points of each time period. In the earliest period 1960 to 1973 labour productivity growth was on average higher in capital intensive industries in both countries. For the years after 1973 this relationship disappears; the correlation is in fact negative (but insignificant) for the period 1973 to 1979 in the UK and for 1979 to 1989 for Germany. Over the long period, 1960 to 1989 the data show a positive correlation but this is significant only for Germany.

In section two above we noted that in total manufacturing there were structural breaks in labour productivity growth in Germany post 1979 and in the UK post 1973. It is interesting to ask if the same result holds when allowance is made for the growth in capital intensity. Joint factor productivity (JFP) growth rates were estimated using the standard growth accounting method of subtracting the growth in capital intensity weighted by capital's share in value added from the growth in labour productivity. In Germany the growth of JFP was 3.01 per cent per annum in 1960-73 but fell to 1.72 per cent per annum in 1973-79 and 1.57 per cent per annum in 1979 to 1989. The comparable figures for the UK were 3.53 per cent, -0.67 per cent and 2.83 per cent respectively. These time patterns are also apparent in the majority of industries. However using annual data we find no evidence of structural breaks in aggregate joint factor productivity in both countries. Also the coefficients on the post 1979 dummy variable were not significant for any of the thirty industries in Germany. The result that there was no statistical evidence of significant structural breaks in trend total factor productivity growth was found by Flaig and Steiner (1994) in a study of twenty five German industries.

Human Capital

The above discussion focused on the role of physical capital. We next consider the role of human capital in explaining labour productivity. To take adequate account of differences in skill levels in the period under consideration in this paper would require data on the number of workers with various skill levels by industry. Unfortunately such detailed information is only available for the last decade. Data on the proportion of workers with various certified qualifications are available from the labour force surveys from the end of the 1970s. Table 11 shows the division of the workforces into those with higher level, intermediate level and those with no qualifications for aggregate manufacturing and summary

M. O'Mahony and K. Wagner

TABLE 11
Proportion of the Workforce with Certified Qualifications

	1978/79			1989		
	Upper Level	Interme- diate	No Quali- fications	Upper Level	Interme- diate	No Quali- fications
Germany						
Total Manufacturing	3.6	60.9	35.5	6.6	67.0	26.4
Mean	3.8	61.1	35.1	6.3	66.2	27.5
Standard deviation	3.9	7.7	9.3	6.1	5.9	8.4
United Kingdom						
Total Manufacturing	4.7	24.4	71.0	7.9	35.2	56.8
Mean	4.9	23.2	71.9	7.7	35.0	57.3
Standard deviation	3.5	10.6	12.1	5.4	12.0	13.8

Notes: Upper level is degree and equivalent or higher degree, Intermediate level is all certified qualifications below degree level but above general schooling, including time-served apprentices.

statistics over the thirty industries for both countries; Appendix table B.5 shows details by industry.

It is immediately apparent that the proportion of the workforce with no certified skills is much lower in Germany than in the UK for both years but that the German advantage is mostly at the intermediate rather than the upper level. If we compare the UK and Germany for 1978/79 we see that only seven German industries had greater proportions of the workforce qualified at the upper level. There were however some quality differences in this category. Most of the British awards were first degrees whereas in Germany the emphasis is on Masters degrees. In addition the number of employees with Doctorates in chemistry, physics, engineering and technology was higher in Germany than in Britain (Prais, 1989; Mason and Wagner, 1993).[3] In 1978/79 all thirty industries

---

[3] These differences do need to be treated with caution since the types of workers included in the upper level category may not be comparable in the two countries. Thus the UK data include persons who are members of professional institutions such as accountants and engineers whose qualifications come from certified institutes rather than from a university degree. The certified qualifications are comparable to those obtained from universities and so should be included in the upper qualification category. However it is not clear if comparably qualified personnel are included in the German data. In Britain members of professional institutions accounted for about a third of those qualified at upper level at the end of the 1970s but this had fallen to about a quarter by 1989.

Germany had higher proportions qualified at the intermediate level. In fact in twenty five industries the German intermediate proportion was more than twice the British and in eleven the ratio of German to British intermediate proportion was more than three.

The growth in skill proportions over the period 1978/79 to 1989 was similar in the two countries at the upper level but was considerably greater in Britain at the intermediate level. Thus the mean annual percent growth rate of the proportion of the workforce with upper level qualifications was 4.6 per cent in Germany and 4.7 per cent in the UK and the corresponding growth rates for intermediate level proportions were 0.8 per cent and 4.6 per cent, respectively. At the upper level fifteen industries witnessed greater annual percent growth rates in Britain. At the intermediate level the British growth rates were higher for twenty nine industries, the exception being textiles. Despite this superior UK growth the German advantage in intermediate skills remained very high in all industries by 1989.

Up to now we have looked at the development of Anglo-German differences in skill proportions but it is worthwhile to consider the development in absolute numbers which shows a very diverse picture in the two countries. In Germany total employment was reduced slightly at an annual rate of 0.2 per cent over the period 1978 to 1989. Decomposing this into skill groups shows that the reduction was concentrated in unskilled workers which declined from 3.03 million to 2.25 million or 2.7 per cent per annum. The number of workers qualified at the upper level increased considerably from 307,000 to 551,000 which represented an annual increase of 5.3 per cent whereas the number of workers qualified to intermediate level increased slightly from 5.2 million to 5.6 million or 0.7 per cent per annum.

In Britain we have already mentioned the huge reduction in employment in manufacturing of about two million workers from 1979 to 1989 - this represented an annual decrease of 3.4 per cent per annum and as in Germany was concentrated among the unskilled which declined at a rate of 5.5 per cent per annum. The number of workers qualified to the upper level did show an increase from 325,000 to 389,000 or 1.8 per cent per annum but the number with intermediate qualifications was virtually static with an increase of less than 40,000 workers or 0.2 per cent per annum. These figures show that in Britain the improvement in the skill structure over this period was due almost entirely to the reduction in unskilled workers and is not based on a policy of improving the skills of the labour force as a whole by companies or the Government.

Detailed data on skill qualifications by industry are only available from the end of the nineteen seventies. We may ask if there have been major changes in the skill proportions in the two countries before then. At the aggregate level we can get some idea of trends in skill proportions by looking at the distribution of skills by age cohort if we make the assumption that most workers acquire their skills before age thirty. Then a comparison of skill proportions of workers in older age cohorts with those less than age thirty can yield some insight into the trends in skill acquisitions. The skill proportions by age cohort[4] are given in table 12, which again are taken from the Labour Force Surveys. This shows that, in both countries, the older the age group the higher the proportion of workers with no skills. But in each age cohort the proportion of workers with qualifications at the intermediate level is considerably higher in Germany which suggests that the German skill advantage has persisted for some time.

TABLE 12
Distribution of Age Cohorts by Skill Proportions.

	1978/79			1989		
	Upper Level	Inter-mediate	No Quali-fications	Upper Level	Inter-mediate	No Quali-fications
Germany						
20-24	0.8	70.0	29.3	0.8	72.5	26.7
25-29	4.9	71.3	23.8	6.5	75.1	18.4
30-34	6.6	68.7	24.7	10.9	71.4	17.6
35-39	6.4	66.2	27.3	9.6	70.4	20.0
40-44	4.8	65.0	30.2	7.8	69.0	23.2
45-49	4.0	62.6	33.4	7.5	68.4	24.1
50-54	3.5	62.2	34.3	5.1	66.9	28.1
55-59	3.6	62.9	33.5	4.9	64.2	31.0
United Kingdom						
20-24	3.5	27.8	68.7	4.3	28.6	67.1
25-29	10.6	34.2	55.2	10.5	34.6	55.0
30-34	8.6	33.8	57.6	10.4	35.4	54.2
35-39	7.6	31.4	60.9	9.1	36.3	54.5
40-44	5.9	31.9	62.2	8.5	34.5	57.0
45-49	6.3	28.8	64.9	8.3	33.4	58.3
50-54	5.7	25.9	68.4	5.3	31.1	63.6
55-59	4.5	25.3	70.2	6.2	32.9	60.9

Sources: Britain from the Labour Force Surveys, Germany from the Microzensus.

Some confirmation of this is provided in Broadberry and Wagner (1994) where it is shown that the German skill advantage, measured by numbers of apprentices trained, was built up across the war and in the 1950s. But that paper also shows that Germany also increased her skill lead in the 1970s. During that decade the

---

[4] The sample size was very small for the youngest (16-19) and oldest (60-65) age groups and hence are not shown.

number of German apprenticeships increased sharply despite a fall in employment whereas in Britain the number of apprentices declined. Unfortunately we have no industry detail on skill proportions before the late 1970s.

It is also interesting that table 12 shows that in Britain all age cohorts showed similar increases in skill proportions over the period 1979 to 1989 whereas in Germany the increases were more concentrated in the younger age groups. This provides further evidence that the improvement in the skill structure in British manufacturing was due primarily to a reduction in unskilled labour rather than to significant new training of younger workers.

The cross section correlation between the skill proportions in the two countries were high at 0.71 for upper level and 0.58 at the intermediate level in 1978/79 and these had not altered significantly by 1989. Therefore, there is some similarity in the relative skill intensity of industries in the two countries. In both countries industries in engineering have the highest percentages of skilled workers followed by the intermediate goods industries with consumer goods having the lowest percentages in particular at the upper level. On the other hand the cross section correlations of the annual percent growth rates in skill proportions in the two countries were insignificant, 0.06 for upper and 0.11 for intermediate levels.

We now come to a consideration of the impact of skills on productivity growth. A series of publications by the National Institute (Daly, Hitchens and Wagner, 1985; Steedman and Wagner, 1987, 1989; and Prais and Wagner, 1988) have exemplified the impact of labour force skills on relative Anglo-German productivity. On the basis of matched plant comparisons it became obvious that skilled shopfloor employees are better equipped than semi-skilled to perform a number of functions which raise productivity. Thus skilled workers raise productivity by operating more machinery and also are better able to do fast and frequent change-overs of production processes or new products, recognise faults in machinery before serious breakdowns take place and adjust machinery to fit different materials. These factors not only raise output per worker but also raise the quality and complexity of products and therefore enhance their value added. In all four matched plant comparisons the matched goods showed, on average, a higher quality and complexity in the German plants.

The qualifications of foremen was also seen as an essential element for an effective work organisation. The German foremen, who had most often passed a higher intermediate examination covering general technological and organisational subjects, could take more responsibility and arrange production more efficiently than his less skilled British counterpart who often lacked any formal qualifications.

O'Mahony (1992b) shows that labour productivity levels in Germany relative to the UK are positively related to differences in skill levels. Here we are concerned to see if skills can help explain labour productivity growth rates. As for fixed capital, it may be the case that productivity growth is higher the greater the skill intensity of the industry. The implementation of new technical processes may be easier the greater the skills of the workforce. Data limitations mean that the 1978/79 skill intensities are used rather than the average of each periods end points. Table 13 shows that in both countries the correlation between labour productivity growth and the proportion of the workforce with no qualifications is negative both for the entire period 1960 to 1989 and the first sub-period 1960 to 1973 thus lending some support to the notion that productivity growth is higher in skill intensive industries. In both countries the relationship is strong only for the sub-period 1960-73; the correlations become insignificant or are positive after 1973.

TABLE 13
Labour productivity and Labour Force Skills

	1960-1989	1960-1973	1973-1989	1973-1979	1979-1989
Germany					
Correlation of dPG with					
Upper level (1978)	0.42	0.42	0.23	0.32	0.05
Intermediate level (1978)	0.08	0.34	-0.25	-0.13	-0.33
No qualifications (1978)	-0.24	-0.45	0.11	-0.02	0.26
dU	-	-	-	-	0.16
dI	-	-	-	-	0.36
dN	-	-	-	-	-0.38
United Kingdom					
Correlation of dPU with					
Upper level (1979)	0.78	0.73	0.41	0.21	0.19
Intermediate level (1979)	0.17	0.12	0.13	-0.18	0.24
No qualifications (1979)	-0.37	-0.31	-0.23	0.10	-0.26
dU	-	-	-	-	-0.10
dI	-	-	-	-	0.02
dN	-	-	-	-	-0.42

Notes: dPG,dPU = growth in labour productivity; dU,dI,dN = growth rates of qualification proportions from 1978/79 to 1989.

The four industries with the lowest proportions of unskilled workers in Britain (ie. mineral oil, office machinery, shipbuilding and aerospace) were some of the best relative productivity performers both in terms of their productivity levels in 1989 and the fact that their productivity growth from 1960 to 1989 were above average.

When we divide the skill data into upper and intermediate level qualifications we see that in all sub-periods productivity growth is positively correlated with the proportion of workers with upper level qualifications and that this correlation is very high for the UK both for the entire period 1960 to 1989 and the subperiod 1960 to 1973. Over long time periods, therefore, industries with high proportions of workers with upper level qualifications tend to experience higher productivity growth. The relationship between intermediate skills and productivity growth is less clear cut - industries with high proportions of workers qualified to intermediate levels achieved higher productivity growth in Germany in the period 1960 to 1973 but the correlation is negative after 1973 and particularly so after 1979. In Britain the correlations are generally positive but insignificant.For the period 1979 to 1989 we can examine the relationship between labour productivity growth and the change in the skill proportions. Table 13 shows that the correlations with the proportion of unskilled workers are significantly negative in both countries. These data therefore provide some evidence that industries whose skills proportions increased most in the period 1979 to 1989 were those who achieved higher labour productivity growth. Dividing the growth in skill proportions into upper and intermediate levels show a significant positive correlation only for intermediate skills in Germany.

Finally in this section we consider the possibility that different skill levels in the two countries lead to different investment patterns. In the clothing industry in the UK, which has a relatively high proportion of unskilled workers, more modern equipment was installed than in Germany to overcome skill shortages. This included costly computer controlled grading of patterns and lay planning. Further as more standardised products were manufactured they were able to use more automated dedicated machinery and to buy specialised machinery. In contrast, in Germany automated machinery had disappeared, they use conventional sewing machines for small batches of highly styled blouses and shirts.

An opposite example became clear in the furniture industry; this time it was more modern in Germany as only the computerised machinery could handle the customised production. Even small German firms used highly sophisticated computer numerically controlled (CNC) woodworking machinery. CNC edge-banders formed part of a linked CNC machinery unit, linked machine lines carried out to cut panels to precise sizes and do two way edge-banding, milling and drilling. In Britain fully linked machine lines with automatic feed and automatic off-line were hardly seen because the managers feared large losses in production if one of the linked machines goes wrong. Thus traditional machinery was found in Britain.

These examples suggest that there may be some connection between skill levels and investment in fixed capital. In Germany capital growth and skill levels, both upper and intermediate, were positively correlated and significant for most periods, the exception being the final decade 1979 to 1989. In Britain the correlations were generally smaller and only significant after 1979. In terms of labour productivity growth it is interesting to look at the correlation with the interaction of fixed capital and skill levels measured by the product of the two. For Germany labour productivity growth was found to be on average highest in industries with combined high levels of skills and high rates of investment for the periods 1960 to 1973 and 1973 to 1979 but not for the years 1979 to 1989. In Britain a significant correlation is only apparent from 1979. In that decade we can also examine the correlation of labour productivity growth with the product of capital growth and skill growth. Here we find a significant positive relationship only for German intermediate skills.

Research and Development

The final explanatory factor considered in this section is research and development expenditure. Periodic surveys of R&D expenditure were available in both countries from the early 1960s and estimates for total manufacturing are available from 1950. Estimates of the gross stock of R&D capital were derived using the perpetual inventory method assuming a life of eight years and sudden death retirements (the use of an eight year life is explained in Appendix A). Table 14 shows R&D per unit of labour input for total manufacturing and summary statistics for the thirty industries - Appendix table B.6 gives the industry details. A discussion of the data sources are given in Appendix A.

In the early 1960s British aggregate manufacturing had higher R&D intensity than German manufacturing but by the early 1970s the relative position in the

TABLE 14
R&D Expenditure per Hour Worked
(1985 £ per 1000 Hour Worked)

	1963	1973	1979	1989
Germany				
Total Manufacturing	225	1,784	3,332	5,288
Mean	353	2,269	3,670	4,711
Standard deviation	1,044	7,011	9,643	9,054
United Kingdom				
Total Manufacturing	967	2,090	2,446	4,481
Mean	1,079	2,391	2,771	4,213
Standard deviation	1,851	4,215	4,983	7,308
N (G > U)	2	10	20	22
Correlation (RDG,RDU)	0.85	0.83	0.82	0.76

Notes: RDG, RDU are R&D expenditures per hour worked in Germany and the UK, respectively.

two countries was reversed. Since then R&D intensity has remained higher in Germany in both aggregate manufacturing and in the majority of industries. An examination of R&D intensity may, however, understate Germany's advantage since the total amount of R&D may confer external benefits which can be of use in more firms than those where the actual research is undertaken - R&D increases the general stock of knowledge available to everyone. These external benefits from R&D have been much emphasised in the recent literature on endogenous growth, for example see Romer (1990a). Since German manufacturing represents a much greater proportion of the total economy than in Britain the total level of R&D expenditure is considerably greater in Germany.

In general the cross industry distribution has a very large variance since R&D intensity is particularly high in a small number of industries, ie. chemicals, mineral oil refining, office machinery, aerospace and electrical engineering. This is confirmed by the cross industry correlations of R&D intensity in the two countries, as shown in the final row of table 14, which is very high in all years. In Germany the R&D intensity of the aerospace industry is about much higher than in Britain but the total research effort is similar in the two countries since employment is considerably greater in Britain. Office machinery in most research intensive industry in Britain and in this industry Britain has a clear R&D advantage since employment is lower than in Germany.

Turning to growth rates table 15 shows that in aggregate manufacturing growth rates of R&D intensity in Germany were considerably higher than in the UK over the period 1960-89 but the growth rates in Britain overtook those in Ger-

TABLE 15
Growth of R&D per Hour Worked

	1960-1989	1960-1973	1973-1989	1973-1979	1979-1989
Germany					
Total Manufacturing	10.89	15.93	6.79	10.41	4.62
Mean	10.79	14.14	8.06	11.47	6.02
Standard deviation	2.44	3.13	3.45	3.96	4.00
United Kingdom					
Total Manufacturing	5.29	5.93	4.77	2.62	6.05
Mean	3.72	5.15	2.55	-0.30	4.26
Standard deviation	2.19	2.61	3.63	4.92	6.05
N (G > U)	29	30	25	30	18
Correlation					
(dRDG,dRDU)	-0.24	0.49	-0.25	0.11	-0.09

Notes: dPG, dPU = labour productivity growth, dRDG, dRDU = growth in R&D expenditures per unit of labour input; all growth rates are in per cent per annum.

many in the final decade 1979-89. The growth in R&D intensity in Britain was pronounced in the iron and steel industry which showed the greatest turnaround in labour productivity growth. However in that decade the coefficient of variation is much higher in Britain so that even then the majority of industries showed higher growth rates in Germany. There was some similarity in the two countries in the cross industry pattern of R&D intensity growth in the period 1960 to 1973 but this disappears after 1973.

We next look at the relationship between labour productivity growth and R&D. The correlations are summarised in table 16. In both countries labour productivity growth is positively correlated with R&D intensity over the entire period 1960 to 1989 and the sub period 1960 to 1973 but the correlations are considerably higher for the UK. In Germany the correlations are close to zero in the post 1973 periods whereas they remain positive for the UK. Labour productivity growth is negatively correlated with the growth in R&D intensity in Germany in the decade 1979/89 but the corresponding correlation is positive and significant in the UK. These results are not significantly altered if we include the absolute levels of R&D expenditure rather than its intensity. Thus only in the UK is there a strong link between R&D activity and labour productivity growth.

TABLE 16
Labour Productivity and Research & Development.

	1960-1989	1960-1973	1973-1989	1973-1979	1979-1989
Germany					
Correlation of dPG with					
R&D intensity	0.22	0.15	-0.03	-0.06	-0.03
Growth in R&D intensity	0.16	0.12	-0.05	0.24	-0.18
Growth in R&D levels	0.18	0.27	-0.16	0.03	-0.29
United Kingdom					
Correlation of dPU with					
R&D intensity	0.66	0.48	0.44	-0.04	0.33
Growth in R&D intensity	0.27	0.08	0.43	0.14	0.31
Growth in R&D levels	0.47	0.21	0.41	0.10	0.16

Notes: dPG, dPU = growth in labour productivity.

Multiple Regression

Combining all the above explanatory factors could be carried out using traditional growth accounting or multiple regressions. O'Mahony and Wagner (1995) present some results using the former. In this paper we concentrate on the latter approach. Therefore we present the results of some multiple regressions showing the influence of the explanatory factors discussed above together with the productivity levels at the beginning of each period. The regressions were run for each country separately and the results are shown in table 17. For the long time period 1960 to 1989 the combination of capital variables and relative productivity levels explain a significant proportion of the variance of productivity growth in the two countries. The signs of the variables are mostly as expected in the German equation but both R&D intensity and intermediate skills are negative and the significance level of fixed capital is low. In contrast fixed capital is highly significant in the UK equation as is the proportion of workers skilled at the upper level but the significance level of most of the other variables is low.

Table 17a
Regression Results: Germany
Dependent Variable is Growth Rate of Labour Productivity

	1960-1989	1960-1973	1973-1989	1973-1979	1979-1989	1979-1989
Constant	0.045	0.012	0.053	0.067	0.047	0.044
	(4.72)	(0.60)	(4.09)	(2.53)	(5.43)	(1.93)
dKL	0.013	0.187	0.149	0.063	0.125	0.083
	(0.16)	(0.94)	(1.35)	(0.33)	(1.30)	(0.81)
dRD	0.082	-0.022	0.068	0.107	0.044	0.055
	(1.42)	(0.26)	(1.40)	(0.97)	(1.21)	(1.74)
KL	0.014	0.055	-0.005	-0.007	0.002	-0.003
	(4.65)	(3.21)	(1.26)	(0.78)	(0.42)	(0.69)
RD	-0.011	-0.013	-0.011	-0.018	-0.004	-0.004
	(2.63)	(1.47)	(4.18)	(4.51)	(2.09)	(2.21)
U	0.240	0.227	0.233	0.421	0.085	0.101
	(2.63)	(2.92)	(3.39)	(3.00)	(1.46)	(2.03)
I	-0.037	0.035	-0.066	-0.096	-0.048	-0.046
	(1.80)	(0.81)	(2.82)	(1.93)	(2.87)	(1.16)
dU	-	-	-	-	-	0.059
						(1.16)
dI	-	-	-	-	-	0.064
						(0.18)
PL	0.022	0.011	0.054	0.086	0.057	0.058
	(1.16)	(0.35)	(1.87)	(1.32)	(1.56)	(1.65)
LEV	-0.015	-0.012	-0.023	-0.026	-0.019	-0.018
	(5.95)	(2.40)	(5.46)	(2.45)	(3.56)	(2.97)
Adjusted R^2	0.57	0.38	0.60	0.45	0.34	0.30

Notes: KL = capital intensity, RD = R&D intensity, U & I are proportions qualified at upper and intermediate levels, respectively, PL = median plant size and LEV = the log of the ratio of German to UK productivity levels at the beginning of each time period. d preceding a variable denotes a growth rate, absolute values of t-ratios in parentheses, standard errors are heteroscedastic consistent estimates.

M. O'Mahony and K. Wagner

For the sub-periods the coefficient on fixed capital is generally insignificant for Germany and smaller than in the UK. The proportion of upper level skills in general has a significant positive effect on labour productivity growth in both countries but is insignificant in the final period, 1979 to 1989. The coefficients on intermediate skills proportions are generally negative, the exception being for the period 1960 to 1973 but then the significance level is not high in either country. This variable is significantly negative in Germany for the period 1979 to 1989. The poor performance of the intermediate skills variable, in particular after 1973, may be because it is likely to be highly correlated with an omitted

Table 17b
Regression Results: United Kingdom.
Dependent Variable is Growth Rate of Labour Productivity

	1960-1989	1960-1973	1973-1989	1973-1979	1979-1989	1979-1989
Constant	0.012	0.020	0.002	0.005	0.008	0.019
	(2.45)	(2.25)	(0.32)	(0.25)	(0.62)	(0.96)
dKL	0.364	0.380	0.462	0.207	0.264	0.338
	(2.52)	(1.94)	(2.84)	(0.62)	(1.26)	(1.25)
dRD	0.041	-0.086	0.127	0.065	0.113	0.117
	(0.42)	(0.61)	(2.36)	(0.60)	(1.36)	(1.19)
KL	-0.004	0.029	-0.020	-0.049	-0.012	-0.008
	(1.75)	(4.10)	(5.77)	(1.74)	(0.96)	(0.52)
RD	0.007	0.004	0.002	-0.013	0.005	0.012
	(1.14)	(0.40)	(0.29)	(0.53)	(0.44)	(0.78)
U	0.173	0.272	0.193	0.513	0.052	-0.070
	(2.73)	(4.24)	(2.88)	(2.23)	(0.31)	(0.30)
I	-0.010	0.012	-0.043	-0.065	-0.033	-0.050
	(1.03)	(0.62)	(2.35)	(1.28)	(1.05)	(0.98)
dU	-	-	-	-	-	-0.064
						(0.66)
dI	-	-	-	-	-	-0.077
						(0.38)
PL	0.001	-0.035	0.075	-0.107	0.190	0.163
	(0.10)	(0.69)	(2.31)	(0.69)	(2.46)	(1.44)
LEV	0.007	0.009	0.012	0.001	0.035	0.037
	(2.06)	(2.87)	(1.81)	(0.08)	(2.93)	(2.74)
Adjusted R^2	0.61	0.54	0.63	0.13	0.47	0.41

Notes: KL = capital intensity, RD = R&D intensity, U & I are proportions qualified at upper and intermediate levels, respectively, PL = median plant size and LEV = the log of the ratio of German to UK productivity levels at the beginning of each time period. d preceding a variable denotes a growth rate, absolute values of t-ratios in parentheses, standard errors are heteroscedastic consistent estimates.

variable, namely that capturing industrial relations conditions. Intermediate skill intensity is highest in industries such as engineering which also have high proportions of the workforce who are members of labour unions. The relatively low productivity in Britain in the years 1973 to 1979 and Germany in the years 1979 to 1989 could be due to the effect of adverse industrial relations.

The coefficient on R&D intensity is generally positive in the UK but not significant and is negative in all periods in Germany. Similarly the growth in R&D intensity has little explanatory power for either country. The coefficient on plant size is always positive in Germany but is negative in the UK for the periods up to 1979. The productivity level variable is the correct sign in all equations and is mostly significant.

The equations perform particularly badly for the UK in the period 1973 to 1979 and Germany in the years 1979 to 1989. In the latter period we also could include the growth in both higher and intermediate skills. These variables have positive signs in the German equation but their inclusion does not improve the explanatory power of the equation. The growth in both types of skilled labour have negative signs in the UK equation.

4. Conclusion

There is a general belief that the productivity performance of German manufacturing industry has been vastly superior to that in Britain since the early nineteen sixties. This paper has shown that at the level of individual manufacturing industries Germany does not so clearly dominate Britain, except in the period 1973 to 1979. On the other hand the British performance was superior in the final decade of the study from 1979 to 1989. Both countries have industries which have performed relatively well in some time periods. The paper shows that industries which perform relative badly in one period on average make up the deficit in subsequent periods.

In attempting to explain relative productivity growth we have concentrated on capital accumulation variables both because these variables are those most often used in traditional growth accounting exercises and the recent emphasis on capital differences in the new growth literature. German manufacturing had an advantage in all three forms of capital by the end of the 1980s and a pronounced advantage in workforce skills. Soskice (1993) suggests that this German superiority in skills is a consequence of some broad institutional differences with the UK which include co-operative industrial relations and a financial system which enables firms to take a more long run perspective. He concludes that these institutional differences make it difficult, and probably undesirable for Britain to imitate the German training system.

The measures of capital accumulation have some power in explaining productivity growth up to 1973 but they perform poorly thereafter. There appears to be a deterioration in productivity performance which is common to all industries in Britain in the period 1973 to 1979 and a deterioration is also evident for Germany in the 1980s. The latter decade, on the other hand, was a period of substantial productivity revival in the majority of British industries. The explanations for these common trends across industries probably lie in differences in the underlying product and labour markets (for discussions see for example Carlin, 1993; Metcalf, 1989; and Giersch et al., 1992).

References

Ark, B. van (1993), "International Comparisons of Output and Productivity", Groningen Growth and Development Centre, *Monograph series No.1*.

Barro, R.J. and X. Sala-i-Martin, (1991), "Convergence across States and Regions", *Brookings Papers on Economic Activity*, 107-182.

Baumol, W.J. (1986), "Productivity Growth, Convergence and Welfare: what the Long Run Data show", *American Economic Review*, Vol. 76, December.

Broadberry, S. (1993), "Manufacturing and the Convergence Hypothesis: what the Long Run Data show", *Journal of Economic History*, forthcoming.

Broadberry, S. and K. Wagner (1994), "Human Capital and Growth in the Long Run: Comparative Skills in Germany and the UK", in B. van Ark and N.F.R. Crafts (eds.), *Quantitative Aspects of Postwar European Economic Growth*, CEPR, Cambridge University Press, forthcoming.

Cameron, G. and J. Muellbauer (1994), "Knowledge, Increasing Returns and the UK Production Function", paper prepared for the Fullbright Colloquium "Sources of Productivity Growth in the 1980s", held at the National Institute of Economic and Social Research, London, February.

Carlin, W. (1993), "West German Growth and Institutions, 1945-90", paper presented to the CEPR conference "The Economic Performance of Europe after the Second World War", Oxford, December.

Daly, A., D. Hitchens and K. Wagner (1985), "Productivity, Machinery and Skills in a Sample of British and German Manufacturing Plants, *National Institute Economic Review*, May.

David, P.A. (1975), *Technical Choice, Innovation and Economic Growth*, Cambridge University Press.

Flaig, G. and V. Steiner (1993), "Searching for the "Productivity Slowdown": some surprising Findings from West German Manufacturing", *Review of Economics and Statistics*, p. 57-65.

Giersch, H. K-H. Paquw and H. Schmiedling (1992), *The Fading Miracle: Four Decades of Market Economy in Germany*, Cambridge University Press.

Jorgenson, D., F. Gollop, and B. Fraumeni (1987), *Productivity and US Economic Growth*, Harvard University Press.

Lansbury, M. and D. Mayes (1994), "Sources of Productivity Growth in the 1980s", in D. Mayes (ed.), *Sources of Productivity Growth in the 1980s*, forthcoming.

Lucas, R.E. (1988), "The Mechanics of Economic Development", *Journal of Monetary Economics*, 22, 3-42.

Maddison, A. (1991), *The Ddynamics of Capitalist Development*, Oxford University Press.

Mason, G. and K. Wagner (1993), *High Level Skills and International Competitiveness. Post-Graduate Engineers and Scientists in Britain and Germany*, National Institute of Economic and Social Research, London.

Metcalf, D. (1989), "Water Notes dry up: The Impact of the Donovan Reform Proposals and Thatcherism at Work on Labour Productivity in British Manufacturing Industry", *British Journal of Industrial Relations*, Vol. XXVII, No.1, pp 1-32.

OECD (1985), *Purchasing Power Parities and Real Expenditures, 1985*, Department of Economics and Statistics, OECD, Paris.

O'Mahony, M. (1992a), "Productivity Levels in British and German Manufacturing ", *National Institute Economic Review*, February.

O'Mahony (1992b), "Productivity and Human Capital Formation in UK and German Manufacturing", National Institute of Economic and Social Research, *Discussion paper No. 28*, October.

O'Mahony (1993), "International Measures of Fixed Capital Stocks: a five Country Study", National Institute of Economic and Social Research *Discussion Paper No. 51*, London.

O'Mahony, M., K. Wagner with M. Paulssen (1994), "Changing Fortunes: An Industry Study of British and German Productivity Growth over three Decades", National Institute of Economic and Social Research, *Report Series No. 7*, London.

O'Mahony, M. and K. Wagner (1995), "Relative productivity levels: UK and German manufacturing industry, 1979 and 1989", *International Journal of Manpower*, no. 1, p. 5-21.

Oulton, N. and M. O'Mahony (1994), *Productivity and Growth: A disaggregated Study of British Industry, 1954-1986*, Cambridge University Press.

Prais, S. (1981), *Productivity and Industrial Structure*, Cambridge University Press.

Prais, S. and K. Wagner (1988), "Productivity and Management: the Training of Foremen in Britain and Germany", *National Institute Economic Review*, February.

Prais, S. (1989), "Qualified Manpower in Engineering: Britain and other industrially advanced Countries", *National Institute Economic Review*, February.

Romer, P. (1986), "Increasing Returns and Long Run Growth" *Journal of Political Economy*, Vol. 94, pp. 1002-37.

Romer, P. (1990a), "Endogenous Technological Change", *Journal of Political Economy*, October, S71-S102.

Romer, P. (1990b), "Capital, Labour and Productivity", *Brookings Papers, Microeconomics*.

Salter, W.E.G. (1966), *Productivity and Technical Change*, 2nd edition, Cambridge University Press.

Schott, K. (1976), "Investment in Private Industrial Research and Development in Britain", *Journal of Industrial Economics*, Vol. 25, No. 2, pp. 81-99.

Smith, A.D., D.M.W.N. Hitchens and S.W. Davies (1982), "International Industrial Productivity: A Comparison of Britain, America and Germany", Cambridge University Press.

Soskice, D. (1993), "Social Skills from Mass Higher Education: Rethinking the Company based initial Training Paradigm. *Oxford Review of Economic Policy*, Vol. 9. No. 3.

Steedman, H., and K. Wagner (1987), "A second Look at Productivity, Machinery and Skills in Britain and Germany", *National Institute Economic Review*, November.

Steedman, H., and K. Wagner (1989), "Productivity, Machinery and Skills: Clothing Manufacture in Britain and Germany", *National Institute Economic Review*, November.

Appendix A: Data Sources and Methods

Some data sources are referred to frequently below and hence we use the following abbreviations.

United Kingdom.
AA: *Annual Abstract of Statistics*, CSO
ACP: *Annual report of the census of production*, CSO
BB: *United Kingdom National Accounts*, the CSO Blue Book
BLY: *British Labour Statistics Yearbook*, Department of Employment
BLH: *British Labour Statistics: Historical Abstract 1886-1968*, Department of Employment
EG: *Employment Gazette*, Department of Employment
HCP: *Historical record of the census of production, 1907-1970*, CSO
LFS: *The Labour Force Survey*
NES: *New Earnings Survey*

Germany
VG: *Volkswirtschaftliche Gesamtrechnungen*, Fachserie 18, Reihe 5, 15, Revidierte Ergebnisse, 1950 bis 1990. Statistisches Bundesamt.
SJ: *Statistisches Jahrbuch*, Statistisches Bundesamt.
MZ: *Microzensus*, Statistisches Bundesamt.

Output

The measure of output used in this paper is gross value added which is defined as gross output minus the cost of materials and fuel, industrial and non-industrial services. Nominal values of gross value added were deflated by the producer price indices in both countries to arrive at real gross value added; 1985 was chosen as the base year.

There are two approaches used by statistical offices in constructing real gross value added (GVA) series using data on gross output (GO), purchases of materials (MAT) and prices. The first, single deflation, calculates GVA as:

$$GVA = (GO - MAT) / PP$$

where PP is the producer price index. This was used for a long time by statistical offices but recently the Americans and Germans have used a double deflation method:

$$GVA = GO / PP - Mat / PM$$

where PM is the price index for materials.

Obviously if producer prices and materials prices rise at the same rate from some base year then PP = PM and GVA = GVA. In general this is not the case - in particular since the early 1970s there have been very large differences in the year to year variation in producer and materials prices. If we subtract the two expressions for GVA we get:

GVA - GVA = MAT (1/PM - 1/PP)

If PM < PP then GVA > GVA.

The reasoning behind double deflation is that since real gross value added is a measure of the volume of output it should be measured as the volume of sales minus the volume of materials purchased. In constructing the latter the value of materials should be deflated by its price index since the value of materials is the price of materials times the quantity of materials and not the price of output times the quantity of materials.

In principle, therefore double deflation is preferable. But there are two major problems with its use. The first is that the method used by the Germans and Americans is not base year invariant - the pattern of output changes over time varies depending on whether say the price indices are set at 100 in 1980 or 1985. The relative performance in the two countries will therefore depend on the which base year is chosen.

The problem of base year invariance can be overcome by using the method outlined in Jorgenson, Gollop and Fraumeni (1987) but this requires reliable prices indices for materials and fuel and bought in services. This brings us to our second objection to using double deflation, ie. we are not convinced that these price indices are measured accurately, in particular, in the United Kingdom. The British central statistical office now produces materials prices which cover all manufacturing industries but prior to 1974 there is little reliable information available. Unfortunately the early 1970s was the period when materials and fuels prices were most variable. Also price indices for bought in services are not available by industry within manufacturing.

International comparability requires that we use the same method in both countries. Our reservations on the accuracy of the materials price indices led us to opt for the easiest alternative of single deflating gross value added in both countries.

Sources:

UK: Nominal GVA from HCP for 1963, 1968 and from 1970 from ACP. Producer price indices AA and unpublished data acquired from the CSO. For missing years in the 1960s we interpolated the census figures using either the index of industrial production from BB or quantity indexes of output from AA. Germany: 1970-89: nominal GVA from VG, producer price indices from SJ. 1960-69: GVA at 1985 prices from VG, spliced onto later series in 1970. The German producer prices in the 1960s included sales taxes and hence are not comparable with later years. We therefore opted to use the double deflated growth in GVA from the official national accounts since the differences in producer prices and materials prices were of minor importance in the sixties.

Employment

Number of employees plus working proprietors.

Sources:
United Kingdom: 1963, 1968, from HCP, 1970-89: from ACP, other years in 1960s were derived by using series in BLH and BLY to interpolate between census years.
Germany: From VG, prior to 1968 we used the growth rates of employment derived by dividing GVA by GVA per worker.

Annual average hours worked

The calculation of average annual hours worked per worker in both the UK and Germany requires data on the average hours worked per week for each type of worker and the average number of weeks worked per year. The former must include not only basic hours worked per week but also overtime hours and an adjustment for short-time working. The latter must allow for days lost due to holidays, sickness and maternity leave and industrial disputes.

United Kingdom:
The starting point for the calculation of annual average hours per week was to first distinguish a number of categories of workers, these were: full-time manual males, full-time non-manual males, full-time manual females, full-time non-manual females and part-time workers. Average weekly hours for all workers were constructed by multiplying the average hours for each type of worker by their proportion in total employment.
    A single time series for all industries within manufacturing was constructed for weeks worked per year using estimates of time lost due to paid leave, sickness, maternity leave and strikes. Van Ark (1993) estimated weeks worked per year by major industry branch for 1984 using unpublished data from the Department of Employment on paid leave and days lost to strikes from the Department of Employment and days lost due to illness from LFS. Van Ark's data on weeks worked per year were used for 1984 and then backdated to 1960 and brought forward to 1989 using our time series for all manufacturing. This approach ensures some cross industry variation in weeks worked per year.

Sources: Manual hours from Annual Enquiry into hours of manual workers, published in EG, from 1968, years prior to that from BLH. Non-Manual hours from NES from 1968; prior to 1968 we used the growth in manual hours. Proportions of employment accounted for by males and females, full and part-time from the Census of Employment, EG, and from BLH, and proportions of manuals and non-manuals from HCP, ACP and BLH. Short-time working from EG. Weeks paid leave and days lost due to strikes from EG and an estimate of days lost due to sickness and maternity was derived using data from Social Security Statistics, Department of Health and Social Security.

Germany:
Series on average annual hours per year were calculated from 1970 to 1989 for the 30 industries by the Deutsches Institut für Wirtschaftsforschung (DIW), published in Görzig, Schintke and Schmidt (1990). These were consistent with independently calculated series by the Institut für Arbeitsmarkt und Berufs-forschung (IAB), published in Kohler and Reyner (1988); this source also includes time series on weeks worked per year for total manufacturing from 1960. Average hours per week from 1960 to 1970 were calculated using manual hours per week from "Arbeitnehmerverdienste in Industrie und Handel" *Preise, Lohne Wirtschaftsrechnungen*, Reihe 15, Statistisches Bundesamt, a single number for each year for non-manual hours from SJ, and proportions of manuals and non-manuals in total employment from SJ. This was combined with the IAB series on weeks per year for all manufacturing to give series for annual average hours. This was spliced onto the DIW series in 1970.

Capital stocks

Gross capital stocks in 1985 prices were calculated using the perpetual inventory method (PIM) which cumulates past investments and subtracts retirements. Capital stocks were calculated separately for equipment (including vehicles) and industrial buildings. The service lives of assets were assumed to be the same in the two countries and were set equal to those currently used by the Statistiches Bundesamt, as given in Tabelle 1, p. 503 of "Reproduzierbares Anlagevermogen in erweiterter Bereichsgliederung", *Wirtschaft und Statistik*, 7/1986. Standar-dising the service lives implies that relative capital stocks are not influenced by uncertain assumed differences in service lives. For a discussion of the PIM and the reliability of international differences in service lives of assets see O'Mahony (1993).

Sources:
United Kingdom: Nominal investment in equipment and industrial buildings by industry within manufacturing for the post war period from HCP, ACP and BB, prewar data unpublished series from the CSO. Investment deflators were derived primarily from unpublished series supplied by the CSO and from Price index numbers for current cost accounting, Business Statistics Office.
Germany: Investment in 1985 prices for 1960-89 from VG, prior to 1960 from Kirner (1968).

Labour force skills

Definitions:
United Kingdom: Higher: degree level and above, membership of professional institutions, 0.17 of "other qualifications"; Upper intermediate: all BTEC HNC/HND qualifications, teaching and nursing qualifications; Lower intermediate: all BTEC ONC/OND, city and guilds, all apprenticeships completed, 0.13 of "other qualifications".

Germany: Higher: Hochschulabschluss, Fachhochschulabschluss; Upper Intermediate: Meister/Techniker gleichwertig Fachschulacschluss; Lower intermediate: Lehr-/Anlernausbildung gleichwertig Berufs- fachschulabschluss, berufliches Praktikum.

Sources:
United Kingdom: LFS.
Germany: MZ.

Wage Rates by skill level

These were only available for Germany. The division into skill groups was as follows: Higher level: average of wage rates for 'Kaufmannliche Angestellte' and 'Technische Angestellte', Leistungsgruppe II,(managers); Intermediate: 0.75 times average of 'Facharbeiten' and 'Angelernten Arbeiten' (skilled manual workers) and 0.25 times average of 'Kaufmannliche Angestellte' and 'Technische Angestellte', Leistungsgruppe III and IV (foremen and skilled non-manuals); Unskilled: 0.75 times 'Hilfsarbeiten' (unskilled manuals) and 0.25 times average of 'Kaufmannliche Angestellte' and 'Technische Angestellte', Leistungsgruppe V, (unskilled non-manuals). The wage rates were for male workers. Sources: SJ

Research and development expenditure

Surveys of research and development expenditures by industry were carried out for the UK for selected years from 1964, available in Business Monitor MO14, "Industrial research and development expenditure and employment", CSO, and by the SC-Gemeinnttzige Gesellschaft ftr Wissenschaftsstatistik, Essen, for Germany from 1963. Missing years data were completed by linear interpolation. A single figure is available for the entire economy from the above source for Germany annually from 1950 to 1964 and from Schott (1976) for the UK for the same time period.

As for physical capital gross stocks of R&D were derived by cumulating investment over a number of years. The difficulty here is in choosing an average service life for these expenditures. No direct information is available on this but we do have a regression estimate of the coefficient on R&D from O'Mahony (1994) of about 0.05. The procedure adopted was to calculate for aggregate manufacturing the number of years R&D expenditure which gives this coefficient value - this turned out to be eight years. This life was then applied to all industries.

Note that we could achieve a similar coefficient value for total manufacturing if we assumed some depreciation rate and cumulated expenditure over a greater number of years. However it is not clear what depreciation rate should be used. For example Schott (1976) used a depreciation rate of under 10 per cent whereas Cameron and Muellbauer (1994) argue that the stock of knowledge does not depreciate in the sense that physical capital does and hence they assume no depreciation. The use of any depreciation rate requires more historical data on R&D by industry than is available to us hence our use of the sudden death assumption. We acknowledge that this assumption is somewhat arbitrary but the regression results presented in the text do not appear to be very sensitive to the service life employed.

Median Plant Size

The measure of average plant size is the median of the distribution of plant employment, ie. it is the plant size for which 50 per cent of the workforce are employed in plants with more than that number of employees. Sources: UK: "Size Analyses of United Kingdom businesses, 1987" BSO, 1988, Germany: Arbeitsstatten und Beschaftigte nach Beschaftigtengrobenklassen, 1987', Statistisches Bundesamt, Fachserie 2, 1989.

Appendix B: Detailed Tables.

TABLE B1.a
Index of Gross Value Added: Germany
(1985 = 100)

	1960	1973	1979	1989
Chemicals	28.6	93.2	104.4	130.1
Mineral Oil Refining	55.1	191.1	152.9	136.7
Plastic Products	13.7	74.1	81.9	132.9
Rubber Products	52.6	115.1	101.2	113.9
Mineral Products	76.6	143.3	132.6	121.7
Ceramic Goods	92.3	122.7	113.0	106.1
Glass	55.5	102.7	108.2	125.5
Iron & Steel	70.8	108.8	112.2	120.0
Non Ferrous Metals	69.1	90.2	97.3	96.1
Plant & Steelwork	75.5	124.2	122.2	128.0
Mechanical Engineering	56.5	97.3	99.1	110.2
Office Machinery	8.6	44.9	60.9	114.7
Motor Vehicles	28.0	70.5	92.3	104.4
Shipbuilding	107.1	166.5	122.3	98.1
Aerospace	14.0	65.0	85.5	133.1
Electrical Engineering	24.9	66.1	82.6	121.0
Instrument Engineering	37.0	80.8	96.8	106.2
Finished Metal Products	60.2	109.3	104.1	124.9
Toys, Musical & Sports Goods	89.2	117.2	121.8	119.1
Timber & Board	64.7	121.0	104.5	105.1
Wood Products	62.4	130.0	129.9	111.5
Paper & Pulp	51.0	85.0	94.0	116.0
Paper Products	70.6	121.5	106.7	109.6
Printing & Publishing	56.9	100.8	101.4	110.7
Leather & Footwear	210.8	153.5	128.5	97.1
Textiles	107.5	122.3	120.6	110.1
Clothing	100.1	124.91	14.9	100.3
Food	60.5	81.3	95.9	112.0
Drink	57.9	109.1	97.8	106.4
Tobacco	96.3	98.0	113.2	107.6
Total Manufacturing	49.1	97.0	102.2	116.4

TABLE B1.b
Index of Gross Value Added: United Kingdom
(1985=100)

	1960	1973	1979	1989
Chemicals	46.4	105.1	98.5	128.1
Mineral Oil Refining	90.2	267.1	231.0	178.9
Plastic Products	17.6	86.5	91.4	144.0
Rubber Products	77.3	154.9	124.9	117.5
Mineral Products	96.6	162.2	122.2	137.5
Ceramic Goods	72.9	102.1	114.0	106.9
Glass	82.6	159.7	131.6	142.2
Iron & Steel	164.5	203.4	93.5	136.0
Non Ferrous Metals	164.8	228.4	170.1	115.8
Plant & Steelwork	51.4	115.0	134.3	97.6
Mechanical Engineering	91.9	146.4	134.2	111.7
Office Machinery	16.0	51.1	66.8	145.8
Motor Vehicles	91.6	137.9	130.4	119.2
Shipbuilding	87.0	114.7	98.7	83.9
Aerospace	79.2	125.5	78.4	165.8
Electrical Engineering	50.6	96.1	95.4	108.6
Instrument Engineering	30.7	72.9	84.9	112.9
Finished Metal Products	93.3	133.0	126.9	113.9
Toys, Musical & Sports Goods	62.9	117.4	122.2	128.3
Timber & Board	76.1	169.1	121.6	129.0
Wood Products	73.6	125.6	114.9	126.2
Paper & Pulp	128.7	153.7	123.5	131.2
Paper Products	67.6	140.4	124.8	113.4
Printing & Publishing	64.0	102.1	93.6	132.0
Leather & Footwear	93.2	122.5	121.1	91.5
Textiles	114.9	145.7	119.4	105.3
Clothing	63.9	96.9	105.1	103.9
Food	59.8	110.5	95.2	118.8
Drink	84.5	162.6	155.0	104.7
Tobacco	119.9	165.3	141.2	99.7
Total Manufacturing	74.0	126.7	112.9	121.0

TABLE B2.a
Numbers in Employment (000's), Germany

	1960	1973	1979	1989
Chemicals	529	637	628	635
Mineral Oil Refining	43	52	34	29
Plastic Products	96	201	206	284
Rubber Products	118	139	118	118
Mineral Products	300	274	226	179
Ceramic Goods	83	67	58	50
Glass	92	97	81	72
Iron & Steel	747	620	564	463
Non Ferrous Metals	266	234	199	176
Plant & Steelwork	234	199	182	178
Mechanical Engineering	1,023	1,195	1,104	1,141
Office Machinery	62	105	75	99
Motor Vehicles	547	863	925	982
Shipbuilding	95	71	58	35
Aerospace	18	40	49	68
Electrical Engineering	937	1,212	1,093	1,195
Instrument Engineering	170	204	219	216
Finished Metal Products	392	389	339	351
Toys, Musical & Sports Goods	94	89	79	65
Timber & Board	85	68	57	45
Wood Products	407	354	353	313
Paper & Pulp	87	67	55	56
Paper Products	137	154	125	119
Printing & Publishing	232	261	227	239
Leather & Footwear	219	140	104	60
Textiles	705	476	338	236
Clothing	469	401	304	206
Food	776	656	682	633
Drink	189	145	119	90
Tobacco	78	34	26	17
Total Manufacturing	9,231	9,444	8,627	8,350

TABLE B2.b
Numbers in Employment (000's), United Kingdom

	1960	1973	1979	1989
Chemicals	446	420	422	331
Mineral Oil Refining	29	26	24	15
Plastic Products	78	128	134	147
Rubber Products	114	118	105	64
Mineral Products	179	185	159	129
Ceramic Goods	61	59	60	46
Glass	69	70	60	45
Iron & Steel	361	320	268	98
Non Ferrous Metals	245	213	187	97
Plant & Steelwork	144	154	168	107
Mechanical Engineering	793	826	781	485
Office Machinery	53	62	47	56
Motor Vehicles	567	563	551	289
Shipbuilding	205	152	131	68
Aerospace	264	213	190	169
Electrical Engineering	624	757	656	491
Instrument Engineering	141	141	142	131
Finished Metal Products	412	442	406	279
Toys, Musical & Sports Goods	92	96	98	82
Timber & Board	77	100	82	63
Wood Products	161	179	164	152
Paper & Pulp	73	59	52	33
Paper Products	150	180	158	123
Printing & Publishing	315	338	323	314
Leather & Footwear	155	122	102	69
Textiles	699	485	368	215
Clothing	447	403	346	252
Food	594	622	579	494
Drink	135	132	113	74
Tobacco	41	39	37	14
Total Manufacturing	7,724	7,604	6,912	4,928

TABLE B3.a
Average Annual Hours Worked, Germany

	1960	1973	1979	1989
Chemicals	2,209	1,869	1,774	1,627
Mineral Oil Refining	2,180	1,806	1,702	1,623
Plastic Products	2,091	1,854	1,739	1,637
Rubber Products	1,997	1,749	1,679	1,620
Mineral Products	2,363	2,101	1,956	1,836
Ceramic Goods	2,033	1,763	1,678	1,611
Glass	2,116	1,821	1,717	1,658
Iron & Steel	2,108	1,867	1,689	1,592
Non Ferrous Metals	2,126	1,871	1,770	1,618
Plant & Steelwork	2,226	1,953	1,789	1,686
Mechanical Engineering	2,191	1,895	1,777	1,642
Office Machinery	1,930	1,700	1,646	1,568
Motor Vehicles	2,039	1,774	1,661	1,550
Shipbuilding	2,194	1,936	1,663	1,728
Aerospace	1,948	1,727	1,669	1,541
Electrical Engineering	2,000	1,732	1,644	1,533
Instrument Engineering	2,079	1,778	1,702	1,590
Finished Metal Products	2,088	1,873	1,741	1,604
Toys, Musical & Sports Goods	1,996	1,736	1,655	1,542
Timber & Board	2,249	2,015	1,867	1,758
Wood Products	2,187	1,925	1,779	1,683
Paper & Pulp	2,280	1,975	1,860	1,727
Paper Products	2,052	1,815	1,749	1,634
Printing & Publishing	2,129	1,842	1,752	1,580
Leather & Footwear	1,923	1,666	1,639	1,565
Textiles	1,953	1,752	1,668	1,600
Clothing	1,820	1,586	1,551	1,483
Food	2,224	1,999	1,879	1,783
Drink	2,261	1,999	1,879	1,783
Tobacco	2,217	2,025	1,904	1,799
Total Manufacturing	2,104	1,839	1,732	1,618

TABLE B3.b
Average Annual Hours Worked, United Kingdom

	1960	1973	1979	1989
Chemicals	2,031	1,820	1,752	1,736
Mineral Oil Refining	1,963	1,781	1,773	1,788
Plastic Products	2,079	1,864	1,761	1,750
Rubber Products	2,078	1,861	1,755	1,709
Mineral Products	2,282	2,068	1,904	1,827
Ceramic Goods	2,008	1,786	1,726	1,778
Glass	2,147	1,899	1,777	1,730
Iron & Steel	2,151	1,956	1,806	1,756
Non Ferrous Metals	2,126	1,927	1,811	1,825
Plant & Steelwork	2,175	1,943	1,800	1,807
Mechanical Engineering	2,127	1,910	1,777	1,785
Office Machinery	2,081	1,868	1,762	1,737
Motor Vehicles	2,065	1,912	1,775	1,802
Shipbuilding	2,173	1,959	1,859	1,753
Aerospace	2,081	1,872	1,804	1,780
Electrical Engineering	2,011	1,777	1,705	1,726
Instrument Engineering	1,999	1,802	1,699	1,724
Finished Metal Products	2,036	1,942	1,746	1,742
Toys, Musical & Sports Goods	1,966	1,737	1,643	1,603
Timber & Board	2,149	1,973	1,806	1,751
Wood Products	2,081	1,900	1,773	1,726
Paper & Pulp	2,224	2,010	1,865	1,791
Paper Products	2,013	1,822	1,740	1,707
Printing & Publishing	2,042	1,826	1,721	1,671
Leather & Footwear	1,946	1,735	1,632	1,652
Textiles	1,997	1,793	1,667	1,673
Clothing	1,862	1,645	1,551	1,572
Food	1,988	1,800	1,704	1,696
Drink	2,067	1,921	1,836	1,765
Tobacco	1,986	1,794	1,644	1,706
Total Manufacturing	2,052	1,855	1,742	1,729

TABLE B4.a
Gross Fixed Capital Intensity, Germany
(1985 £ per 1000 Hour Worked)

	1960	1973	1979	1989
Chemicals	13,429	31,644	39,048	43,189
Mineral Oil Refining	21,345	93,152	185,777	217,191
Plastic Products	3,222	11,667	17,345	21,336
Rubber Products	8,141	17,989	23,563	24,719
Mineral Products	9,561	24,724	33,384	39,446
Ceramic Goods	3,766	10,994	14,376	18,561
Glass	5,215	16,112	24,802	34,346
Iron & Steel	8,542	25,468	32,795	39,331
Non Ferrous Metals	6,632	18,893	26,432	34,537
Plant & Steelwork	2,101	7,623	11,059	13,907
Mechanical Engineering	4,809	11,001	14,602	18,856
Office Machinery	6,449	18,509	37,399	42,209
Motor Vehicles	8,298	16,651	20,226	32,740
Shipbuilding	2,501	9,418	18,856	32,757
Aerospace	1,244	7,825	10,753	20,490
Electrical Engineering	2,927	8,607	13,360	19,939
Instrument Engineering	3,299	7,603	9,354	14,753
Finished Metal Products	3,858	10,976	15,698	19,733
Toys, Musical & Sports Goods	2,209	8,410	12,486	21,076
Timber & Board	10,342	22,565	31,189	37,728
Wood Products	3,498	10,325	12,801	15,615
Paper & Pulp	15,547	40,516	55,544	70,246
Paper Products	4,790	13,793	21,576	30,230
Printing & Publishing	5,636	12,215	17,631	24,082
Leather & Footwear	5,207	13,069	17,247	27,837
Textiles	7,627	17,944	25,601	33,840
Clothing	2,497	6,044	8,417	12,510
Food	7,501	18,003	20,070	23,685
Drink	14,901	43,041	61,965	86,257
Tobacco	3,538	15,502	26,591	51,387
Total Manufacturing	6,470	16,363	21,774	27,828

TABLE B4.b
Gross Fixed Capital Intensity, UK
(1985 £ per 1000 Hour Worked)

	1960	1973	1979	1989
Chemicals	11,072	26,815	31,752	44,304
Mineral Oil Refining	54,697	115,392	128,345	215,362
Plastic Products	4,069	8,690	11,761	16,963
Rubber Products	6,192	12,308	14,641	20,330
Mineral Products	6,697	15,405	21,108	30,909
Ceramic Goods	3,667	7,884	9,256	12,881
Glass	4,250	10,066	14,980	21,281
Iron & Steel	12,206	24,494	34,202	75,620
Non Ferrous Metals	6,687	14,442	18,001	29,581
Plant & Steelwork	4,347	6,046	6,979	13,229
Mechanical Engineering	4,529	7,769	10,162	16,515
Office Machinery	2,968	6,548	10,323	19,883
Motor Vehicles	5,589	9,476	10,869	26,294
Shipbuilding	3,445	7,352	10,509	24,297
Aerospace	4,577	7,694	8,670	11,613
Electrical Engineering	3,906	6,455	9,290	15,762
Instrument Engineering	1,904	5,384	7,595	12,559
Finished Metal Products	4,819	7,543	10,267	15,550
Toys, Musical & Sports Goods	3,495	6,816	8,311	10,987
Timber & Board	3,894	5,937	10,460	17,806
Wood Products	3,184	4,853	6,695	8,641
Paper & Pulp	12,342	24,937	30,008	56,210
Paper Products	3,931	7,829	11,196	19,465
Printing & Publishing	4,146	7,349	9,305	16,064
Leather & Footwear	2,298	4,285	5,556	8,027
Textiles	4,379	9,251	13,382	17,936
Clothing	1,776	2,798	3,640	5,541
Food	6,790	11,049	14,447	21,061
Drink	8,556	23,102	35,236	61,273
Tobacco	6,679	16,314	21,249	49,563
Total Manufacturing	5,610	10,698	14,009	21,866

TABLE B5.a
Skill Proportions of Workforce: Germany

	1978			1989		
	Upper Level	Inter-mediate	No Quali-fications	Upper Level	Inter-mediate	No Quali-fications
Chemicals	7.4	62.3	30.3	12.0	66.7	21.3
Mineral Oil Refining	6.5	72.2	21.4	14.3	71.4	14.3
Plastic Products	2.9	50.4	46.8	5.1	57.0	38.0
Rubber Products	2.9	55.7	41.4	3.3	61.0	35.7
Mineral Products	1.8	62.0	36.2	3.9	65.9	30.2
Ceramic Goods	3.2	56.2	40.7	4.3	62.9	32.9
Glass	1.3	53.3	45.3	4.0	61.4	34.7
Iron & Steel	2.8	63.3	33.9	4.0	70.2	25.8
Non Ferrous Metals	1.5	65.0	33.5	5.2	61.5	33.3
Plant & Steelwork	3.9	67.7	28.5	4.0	69.8	26.2
Mechanical Engineering	4.3	64.6	31.0	8.2	72.2	19.6
Office Machinery	15.4	64.6	20.0	23.0	64.4	12.6
Motor Vehicles	3.3	67.5	29.2	6.1	68.3	25.6
Shipbuilding	1.8	75.8	22.4	6.1	73.5	20.4
Aerospace	6.9	63.4	29.7	26.9	62.7	10.4
Electrical Engineering	6.1	57.8	36.0	12.8	61.9	25.3
Instrument Engineering	3.3	62.0	34.7	6.3	69.4	24.3
Finished Metal Products	2.0	55.3	42.7	3.1	67.8	29.1
Toys, Musical & Sports Goods	1.1	60.4	38.5	3.8	67.1	29.1
Timber & Board	1.0	68.9	30.1	1.2	74.4	24.4
Wood Products	1.0	71.6	27.4	1.3	71.9	26.8
Paper & Pulp	2.3	51.4	46.2	3.6	64.3	32.1
Paper Products	1.7	70.3	28.0	3.3	64.8	32.0
Printing & Publishing	7.6	67.4	25.0	7.2	72.9	19.9
Leather & Footwear	1.1	43.5	55.4	1.3	60.3	38.5
Textiles	1.3	45.1	53.6	2.2	58.0	39.8
Clothing	0.7	53.8	45.5	2.2	65.5	32.4
Food	1.4	59.4	39.2	1.2	67.0	31.8
Drink	2.5	63.1	34.4	4.0	72.0	24.0
Tobacco	2.8	65.9	31.3	6.7	73.3	20.0
Total Manufacturing	3.6	60.9	35.5	6.6	67.0	26.4

Notes: U = upper level, I = Intermediate level, N = no qualifications

TABLE B5.b
Skill Proportions of Workforce: UK

	1979			1989		
	Upper Level	Inter-mediate	No Qualifications	Upper Level	Inter-mediate	No Qualifications
Chemicals	10.4	21.5	68.1	15.7	31.1	53.1
Mineral Oil Refining	12.3	27.0	60.7	17.8	47.9	34.3
Plastic Products	4.5	22.0	73.5	3.7	30.9	65.4
Rubber Products	3.6	19.6	76.7	5.0	27.4	67.5
Mineral Products	2.1	16.9	81.0	6.2	29.9	64.0
Ceramic Goods	2.0	7.9	90.1	7.0	19.8	73.2
Glass	7.0	15.0	78.0	6.0	36.4	57.5
Iron & Steel	4.0	24.9	71.1	5.2	45.1	49.7
Non Ferrous Metals	3.4	22.1	74.6	5.8	39.6	54.7
Plant & Steelwork	8.4	43.2	48.4	4.7	46.9	48.4
Mechanical Engineering	4.0	34.9	61.1	6.2	47.5	46.2
Office Machinery	16.5	27.9	55.6	27.5	38.4	34.1
Motor Vehicles	2.8	27.5	69.7	5.2	39.0	55.8
Shipbuilding	3.6	52.2	44.2	4.5	64.1	31.5
Aerospace	9.8	40.6	49.6	11.4	56.4	32.2
Electrical Engineering	5.5	24.5	70.0	10.9	35.9	53.2
Instrument Engineering	8.6	24.9	66.5	8.3	40.0	51.7
Finished Metal Products	2.5	23.2	74.3	4.5	34.0	61.6
Toys, Musical & Sports Goods	4.4	14.8	80.8	6.2	27.5	66.4
Timber & Board	2.1	35.7	62.2	3.6	53.6	42.8
Wood Products	1.4	32.8	65.8	3.3	37.1	59.6
Paper & Pulp	2.7	17.4	79.8	9.7	31.4	58.9
Paper Products	3.3	13.8	82.9	4.8	27.7	67.4
Printing & Publishing	6.0	30.1	63.9	13.6	36.1	50.3
Leather & Footwear	2.4	8.5	89.2	2.8	13.7	83.5
Textiles	2.8	13.9	83.3	4.3	16.9	78.8
Clothing	1.7	7.7	90.6	3.6	17.7	78.7
Food	3.4	13.2	83.5	4.2	22.6	73.2
Drink	3.4	16.0	80.6	12.8	23.3	63.9
Tobacco	2.8	15.4	81.8	5.5	32.6	61.9
Total Manufacturing	4.7	24.4	71.0	7.9	35.2	56.8

Notes: U = upper level, I = Intermediate level, N = no qualifications

TABLE B6.a
R&D Expenditure Intensity: Germany
1985 £ per 1000 Hours Worked

	1960	1973	1979	1989
Chemicals	1,179	7,209	11,617	16,581
Mineral Oil Refining	276	1,792	4,956	15,280
Plastic Products	89	410	704	1,375
Rubber Products	115	932	1,590	2,278
Mineral Products	35	224	463	1,131
Ceramic Goods	70	523	1,062	1,218
Glass	55	314	663	2,004
Iron & Steel	141	751	897	1,495
Non Ferrous Metals	157	789	1,051	1,208
Plant & Steelwork	14	265	709	1,826
Mechanical Engineering	87	1,216	3,145	4,092
Office Machinery	632	3,159	8,984	12,183
Motor Vehicles	371	2,809	4,166	8,404
Shipbuilding	20	316	676	1,851
Aerospace	6,090	39,151	53,401	47,202
Electrical Engineering	633	3,915	7,314	10,247
Instrument Engineering	193	1,448	2,748	3,302
Finished Metal Products	117	841	1,582	1,848
Toys, Musical & Sports Goods	63	490	877	1,116
Timber & Board	8	40	101	419
Wood Products	17	76	163	511
Paper & Pulp	25	129	330	666
Paper Products	17	59	148	436
Printing & Publishing	6	23	55	149
Leather & Footwear	67	267	400	369
Textiles	33	120	242	409
Clothing	13	39	58	149
Food	12	78	155	369
Drink	26	182	457	826
Tobacco	43	514	1,386	2,383
Total Manufacturing	225	1,784	3,332	5,288

M. O'Mahony and K. Wagner

TABLE B6.b
R&D Expenditure Intensity: United Kingdom
1985 £ per 1000 Hours Worked

	1960	1973	1979	1989
Chemicals	2,428	6,305	7,696	14,541
Mineral OilRefining	5,293	12,227	10,887	14,837
Plastic Products	807	907	930	571
Rubber Products	394	699	843	951
Mineral Products	253	486	502	588
Ceramic Goods	600	1,266	999	922
Glass	661	1,336	1,311	1,317
Iron & Steel	114	196	177	1,736
Non Ferrous Metals	340	696	532	990
Plant & Steelwork	652	1,128	608	798
Mechanical Engineering	569	1,141	1,096	2,008
Office Machinery	3,477	8,732	17,079	30,609
Motor Vehicles	1,042	2,167	2,108	5292
Shipbuilding	92	587	1,071	313
Aerospace	8,881	19,560	20,724	21,589
Electrical Engineering	2,339	4,949	6,519	14,195
Instrument Engineering	1,325	2,953	2,360	2,552
Finished Metal Products	178	408	397	427
Toys, Musical & Sports Goods	261	527	740	1,649
Timber & Board	81	78	61	179
Wood Products	21	24	17	40
Paper & Pulp	111	199	165	290
Paper Products	134	161	130	182
Printing & Publishing	248	336	252	286
Leather & Footwear	23	42	27	94
Textiles	68	201	234	271
Clothing	27	43	28	87
Food	223	461	577	544
Drink	509	1,096	1,473	1,888
Tobacco	1,232	2,812	3,574	6,654
Total Manufacturing	967	2,090	2,446	4,481

International Productivity Differences
K. Wagner and B. van Ark (editors)

Comparative Productivity in Ireland: The Impact of Transfer Pricing and Foreign Ownership

*J.E. Birnie**
Queen's University Belfast

1. Introduction

The relatively low level of living standards in the Republic of Ireland (ROI) and the chronic nature of this shortfall relative to the UK provide a *prima facie* case for investigation of the ROI's comparative productivity performance.[1] It is also of note that the measurement of the comparative level of output per head in the ROI economy has been the subject of less attention than consideration of the growth of those productivity levels over time (Kennedy, 1971; Baker, 1988; NESC, 1993). This contrasts greatly to the UK case where the reasons for a productivity gap relative to other industrial countries has been the subject of intense research study over at least half a century (summarised in Matthews, 1988; Hitchens and Birnie, 1989; Crafts, 1991, 1993; Broadberry, 1994).

One reason for concentrating on comparisons of ROI productivity levels with those in the UK is therefore to test whether the UK experience can yield any lessons for the ROI. One particular hypothesis would be that the ROI, given a shared administration up to 1921 and extensive institutional legacy from the pre-Independence period of British rule, has also fallen victim to the so-called "British disease" of comparatively low productivity performance especially in

---

* **Acknowledgments**
This paper summarises the results of a comparison of ROI and UK productivity conducted during 1988-1994 (Birnie, 1994). I would like to thank the following who assisted in the development of that research: Bart van Ark, Noel Cahill, David Hitchens, Professor Kieran Kennedy, Liam Kennedy, Mick Lucey, John McMahon, Gerry O'Hanlon, Professor Dermot Mc Aleese, Professor John Spencer and Professor Paul Stoneman. The editors also provided very helpful advice. Eileen Maguire very kindly produced the text in the required WP format. The usual disclaimer applies.
[1] The subject of this chapter is the productivity record of the industries located in the twenty six southern counties of Ireland which gained independence from the United Kingdom in 1921. The six counties of Northern Ireland remained within the United Kingdom and the comparative productivity of Northern Ireland industry is considered in Hitchens and Birnie (1994). The modern designation of the state, Republic of Ireland, is applied anachronistically throughout the post First World War period.

manufacturing (Hitchens and Birnie, 1994).[2]

None of this is to deny that comparisons of ROI to continental European economies are also of interest and we include some in this paper, linking our own estimate of ROI productivity compared to the UK with the results of earlier studies which indicated the UK's productivity relative to another economy. Where the results of earlier studies allow, the ROI is compared with the productivity performance of the United States. In most sectors the USA performance can be taken to represent best practise in the world economy.[3]

ROI Comparative Living Standards

Living standards in the ROI have persistently lagged behind those of most other industrial economies (Kennedy, 1993). This is significant given that relative living standards are in part related, as a number of American commentators have noted, to the comparative productivity of the economy (Baumol, Blackman and Wolff, 1989; Porter, 1990). Admittedly, the gap between levels of GDP per capita in the ROI and the average for the UK as a whole has narrowed albeit the progress over almost seven decades has been quite modest. In the case of the ROI most of these gains have been concentrated in the period since 1986 and especially during 1989-1992.[4]

Given the relative economic decline of the UK economy (Crafts, 1991), the ROI was failing to sustain significant catch up relative to other industrial economies such that by the end of the 1990s it represented one of the poorest parts of the western industrial world. The relatively low standing of levels of GDP per capita in the ROI by comparison with the European Community (EC) average is illustrated by the following table which also includes data on the other Objective I members of the EC.

The ROI's level of GDP per capita is equivalent to about 70 per cent that of the average for the EC as a whole and the economy made little progress in narrowing the GDP per capita relative to the more prosperous members of the EC during the 1970s and 1980s. Comparisons based on GDP per head in fact overstate the ROI's relative position given the substantial outflow of net factor income in recent years. The ROI's performance in terms of comparative GNP per capita is even worse and, as the table shows, is broadly similar to that of two other peripheral members of the EC (Portugal and Greece) whilst having fallen

---

[2] An earlier study came to this conclusion regarding Northern Ireland. See Hitchens, Wagner and Birnie (1990).

[3] On the extent to which this position has been challenged by Japan, see van Ark and Pilat (1993) and van Ark (1993).

[4] ROI GDP per capita as a percentage of the UK average level stood at 52 in 1911, 51 in 1926, 54 in 1973, 61 in 1986 and 76 in 1991. Commission of the European Community (1992, 1994), Kennedy (1994).

TABLE 1
ROI comparative living standards relative to the EC
(EC12 average = 100)

	GDP per capita		GNP per capita	
	1986	1990	1986	1990*
ROI	63	69	56	62
UK	104	100	104	103
Greece	56	47	56	n.a.
Spain	73	75	72	n.a.
Portugal	53	56	51	n.a.

* Comparative GNP per capita estimates were not readily available for 1990, however, ROI GNP can be estimated to have been 60 per cent of the UK level.
Source: NESC (1989), Kennedy (1993), Murshed, Noonan, Thanki, Gudgin and Roper (1993), SOEC (1993).

behind that of Spain. In fact, previous studies have suggested that the ROI has been outperformed in terms of growth of GDP per capita by the other low income economies of Western Europe which have constituted a so-called "convergence club" (O'Grada and O'Rourke, 1993; Walsh, 1993).[5] This illustrates the dimensions of the economic problem confronting policy makers in the ROI. It is no longer simply a question of catching up with Great Britain, let alone West Germany, but also with some other European economies which traditionally would have been considered as backward.

Comparative Aggregate Productivity

While GDP per capita in the ROI in the early 1990s stands at roughly 70 per cent of the UK average, the relative aggregate productivity achieved is more impressive. GDP per worker has risen to about 90-100 per cent of the level attained in the UK (Birnie, 1994). Similarly, GDP per worker was 89 per cent of the EC average in 1990 whereas GDP per capita was only 69 per cent of the EC average. The relatively low living standards attained are partly a function

---

[5] GNP is probably a better indicator of relative living standards in the ROI context since it makes allowance for the substantial outflow of profits from, and payment of interest on international debt by, the ROI economy. However, data availability usually implies that long run comparisons are restricted to the use of GDP statistics (Murshed, Noonan, Thanki, Gudgin and Roper, 1993).

of comparatively high dependency ratios[6] and low participation rates[7] as well as the relatively low productivity of those who are in work (Haughton, 1991).

It should be stressed that the low participation rate is itself partly the result of relatively low productivity, i.e. a lack of competitiveness constrains the growth of the tradeable sectors and therefore these activities employ fewer people in the ROI than might have been expected though productivity growth could in principle occur without any expansion of tradeable activities, for example through the shedding of surplus labour (O'Donnell and Kenny, 1993). The fact that the ROI is the only Western European country where the total number of persons employed today is lower than it was in the 1920s testifies to dismal performance as well as the structural disadvantage arising from the initial preponderance of the declining agricultural sector (Kennedy, 1993). The lack of employment growth in turn reflects the inadequate expansion of the high productivity sector, particularly manufacturing.

How our Results Differ from Previous Comparisons

Only a small number of previous studies of ROI comparative productivity have been made (NESC, 1975; Ferris, 1989; Roy, 1989). Our own study sought to move beyond those earlier comparisons in several respects. For example, as far as the data allowed, an industry of origin approach was adopted. This meant that output and employment data were taken whenever possible from a common statistical source such as the *ROI Census of Industrial Production* (or its UK counterpart, the *Census of Production*) so as to ensure greater reliability. Attempts were also made to make detailed comparisons of output price levels, i.e. unit value ratios, so as to facilitate estimates of comparative real output per head. Productivity levels were compared at as fine a degree of disaggregation as was possible as well as for broader branches and sectors. In addition to such cross-sectional comparisons there was also a longitudinal review of comparative productivity levels. Where the data allowed benchmark comparisons were made for the mid 1930s, late 1960s and mid to late 1980s. Such comparisons allowed the development of ROI comparative industrial productivity to be traced through the key stages of post-Independence development: protectionism in the mid 1930s, the onset of free trade during the 1960s, and the impact of large scale inward investment by the mid 1980s.

---

[6] Dependent age groups (i.e. less than 15 or older than 64) represented 39.3 per cent of the total ROI population in 1988 compared to 32.7 per cent of the EC12 population.

[7] The employed labour force represented only 30 per cent of the ROI's population in 1986 compared to 43 per cent in the UK (the unweighted average for the US, Japan, West Germany, Canada and France was 43.6 per cent).

Summary of Principal ROI/UK Comparative Productivity Results

Table 2 summarises our productivity results. It also includes an assessment of the likely reliability of such measurements, namely A is good; B is moderate; C is poor. These assessments are necessarily somewhat subjective but have been guided by data issues such as the extent of coverage of sample price comparisons

TABLE 2
ROI Comparative Productivity by Industrial Sector, 1935-1990
(Net Output per Head as a per cent of the Level in the UK, UK=100)

	1935	1968	1985	1990*
Manufacturing	88^B	82^A	128^B	151^C
Agriculture[a]	61^C	55^B	77^B	80^B
Construction	n.a.	66^{bC}	91^{cC}	96^C
Mining and quarrying	65^B	132^A	57^A	53^{C1989}
Utilities	54^A	47^A	27^{dA}	39^{B1989}
Transport	n.a.	64^{eC}	57$^{fB1986-89}$	
Telecommunications	n.a.	n.a.	54^{gB1987}	
Postal services	n.a.	n.a.	62^{hA1987}	

Reliability of the measure: A = good, B = modest, C = poor
* Estimates were based on relative prices of principal products, i.e. unit value ratios, and geometric averages if both UK and ROI weights available. Indices of the change in the volume of net output during 1985-1990 and of the change in the level of employment were used to update the 1985 benchmark comparisons (details in Birnie, 1994).
[a] Fishing and forestry are not included in these comparisons. However, given the relatively small size of these activities in both the ROI and UK the comparative productivity ratio for agriculture alone is a good indicator of that for the whole of agriculture, fishing and forestry. The 1935 comparison in fact relates to 1938 (the result of the comparison for 1955 was projected backwards using national series of the volume of output and employment).
[b] Using the comparative output price level of the building products industry to proxy for the comparative output price level of the building and construction sector.
[c] Gross value added per head using the building products industry unit value ratio as a proxy for output prices.
[d] When the high productivity level gas extraction industry is excluded in both the ROI and UK the ROI comparative productivity rises to 45, which implies a comparative productivity of 58 in 1989.
[e] Weighted average of physical productivity ratios for railways (1968), buses (1968) and road freight (1969).
[f] Weighted average of physical productivity ratios for railways (1989), buses (1986), road freight (1987-1988), ports (1986), airports (1988) and airlines (1989).
[g] Telecommunications revenues per head in 1987 compared using PPP.
[h] Physical productivity of postal services in 1987 (items carried).
Sources: *Agricultural Census* (UK) and *Agricultural Survey* (ROI), *Census of Industrial Production* (ROI) and *Census of Production* (UK), all for relevant years. SOEC (1988a, 1988b), Commission of the European Communities (1992), Department of Transport (1990) and Birnie (1994).

or the likely quality of the weighting procedures used. Most attention is given to the benchmark comparisons for 1935, 1968 and 1985 which formed the focus of earlier attention. However, where indices of the change in output and employment were available these were used to update the results to 1990.

Benchmark productivity measures were established for all the sectors in the mid 1980s. Sectoral comparative productivity levels ranged from 27 per cent of the level attained by the UK in utilities up to 128 per cent of the UK level in manufacturing. Manufacturing was the only sector where ROI productivity was indicated to exceed that of the UK counterpart. While ROI productivity in construction was close to that of the UK, productivity in all the other sectors was substantially lower than that in the UK. Whilst it was not possible in every case to make comparisons for 1935 and 1968 a number of trends could be identified. In manufacturing there was strong productivity convergence between 1968 and 1985 and the same applied to agriculture though agricultural productivity remained substantially lower than that in the UK at the end of the period. There was probably some productivity convergence in construction during the same period.[8] On the other hand, in mining and quarrying, utilities and transport the productivity shortfall relative to the UK increased between 1968 and 1985 and perhaps over a longer period as well.

Table 2 shows, where the mid 1980s results have been brought forward to later years by using the available data on the growth of the volume of output and employment, the broad conclusions remain the same. Indeed, the ROI's productivity advantage in manufacturing relative to the UK is even further enhanced.

2. ROI Manufacturing Productivity Comparisons in 1985

Deviations from the Unit Value Ratio Method

In one sense the quality of data used for the manufacturing productivity comparisons in 1985 improved relative to those for the years 1935 and 1968: the available data allowed the level of disaggregation to be greater, namely 70 industries and activities within manufacturing compared to only 42 in 1968 and 34 in 1935. However, whereas in the case of the 1935 and 1968 comparisons it was possible to rely exclusively on production census based unit values (UVRs) to measure comparative output prices and hence real output, in the case of 1985 the extent to which UVRs could be estimated was much more limited.[9] Van Ark

---

[8] Uncertainty arises because the basis of comparisons differs between the two years.
[9] The matched products on which the calculations of UVRs were based represented 77 per cent of total ROI gross output in manufacturing in 1935, 45 per cent in 1968 and 15 per cent in 1985. All these shares were based on ROI sales weights. Using UK sales weights the rates of coverage were: 31 per cent in 1935, 24 per cent in 1968 and

(1993) has discussed why UVRs are the preferred measure, and so UVRs were used for those industries and activities where the data allowed them to be estimated.[10]

In the absence of UVRs the next best measure was to proxy the UVR of a given industry or activity by the known UVR of a closely related branch or activity. Where such a proxy was not available, the next best measure was an estimate of relative export prices (RXPs) as provided by SOEC (1986). There were several reasons why these were likely to be reliable indicators of UVRs. The extent to which the RXPs of matched products covered the total sales of each activity in the ROI was generally high which reflected the high export orientation of much of ROI manufacturing. Moreover, for those activities where the results of the two methods of comparison could be compared the estimated UVRs and RXPs were usually close to each other.

If there were no UVR or RXP data then an expenditure PPP was used. The limitations of the use of PPPs for industrial productivity comparisons have been noted in van Ark (1993).[11] Nevertheless, in a few cases PPPs were preferred to the available RXP measures, this was for example the case when the coverage of the RXPs was low, i.e. less than 10 per cent of total activity sales, or where

TABLE 3
Methods of Output Price Comparison Used in 1985
Manufacturing Productivity Comparison

Price indicator	Number of activities where it was used
Unit Value Ratios (UVRs)	17
UVR proxied by the UVR of another activity	3
Relative Export Prices (RXPs)	33
RXP proxied by the RXP of another activity	2
PPPs	14
Exchange rate	1
Total manufacturing	70

---

3 per cent in 1985. As noted in the text, the very low rates of coverage in 1985 led to the UVRs being supplemented by a range of other indicators of relative output price levels (i.e. RXPs and PPPs). Use of the range of price indicators increased coverage in 1985 to 35 per cent, using ROI weights, and 19 per cent, using UK weights.

[10] Van Ark (1993) pointed at consistency of UVR data with the source of measures of productivity levels and the closeness to an "ideal" measure of ex-factory prices. See also chapter 2 in this volume.

[11] They may include transport and retail margins and imports and they exclude intermediate goods and that part of domestic output which is exported.

RXPs indicated a widely different result according to whether ROI or UK export sales were used to weight up the individual product RXPs. Finally, for a single activity (fur) the average market exchange rate was used in the absence of any UVR, RXP or PPP data.

Table 3 summarises the methods of price comparison which were used. Having thus selected the best price comparison for each activity comparative price levels for total manufacturing were estimated. The price ratios for the 70 individual branches were weighted using first ROI net output weights and then weights for the UK. A geometric average was then taken of these two results.

ROI Productivity Compared to International Best Practice

Comparisons of the productivity of the ROI with that of the UK form the main subject of this paper. However, given that in most cases UK productivity levels themselves fell short of the standards of international best practice, ROI productivity performance should also be placed in a wider perspective. In general UK manufacturing productivity levels are lower than those in continental West Europe, such as in West Germany, the Netherlands and France (van Ark, 1990a, 1990b; O'Mahony, 1992), which in turn are less than those in the USA (van Ark, 1992).[12] Table 4 presents our own results updated to 1987 alongside those of van Ark for the UK relative to the USA in the same year so as to illustrate the implied comparative productivity of the ROI relative to the USA.

A comparison of this kind which combines the results of two different studies should be regarded with caution. Although the same method of comparison of real output was used in both cases, the UVRs between the UK and the ROI and between the UK and the USA are not likely to be transitive. This means that for each matched industry the sample of products being considered could be different in the case of the USA/UK comparison as opposed to the ROI/UK comparison. The potential for further unreliability was introduced by the fact that our results related to 1985 whereas van Ark's results to 1987. It was therefore necessary to use ROI and UK Census data for 1985 and 1987 to update the ROI/UK productivity ratio to the later year. Nominal net output data, employment series and product price indices were used to estimate the growth of output per head in real terms between 1985 and 1987. The variability in results derives from the indices of real output change, especially those for the ROI. Previous studies have confirmed that direct productivity comparisons in a given year are usually more reliable than the implied results produced by the updating (or "backcasting") of the results for an earlier (or later) year. Measures of ROI real net output are especially sensitive to variations in the number of plants in operation. The absolute size of output in the ROI is small and so that inward investment projects

---

[12] See also van Ark in chapter 2 of this volume.

can strongly affect the level of output.

Notwithstanding the qualifications to the results certain conclusions seem clear. The average productivity of manufacturing in the ROI is indicated to have been about seven-tenths of the level in the USA in 1987. Around this average

TABLE 4

Comparative Manufacturing Productivity (Net Output Person Engaged)
ROI, UK and USA, 1987

	ROI/UK 1985[a] (UK=100)	ROI/UK 1987[b] (UK=100)	USA/UK[c] (UK=100)	ROI/USA[d] (USA=100)
Mineral Oil Refining	28	53	72	73
Non-Metallic Mineral Products	119	101	138	73
Chemicals and Man-made Fibres	174	147	174	84
Production and Preliminary Processing of Metals and Metal articles	86	82	166	50
Mechanical Engineering, Office & Data Processing Machinery, Motor Vehicles and Other Means of Transport	182	232	176	132
Electrical Engineering	118	146	209	70
Food Products	122	148	255	58
Drink	108	96	168	57
Tobacco Products	93	92	183	51
Textile Industry	97	100	170	58
Clothing	79	73	198	37
Footwear and Leather Products	104	82	142	58
Timber and Wooden Furniture	81	91	193	47
Paper and Paper Products, Printing and Publishing	74	69	241	29
Rubber and Plastics	112	107	128	84
Instrument Engineering, Other Manufactures	188	208	258	81
Total Manufacturing	128	137	187	69

[a] Derived as in our own productivity comparisons shown in Hitchens and Birnie (1994). The definitions of industries are chosen so as to be compatible with those used by van Ark, (1993). ROI/UK comparative productivity for 1985 was estimated using unit value ratios.

[b] 1985 results were updated using indices of real net output (1985-1987, estimated by using series of nominal net output deflated by appropriate wholesale price indices) and employment.

[c] Taken from van Ark (1993).

[d] A simple division of our own estimate of the ROI/UK comparative productivity for 1987 by van Ark's for the USA/UK comparative productivity for that year.

Source: As in text.

there was considerable variation in performance. Only one major branch of manufacturing, i.e. mechanical engineering, office and data processing machinery, motor vehicles and other means of transport is indicated to have a productivity advantage relative to the USA in 1987. The comparative performance of this industry was dominated by the very high productivity levels of office equipment and data processing machinery which in turn reflects the impact of foreign owned plants in the ROI. In a further four industries, mineral oil refining, chemicals plus man-made fibres, rubber and plastics, and instrument engineering plus other manufacturing, ROI comparative productivity levels are implied to exceed the average for manufacturing as a whole, i.e. the comparative productivity ratios were greater than 69 per cent. In the case of chemicals performance would be driven by the very high productivity levels of externally owned plants in pharmaceuticals. Externally owned plants in instrument engineering would have a similar effect, and in the case of rubber and plastics it is notable that the US productivity advantage is small relative to both the ROI and UK.

The remaining branches are predominantly indigenously owned and in some cases could be considered as operating within the more sheltered part of manufacturing, i.e. the ratio of imports and exports to output is relatively low in branches such as paper, printing and publishing or timber and furniture (O'Malley, 1989). In these sectors comparative productivity levels relative to the USA are implied to be low, for example less than two-thirds of the American productivity level in food, drink, tobacco and textiles and only about one-third of the USA level in clothing and paper, printing and publishing. One could conclude that ROI manufacturing productivity levels generally lag those in the USA by a substantial margin except for the very high productivity industries such as pharmaceuticals and office equipment and data processing machinery which are almost entirely foreign owned.[13]

Although comparisons of the ROI with the USA are of interest in placing ROI performance relative to standards which are still, notwithstanding catch up by Japan, representative in most cases of best practice at the world level (van Ark and Pilat, 1993; Baily, 1993), it is also important given such considerations as the Single Market and any moves towards European Monetary Union to indicate comparative productivity relative to major competitors within the EC. The following table illustrates the implied comparative productivity of the ROI in 1987 relative to West Germany. Once again, our own comparisons using UVRs in 1985 were updated using net output, output price and employment data and set alongside West Germany/UK comparisons (O'Mahony, 1992; van Ark, 1993).

---

[13] The importance of ownership type and the associated possibility of transfer pricing are considered as potential explanations of comparative labour productivity, which is more fully discussed in section 3.

TABLE 5
ROI Comparative Manufacturing Productivity (Net Output Person Engaged)
ROI, UK and West Germany, 1987

	ROI/UK 1985[a] (UK=100)	ROI/UK 1987[b] (UK=100)	West Germany/UK[c] (UK=100)	ROI/West Germany[d] (WG=100)
Mineral Oil Refinery	28	53	n.a.	n.a.
Non-Metallic Mineral Products	119	101	103	98
Chemicals and Manmade Fibres	174	147	89	166
Production and Preliminary Processing of Metals	74	76	96	79
Metal Articles	98	94	119	79
Mechanical Engineering and Office & Data Processing Machinery	233	310	121	256
Motor Vehicles and Other Means of Transport	68	70	119	59
Electrical Engineering	118	146	90	161
Food Products, Drink and Tobacco Products	117	139	114	122
Textile Industry	98	100	104	95
Clothing, Footwear and Leather	79	73	113	65
Timber and Wooden Furniture	81	91	148	62
Paper and Paper Products, Printing and Publishing	74	69	188	37
Rubber and Plastics	112	107	114	94
Instrument Engineering	200	216	142	153
Total Manufacturing	128	137	113	121

[a] Derived as in our own productivity comparisons shown in Hitchens and Birnie (1994) (the definitions of industries are chosen so as to be compatible with those used by van Ark (1993), two outstanding definitional differences are the exclusion of publishing and miscellaneous manufacturing from the West Germany/UK estimates for total manufacturing, and the exclusion of publishing from the West Germany/UK estimate for paper etc.). ROI/UK comparative productivity for 1985 was estimated using unit value ratios.

[b] The 1985 results were updated using indices of real net output (1985-1987, estimated by using series of nominal net output deflated by appropriate wholesale price indices) and employment.

[c] Taken from van Ark (1993).

[d] A simple division of our own estimate of the ROI/UK comparative productivity for 1987 by van Ark (1993) for the West Germany/UK comparative productivity for that year.

Source: As in text.

By 1987 manufacturing in the UK had made considerable progress in narrowing the productivity gap relative to West Germany, which has been called "productivity miracle" of the 1980s. By implication average ROI manufacturing productivity in 1987 is indicated to have been 20 per cent greater than the level attained in West Germany. The results in the table indicate that as in the case of the ROI/USA comparisons, high performance in the ROI is concentrated in those sectors where inward investment has been particularly important. For example, the productivity of mechanical engineering and office and data processing machinery in the ROI is indicated to have been more than two and a half times the West German level while the productivity of chemicals and man-made fibres and electrical engineering is indicated to be about two-thirds higher than the West German level. ROI instrument engineering has a productivity level about one and a half times that of its counterpart in Germany.

Perhaps more surprising are the relatively good productivity performances of food, drink and tobacco, non-metallic mineral products, and the textile industry. In contrast, the ROI is implied to have low comparative productivities relative to West Germany in paper and printing (less than one-half of the West German level), timber and furniture, motor vehicles and transport equipment and clothing (about two-thirds of the West German level).

3. The Contribution of Transfer Pricing and Foreign Ownership

Transfer pricing, i.e. manipulation of the intra-company distribution of profits within an international firm in order to minimise its total tax liability, in principle could occur in any economy where international firms are present though a number of commentators have cast doubt on whether it is common in practice (Hood and Young, 1979; Dunning, 1981). However, the ROI is usually considered to offer great potential for transfer pricing given the low rate of taxation on company profits (10 per cent), the high proportion of total manufacturing in external ownership and the extent to which the subsidiaries in the ROI either buy from, or sell to affiliates within the same firm. If transfer pricing does occur it would take the form of artificially high output prices or artificially low input prices on these intra-firm sales. Mc Aleese (1977) noted that USA subsidiaries in the ROI sold 77 per cent of their exports to affiliates and bought 46 per cent of their material inputs from the same thus providing scope for transfer pricing.

The Growth of the Foreign Owned Manufacturing Sector

The growth of the foreign owned sector in the ROI has increased the possibility of transfer pricing. This growth has received extensive attention from commentators (O'Malley, 1989) who have noted that this component of manufacturing has become the main driving force for the growth of output, employment, and exports of the sector as a whole (Foley, 1991). The manufacturing sector in the ROI is notably more dependent on externally controlled firms than is the case for its counterparts in the major industrialised economies. In 1985 foreign owned plants represented 40 per cent of total manufacturing employment and by 1988 this share had increased to 44 per cent (*Census of Industrial Production*). Their share of total net output was even higher, namely 63 per cent in 1985 and 69 per cent in 1989, which is a reflection of the relatively high productivity of the foreign sector. In 1987 almost three-quarters of manufacturing exports were produced by foreign subsidiaries.

In contrast, in 1985 foreign owned firms represented 14 per cent of total manufacturing employment in the UK and 16 per cent of the total in West Germany (*Census of Production*; Olle, 1985). Dunning (1981) estimated that foreign firms accounted for 31 per cent of total UK manufacturing exports. The extent of foreign ownership in the ROI compares with that of such newly industrialised economies as Singapore and exceeds that in other small European economies.[14] The capital assets of foreign affiliates were equivalent to 21.7 per cent of GNP in 1981 compared to 3.0 per cent in Denmark (1983), 4.4. per cent in Austria (1981), 0.9 per cent in Finland (1983), 0.9 per cent in Sweden (1981) and 8.2 per cent in Switzerland. Employment in foreign affiliates represented 34.6 per cent of total manufacturing employment in 1981 compared to 14.8 per cent in Denmark (1984), 26 per cent in Austria (1981), 3.7 per cent in Finland (1981) and 5.7 per cent in Sweden (1975-1976) (NESC, 1992).

Analysis of trends in the ROI's comparative productivity at the level of branches of manufacturing strongly implies an association between inward investment and productivity catch up relative to the UK (Hitchens and Birnie, 1994). Indeed, the comparatively high level of productivity of ROI manufacturing on average is primarily the responsibility of foreign owned firms in a limited number of branches of manufacturing, especially pharmaceuticals, electronics, office and data processing machinery and miscellaneous foods, such as concentrates for the soft drinks industry.

Table 6 shows the gulf separating the average productivity performance of ROI-owned and externally owned firms in the ROI. During the late 1980s levels of output per head in the external sector were about twice as high as those achieved by manufacturing in the UK. However, productivity levels in the indigenous sector remained 15-20 per cent below those in the UK. Table 7 provides detail on the comparative productivity performance of externally and indigenously owned plants at a disaggregated level.

In 1989 the productivity of externally owned firms in the ROI was more than twice as high as the manufacturing average in the UK on the basis of market ex-

---

[14] In Singapore 70 per cent of manufacturing output and 82 per cent of exports was realised by foreign owned firms, Foley and McAleese (1991).

J.E. Birnie

TABLE 6
ROI's Comparative Manufacturing Productivity by
Ownership Type (ROI/UK, UK=100)*

	1985	1987	1988
Indigenous ROI	81 (75)**	85	79
External ROI	198 (184)**	211	210
All ROI	128 (119)**	139	137

*   Net output per head using average market exchange rates. Given that the data by ownership type was not also broken down by size of establishment, the ROI estimates of net output per head include establishments in the 3-19 employees size band while the UK data does not.
** Using the estimated average unit price for total manufacturing. Average unit prices would ideally have been re-estimated for the indigenous and externally owned sectors separately. This would have made allowance for the different product compositions of the two sectors.

Source: ROI: *Census of Industrial Production* 1985, 1987 and 1988; UK: *Census of Production* 1985, 1987 and 1988.

change rates (PPP or unit price data not yet being available for that year). However, the average productivity of indigenous firms in the ROI was only 85 per cent that of average manufacturing productivity in the UK. It was also striking that the ROI retained a substantial productivity advantage when the externally owned firms in the ROI are compared to the foreign owned part of manufacturing in the UK, namely 69 per cent higher. In contrast the productivity of indigenous firms in the ROI was only 92 per cent of the level attained by domestically owned firms in UK manufacturing. The so-called high technology activities stand out as the cases where the gap between the foreign owned plants in the ROI and those in the UK is largest. It is in these cases that transfer pricing is most likely to be occurring. In almost all cases the productivity of indigenous firms falls short of that of the counterpart plants in the UK. By implication the spread between productivity levels in the foreign and domestically owned sectors is much wider in the ROI than in the UK. On average externally owned plants in the ROI have a productivity level more than two and a half times that of indigenous plants, this compared to the UK where the productivity of foreign owned plants is one and a half times that of the indigenous plants. However, it is the high technology activities which once again stand out as cases where something unusual seems to be happening in the ROI: productivity in the foreign owned plants is between twice and eight times that of the indigenous plants. In miscellaneous foods, i.e. reflecting the impact of the cola concentrates activity, externally owned productivity is thirteen times that of domestic.

TABLE 7
Comparative Productivity by Ownership Type (Net Output per Person Engaged),
ROI/UK (UK=100), 1989*

	ROI/UK				External/ indigenous (indigen.=100)	
	Exter-nal/all[a]	Indige-nous/all[b]	Extern./extern.[c]	Indigen./indigen.[d]	ROI[e]	UK[e]
High Technology Branches:[f]						
Pharmaceuticals	345	44	n.a.	n.a.	791	n.a.
Office and Data Processing Machinery	286	65	288	65	441	99
Electrical Engineering	281	75	249	77	375	116
Instrument Engineering	202	88	179	91	229	116
Medium Technology:[f]						
Production and Preliminary Processing of Metals[g]	106	93	113	92	114	92
Chemicals[h]	93	89	85	93	105	115
Mechanical Engineering[i]	134	78	104	83	173	137
Motor vehicles	120	35	83	47	339	194
Other Means of Transport	92	104	112	103	89	82
Rubber and Plastics and Other Manufacturing	118	98	90	104	120	140
Low Technology:[f]						
Non-Metallic Mineral Products	164	82	158	83	199	104
Metal Articles	115	82	81	85	139	146
Food, Drink and Tobacco Products[j]	126	106	71	117	119	196
Miscellaneous Foodstuffs	581	45	n.a.	n.a.	1,303	n.a.
Textile Industry	106	91	70	94	115	154
Clothing, Footwear and Leather	84	89	49	91	95	176
Timber and Wooden Furniture	197	75	130	76	264	153
Paper and Paper Products, Printing and Publishing	90	84	67	89	108	145
Total Manufacturing	238	85	169	92	278	152

* Average market exchange rate used in all cases.
[a] ROI externally owned plants compared to the average for the entire industry in the UK.
[b] ROI indigenously owned plants compared to the average for the entire activity in the UK.
[c] ROI externally owned plants compared to the externally owned in the UK.
[d] ROI indigenously owned plants compared to the indigenously owned in the UK.
[e] Ratio of externally owned productivity to that in indigenously owned plants.

Notes and sources table 7 continued:
f As classified by NESC (1993a) on the basis of data on performance at the OECD level.
g Including boilermaking in the ROI but not in the UK.
h Excluding pharmaceuticals in the ROI but not in the UK.
i Including boilermaking in the UK but not in the ROI.
j Excluding miscellaneous foodstuffs in the ROI but not in the UK.
Source: *Census of Industrial Production 1989* (ROI), *Census of Production 1989* (UK), and NESC (1993).

O'Leary (1984) argued that the price of output and hence the level of value added of foreign subsidiaries in the ROI might be raised because that price included an implicit charge for marketing and R and D activities completed within the same firm but outside of the ROI. The impact of such pricing policies on measured value added would be similar to transfer pricing though the firm would not necessarily have the same intention to redistribute profits within the company.[15] In such cases the very high value added per head of international firms in the ROI does not reflect financial manipulation but rather the fact that as plants mainly concentrate on production, some of the costs incurred in bringing the final product to the market are carried elsewhere within the organisation.

Below we adopt three methodologies which afford rough indications of the maximum extent of intra-company "transfer pricing" by the foreign owned subsidiaries in the Republic. While these methods are relatively crude it is significant that they all three indicate that even on the most generous assumptions transfer pricing can explain only part of the ROI's productivity advantage.

Method 1. Using International Best Practice Productivity Levels

The very high levels of productivity attained by certain branches of manufacturing in the ROI, particularly those relating to computers, soft drink concentrates and pharmaceuticals where output is almost entirely from externally owned plants, has often been taken as *prima facie* evidence that substantial transfer pricing is in fact happening (Foley, 1991). What stands out is that the productivity levels for some industries and activities are high even by the standards of best practice economies.

Table 8 illustrates the ROI productivity advantage when comparison is made at a lower level of aggregation albeit this data is restricted to EC countries. There could still be some heterogeneity between the activities being compared, in particular in the case of miscellaneous foodstuffs which in the ROI is domi-

---

[15] The ROI subsidiary might make a royalty payment to cover these marketing or R and D charges incurred outside of the ROI. Indeed, in the case of USA firms the domestic revenue authorities may force them to do this.

TABLE 8
Comparative Productivity in Selected Industries, ROI Relative to the EC,
1988 (Gross Value Added per Employee at 1,000 ECU)*

	Pharmaceuticals	Office & Data Processing Machinery	Miscellaneous foodstuffs
ROI	166.0	165.4	347.8
Belgium[1987]	56.5	39.0	39.5
Denmark	67.7	43.8	51.6
West Germany	52.4	50.5	40.4
France	50.3	79.5	44.4
Italy	57.0	78.6	50.5
UK	63.4	70.4	40.4
EC-12	54.3	n.a.	42.5
ROI as % EC average	306	n.a.	818
ROI as % next highest	245	208	674

* Using exchange rate.
Source: NESC (1993).

nated by a single plant making cola concentrates for soft drinks. Never-theless the measured productivity gaps between the ROI and the rest of the EC are sufficiently large to suggest either transfer pricing or a "genuine" productivity advantage when like is compared with like.

It might be argued that the substantial superiority of the ROI relative to the rest of the EC in these industries is less surprising when the large representation of USA owned plants in these activities in the ROI is considered. We have already indicated that in 1987 ROI comparative productivity in a combination of engineering industries, including office and data processing machinery, stood at least equal to that in the USA and was considerably better than that attained by counterpart branches in West Germany.[16] If it is argued that American industry does indeed represent the frontier of international best practice (van Ark and Pilat, 1993) then the apparent ROI advantage could be attributed to transfer pricing. However, it should be stressed that the comparisons of the ROI with the USA and West Germany are at a high level of aggregation. The ROI advantage could therefore be a function of a structural advantage within each broadly de-

---

[16] In a combination of chemicals industries, including pharmaceuticals, value added per head was indicated as 84 per cent of the USA level but considerably higher than the level attained by the West German industry.

J.E. Birnie

TABLE 9
ROI/USA Comparative Productivity Performance, 1985

	USA			ROI		
	Value Added (mln. IR £)[b]	Persons Employed[a] (000s)	Value Added per Head (IR £)[b]	Net Output (mln. IR £)	Persons Employed[a] (000s)	Net Output per Head (IR £.)
Pharmaceuticals[c]	1,1432.1	128	89,313	650.8	4.3	151,200
*Implied Transfer Pricing in the ROI**				265.7		
Office and Data Processing Machinery[d]	25,614.8	407	62,936	631.4	6.1	104,003
*Implied Transfer Pricing in the ROI**				248.7		
Radio & TV Receivers incl. Microelectronic Circuits[e]	28,035.6	617	45,439	185.9	2.9	64,059
*Implied Transfer Pricing in the ROI**				54.1		
Miscellaneous Foodstuffs	n.a.	n.a.	98,806[f] 30,705[g]	336.3	2.1	161,527

* Estimated by method described in the text.
a Total number in employment. The US industrial census attempted to provide a complete coverage while its ROI counterpart includes plants with 3 or more persons engaged).
b Converted at the average market exchange rate; IR £ 1 = 1.067 $.
c Matched with USA 283 Drugs.
d Matched with USA 357 Office and computing machinery.
e Matched with USA 365, 367 Radio and TV equipment.
f USA data was not disclosed for miscellaneous foodstuffs (or soft drink concentrates) separately. This figure is the level of value added per head in 208 Beverages.
g An estimate of US productivity based on the assumption that US miscellaneous foodstuffs productivity was in the same proportion to drinks productivity as was the case in the ROI, i.e. the ratio of net output per head in NACE 417-418 and 423, to that in NACE 424-428; this was 3.1: 1.

fined industry in terms of a greater representation of activities which generally have a high level of output per head. For example, the share of fine chemicals within ROI chemicals might be larger than in the US.

Ideally ROI and USA productivity levels would be compared directly using the kind of Census based approach, i.e. the industry of origin approach, which we have already applied to the ROI/UK comparisons. The following comparisons should be taken as indicative of what such a comparison might produce.[17] For all their limitations these figures do confirm that the ROI has a substantial productivity advantage in at least three of these activities, the case of miscellaneous foodstuffs being more doubtful. Indeed, these are the only cases where the ROI has a manufacturing productivity advantage relative to the USA. Total manufacturing in the ROI was indicated to have a productivity level only 60 per cent that of its counterpart in the USA.

Table 9 shows that in 1985 productivity in ROI pharmaceuticals was at a level 169 per cent that of its counterpart in the USA, office and data processing machinery productivity was 165 per cent higher, and radio and TV receivers, etc., 141 per cent greater. If it is assumed that these measured productivity advantages are entirely the consequence of transfer pricing then it is possible to calculate by how much net output in the ROI would be lower if output per head was equal to that of the US counterpart. The total gain to ROI net output is estimated to have been 589 million IR £.[18] This would have been equivalent to 11 per cent of the measured net output of ROI plants with 3 or more persons engaged. In the absence of transfer pricing on this scale the ROI/UK comparative productivity ratio for total manufacturing would decline from 128 per cent of the UK level (as estimated in section 1) to 114 per cent.

Method 2. Using Net Output/Gross Output Ratios

This second method focuses on comparison of the ratio of net output to gross output in the ROI and UK. Since transfer pricing involves the inflation of value added of the international firms by either increasing the selling price of outputs of the ROI subsidiary or by decreasing the buying price of inputs it will, *ceteris paribus*, be indicated by the net output/gross output ratio being higher than it would otherwise have been. However, when net output/gross output ratios in the ROI are compared to those in the UK there is apparently little evidence of transfer pricing. In both 1980 and 1985 the ratios for all manufacturing were lower in the ROI, namely 37 per cent compared to 41.8 per cent in the UK in

---

[17] We have not attempted to match the ROI and USA industrial classifications in great detail and the average market exchange rate has been used in the absence of detail on relative unit prices.

[18] That is leaving aside any transfer pricing in miscellaneous foods where it is unclear whether ROI productivity was higher than the level in the USA.

1980, and 38.8 per cent compared to 41.6 per cent in the UK in 1985, which was the opposite of the expected result if transfer pricing was occurring. In 1980 most individual finely disaggregated industries in the ROI (34 out of 66) also had lower net output/gross output ratios than their UK counterparts. Whilst in 1985 a majority of ROI industries had higher net output/gross output ratios than their counterparts this advantage was still slight (in 36 industries out of 70). In any case, a range of other factors also influence the net output/gross output with the result that its value as an indicator of transfer pricing may be limited.

The data used is still insufficiently disaggregated to ensure that the industries being compared are sufficiently similar in structure to ensure net output/gross output ratios do not differ for reasons other than transfer pricing, such as for example differences in the types of products and activities represented. To the extent that ROI manufacturing tends to concentrate on simple fabrication as opposed to the product development of high value-added goods, as evidenced in the survey studies of O'Farrell and Hitchens (1989) and Hitchens and Birnie (1993), then it might be anticipated that on an industry by industry basis the ROI will show a systematic tendency to have a lower net output/gross output ratio than the UK. This ratio's usefulness is further diminished by variations in the extent of vertical integration between the ROI and the UK. For example, a highly integrated motor vehicle manufacturer might smelt its own steel, make its own components and then produce some of the furnishing and electricals for the cars. This firm would thus extract value added at each of these stages of production whereas if it had bought in the steel, the components, the seats and the lamps then the value added would have been attributed to the firms supplying these inputs. Hence the distribution of value added across industries would have been very different. Whilst it is not clear to what extent vertical integration in the ROI differs from that in the UK it is at least plausible to suggest that the much larger absolute size of industry in the UK (allied to the existence of a number of large engineering firms) makes it likely that it will be more important in the UK. This is a further reason why use of the net output/gross output ratio as an indicator transfer pricing fails the *ceteris paribus* condition.

Despite these qualifications on the use of the ratio it may still be notable that the ROI has a very much higher net output/gross output ratio in four activities where production is dominated by foreign owned branch-plants, namely chemicals for industrial and agricultural use, pharmaceuticals, radio, TV and sound reproduction etc., and miscellaneous foods. As an experiment the net output of these industries was recalculated to show how much lower it would have been in 1985 if the net output/gross output ratio had been that ruling in the counterpart industry in the UK rather than that actually applying to the ROI industry. The results are illustrated in table 10 below.

A total 344.5 million IR £ of net output would be "lost" if the net output/gross output ratios in these activities were as low as those of the counterparts in the UK. Since ROI total manufacturing net output in the plants

TABLE 10
Impact on Levels of Net Output of Variations in
the Net Output/Gross Output Ratio of Selected Activities, 1985

	Net Output as a Per Cent of Gross Output		"Excess" Net Output in ROI (mln. IR £)
	ROI	UK	
Chemicals for Industrial & Agricultural Use	51.8 (43.5)	39.8	10.0
Pharmaceuticals	71.4 (646.2)	60.0	103.4
Miscellaneous Foodstuffs	77.3 (322.5)	40.0	155.7
Radio & TV receivers, Sound Reproduction etc.	61.6 (179.5)	35.7	75.4
Total Manufacturing	(5,191,215)		

Note: All estimates are adjusted to exclude the smaller establishments in the ROI (i.e. those with 3-19 persons engaged). Values in parenthesis are the absolute levels of net output in each of the industries in the ROI.
Source: ROI: *Census of Industrial Production 1985*; UK: *Census of Production 1985*.

with 20 or more employees in 1985 was about IR £ 5,200 million the implication of this measure is that 6.6 per cent of this was contributed by transfer pricing. In other words instead of having a level of net output per head of 128 per cent that of the UK, the ROI productivity level without transfer pricing would sink to 120 per cent. This implies that whilst transfer pricing is a not insignificant factor, when explaining the ROI's productivity superiority most of the gap is caused by other factors.

One problem which arises is that of the relationship between this finding that transfer pricing inflates the ROI net output by about seven per cent and our estimation that ROI manufacturing product prices were on average 5-11 per cent greater than those in the UK. More specifically, the question is whether this implies the ROI's nominal level of value added is inflated by 12-17 per cent through financial factors, i.e. 6.6 per cent for transfer pricing plus a further 5-11 per cent for higher unit product prices. Or is the 6.6 per cent arising from transfer pricing entirely included within the 5-11 per cent effect arising from the higher prices of the ROI's goods? In principle the effect of transfer pricing arising from higher product selling prices should be captured by the calculation based on PPPs, RXPs or UVRs. However, the PPPs, RXPs and UVRs will fail to allow for the extent to which transfer pricing results from the prices of inputs being lower than what they would otherwise have been. Thus a straightforward addition of the effects of higher prices in the ROI to those of transfer pricing is likely to exaggerate the "financial" contribution to higher productivity to the extent that there is double counting. At the same time, merely to use the PPPs and UVRs would be to underestimate that financial contribution.

A further uncertainty relating to the use of this method to estimate the scale of transfer pricing lies in the selection of the activities where the impact of variations in the net output/gross output ratio was investigated. While, the four activities shown in table 10 were characterised by both high rates of foreign ownership and a relatively high net output/gross ratio in the ROI there were other activities where transfer pricing might have been anticipated, for example office machinery and data processing equipment, and yet the net output/gross output ratios in the ROI and UK were similar. Moreover, our estimate of transfer pricing depends critically on the assumption that there is enough structural similarity between the ROI and UK chemicals, pharmaceuticals and miscellaneous foods industries for one to neglect other influences on the net output/gross output ratio. Given uncertainty as to the validity of this assumption it is worthwhile pursuing an alternative method for measuring the impact of transfer pricing.

Method 3. Using Comparative Profit Rates

The method is based on the assumptions that the incentive to engage in transfer pricing is greatest for American owned companies. This is because the tax systems of non-American countries heavily penalise any company attempting to repatriate the profits made through transfer pricing to its ROI subsidiary.[19] Whilst American companies would also be heavily taxed if they attempted to repatriate into America the inflated profits of their Irish subsidiaries, given the generally larger scale of their global operations than, say, the German firms operating in ROI they will have more opportunities to recycle those profits to their operations in some third country.[20]

If the incentive to transfer pricing is effectively limited to some American subsidiaries this implies that the sectors where it will have greatest impact are chemicals (NACE 25 and 26), and electrical engineering, office and data processing machinery, and instrument engineering (NACE 34, 33 and 37). We

---

[19] Admittedly this would not affect the incentive to transfer price if the company wished to keep profits enhanced thereby within the ROI but, given the extent of profit repatriation from the ROI, we assume that this motivation is not significant.

[20] A complication is that the US Revenue Service limits the extent of transfer pricing between the USA and ROI by monitoring the divergence between intra-company profit rates in the two locations. If it judges a subsidiary in the ROI to be making an unacceptably high profit rate then this is reduced by the imposition of a compulsory royalty payment by that subsidiary to the US parent which can then be taxed.

therefore consider transfer pricing only in relation to these sectors.[21] Differences between companies sales and gross output were assumed to be negligible.

The maximum possible extent of transfer pricing is indicated by the degree to which subsidiaries in the ROI have higher profit rates than their American parents, that is after allowance for differences in costs between the two countries. The IDA Survey, which represents a sample of firms employing more than 29 persons representing 65 per cent of the population's employment, suggests that foreign owned chemicals plants in the ROI earned profits of 29 per cent of sales in 1984 compared to 18 per cent for their parent companies.[22]

Thus the ROI plants had excess profits equivalent to 11 per cent of sales. Unfortunately, there is no readily available data which would allow one to determine how much of this 11 per cent is the result of differences in fuel and material inputs, interest charges and the absence of charges for certain higher order services (e.g. management, research and development, designing, marketing) provided by the American headquarters of the companies to the ROI subsidiaries. Whilst some international companies may charge their subsidiaries fees for these services the level of these may be set in such a way as to reallocate profits to the least tax location, i.e. they become part of the process of transfer pricing. In principle these differences in inputs should be picked up by the ratio of materials, fuels and industrial services to gross output. This ratio is by definition equal to one minus the net output/gross output ratio and so is subject to all the difficulties of interpretation already discussed when considering our second method.

However, it is possible to estimate the extent to which the ROI profitability is boosted by lower labour costs. Using ILO (1987) and Ray (1987) total labour costs were estimated as 8.9 per cent of the ROI's gross output in chemicals and 15.5 per cent in the United States. In other words, of the excess of 11 per cent, 6.6 per cent could be accounted for by lower wages, salaries and social charges in the ROI. This therefore leaves 4.4 per cent of American subsidiary gross output/sales as unexplained and this was assumed to reflect transfer pricing. This was equivalent to IR £ 39.8 million out of a total net output of IR £ 906.5 million and therefore the ROI's chemicals' net output without transfer pricing is estimated to be 95.6 per cent of the unadjusted level in 1984.

This method can be repeated for the office and data processing machinery, electrical engineering and instrument engineering industries (NACE 33, 34 and 37). In this case the ROI's excess profit rate was 28.9 per cent minus 14 per cent, that is 14.9 per cent of sales. Lower labour costs in the ROI amounted to

---

[21] Limitations on the available data did not allow us to include NACE 417-418, 423 miscellaneous foodstuffs within the scope to this method which is unfortunate given that an American soft drinks manufacturer dominates this industry.

[22] These figures represent the pre-tax average of the 20 most important foreign companies in this industry which are located in the ROI.

13.1 per cent of gross output which leaves 1.8 per cent of gross output as the maximum possible extent of transfer pricing. This is equivalent to IR £ 41.8 million out of a total net output of IR £ 1261.1 million and therefore the ROI's net output per head in the electrical and electronic industries is estimated as 96.7 per cent of the unadjusted level in 1984.

When these two sectoral estimates are combined one has an estimate of the maximum possible impact of transfer pricing on manufacturing value added in the ROI. This is equivalent to IR £ 81.6 million out of a total net output of about IR £ 4710.4 million in the firms of 20 or more employees and therefore the ROI's manufacturing net output per head is estimated as 98.3 per cent of the unadjusted level in 1984. In other words, this method suggests that the total impact of transfer pricing is much smaller than was estimated by the net output/gross output ratios used in the previous section which in turn was smaller than the result of method (1). Unfortunately these three results are not strictly comparable given that in each case a different set of industries were considered. In method (1) pharmaceuticals, office and data processing machinery and radio and TV receivers etc. were considered. In method (2) chemicals for industrial and agricultural use, pharmaceuticals, and radio, TV etc. and miscellaneous foods were considered. In the third method all chemicals and all the electrical engineering, office and data processing machinery and instrument engineering industries were considered. In each case the selection was quite pragmatic, i.e. the industries considered were those which according to the chosen indicator displayed the greatest apparent evidence of transfer pricing though in all cases only those activities were considered in which foreign and particularly US ownership was substantial. The variations in the activities and the differences in the indicated scale of transfer pricing are causes for concern. Whilst some doubt therefore remains as to the precise size of the impact of transfer pricing and greater research is required in this area, whichever measure is used the implication is that much of the relatively high productivity in the ROI appears to be attributable to factors other than transfer pricing.

4. Conclusion

This paper first outlined the ROI's sectoral comparative productivity performance in the perspective of the ROI's failure to achieve significant catch up and convergence with respect to levels of relative living standards.

Our own results were presented in the final part of section 1. In most of the sectors considered, ROI productivity levels remained substantially lower than those attained by the UK counterpart throughout the period from the 1930s to 1990. Manufacturing, however, provides a notable exception to this pattern. Productivity levels caught up with those in UK manufacturing and by the late 1980s a very substantial advantage had been established. Disaggregated comparisons, including those of the ROI to the USA and West Germany, as shown in section 2, illustrate that the high average productivity level of ROI manufacturing is largely attributable to a narrow section of manufacturing which has been dominated by inward investment. We provide indications in section 3 that some but not all of the ROI's manufacturing productivity advantage relative to the UK in 1985 can be attributed to transfer pricing by international firms in favour of subsidiaries in the relatively low profit tax ROI location. If transfer pricing is occurring the reason would be a wish by international firms to maximise their total post-tax company profits. Having increased their net profits through redistributing gross profits in favour of plants in the ROI they might choose to keep profits within the ROI, i.e. to re-invest them there. However, repatriation of such profits might well appear more attractive assuming, that is, that any taxation in the USA, Germany or Japan etc. on profits brought back from the ROI does not negate the benefits derived from transfer pricing. The volume of repatriated profits, dividends and royalty payments leaving the ROI increased dramatically over the 1980s: 47 million IR £ in 1975, 659 million IR £ (14.6 per cent of manufacturing net output) in 1983, 1,321 million IR £ (23.7 per cent of net output) in 1985 and 1908 million IR £ (24.6 per cent) in 1988 (Foley, 1991; Central Bank, 1992). The scale of such outflow is often taken as *prima facie* evidence of the significance of transfer pricing.

If it were assumed that every IR £ of profit outflow had been generated by transfer pricing, then net output in the absence of such profits would have been one-quarter lower in the mid 1980s. In other words almost all of the productivity superiority relative to UK manufacturing would have disappeared. However, such an adjustment may exaggerate the scale of transfer pricing (NESC, 1993) given that not all of the outflow originates from the manufacturing sector. About 90 per cent of the total has been estimated to originate from within the combination of agriculture and the other sectors. It is likely that international firms would wish to repatriate substantial profits from ROI operations regardless of whether these have been generated by transfer pricing or otherwise. Moreover, it is known through the IDA Irish Economy Expenditures Survey that part of the capital outflow reflects the royalty payments which some ROI subsidiaries make to the home country operations which supply marketing and R and D services. In such cases the very high measured value added of the ROI subsidiary could be considered a "real" as opposed to a financial phenomenon albeit an organisational phenomenon reflecting the concentration on purely production functions in most ROI plants.[23]

In view of some of these factors NESC (1993) decided to reckon that half of the total outflow from agriculture and other sectors represented an upper bound on the possible transfer pricing occurring. When such an adjustment was made

---

[23] O'Leary (1984) considers the latter a case of the ROI national accounts GDP measures giving an unduly favourable impression of the total level of output since rewards to factor inputs located outside of the ROI are being included.

to rates of output and output per head growth in ROI manufacturing it had the effect of reducing the average growth rates for 1984-1990 to 6.2 and 5.5 per cent per annum respectively, the actual rates of growth being 7.6 and 6.9. In other words, the indicated impact of transfer pricing is significant but even in its absence productivity growth would still have been very considerable. If the NESC (1993) approach is applied to levels of net output per head in ROI manufacturing it implies that half of 90 per cent of the total outflow of 1321 million IR £ in 1985 (i.e. 594.5 million IR £) should be regarded as the consequence of transfer pricing. Given that total net output was 5,191.2 million £ IR (for plants employing more than 19 persons) the implication would be that 11 per cent of this "value added" is indicated to be the result of transfer pricing. In the absence of such transfer pricing the comparative productivity of the ROI would drop from 128 per cent of the UK level to 113 per cent.

It is notable that this application of the method used by NESC (1993) indicates a larger scale of transfer pricing (up to 11 per cent of net output) as compared to our own estimations which are 2, 7 or 11 per cent depending on the method employed. It should be stressed that all these approaches are still unrefined. Whilst the NESC approach may overestimate the scale of transfer pricing, our own estimates, which exclusively concentrated on a couple of industries where foreign ownership was predominant, may underestimate the effect through failure to allow for any transfer pricing activity by foreign subsidiaries across the entire range of manufacturing activity in the ROI. It should be stressed that even with the most generous assessment of the scale of transfer pricing there would still be a sizeable productivity gap relative to the UK albeit one which is much reduced and might probably be explained largely by the differences between the structure of manufacturing in the ROI relative to the UK.

References

Ark, B. van (1990a), "Comparative levels of labour productivity in Dutch and British Manufacturing", *National Institute Economic Review*, no. 131, pp. 71-85.

Ark, B. van (1990b), "Manufacturing Productivity levels in France and the United Kingdom", *National Institute Economic Review*, no. 133, pp. 62-77.

Ark, B. van (1992), "Comparative Productivity in British and American Manufacturing", *National Institute Economic Review*, no. 142, pp. 63-73.

Ark, B. van (1993), "International Comparisons of Output and Productivity: Manufacturing Productivity Performance of Ten Countries from 1950 to 1990", *Monograph Series*, no. 1, Growth and Development Centre, Groningen.

Ark, B. van, and D. Pilat (1993), "Productivity Levels in Germany, Japan and the United States: Differences and Causes", *Brookings Papers on Economic Activity*, Microeconomics no. 2, pp. 2-48.

Baily, M.N. (1993), "Competition, Regulation and Efficiency in Service Industries", *Brookings Papers on Economic Activity*, no. 2, pp. 71-159.

Baker, T.J. (1988), "Industrial Output and Wage Costs", *Quarterly Economic Commentary*, October, Economic and Social Research Institute, Dublin.

Baumol, W.J., S.A.B. Blackman and E.H. Wolf (1989), *Productivity and American Leadership*, MIT Press, Cambridge (MA).

Birnie, J.E. (1994), "British-Irish Productivity Differences, 1930s-1990s: ROI and UK Labour Productivity Levels in the Industrial Sectors", *QUB Papers in Economics Working Paper*, no. 47, Queen's University Belfast.

Broadberry, S.N. (1994), "Manufacturing and the Convergence Hypothesis: What the Long Run Data Show", *Journal of Economic History*, vol. 53, no. 4, pp. 772-795.

Central Bank (1992), "Submission on Industrial Policy", *Submission to the Industrial Policy Review Group*, Stationery Office, Dublin.

Commission of the European Communities (1992), *Panorama of EC Industry 1992-1993 Statistical Supplement*, Office for Official Publications of the European Communities, Luxembourg.

Commission of the European Communities (1994), *European Economy*, 1993, no. 55, Office for Official Publications of the European Communities, Luxembourg.

Crafts, N.F.R. (1991), "Reversing Relative Economic Decline? the 1980s in Historical Perspective", *Oxford Review of Economic Policy*, vol. 7, no. 3, pp. 81-98.

Crafts, N.F.R. (1993), "Can De-Industrialisation Seriously Damage your Wealth?", *Hobart Paper*, no. 120, Institute of Economic Affairs, London.

Department of Transport (1990), *Transport Statistics Great Britain 1979-1989*, Department of Transport, London.

Dunning, J.H. (1981), *International Production and the Multinational Enterprise*, Allen and Unwin, London.

Economist (1994, February 5), "European Airlines: Flights of Fancy".

Ferris, T. (1989), "Changes in Productivity and Living Standards: 1971-1986", *Irish Banking Review*, Spring.

Financial Times (1994, February 24), "Can Europe Compete? The Challenge".

Foley, A. (1991), "Interpreting Output Data on Overseas Industry", in A. Foley and D. Mc Aleese (eds.), *Overseas Industry in Ireland*, Business and Economic Research Series, Gill and Macmillan, Dublin.

Haughton, J. (1991), "The Historical Background", in J.W. O'Hagan (ed.), *The Economy of Ireland Policy and Performance*, Irish Management Institute, Dublin.

Hitchens, D.M.W.N. and J.E. Birnie (1989), "The United Kingdom's Productivity Gap: its Size and Causes", *Omega*, vol. 17, no. 3, pp. 209-221.

Hitchens, D.M.W.N. and J.E. Birnie (1994), *The Competitiveness of Industry in Ireland*, Avebury, Aldershot.

Hitchens, D.M.W.N., K. Wagner and J.E. Birnie (1990), *Closing the Productivity Gap: A Comparison of Northern Ireland, the Republic of Ireland, Britain and West Germany*, Gower-Avebury, Aldershot.

Hood, N.S. and S. Young (1979), *The Economics of Multinational Enterprise*, Longman, London.

Kennedy, K.A. (1971), *Productivity and Industrial Growth: The Irish Experience*, Clarendon Press, Oxford.

Kennedy, K.A. (1993), "Facing the Unemployment Crisis in Ireland", *Undercurrents*, no. 1, Cork University Press, Cork.

Kennedy, K.A. (1994), "The National Accounts for Ireland in the 19th and 20th Centuries", *Paper for N.W. Posthumus Institute Seminar "Comparative Historical National Accounts for Europe in the 19th and 20th Centuries"*, University of Groningen, June 10-11.

Matthews, R.C.O. (1988), "Research on Productivity and the Productivity Gap", *National Institute Economic Review*, no. 124, pp. 66-71.

McAleese, D. (1977), *A Profile of Grant-aided Industry in Ireland*, Industrial Development Authority of Ireland, Dublin.

Murshed, M., P. Noonan, R. Thanki, G. Gudgin and S. Roper, (1993), "Growth and Development in the Two Economies of Ireland: An Overview", *NIERC Report*, Belfast.

NESC (1975), "Jobs and Living Standards: Projections and Implications", *Report*, no. 7, National Economic and Social Council, Dublin.

NESC (1989), "Ireland in the European Community: Performance, Prospects and Strategy", *Report*, no. 88, National Economic and Social Council, Dublin.

NESC (1992), "The Irish Economy in a Comparative Institutional Perspective", *Report*, no. 93, National Economic and Social Council, Dublin.

NESC (1993), "The Association between Economic Growth and Employment Growth in Ireland", *Report*, no. 94, National Economic and Social Council, Dublin.

O'Donnell, R. and S. Kenny (1993), "Ireland's Competitive Advantage: A Review of Some Measures", *Working Paper*, Industrial Development Research Centre, Economic and Social Research Institute, Dublin.

O'Farrell, P.N. and D.M.W.N. Hitchens (1989), *Small Firm Competitiveness and Performance*, Gill and Macmillan, Dublin.

O'Grada, C. and K. O'Rourke (1993), "Irish Economic Growth 1945-1988", *Working Paper*, WP93/27, Centre for Economic Research, University College Dublin.

O'Leary, J.P. (1984), "Some Implications of the Revisions to the Balance of Payments on National Accounts", *Irish Banking Review*, September, pp. 13-34.

Olle, W. (1985), "The Development of Employment in Multinational Enterprises in the Federal Republic of Germany", Multinational Enterprises Programme, *Working Paper*, no. 33, International Labour Organisation, Geneva.

O'Mahony, M. (1992), "Productivity Levels in British and German Manufacturing Industry", *National Institute Economic Review*, no. 138, pp. 46-63.

O'Malley, E. (1989), *Industry and Economic Development: The Challenge for the Latecomer*, Gill and Macmillan, Dublin.

Porter, M. (1990), *The Competitive Advantage of Nations*, Free Press, New York.

Roy, D.J. (1989), "Labour Productivity in 1985; An International Comparison", *Paper presented to the Twenty First Conference of the International Association for Research in Income and Wealth*, Lahnstein, August.

SOEC (1986), *External Trade: Export NIMEXE*, Parts A to Z, Statistical Office of the European Communities, Office for Official Publications of the European Communities, Luxembourg.

SOEC (1988a), *Price Structure of the Community Countries in 1985*, Statistical Office of the European Communities, Office for Official Publications of the European Communities, Luxembourg.

SOEC (1988b), "Appendix", in, *Research on the Cost of Non-Europe: Basic Findings*, vol. 2, Statistical Office of the European Communities, Office for Official Publications of the European Communities, Luxembourg.

Walsh, B.M. (1993), "The Contribution of Human Capital Formation to Post-War economic Growth in Ireland", *Working Paper*, no. 93/8, Centre for Economic Research, University College Dublin.

International Productivity Differences
K. Wagner and B. van Ark (editors)

Explanations of International Productivity Differences: Lessons from Manufacturing

Hans Gersbach and *Martin N. Baily*[**]
[*] *University of Basel, University of Heidelberg and McKinsey Global
    Institute*
[**] *University of Maryland, The Brookings Institution, McKinsey
    Global Institute, and NBER*[*]

1. Introduction and Relation to the Literature

There has been a renewed interest in why productivity grows over time within
countries, and the related issue, why productivity varies across countries at a
point of time. In this paper, we summarise findings from a recent study to
measure and explain productivity differences across Germany, Japan, and the
United States at the industry level. Our main results are as follows:

- Large productivity differences exist at the industry level.
- The differences in industry productivity are caused primarily by
  differences in the technology used, the design of products for
  manufacturing and the way functions and tasks are organised.
- Achieving and maintaining high relative productivity requires that
  companies compete directly against the best practice production in the
  global economy.

Our results fit into three major developments in the literature. First, there
is a renewed emphasis on the role of catch-up in growth. The pattern of
economic convergence among the major industrial countries after World War
II shows that the USA had by far the highest level of productivity in 1945.
but Japan and the European economies were able to grow more rapidly in
subsequent years than the USA (see e.g. Baumol et al. 1989). However, the

---

[*] **Acknowledgement**
    This paper is based on the McKinsey manufacturing project (McKinsey Global
    Institute 1993) and all data, unless otherwise indicated, is derived from that
    project. The project was directed by William Lewis, Heino Fassbender, and Martin
    Neil Baily. Hans Gersbach was the project coordinator. Other members of the team
    were Kathy Huang, Tom Jansen and Koji Sakate. Robert Solow, Francis Bator,
    and Ted Hall were advisors to the project. We also benefited from comments and
    suggestions by the editors of this volume, Bart van Ark and Karin Wagner, and by
    the participants of the workshop on International Productivity Differences at the
    Wissenschaftszentrum in Berlin.

catch-up has slowed or stopped since 1980. As shown by Baily (1993), McKinsey Global Institute (1992) and Dollar and Wolff (1993) the remaining differences in output per hour worked can be attributed to a large extent to the service sector. Our results indicate that the manufacturing sector contributes as well to the explanation of aggregate productivity differences.

Second, there have been many international studies on manufacturing productivity on a more aggregate level. A sample of estimates from various cross-country comparisons agree on the rank order of manufacturing productivity levels for Germany, Japan and the USA, but there is considerable disagreement over the magnitude of the gap. For instance, results from van Ark and Pilat (1993) report that German operations are within 20 per cent of the US level, but a study by Dollar and Wolff (1993) suggests that the same operations are almost only half as productive at the end of the 1980s. Our industry case studies show that productivity gaps of 10 to 50 percentage points are common at the industry level across Germany, Japan, and the USA Moreover, our study points out that labour productivity in a number of manufacturing industries in Germany has fallen behind. This theme is also addressed in this volume by O'Mahony and Wagner, and by Freudenberg and Ünal-Kesenci.

Third, there is an ongoing, unresolved debate about the reasons why productivity levels differ and whether or not the traditional growth accounting based on Solow-type growth theory should be replaced (e.g. Abramovitz, 1993; Maddison, 1991; Romer, 1990; Mankiw, Romer and Weil, 1992; Costella, 1994). In recent years, there have been some attempts to isolate the factors that account for observed productivity differences among countries in the triad in a given year. Van Ark and Pilat, 1993 found that while plant size and capital intensity can help explain part of the productivity gap between Japan and the USA, these factors as well as basic labour force qualifications or industry composition have little explanatory power why the productivity gap between Germany and Japan should be as large as it is. Caves et al. (1992) carried out various industry studies comparing six countries by estimating the degree of technical efficiency as distinguished from allocative inefficiency. They found that technical efficiency plays a substantial role in explaining international differences. Dale Jorgenson with various co-authors have produced a range of papers on the technology gap among Germany, Japan, and the USA. For instance, Jorgenson and Kuroda (1992) found the technology gap, which is the difference between the productivity level in the USA and Japan after correction for the use of labour, capital and intermediate inputs, was almost 50 percentage points in 1985. Our analysis suggests that the major part of productivity differences can be attributed to the way functions and tasks are organised and to the design of products for manufacturing which can be summarised under intangible capital in the widest sense.

2. The Approach

The starting point for our study was the industry-of-origin approach (e.g. van Ark and Pilat, 1993). This approach is based on data from the Census of Manufacturers of different countries. Using the approach on the level of four- or three-digits industries requires modifications in two different directions. First, to make labour input and value added data comparable across countries, a series of adjustments are necessary regarding industry coverage, definition of value added, mix of finished goods and parts, differences in distribution and other service-oriented activities, and differences in the way headquarters are treated (see e.g. van Ark and Pilat, 1993; Gersbach and van Ark, 1994). Furthermore, we modified the industry PPPs as they were calculated from the Census of Manufactures. The industry PPP represents the number of units of different currencies needed to purchase an equivalent amount of industry's output. It therefore requires to measure product prices of manufacturing industries at the factory gate. Since the data from the Census of Manufactures does not always provide sufficiently detailed prices to compile industry PPPs, we used additional price comparisons from consulting work to calculate the industry-specific currency conversion. Hence, our objective was to refine the existing industry-of-origin approach as much as possible until it can be used on the industry level.

We used the case study method to both test existing hypotheses on manufacturing productivity and develop our own understanding of the aggregate productivity differences. A sample of nine industries was selected that comprise between 15 and 20 per cent of employment and between 17 and 22 per cent of value added of the manufacturing sector in the three countries Germany, Japan, and the USA. The industry studies - automotive cars, automotive parts, computer, consumer electronics, metalworking, steel, processed food, beer, and soap and detergent - were selected on the basis of the following criteria. First, we tried to cover the entire range of the manufacturing sector as broadly as possible. Second, we were aiming to include different types of manufacturing production methods, including assembly and process industries. Third, we only undertook case studies where the consulting company McKinsey had sufficient knowledge to understand and determine the causality of productivity differences. Hence, while our case studies account for a broad variety of manufacturing industries, they were not chosen by representativity concerns alone.

We focused exclusively on calculating the productivity of labour. However, labour productivity is not a complete measure of productivity; in the cases where capital productivity is important, we provide discussions on capital intensity and its impact on productivity.

In order to identify and explain the causes of observed productivity differences, we developed a framework, introduced in the fifth section, that captures all major possible causes and reflects their relationship to each other within a given hierarchy.

Testing and revising our hypotheses and assessing the relative importance of the different causal factors were done through data analysis of publicly available data and benchmarking studies by a team of McKinsey consultants. Benchmark studies (e.g. Joly, Kluge and Stein, 1994) consist of the following key elements: (1) identifying the manufacturing and managerial processes that needed to be assessed, (2) selecting facilities for comparison, (3) observing and measuring in detail how well these processes - and specific tasks within processes - are performed, and (4) interpreting the results. Prior McKinsey work provided some benchmarking results for the study - e.g. for the automotive, metalworking, computer, and consumer electronics industry (e.g. Joly, Kluge and Stein, 1994). In some industries the project team conducted small-scale benchmarking studies of their own, geared to productivity differences. Moreover, the results were scrutinised through meetings and discussions with other McKinsey consultants who also brought in additional data or evidence. Hence, our approach is certainly non-standard from an economists point of view. We hope, however, that this approach can reveal valuable insights for what has happened to productivity on a disaggregated level.

3. Productivity Results

Graph 1 shows the case study comparisons for all nine of our industries. Looking first at the German-USA comparisons, there are two industries (metalworking and steel) in which labour productivity in 1990 was virtually identical and where a convergence of productivity occurred. Such equalisation of productivities is not, however, because the industries in the two countries are identical in their production processes, but rather because of offsetting differences, as we will see shortly.

Graph 1 also reveals that productivity in Germany is substantially lower than productivity in operations in the USA in six of the industries. And since the graph also shows that productivity in operations located in Japan is ahead of those in the USA in five of these industries, it is clear that productivity in some operations in Germany is far lower than the international productivity leader. One of the important questions addressed in this report is why manufacturing operations in Germany have failed to catch up to best practice or have fallen behind in many industries.

Turning to the US-Japan comparison, the wide variations in productivity relative to the USA are striking. In food processing, for example, operations in Japan have only a third of the US level of output per hour, whereas in the steel industry, operations in Japan are 45 per cent above the US level.

GRAPH 1
Value Added per Hour Worked, using Industry PPP
(USA = 100)

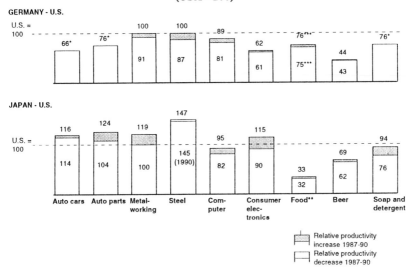

* Only 1990
** Based on shipment
*** Could be 5 to 10 percentage points lower if precise data for companies with less than 20 employees available

Source: McKinsey analysis

Another notable feature of this bilateral comparison is that operations in several industries in Japan have made productivity gains relative to the corresponding US industries from 1987 to 1990, despite the brief time period (graph 1). Furthermore, the average labour productivity in automotive assembly, automotive parts, metalworking, computer and consumer electronics in Japan was already close to, or above, the average of plants in the USA.

One possible explanation for this growth pattern is that the economies were at different points in the business cycle. The US economy was weakening in 1989 and went into recession in 1990, while in Japan, output was low in 1987 and very high in 1990. To address this, we examined capacity utilisation data, and adjusted the car, car parts, and metalworking figures for the business cycle. These adjusted figures are reported in graph 1. In steel, capacity utilisation in the USA remained high in 1990, so that a cyclical adjustment was not appropriate. Since we have removed the effects of the business cycle, it follows that the Japanese car parts, metalworking and consumer electronics industries must have achieved large gains in productivity by changing their production methods.

GRAPH 2
Employment Share and Relative Productivity
Levels in Japan for Nine Case Studies, 1990
(USA=100)

RELATIVE PRODUCTIVITY LEVELS

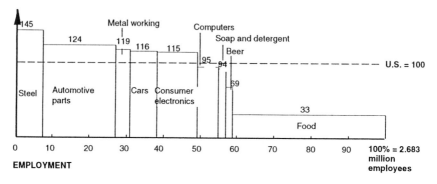

Source: McKinsey analysis

GRAPH 3
Value Added per Hour Worked, Weighted Average of Case Studies
(USA=100)

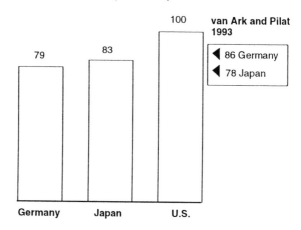

Source: Census of Manufactures; McKinsey analysis

We chose case studies that covered a range of different types of industries, but did not select an equal number of industries in each part of the manufacturing sector. In fact, it is apparent in graph 2 that the case studies represent very different shares of employment as well as different levels of productivity. For example, food processing in Japan has more employment than the combined total of steel, car assembly, car parts, and metalworking. Therefore, when we calculated the weighted average of our case study productivity results, the employment and productivity of food processing substantially affect the outcome. Hence, our results are not a comprehensive test of the aggregate productivity results for manufacturing. As graph 3 shows, the weighted average of our case studies shows rough comparability between our findings for a sample of industries and the aggregate results of labour productivity for total manufacturing (as reported by van Ark and Pilat, 1993). The results are comparable despite the fact that we made changes in some of the original industry PPPs on the order of 30 to 40 per cent. The adjustments to the original Census UVR are most substantial in the case of investment goods and durable consumer goods (e.g. automotive industry, machinery, computers). On average, a downward bias exists in the ICOP UVRs compared to the MGI PPPs, which, however, cannot be used directly as a statistical test due to the small sample size and the overrepresentation of the machinery and transport equipment branches in the industry sample of the MGI study (for more details see Gersbach and van Ark 1994; appendix to this paper).

Our results confirm that productivity in Japan and Germany is lower than in the USA on average. However, our results suggest a different order in productivity levels in Germany and Japan. Due to the use of different industry PPPs and the relatively low coverage of manufacturing as a whole by our case studies, the average productivity result of our case studies does not allow us to draw any sharp conclusions about the validity of existing aggregate productivity results.

4. Causes of Productivity Differences at the Production Process Level

The General Framework

To see what has led to the pattern shown in graph 1, we developed a framework that attempts to capture all major possible causes and reflects their relationships to each other within a given hierarchy. In constructing this framework, we distinguished three hierarchical levels of causality. First, observed productivity differences must have some causes at the production process level, meaning that operations in Germany, for example, must do something different that makes output per hour worked higher or lower relative to their counterparts in Japan or the USA. Second, differences at the production process level can be the result of past and present industry structure and behavior which is captured under the nature of competition.

Third, competition and the behaviour of managers are heavily influenced by the external forces confronting and constraining managers, in both the market and policy environment. We call this third layer of causality external factors.

The First Level of Causality

In this section we examine the first level of causality. Causes of productivity differences at the production process level are sometimes called proximate causes in order to distinguish them from causes at higher causality level. On this first level of causality we can again distinguish three basic elements that explain possible differences in productivity.

First, the estimates of labour productivity can differ because of output differences as seen from the buyer's perspective. We call this first basic element output. Differences in output can influence labour productivity in three different ways: output mix, output quality, i.e. essentially the same sort of products, but tangible features that differ for which consumers are willing to pay price differences, and output variety at the plant level.

Second, labour productivity differences can be caused by differences in the mix of basic inputs, such as capital, the way products are designed, labour skills and intrinsic motivation, raw materials and parts. We call this second element, mix of production factors. We also include economies of scale since it is tied to physical capital. We use the term "economies of scale" to describe the situation in which a plant or a firm can increase its value added (or output) with less than a proportional increase of all inputs.

The third element which can cause differences in labour productivity is caused by the way the basic inputs are combined. We call this category operations. Since we made cyclical adjustments for those industries greatly affected by business cycles organisation of functions and tasks is the major component. This category describes the effectiveness and efficiency with which labour and other inputs are brought together in the production process.

Graph 4 shows a summary of the factors at the production process level that led to productivity differences in the nine industries studied. These causes have been collected into three groups. Shaded circles indicate factors that are of major importance for at least one of the bilateral productivity comparisons, clear circles indicate factors that are of lesser importance and crosses indicate factors that were not important sources of productivity differences. A cross next to some factor does not imply that this aspect of the production process is unimportant to overall performance. It simply indicates that we did not find this factor to be a source of productivity difference across the countries.

The assignment of circles and crosses was done at the case study level. It was made on the basis of the relative importance of each of the elements of the production process in explaining the productivity differences for that industry. By looking down a column, therefore, one can determine which are the one or two key causes of productivity difference within that industry. For example, design for manufacturing and organisation of functions and tasks are the two most important sources of productivity difference in car parts. In this synthesis chapter, however, we will draw out the common themes across the case studies, indicated along the rows in graph 4.

For this purpose, we have constructed an average column which summarises the overall importance of each factor. The organisation of functions and tasks is an important source of productivity difference in steel, metalworking, car assembly, car parts, and consumer electronics, and it is also of some importance in all of the other industries. We therefore judged it to be of high importance on average. Output mix, variety, and quality, by contrast, are very important in the consumer goods industries, but they are of significantly less importance to the other industries and were therefore judged to be of only some importance on average. In the next sections of this chapter, we examine each row in turn in order to understand the most important production process factors which account for differences in productivity in manufacturing operations across the three countries.

GRAPH 4
Causes of Labour Productivity
Differences at the Production Process

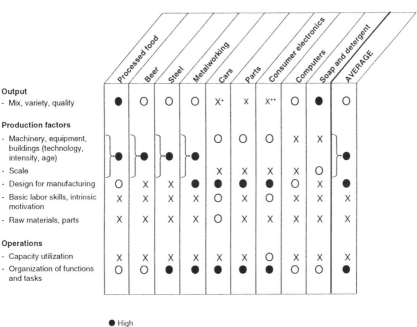

● High
O Low
X Undifferentiated

*   Adjustment for quality made to the productivity data
** Influence is high in opposite direction

Output Mix, Variety and Quality

As a practical matter, we used census data for our productivity comparisons. These data provide information on the outputs and inputs of a group of plants that are defined to be in the same industry. Industries and products are not synonymous, however, since all of the industries in our case studies produce a variety of products. For example, TVs and VCRs are different products, but are both manufactured within the consumer electronics industry.

The productivity results reported in graph 1 therefore reflect, in part, the impact of differences in product mix, variety and quality. The role of these three elements on the case study results is summarised in graph 5.

GRAPH 5
Causes of Labour Productivity Differences at the
Production Process Level: Product Differences

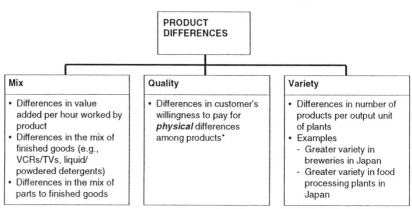

* We have used a methodology that incorporates these quality differences in our productivity measure

1) Output mix. Within a given industry, some products have higher value added per hour worked than others. As a matter of simple arithmetic, the value added per hour for the industry is the average of the values added per hour by each product, with the products weighted by their share of the industry's total employment. This means that if the mix of output is different among the countries, then overall value added per hour will differ, even if the productivity of each good viewed separately was exactly the same in the countries. We did find that product mix differences were of some importance in several case studies.
- In the soap and detergent industry, Germany suffers a significant productivity disadvantage because German consumers demand much more

powdered detergent than is the case in the other countries. If the German productivity figure is adjusted to remove this product mix penalty, then it would increase to 88 per cent of the US figure.

- In consumer electronics, mix differences were also important, but they do not help explain why productivity is so high in Japanese operations. The production of VCRs and audio equipment has lower value added per hour than the production of TVs, and operations in Japan have a larger share of production in VCRs and audio equipment than do operations in Germany or the USA. If productivity were calculated on a comparable product by comparable product basis, therefore, the productivity advantage for operations in Japan would be even greater than the industry average figure shown in graph 1 (see the consumer electronics case study in McKinsey Global Institute, 1993, for a comparison of productivity in TV production).

- In food processing, even though product mix is not the most important source of productivity difference, it still has a significant effect. Japan has lower productivity, in part, because of its high share of output in product categories such as seafood, which have relatively low productivity in all countries.

- In metalworking, product mix differences were also somewhat important, but this effect is tied to the changes in technology that are taking place in that industry and to the way products are designed. Output per hour is higher in standard machine tools than in customised tools, and the output of Japanese operations contains a larger share of standard machine tools. Productivity differences due to these factors are attributed to technology and design for manufacturing and discussed later in this section.

2) Output quality. In order to make meaningful productivity comparisons across countries, adjustments must be made for differences in quality. Our procedure accomplishes this in the following way. First we try to construct the industry PPPs by comparing products where quality differences are not significant. We compare like products to like products for that part of industry output where this was possible. For example, we looked at the producer prices of a given type of steel in the three countries.

The first issue of quality then arises for these comparable items. Are they really of the same quality when we compare across countries? We decided to assume quality was the same across countries unless there are differences that meet the following two-part test. The differences in quality are: 1) recognised by consumers and such that they are willing to pay a price premium; and 2) are a result of differences in the production process and not of taste. We adjust our comparable products for quality only if the product differences meet these two conditions; other notions of "quality" are regarded as consumer preference differences and treated as explanatory factors for productivity differences. The most important adjustment of quality arises in the carmotive industry. Even with similar basic features, cars can differ with respect to reliability, functionality, etc. Quality differences are defined by the price differential an average consumer is willing to pay for a content-equivalent car. For this study, estimates for the price premium associated with quality could be obtained from specific surveys (see Gersbach, Lewis, Mercer, and Sinclair, 1994). In 1987 Japanese cars commanded a quality price premium of 12 per cent over US cars, whereas German cars were perceived 10 per cent better in quality than US cars. The quality price premiums shrunk to 8 (Japan/USA) and 5 per cent (Germany/USA) in 1990.

The second step in accounting for quality differences across countries arises with products that are not comparable. We argue that, provided the PPP has been correctly estimated for the standard products of the industry, there is no further adjustment necessary to take account of specialty products that are either higher or lower in quality than the standard products. The basis for this is that specialty products will command a higher or lower price in the market than the standard industry products and will consequently add more or less to value added per unit than the standard industry products. The price system in market economies automatically provides a quality adjustment because it reflects value as perceived by customers.

Our procedure is based upon an idea similar to that of hedonic prices, which rely on the market to reveal the value of products attributes to consumers. It works properly only if the products made in an industry are close substitutes for each other, the markets are competitive and customers have unrestricted access to the entire product set. These conditions will not be satisfied completely, but using the price system does give us our best available information.

Obviously, customers may value products differently simply because they perceive and experience products in diverse ways, even though these distinctions are not based on measurable product differences. These are generally due to differences in taste, advertising, brand image, tradition or custom, and information. Product differences of this type can differ substantially across countries and are frequently important in consumer goods, where consumer perceptions and brand image are major buying factors. Product differentiation based upon these differences in preferences can also provide value to customers, but these differences were treated as causal factors at the external factors level of the framework since they are not primarily based on the production process.

3) Output variety. Product variety on the plant level was a source of productivity differences in two industries, beer and food, and in both cases it helped explain lower Japanese productivity. A remarkable proliferation of products in the food industry in Japan hurts efficiency. In the beer industry, producers in Japan have introduced a large number of new products to try to build market share. These new products reduce lot sizes for production and delivery, creating inefficiency (e.g. by increasing set-up time).

Production Factors

Within the category of production factors there were two main sources of productivity difference: capital and technology associated with different generations of manufacturing equipment on the one hand, and design for manufacturing on the other.

1) Capital, technology and scale. Periodically the process technology in an industry undergoes a major transformation that results in large increases in productivity. In the industries studied there were large variations in the extent to which such new technologies have been adopted across countries. In one country there may be a substantial fraction of output that is manufactured using a process that has been largely superseded elsewhere. Since productivity varies with these different generations of technology, we found that the mix of generations of technology is an important source of productivity difference across the countries.

- Industrial-scale food processors dominate the industry in the USA, but account for only a small fraction of output in Japan. German output comes heavily from multinational food companies, but a sizeable craft industry remains in certain food categories (e.g., bakery, meats).
- Large-scale breweries have taken over the beer industries in the USA and Japan, but beer production in Germany remains largely in small plants. US plants have been able to take full advantage of the high speed canning and bottling lines that require very large volumes.
- Minimills were developed as an industry in the USA and are now widely used there and in Japan. Very little minimill production existed in Germany in 1990.
- Most metalworking plants located in Japan have introduced methods for producing standard machine tools on production lines. Many machine tool makers in Germany have not yet adopted this innovation.

We found that shifts to new generations of technology in our case studies were usually accompanied by large increases in capital intensity, as measured by the amount of capital per worker employed (or by the amount of capital per hour). Modern food processing plants are highly automated compared to traditional food processing methods, for example. But the amount of capital required per unit of output (the capital output ratio) is often not higher with the new generation of technology. For a given level of output, the innovation may save capital, and it saves even more labour. For example, minimills in the steel industry require less capital per dollar of value added than integrated mills (even though they are more capital intensive).

In graph 6 we show capital intensities in metalworking, steel, beer and food to illustrate the fact that the technology shifts described above for these industries usually involved a substantial increase in capital per hour or per employee (higher capital intensity). The main exception to this rule was metal-

GRAPH 6
Capital Stock per Hour Worked, 1987

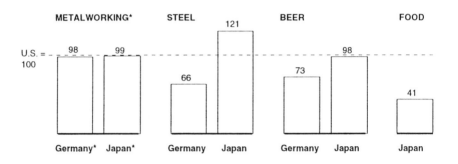

* Per employee

working, where the industry in Germany was just as capital intensive as that in Japan, but few companies in Germany had linked machines into a production line, resulting in lower productivity. The same picture is also reflected in investment intensity from 1987 to 1990 (graph 7). The only exception is beer where operations in Japan embarked on a massive investment campaign during this period, an investment surge that helped their productivity move closer to the US level. Because of inefficient labour organisation, however, labour productivity remained substantially lower than in the USA.

2) Design for manufacturing. An important source of productivity advantage for many companies has been their ability to create product designs that are less complex, use fewer parts and are easier to assemble, without producing products that are different from the customer's perspective. Innovations in this area have usually been introduced first in manufacturing operations in Japan.

Techniques that are used to raise productivity through product design include standardising components, optimising the number of parts, and designing the product so that its manufacture can be automated and its assembly done with no or few tools. The industries where this has been important are metalworking, car assembly, car parts, and consumer electronics. While companies based in Japan have been the leaders, some in the USA have been changing as a result of transplants and the adoption of the new methods. The Ford Taurus is one of the most successful examples of a product designed car for easy manufacture by a US-based company.

GRAPH 7
Investment per Hour Worked in 1987 dollars, 1987-1990

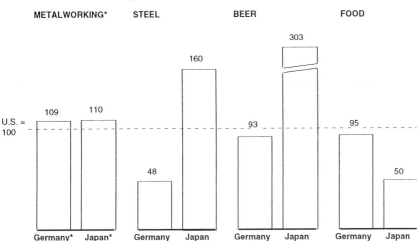

* Per employee

Operations in Germany have been slow to adopt the innovations in product design. German-built cars, for example, required more parts and more complex assembly than cars designed in Japan. We observed similar disadvantages in product design in both the consumer electronics and metalworking industries in Germany.

3) Basic labour skills and intrinsic motivation. We did not find evidence that intrinsic motivation and basic labour skills were major explanations for the cross-country productivity differences that we observed in our case studies.

As we noted earlier, this finding does not mean that managers can ignore these factors, but rather that manufacturers were able to recruit workers that could be trained and motivated adequately to achieve international productivity standards.

In recent decades, the average years of education completed by the workforce in Germany and the USA has increased. In both countries, however, there is a growing concern over the performance of the education system and the relative skills of those educated (see also Mason, van Ark and Prais, 1992, for comparisons across Europe). Companies in both countries echo these concerns and stress the difficulties of recruiting workers. In the USA, there has been a sharp increase in the wage premium associated with skill and education.

Against this backdrop, our conclusion that basic labour skills are not an important causal factor for explaining productivity differences in any of our nine case studies seems somewhat surprising. In the following we provide a reconciliation of the popular view with our findings.

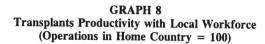

GRAPH 8
Transplants Productivity with Local Workforce
(Operations in Home Country = 100)

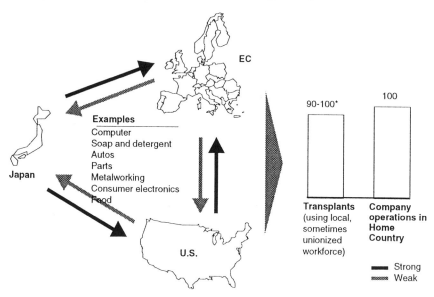

* In most cases
Source: Interview with industry and McKinsey experts; case studies

The "basic skills" we measured refers only to the basic, pre-hiring skills of production workers. Differences in post-training worker skills and in management and engineering skills are largely accounted for in the "organisation of functions and tasks" and in "design for manufacturing". Furthermore, we were interested only in the skills of workers actually hired, not those rejected. We found no differences in the trainability of the blue-collar workers that explain productivity differences in our cases.

For example, transplants achieved productivity levels similar to those in their originating countries (see graph 8). In addition, car companies originating in the USA have achieved best-practice productivity levels in the USA using the existing (often unionised) workforce (e.g., Ford-Atlanta, GM/Toyota-NUMMI). Finally, these findings were confirmed in our interviews with companies across the Triad. Managers in all three countries (even those managing transplants) confirmed that the basic skills of their production workers were not an obstacle to achieving best-practice productivity levels. With the exception of computers, the industries we studied did not include any small, high-tech or rapid-growth manufacturing industries. By and large, we chose developed industries, operating in slowly growing or stable markets, that hired few new workers.

However, differences in labour reliability and absenteeism can affect labour productivity. For instance, small factories can get a productivity penalty in the range of 5 per cent if they experience a 10 to 15 per cent higher absentee rate than comparable factories in other countries. Moreover, companies operating in the USA experienced higher turnover rates than companies operating in Germany and Japan. This lack of reliability could reduce productivity by as much as 10 per cent.

In all three countries, companies (including transplants) screen potential new employees to find the most attractive. They find large numbers with the necessary basic skills. The critical factors that drive their hiring decisions, however, are attitudinal factors that make workers more flexible, less likely to call in sick, and committed to remaining on the job for a long period of time. Others often define these attributes as "skills". In our study, employee screening and motivation are captured under the "organisation of functions and tasks".

This general conclusion about the lack of impact of labour skills and motivation is subject to two qualifications:
- Japanese transplants in the USA do report a small productivity disadvantage with US workers, resulting from higher turnover than in Japan.
- Some companies in Japan have achieved higher levels of worker motivation that give them a small productivity advantage. For example, some workers in the car industry in Japan work additional unpaid time devoted to meetings and discussions about ways to achieve higher productivity and quality. This behavior is partly because of incentives generated within the company (e.g., quality circles) and partly because of intrinsic motivation. Toyota selects workers who devote themselves to the company in a way that is not seen in the USA or Germany, or even in other Japanese companies.

4) Raw materials and parts. The use of raw materials and parts only played a role in explaining productivity differences in car assembly. In car assembly in Japan, the lack of defects and high quality in parts helps companies avoid inspections of incoming parts and rework and thus achieve higher labour productivity.

Production factors tell us about the equipment, parts and labour which are available for use. We now turn to a comparison of operations. Operations describe how the factors of production are combined to produce the output.

Operations

Within operations, there are two main sources of productivity differences: capacity utilisation, and the organisation of functions and tasks.
1) Capacity utilisation. Metalworking, cars, car parts, and consumer

electronics are all industries that are rather sensitive to the business cycle. And, as we noted in the introduction, these industries in the USA experienced the effects of a downturn in 1990. Based on official and a sample of company utilisation data we made rough estimates of the likely effect on productivity from differences in utilisation that were caused by the recession and the unusual upturn in Japan. The resulting cyclical adjustment reduced the gap between Japan and the USA In the case of cars, the cyclical adjustment was about 8 per cent, but in the other cases the effect was smaller. We have reported the cyclically adjusted figures for metalworking, cars, and parts since the influence of the business cycle turned out to be significant.

2) Organisation of functions and tasks. Somewhat surprisingly, there are very large differences in productivity among plants that look similar and that produce similar products (after accounting for differences in design for manufacturing). These productivity gaps result from the way in which work is organised. The most productive operations in Japan have refined and refined their production methods in order to pull as much labour out of the process as possible. There is no one large change that has been implemented, so that the nature of the improvements seems mysterious. It is the accumulation of thousands of small changes, to the point where the placement of every small part and every machine and the movements of every worker are optimised for productivity. It not only includes the optimisation of time and motion, but also the management structure. For instance, the delegation of responsibilities, such as production worker empowerment and suggestion systems where improvements are directly implemented, played a large role in the way operations in Japan were able to achieve high productivity. In addition, these advances in organisational efficiency can only be achieved by cross-functional training in multiple tasks as well as on-the-job training in specific tasks.

To get more insight into the nature of the differences we summarise in table 1 the main differences between more traditional ways to produce goods, often termed mass production, and leading edge modes of production sometimes called lean, or as we call it more generally, agile manufacturing.

Obviously, table 1 does not apply uniformly for all industries and describes more the assembly production processes. Moreover, some elements of agile manufacturing were introduced by companies decades ago while they were still viewed as mass producers.

The Toyota production system is predominantly a method of organisation, not a new patented or proprietary technology. Other Japanese companies and some US companies have been able to adopt similar innovations and have achieved very large productivity increases. The US minimills are run with very agile methods; one firm with over $1 billion in sales operates with fewer than 20 employees in their headquarters, a much lower ratio than for the integrated mills. The high productivity of minimills has much to do with their organisation of functions and tasks.

TABLE 1

Characteristics of Agile Manufacturing and Mass Production

	Agile Manufacturing	Mass Production
Production Factors		
Workers	Team	Rigid Work Rules
Workers/training/skills	Integration	Specialisation
Machinery	Flexible	Specialised
Raw materials, Parts	Low inventory, flexible variations of inventory	High inventory
Connecting Production Factors and Tasks		
Workers (decisions)	Flat hierarchies, self-regulation	Hierarchical
Workers (communication)	Horizontal and vertical	Vertical
Workers (responsability)	High commitment, delegation quality and volume objectives	Low commitment volume objectives
Machinery	Flexible rules for automation	Rigid rules for automation
Functions and tasks	Flexible rules for integration	Separation
Implementing Changes		
Operational improvements	Continuous improvements, decentralised and centralised	Static optimisation, centralised
Product changes	More frequent, simultaneous across functions	Less frequent, sequential
Design and Managing of Relationships		
Suppliers	Long-term fewer, but more intense, direct relationships	Arm's length, short term, many suppliers
Customers	Make-to-order, early communication	Make-to-stock, less communication

The organisation of functions and tasks was seen as a factor affecting relative productivity in all of our case studies. It is particularly important in steel, metalworking, cars, car parts and consumer electronics. Based on McKinsey benchmarking studies and surveys, it is clear that there are many companies in all three countries that can make large improvements in productivity by improving the organisation of their factories.

Not all manufacturing operations in Japan score high on the organisation of functions and tasks. Beer producers in Japan adopted process technologies in recent years that are similar to those used in US operations, but many workers were retained in spite of these labour-saving investments and are now being used for labour-intensive marketing programs. Other examples of inefficiently organised functions and tasks in Japan are the food, and soap and detergent industries, where sales administration requires more labour than in the USA.

In the automotive industry, we concluded that the subcontracting system used with parts suppliers in Japanese operations creates efficiency advantages. There is a "pyramid" structure, in which the small plants supply simple parts to the large plants, and the large plants then assemble more complex parts to be sold to the OEMs. This appears to be a better way to organise functions and tasks when final products are highly complex and when the first tier suppliers have the ability to manage the second tier suppliers. It facilitates the transfer of technology from the OEMs to the first tier suppliers and it simplifies the OEMs' supplier relationships.

Our findings about the proximate causes graph several important features. First, despite that the levels of aggregate capital intensity are relatively close among the countries studied (e.g. van Ark and Pilat 1993), there exists wide variations at a more disaggregated level. Second, most of the productivity differences are disembodied from physical capital. They are related to intangible and human capital.

The last observation may point to a fundamental change in the way productivity improvements occur today. Whereas capital intensity and vintage differences dominated the set of explanations until very recently, differences in intangible capital appear to play the dominant role for explaining productivity differences today.

5. Productivity Differences and the Nature of Competition

Defining the Nature of Competition

As we examined the results of the nine case studies, a relationship emerged between the competitive environment in which industries operate, and their productivity performance. To explore the ways in which competition has affected productivity in our case studies, we set up a three-way classification, depending upon whether the manufacturing operations located in a given country are managed by companies that compete only locally, in regional markets, or globally.

1) Local competition. Companies that compete locally are part of unconsolidated national industries, where small companies serve local markets. In some locally competitive industries there are several small companies serving the same local market which provides some pressure for cost cutting. In other cases, companies are essentially the sole suppliers to different local markets.

2) Regional competition. Companies that compete regionally sell directly against the most productive companies in their own national or regional

market, but do not face the best external producers. Regionally competitive companies may export, but they do not export substantially to third markets where they have to compete against the best external producers. For companies that operate primarily in the USA, regional competition means that the companies are selling in the USA or North America; in Germany it means that they are selling in Europe; and in Japan it means selling in Japan. An industry is regional if most of its production is managed by regionally competitive companies.

3) Global competition. We classify companies as globally competitive if they compete in their own region and also against the best external producers. Such companies have an external, global orientation and the nature of this global competition can take several forms. (i) Globally competitive companies can sell in their domestic market against transplant production or imports from the best external producers. These external producers must have a substantial market share. External competitive pressure is weakened if trade restrictions, particularly VRAs, limit import market shares. (ii) Globally competitive companies can export a substantial share of their production to the home market of the best external producers. (iii) Globally competitive companies can set up transplants that compete directly against the best external producers. (iv) Globally competitive companies can compete against the best external producers, either through trade or transplants, in third countries. An industry is global if most plants are run by global companies.

The Nature of Competition in the Case Studies

Using the information from the case studies, we made a subjective judgement and assigned each of the twenty-seven industries in our study (nine industries times three countries) to one of these three broad classifications. This purpose of the judgmental component is to give an insider view on the industries and to create the hypotheses about the nature of competition. A more rigorous measuring and testing of the extent of globalisation of the case studies has been performed in Gersbach (1994a).

The specifics of our assessment of all of the industries in the three countries are described as follows.

- Japan. The steel, metalworking, cars, car parts, consumer electronics, and computer industries in Japan are globally competitive. These industries sell world-wide and build transplants in other countries; they meet their best external producers in a substantial manner. We also view the soap and detergent industry in Japan as heavily exposed to global competition because transplants from the USA and Europe in this industry have a significant market share in Japan and now set the competitive environment for the industry as a whole. The beer industry located in Japan has consolidated and competes regionally. However, the government regulates prices and prevents full competition, even in the regional market. In the food industry a consolidation process is just beginning with the growth of some national companies and the entry of multinational food processors. The bulk of the industry competes locally, however.

- Germany. Two of the nine industries in this country compete intensively with world productivity leaders: computers and soap/detergents. The bulk of mainframe computer production is either produced in transplants from multinationals originating in the USA or assembled by companies headquartered in Germany using parts imported from Japan. The personal computer market faces world-wide competition. The soap and detergent industry consists of a large Germany-based producer competing head-to-head with multinational companies. The majority of industries in Germany (processed food, steel, metalworking, cars, car parts, and consumer electronics) have most of their production managed by companies competing regionally in Europe. Car companies originating in Germany did not compete extensively in the main segments of the industry against Japanese producers until recently, and the car parts suppliers were tied to the OEMs in Germany with no large segment competing globally. Germany had the world's leading metalworking companies in earlier decades but these companies did not face until recently the strength of the Japanese industry. Multinational food processing companies produce and sell in Germany to a certain extent and are growing, but there is also a substantial unconsolidated segment of the industry. In general, due to the intensive competition between Japanese and US companies in the US market, German industries experienced less pressure from the emerging productivity leaders from Japan. Beer is the only industry in Germany that we studied that faces only local competition. Small breweries are either the sole local supplier or face competition from other small local breweries.

- United States. The processed food, automotive assembly, computer, soap and detergent and consumer electronics industries in the USA compete globally. The major domestic operations in food processing, consumer electronics, and soap and detergents belong to multinationals that have transplants in the leading economies in the Triad. The computer industry in the USA also has transplants overseas and competes worldwide in export markets. The US beer industry has thus far competed mainly in the regional North American market. Beer is a product where exports are uneconomic except to serve niche markets because of transportation costs. Transplants, until recently, have been uncommon. The bulk of output in the metalworking, steel, and car parts industries in the USA is produced by companies that compete regionally. There are some companies that are global. The metalworking industry is in transition. Substantial production is performed by companies originating in the USA, but transplants managed by globally competitive companies headquartered in Japan also play an active role. Steel operations located in the USA are a mix of globally competitive minimills and integrated producers that still use work practices that date from a time when the industry was not globally competitive.

GRAPH 9
Changing Nature of Competition

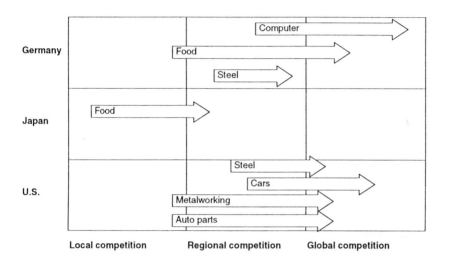

In making these assignments, however, we judged that there is an important dynamic component that is still missing. Several industries are in transition as they adjust to changes in the competitive environment and thus our assignments represent an "average."

The case studies in which the evolution of an industry was important in 1990 are shown in graph 9. The arrows indicate that companies in these industries are facing increasing competitive pressure. The lengths of the arrows indicate the extent to which the competitive environments facing the various companies within each industry are changing.

- In Germany, some computer production is still moving towards global competition. In the food processing industry small craft companies are consolidating and the multinationals are expanding. In addition to the regional component, the steel industry is facing increased competition from abroad as the EC restrictions are breaking down.
- In Japan, the food processing industry is gradually consolidating and multinationals are entering.

- In the USA, the steel and partially the car industries have a legacy from the era of regional competition where 2-3 large companies were slow to adjust to the challenge of global competition. These large companies still have a significant share of total output. In metalworking the transplants are growing and will influence industry productivity within a few years. The car parts industry is also still in transition. Transplant production is growing, but the group of companies originating in the USA have not yet responded to the increased global competition with improvements in productivity.

Consideration of how the industries had evolved in recent years led us to adjust their classifications. An industry may be largely global, but may have a regional component if it is in transition.

Productivity and the Nature of Competition

To see whether our classifications of the industries were related to their productivity, we plotted them against the industries' productivity rankings. The results are summarised in graph 10. The graph suggests that there is a strong relationship: local or regional industries are lower in productivity than the same industries competing globally.

A few cases deserve special mention. The soap and detergent industry in Germany is ranked lowest of the three in productivity within the industry despite being globally competitive. The low productivity is largely the result of its large share of powdered detergent, not weak competitive intensity.

The food industry in Japan and the beer industry in Germany are ranked third in productivity, similar to several regionally competitive industries. In fact, their productivities (at 33 and 44 per cent) are by far the lowest of the group (see graph 1). Local competition with its associated lack of consolidation exacts a large productivity penalty. This penalty is not fully revealed by a simple productivity rank ordering within an industry. To clarify our hypothesis and to create a more quantitative and objective measure of the intensity of competition, we refined this analysis with two definitions. The productivity leaders are the most productive manufacturing operations within the Triad. In each of the nine industries there is a productivity leader: metalworking, steel, cars, car parts, and consumer electronics in Japan; computers, soap and detergents, beer and food in the USA.

The productivity followers are the manufacturing operations whose productivity on average is below that of the leaders. The productivity followers are the remaining eighteen industries.

Dividing the industries into these two groups allows us to see more clearly the effect of the competitive environment on productivity. We start by looking at the productivity leaders.

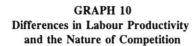

GRAPH 10
Differences in Labour Productivity
and the Nature of Competition

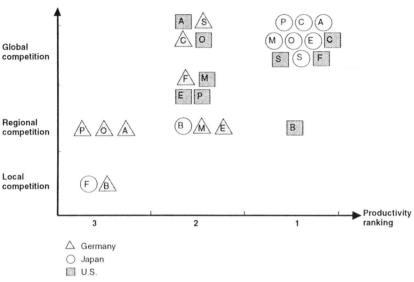

C: Computer   O: Consumer electronics
S: Soap/detergent   F: Food
A: Auto cars   B: Beer
P: Parts   E: Steel
M: Metalworking

Globalisation Among the Productivity Leaders

Maintaining leadership. With the exception of beer, all of the industry productivity leaders studied are exposed to both the best internal and external producers. Through continuous improvement in their production processes, they have been able to develop and maintain their labour productivity lead.

1) Exposure to best external and internal producers. The companies exposed to the best external competition compete head-to-head through transplants, exports and, to a lesser degree, imports.

- All of the operations in Japan that are leaders export large fractions of their output to sell in direct competition with their best external producers. In the cases we studied this has meant competing in the US market. Several companies in these industries have established transplants in the USA and Europe.

- The large computer companies originating in the USA have long exported around the world, set up transplants, and faced competition from imports. The companies that manage soap and detergent and food processing operations in the USA are multinationals, meeting competitors around the globe.

- The beer industry based in the USA is the only exception where the North American operations mainly compete regionally. However, operations in Germany and Japan are not exposed to greater global competition than the USA.

2) Continuous improvement of the production process. The nine industry leaders have maintained their productivity advantage by continually improving their production processes. This improvement is achieved through either increasing efficiency within the existing process or incorporating innovations.

- In the automotive industry, Toyota has maintained its productivity lead through refining its lean manufacturing process. The beer industry in the USA uses the same production process as years ago, but increasingly with the addition of computer controls.
- Productivity improvements have also come through innovations in the product or in the production process itself, and can originate from suppliers. The productivity leadership of computer companies originating in the USA has been maintained largely through product innovations such as new standards of workstations and client-server networks.
- Leadership in integrated steel has required innovations in continuous production systems and in the size of blast furnaces. Integrated plants in Japan are newer than in the USA and Germany, and by virtue of their youth they have been productivity leaders since they were built. But these plants have maintained their leadership through further innovations in the production process.

Becoming a leader. In the computer, soap and detergent, food and beer industries, productivity leadership has not changed, but has remained with the USA for a long period of time. In the other five cases Japan overtook competitors in productivity within the last two decades.

1) Exposure to past leaders. Prior to becoming productivity leaders, most of these operations in Japan were competing against their best external producers in Europe and the USA.

- When the metalworking, cars, car parts, and consumer electronics industries in Japan were followers, they were exporting and competing extensively with the productivity leader at that time.
- During this period, operations in Japan were well below the highest productivity operations world-wide, and imports and transplants were discouraged. This "protection" lasted well beyond the point where operations in Japan could be described as infant industries. However, given their external orientation through exports, the limits to competition did not prevent these operations from becoming productivity leaders.

2) Reasons for becoming leaders. Followers improve their productivity by competing with and learning from the leaders. However, revolutionary

innovations appear to be important in leap-frogging the leaders. Innovation is intrinsically hard to predict and the reasons why particular leaders became leaders may be impossible to determine. However, we do have a few concrete examples of how operations in Japan surpassed the leader at that time through a significant innovation.

- Lean manufacturing and design for manufacturing, which originated in car operations in Japan, have proven to be enormously significant innovations. They use continuous incremental improvement and integrate product design engineering and process engineering. They also utilise suggestions from line workers. These innovations have spread among the car makers, to car parts and metalworking (all major suppliers to cars) and have been adapted by other industries for their own production.
- Sweeping innovations such as standardisation and automation in metalworking were largely responsible for the operations in Japan overtaking those in Germany and the USA for productivity leadership.

Exposure to the best internal and external producers and innovation appear to be important for maintaining leadership, and innovation appears to be important for gaining leadership in the first place. Innovations may well be triggered by the pressure generated by the competition with the productivity leader, although we do not have data to confirm this. We do argue, however, that the intensity and scope of competition greatly affects the speed of diffusion of innovations, and hence the size of the gap between follower industries and the productivity leaders that are observed across countries at a point in time. We turn now to an examination of the productivity followers among our case studies in order to show this.

Productivity and Globalisation Among the Productivity Followers

Our hypothesis for the productivity followers is that, the greater the exposure of a productivity follower to competition with the productivity leader, the closer this industry's productivity will be to that of the leader.

We constructed a globalisation index for each of the eighteen productivity followers in the case studies. The globalisation index is derived by using the following construction principle. Assume the only connection of the domestic industry with the productivity leader are imports from the productivity leader. This volume is denoted by D. Let C be the total production volume of the domestic operations which is assumed to be sold entirely in the home market. Then, we define the globalisation of the domestic industry as:

$$G = \min \left[1, \frac{2D}{D+C} \right]$$

The globalisation index measures the exposure of the domestic operations.

GRAPH 11
Globalisation vs. Relative Productivity*
Transplant, Transplant Exposure, and Trade

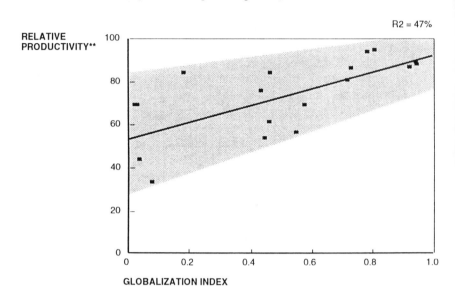

Data points are nine case study industries in countries without productivity
leading edge
Relative to industry leader at 100
Source: McKinsey analysis

If the exports from the productivity leader reach the same level as domestic
incumbent production the globalisation index represents the notion of head-to-
head competition of two companies of equal size. This is interpreted as full
exposure or $G = 1$. Otherwise, if D is zero, G is obviously zero as well.

The construction principle is now used to construct the globalisation index
for the general case by measuring the exposure for each part of the production
volume and through aggregation (for more details see Gersbach, 1994a,
1994b).

Graph 11 shows that there is a high correlation between globalisation and
relative productivity. The horizontal axis measures the degree to which a
country's production volume comes from the productivity leader (transplants),
or is exposed to competition with the productivity leader. The vertical axis is
the productivity for each industry normalised to the leader at one hundred.
graph 11 suggests that all of the industries where the globalisation index was
above about 0.7 have productivities very close to the productivity leaders.
The globalisation index for a domestic industry takes the following factors
into account:

- The volume of production in transplants operated by productivity leaders;
- The exposure of domestic operations to the productivity leader's transplants;
- The exposure of domestic operations to competition with the productivity leader through trade: imports from the leading country, exports to the leading country, and exports to third countries where head-to-head competition with the productivity leader exists.

Graph 12 shows the factors considered in calculating the index, which is a weighted sum of all the components. Other factors were also taken into account:

GRAPH 12
Exposures of Industries to Productivity Leader

VEHICLE OF EXPOSURE

Trade
- From leader
- To leader
- From transplant of leader in third country
- To third country with transplant of leader
- To third country with trade from leader

Foreign direct investment
- Into domestic market
- Into third country

Exposure to productivity leader

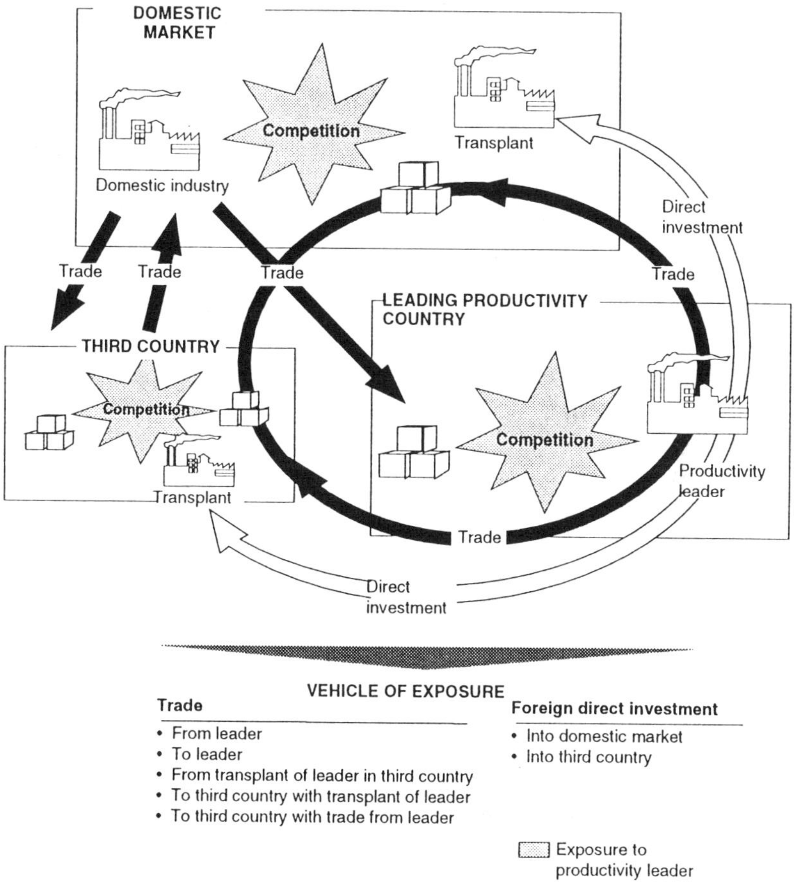

- The extent of trade protection, as measured by the difference between the PPP and the market exchange rate, was included in the import component (for details see Gersbach 1994b).
- Transplants from third countries added to the globalisation of domestic company production if operations in the third country have higher productivity than that of the domestic industry.
- The globalisation of the car parts industry was adjusted for the globalisation of the car industry (the OEMs), due to their strong influence on supplier productivity.

We have constructed country-level globalisation indexes for productivity followers, with each industry's globalisation index weighted by its employment share. The results of these calculations are shown in graph 13.

GRAPH 13
Globalisation of Productivity Followers
Globalisation Index Weighted by Employment Share for Followers

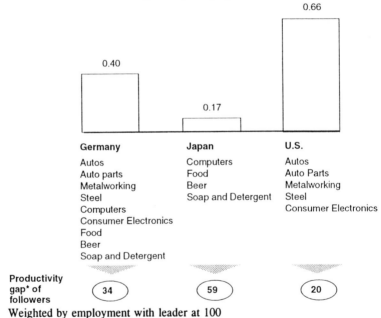

* Weighted by employment with leader at 100
Source: McKinsey analysis

We find that productivity followers in the USA have the highest overall level of globalisation, with follower industries in Germany next. Productivity followers in Japan are low in overall globalisation, held down by the large food industry. Some German industries have faced limited direct competition with productivity leaders. We believe that this has been an important reason for the lower productivity found in those industries.

Determining the Direction of Causality

It seems clear that there is a strong association between productivity and degree of competition with the productivity leaders. However, we need to probe carefully into the reasons why this association exists and why we believe that competition with the productivity leader determines productivity rather than vice versa.

A possible criticism of our conclusion is that the direction of causality is the opposite of that stated above. This would imply that competitive industries became highly productive first and then started to export or to make foreign investment in order to exploit their cost advantages. We disagree with this alternative perspective for the following reasons.

- It is possible to be externally oriented and to export well before levels of productivity are achieved that rival the world frontier. This is certainly the case for countries in South East Asia today and was true for Japan and Germany in the 1960s and 1970s. The decision to participate in the global economy typically preceded the high productivity levels rather than vice versa.

- In those German industries that were competing against the leading edge in the 1960s and 1970s, productivity growth was very rapid. During the eighties productivity growth slowed down and some German industries faced substantial productivity gaps. One reason is that they did not take part in some industries in the global productivity race between Japan and USA since they were mostly focused on Europe.

TABLE 2
Responses of US-based Industries to
Japanese Competition until 1990

Industry	Faced	Reaction
Cars	√	Reform
Parts	√	No major improvement
Steel	√	Reform (minimills)
Metalworking	√	Partial exit
Computers	√	Reform, partial lead
Consumer electronics	√	Exit, no growth
Processed food	-	-
Beer	-	-
Soap and detergents	-	-

These arguments about why we believe that it is globalisation that leads to high productivity, rather than vice versa, can be greatly strengthened by examining what actually happened to USA industries that faced leading edge competition from Japan.

Table 2 summarises the impact of increased competition on industries operating in the USA. Six of these have faced strong competition in recent years from industries in Japan with high productivity.

- Of these six, there are two that have clearly responded to the Japanese challenge and improved the productivity of their operations i.e. computers and cars.
- A third industry, steel, has changed dramatically. The US-integrated mills did not invest heavily to upgrade their facilities, but they have responded, albeit slowly, by streamlining their operations and retiring many integrated mills. Minimills entered the industry, which can be seen as a response to the need for lower-cost production in the face of increased international competition.
- At present there is still a large car parts industry consisting of plants that originated in the USA, but transplants are being set up to compete with these. Our data suggest that the original US plants have fallen well behind the average of Japanese operations in productivity. This industry may be one where existing plants adjust in response to the increased competitive intensity, or it may be one where these plants exit. Either way, we expect productivity to rise in US operations in car parts.
- Companies founded in the USA have almost completely exited the consumer electronics industry, and to some extent, left metalworking too, as transplant entry and import competition has occurred.

Local Competition and Productivity

In the case studies we found that two industries, beer in Germany and food in Japan, showed large productivity shortfalls compared with the productivity leaders. They have a common feature which distinguishes them from the rest of the productivity followers: they have remained local and unconsolidated with mostly small companies serving local markets.

These two industries also lack the scale and technology of the productivity leaders. But to achieve high productivity it may be necessary for most of the companies in the industry to go out of business, creating worker dislocation and lower total employment in the industry as it is e.g. happening in the German beer industry. Barriers to consolidation can be found mainly in the regulatory environment protecting existing players and/or customers taste for locally produced and specialty goods.

We conclude that within the productivity followers, there are essentially two groups: unconsolidated industries which show a substantial gap and which are at most competing on a local basis, and others which are consolidated nationally or regionally and serve national or regional markets.

Importance of Factors in the Globalisation Index

If we look at the three main components of the globalisation index in graph 14 (leading edge transplants, exposure to leading edge transplants, and exposure through trade to the productivity leader), we can see that the USA's high overall globalisation index is mainly due to the high level of transplants. The exposure factors contribute similarly to Germany's overall index value, but at lower levels. In those industries where Japan is a productivity follower, however, there is significantly less transplant production relative to trade as well as low exposure to the productivity leader through trade.

GRAPH 14
Importance of Factors in the Globalisation Index

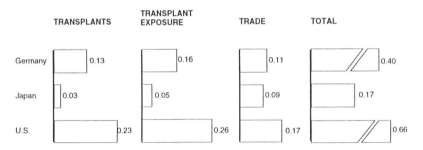

6. Conclusions

The main effort to understand causality in this report has been directed at the production process level. We wanted to know what companies were doing differently in these countries. Several themes have emerged from the case studies. First, the products manufactured are somewhat different and this helps explain some of the productivity gaps. Second, very different production technologies coexist within a given industry and productivity varies greatly among these generations of technologies. Third, innovations in product design for manufacturing have sharply reduced cost and raised productivity for companies that have adopted the new techniques. Fourth, even with a given technology and product design, there are very large increases in productivity that can be achieved through the efficient organisation of functions and tasks. Fifth, we did not find that intrinsic motivation and skill differences were a major source of the productivity gaps, although improved organisation of functions and tasks will require on-the-job training.

Moving beyond the production process level we found a strong association between the degree of competition with the world's productivity leader and relative productivity. Also, unconsolidated local industries have very low productivity. Global competition appears to be very important in achieving and sustaining best practice productivity levels.

References

Abramovitz, M. (1993), "The Search for the Sources of Growth: Areas of Ignorance, Old and New", *Journal of Economic History*, 53 (2), pp. 217-243.

Ark, B. van and D. Pilat (1993), "Cross Country Productivity Levels: Differences and Causes", *Brookings Papers on Economic Activity: Microeconomics, 2*, December.

Baily, M.N. (1993), "Competition, Regulation and Efficiency in Service Industries", *Brookings Papers on Economic Activity: Microeconomics, 2*, December.

Baily, M.N., C. Hulten and D. Campbell (1992), "Productivity Dynamics in Manufacturing Plants", *Brookings Papers on Economic Activity: Microeconomics*, pp. 187-267.

Barro, R.J. (1991), "Economic Growth in a Cross Section of Countries", *The Quarterly Journal of Economics*, CV, May, pp. 407-443.

Baumol, W.J., S.A.B. Blackman and E.N. Wolff, (1989) *Productivity and American Leadership. The Long Run View*, MIT Press, Cambridge Massachusetts.

Caves, R.E. and Associates (1992), *Industrial Efficiency in Six Nations*, MIT Press, Cambridge Massachusetts.

Dollar, D. and E.N. Wolff (1993), *Competitiveness, Convergence, and International Specialisation*, MIT Press, Cambridge Massachusetts.

Gersbach, H. (1994a), "Does and How Does Globalisation matter", *Working paper*, University of Basel.

Gersbach, H. (1994b), "Import Protection as Growth Promotion?", *Working paper*, University of Basel.

Gersbach, H. and B. van Ark (1994), "Microfoundations of International Productivity Comparisons", *Research Memorandum*, Groningen Growth and Development Centre, University of Groningen.

Gersbach, H., B. Lewis, G. Mercer and J. Sinclair (1994), "Production in the Automotive Assembly Industry", *International Motor Business*, 1st quarter, EIU, chapter 7, pp. 102-132.

Grossman, G.M. and E. Helpman (1991), *Innovation and Growth in the Global Economy*, MIT Press, Cambridge Massachusetts.

Jorgenson, D.W. and M. Kuroda (1992), "Productivity and International Competitiveness in Japan and the United States, 1960-1985", *Economics Studies Quarterly*, 43, pp. 313-325.

Joly, H., J. Kluge and L. Stein (1994), "Excellence in Electronics, Europe's Structural Weakness", *The McKinsey Quarterly*, 1, pp. 33-38.

Mason, G., S.J. Prais and B. van Ark (1992), "Vocational Education and Productivity in the Netherlands and Britain", *National Institute Economic Review*, No. 140, May, pp. 45-63.

McKinsey Global Institute (1992), *Service Sector Productivity*, McKinsey & Co., Washington D.C.

McKinsey Global Institute (1993), *Manufacturing Productivity*, McKinsey & Co., Washington D.C.

Maddison, A. (1991), *Dynamic Forces in Capitalist Development*, Oxford University Press.

Mankiw, N.G., D. Romer and D.N. Weil (1992), "A Contribution to the Empirics of Economic Growth", *Quarterly Journal of Economics*, CVI May, pp. 407-437.

Milgrom, P. and J. Roberts (1990), "The Economics of Modern Manufacturing: Technology, Strategy, and Organization", *American Economic Review*, 80 (3), pp. 511-528.

Pilat, D. (1994), "The Economics of Rapid Growth: The Experience of Japan and Korea", Edward Elgar Publishers.

Scott, M.FG. (1992), "Policy Implications of a New View of Economic Growth", *Economic Journal*, 102, pp. 622-632.

Solow, R. (1957), "Technical Change and the Aggregate Production Function", *Review of Economic Statistics*, 47, pp. 312-320.

Spence, M.A. and H.A. Hazard (eds.) (1990), *International Competitiveness*, Ballinger Publishing, Cambridge Massachusetts.

Summers, R. and A.W. Heston (1991), "The Penn World Table (Mark 5):An Expanded set of International Comparisons", 1950-1988, *Quarterly Journal of Economics*, 106, pp. 327-368.

Appendix - A Micro Approach towards the Calculation of Industry PPPs[1]

In the study of the McKinsey Global Institute, industry PPPs were calculated, tested and modified for nine case industries. In addition, PPPs for three other industries were derived or adapted from other McKinsey studies. Four methods were considered to arrive at industry PPPs, which will be dealt with subsequently in the following sections:
1) Existing products UVRs based on census information were adjusted for differences in terms of product mix and product quality between countries:
- adjustment of existing UVRs for differences in product mix;
- adjustment of existing UVRs for differences in product quality;
- reshuffling product matches on the basis of industry expert information.
2) New PPPs were obtained from surveys specifically carried out for this study or from existing McKinsey studies.
3) Indirect methods were used to obtain proxy PPPs, for example by using company estimates on cost and profit, or by adjusting ICP expenditure PPPs for distribution margins and taxes.
4) PPPs were adjusted for price differentials of intermediate inputs. Table A1 gives an overview of these four approaches and to which industries they were applied.
It needs to be emphasised that some of these methods, in particular the indirect ones under 3), are not necessarily superior over original census UVRs. In some cases census UVRs are not available at the micro-industry level, so that there is no alternative to the indirect procedure suggested in the MGI study. The use of proxy expenditure PPPs for food products was mainly motivated by the need to circumvent quality problems in the UVRs derived from the census.

ad 1) Adjusting Existing Product Matches

"Existing" product UVRs were mostly derived from the ICOP studies as described by van Ark and Pilat (1993). Three steps were considered to adjust these existing PPPs. Firstly, they were adjusted for differences in product mix between countries (1.1); secondly for differences in product quality (1.2); and thirdly existing PPPs were reshuffled to obtain a better match of product items in two countries (1.3).

---

[1]   This appendix is derived from H. Gersbach and B. van Ark (1994), "Microfoundations of International Productivity Comparisons", *Research Memorandum GD-11*, Groningen Growth and Development Centre, University of Groningen.

Table A1

Methods for Industry PPPs in the McKinsey Global Institute Study of
Manufacturing Productivity in Germany, Japan and the United States

Industry	(1) Adjusting Existing Product Matches		(2) Adding New Product Matches		(3) Indirect Proxy PPPs		(4) Including PPPs for Intermediate Inputs	
	Germany/USA	Japan/USA	Germany/USA	Japan/USA	Germany/USA	Japan/USA	Germany/USA	Japan/USA
Food Manufacturing					adjusted ICP PPP	adjusted ICP PPP		
Breweries	*no quality adjustment*	*no quality adjustment*	using physical quantities	using physical quantities				
Soap and Detergents	reshuffling	reshuffling					*no effect*	*no effect*
Iron and Steel	reshuffling	reshuffling					negligible effect	neglible effect
Machine Tools			McK survey domestic prices	McK survey domestic prices	domestic vs. export price	domestic vs. export price		
Computers			PCs: producer and wholesale prices, McK survey	PCs: producer and wholesale prices, McK survey			imported inputs at exchange rate	negligible effect
Audio and Video Equipment	reshuffling and mix	reshuffling and mix					imported inputs at exchange rate	no effect
Passenger Cars	{mix/quality	mix/quality						
Parts and Components of Cars	{mix	mix						
Other Machinery			McK survey					
Industrial Electronics			McK survey					
Wired Communication Equipment				McK survey				

1.1 Adjustment of existing UVRs for differences in product mix

In various cases it was possible to obtain information from trade sources or from McKinsey studies to adjust the census-based product matches for differences in the mix of product varieties between two countries. Mix adjustments were made in the MGI study for passenger cars and parts and for audio and video equipment. As an example we illustrate passenger cars.

Passenger Cars and Parts.

Product mix was defined according to the European ABCDE market segmentation, which classifies cars according to size and basic features (See Gersbach, Lewis, Mercer, Sinclair, 1994). This standard is normally used only in European countries, but it provides a worldwide yardstick against which cars from other countries can be classified as well. After classifying cars in Japan and the USA according to the ABCDE standard, and applying production value weights from standard automotive statistics to each of the market segments, the appropriate mix adjustment was obtained. The adjustment for mix showed that in 1987 Japanese cars were on average 37 percent "lighter" than in the United States. By 1990, this adjustment was smaller (29%), reflecting the shift of Japanese producers into larger luxury cars. A similar but smaller adjustment in the same direction was made for the Germany/US comparison (11%).

1.2. Adjustment of existing UVRs for differences in product quality

In the MGI study the quality concept applied was related to the valuation of the product by the users, but only in so far as it could be connected to characteristics of the product itself or the production process. PPPs were adjusted for quality differences when these were recognised by consumers in such a way that they were willing to pay a price premium, and when these quality differences were the result of differences in the products and production process, and not of advertising or taste. The remaining notions of quality were treated as differences in consumer preferences which may *explain* the differences in productivity and which can improve the competitive situation of companies, but which are not used in adjusting the productivity measure itself. Moreover, quality premiums were only measured in markets where two products under consideration are sold with equal access. Otherwise quality premiums and price markups are not distinguishable. As an example we consider passengers cars.

Passenger Cars.

There are substantial differences in reliability, functionality, and basic quality among the cars produced in the three countries within each individual market segment. The quality difference is defined as the price differential which a consumer with unrestricted access to foreign products would be willing to pay for a car of the same category, based on his/her perception of quality differences like reliability and functionality, etc. This definition made it possible to distinguish between consumer preferences which were related to tangible product differences, and those related to differences based on intangible product characteristics. For both country comparisons the MGI study relied on proprietary information about the quality premium, although a much wider range of models was covered in the Japan/USA comparison than in the Germany/USA comparison. In the Japan/USA comparison the quality adjustment on the basis of this procedure was 12 per cent, which was the price premium which American consumers with ready access to all models were willing to pay for a Japanese car over a similar US car in 1987. By 1990 this price premium had been reduced to 8 per cent. In Germany, consumers valued the quality of German-made cars almost equal to that of Japanese cars, i.e. they commanded a 10 per cent quality premium against US cars in 1987. This quality premium had shrunk to about 5 per cent in 1990. This procedure relies on a market valuation to reveal the value of product attributes to consumers, and can only be used when the products are close substitutes, the markets are competitive and customers have unrestricted access to the entire product range.

The MGI study also observed significant differences (between Germany and the USA) in quality of products in various machinery industries. For example, a machinery survey by McKinsey (*Total Quality Management*) showed that part of German machine tools commanded a price premium of on average 8 per cent over comparable US products in Germany. However, for total metalworking this quality premium had only a very small impact of 1 to 2 per cent.

1.3. Reshuffling Product Matches

In some industries specialist industry knowledge was used to check the original product matches when the product specifications given in the censuses were not exactly comparable across countries or when they were subject to different interpretations. The reshuffling of existing product matches was done for audio and video equipment, for soap and detergents and for steel. In practice the overall impact of these reshuffles on the PPPs were relatively small.

ad 2) Adding New Product Matches

Another way to derive industry PPPs is to make new product matches next to the existing ones from ICOP on the basis of information from other public sources than the census or on the basis of McKinsey data bases. These new matches can be combined with the (adjusted) product matches derived from the census or they can serve as the basis for a new industry PPP. The MGI study made new matches for computer and for beer. In addition to the case studies some new product matches were obtained for various machinery items and for industrial electronics.

ad 3) Indirect Methods

When industry PPPs could not be obtained by way of direct observation, proxy PPPs were calculated for some items through indirect methods. In the MGI study two indirect methods were applied. Firstly, PPPs were estimates by separating exports and domestic sales, and by making price comparisons on the basis of cost and profit estimates. Secondly, proxy PPPs were derived from adjusted expenditure ICP PPPs.

3.1. Using exports and domestic sales PPPs
Separate PPPs are calculated for exports and for domestic sales and weighted according to their share in total sales. The export PPP is mostly close to the current exchange rate, but is adjusted for differences in distribution margins or price setting behaviour. The PPP for domestic sales can be calculated in two different ways, i.e. either by gathering information about price differentials between export and domestic sales, or by deriving the PPP from cost and profit comparisons of companies producing the same products.

3.2. Using final expenditure PPPs
A second indirect method is to make use of existing expenditure ICP PPPs from the International Comparisons Project (ICP). In order to derive industry PPPs from final expenditure PPPs, certain adjustments were required. Final expenditure PPPs reflect price ratios at the retail level and need to be adjusted for differences in relative distribution margins and differences in sales and value added taxes. In addition, one needs to check the impact of included import prices and excluded export prices in expenditure PPPs. Despite such adjustments, a major problem remains that expenditure PPPs do not include observations for prices of products which are used in intermediate stages of the production process, such as wheat flour, fats, etc. The ideal method should therefore be to derive direct observations of ex-factory prices adjusted for differences in quality.

ad 4) Accounting for Double Deflation

In addition to modification of PPPs based on gross output or sales, some industries were characterised by different price relatives for inputs and output. For instance, in some industries inputs are traded more freely on the world market than output, so that the former were priced more closely to world market exchange rates. In such cases the MGI study calculated a separate input PPP to convert intermediate inputs to a common currency. This has been done for soap and detergents, metalworking, computers, audio and video equipment and steel.

The MGI study also observed the necessity for double deflation in the food manufacturing industry, but in contrast to the original ICOP measures it did not undertake such estimations, so that MGI PPPs for food products are for shipments and not for value added.

Table A2a shows the changes in DM/US$ PPPs and table A2b shows the changes in Yen/US$ PPP for the selected industries following the adjustments made in the MGI study as described above. The first column with unit value ratios in tables A2.a and A2.b shows the original ones as derived from the censuses.

Table A2.a shows that for the Germany/USA comparison the differences between the census UVRs and the MGI industry PPPs are moderate for most of the industries. The only big exception is computers, for which the adjusted PPP was 41 per cent higher than the census UVR. However, it needs to be emphasised that we were not able to compare the PPPs for machinery and industrial electronics with a census UVR, as it was not possible to obtain an estimate for this specific industry from the census. On the other hand, even the adjustment for durable consumer goods (audio and video equipment and passenger cars) appeared surprisingly small.[2]

In the case of the Japan/USA comparison (table A2.b) the changes were biggest in the cases of metal working, cars and car parts, and smaller for iron and steel and breweries. In this case no comparison with census UVRs could be made for computers and for communication equipment.[3] A surprisingly large downward adjustment was made to the original census UVR for food products, for which no single explanation can be given. The much lower expenditure PPP suggests a higher quality of food products in Japan, which may be related to the greater freshness and a lower degree of standardisation of the goods in Japan. On the other hand, the expenditure PPPs may not reflect the relatively high prices of intermediate food products which are more directly associated with the excessively high prices of Japanese agricultural products. As the "pro memoria"-column shows, an adjustment for higher agri-

---

[2]   The "pro memoria" column in table A2a shows the ICOP UVRs which were used in the ICOP aggregation procedure from industry to branch level (see van Ark and Pilat (1993) and the chapter by van Ark in this volume). The ICOP DM/US$ UVRs for metal working and machinery can therefore not be used at the industry level, because they represents products in more aggregate groups of industries.

[3]   The ICOP UVRs for metal working, computers and wired communication equipment in the "pro memoria" column cannot be used at the industry level as they represent UVRs of products from more aggregate groups of industries.

Table A2a
Census UVRs and PPPs of McKinsey Global Institue for
selected industries Germany/USA, 1987 (DM/US$)

Industry	Industry Codes		DM/US$ 1987			Pro Memoria
	Germany	USA	Census UVR	MGI Industry PPP	% Difference Between MGI PPP & Census UVR	*ICOP UVR*
Food Products	6811-60 6882 6889	201-209 excl. 208	1.952	2.071	6.1%	*1.952*
Breweries	6871	2082	2.140	2.080	- 2.8%	*2.215*[a]
Soap and Detergents	4036 (part)	2841	2.204	2.204	0.0%	*2.204*
Iron and Steel	2711 2715 2720 3015	3312 3316 3317	2.018	1.880	- 6.8%	*2.018*
Metal Working	3220	3541-45 3549	2.241	2.280	1.7%	*1.913*[b]
Construction Machinery; Textile Machinery; Food Product Machinery; Ball and Roller Bearings	3230 3240 3256 3257 3260	353 3552 3556 3562	n.a.	2.460	n.a.	*1.913*[b]
Computers	5080	3571-77	1.624	2.290	41.0%	*1.624*
Audio and Video Equipment	3670	3651 3652 3695	2.787	2.930	5.1%	*2.787*
Industrial Electronics	3660	3625 3661-69 3812-26 3829-45	n.a.	2.670	n.a.	*2.503*[c]
Cars, incl. Parts	3311 3314	3711 3714	1.968	2.030	3.2%	*1.968*

[a] ICOP UVR differs from census UVR because the former is the quantity weighted UVR for beer <u>and</u> malt and can therefore not be used for the beer industry separately.
[b] ICOP UVR differs from census UVR because the former is the quantity weighted UVR of <u>all</u> items in machinery and transport equipment and can therefore not be used for metal working and machinery industries separately.
[c] ICOP UVR refers to the quantity weighted UVR of <u>all</u> items in electrical engineering and can therefore not be used for industrial electronics separately.

Table A2b
Census UVRs and PPPs of McKinsey Global Institue for
selected industries Japan/USA, 1987 (Yen/US$)

Industry	Industry Codes		Yen/US$ 1987			*Pro Memoria ICOP UVR*
	Japan	USA	Census UVR	MGI Industry PPP	% Difference Between MGI PPP & Census UVR	
Food Products	12	201-209 excl. 208	384.2	252.5	- 34.2%	*266.2*[a]
Breweries	1322	2082	184.9	205.0	10.9%	*184.9*
Soap and Detergents	2052	2841	210.0	210.0	0.0%	*210.0*
Iron and Steel	261 263 264 265	3312 3316 3317	145.6	149.0	2.3%	*145.6*
Metal Working	2941-44 2996 2998	3541-45 3549	116.4	140.0	20.3%	*133.3*[b]
Computers	3051	3571-77	n.a.	153.3	n.a.	*133.3*[b]
Audio and Video Equipment	3043-44 3062	3651	138.9	138.9	0.0%	*138.9*
Wired Communication Equipment	3041	3663	n.a.	168.7	n.a.	*138.5*
Cars	3111	3711 3751	96.1	114.3	18.9%	*97.4*[c]
Car Parts	3113	3714 3592 3694	110.0	126.0	14.5%	*97.4*[c]

[a] ICOP UVR differs from census UVR because the former is adjusted for the PPP of agricultural inputs.
[b] ICOP UVR differs from census UVR because the former is the quantity weighted UVR for all items in machinery and can therefore not be applied to metal working and computer industries separately.
[c] ICOP UVR differs from census UVR because the former is the quantity weighted UVR for cars and parts and can therefore not be applied to cars and car parts separately.

cultural input prices in the food processing industry in Japan suggests a reduction of the gross output UVR by almost one-third.

The overall results suggest that for both the Germany/US as well as the Japan/US comparison the adjustments to the original census UVRs are most substantial in the case of investment goods and durable consumer goods, but (with the obvious exception of food products in Japan) less so for non-durable consumer goods and basic goods.

One can therefore conclude that for the latter category of products, comparisons of output and productivity at the disaggregated industry level even when exclusively based on census information give more robust results. However, for comparisons of industries producing durable consumer goods and investment goods detailed adjustments for differences in product variety and quality are required.

International Productivity Differences
K. Wagner and B. van Ark (editors)

The Comparative Productivity of East and West German Manufacturing: A Matched Plant Comparison

D.M.W.N. Hitchens[*], *K. Wagner*[**] *and J.E. Birnie*[*]

[*] *Department of Economics, Queen's University of Belfast*
[**] *Wissenschaftszentrum Berlin für Sozialforschung and Fachhochschule für Technik und Wirtschaft Berlin*[*]

1. Introduction

If the East German economy is to perform satisfactorily in terms of generating socially acceptable levels of employment and living standards it will be necessary for it to develop a tradeable sector which is competitive within Germany and the rest of the European Union (Siebert, 1991). This paper focuses on manufacturing productivity performance and examines levels achieved by a sample of East German firms shortly after unification, and measures progress in productivity made since 1989. An important objective is to update the data presented here in order to examine how East German firms close the productivity gap with West Germany, to draw lessons which will have wider application throughout the Eastern European economies. Despite problems currently being experienced by the East German economy the speed of transition to a market economy and rate of convergence to Western productivity levels is expected to be faster.

The principal aim is to establish a benchmark measure of relative manufacturing productivity for 1990-91 and measure productivity change since 1989. A further purpose is to examine sources of productivity differences including: machine type, age, and manning. Also labour force characteristics including managerial qualifications, labour skills, turnover, absenteeism; and work organisation and production methods.

Table 1 provides background data relating to trends in relative investment, labour costs, productivity and competitiveness in the East German economy as a whole.

---

[*] **Acknowledgement**
These results are largely based on a one year study of matched companies (in East and West Germany) and Northern Ireland funded by the European Commission (DG Regional Policy). The authors are also grateful for the research assistance provided by Jörn Mallok during that project. Eileen Maguire of Queen's University kindly helped with production of the camera-ready copy.

TABLE 1
East German Investment Rates, Labour Costs, Productivity and
Competitiveness Compared to West Germany
East Germany as a per cent of the West German level

	1991	1992	1993
Investment per head of the population	62	80	103
Total labour per employee	46	60	66
Output per employee	28	39	46
Unit labour costs[a]	164	154	153

[a] Comparative total labour costs per employee divided by relative output per employee.

Source: Investment rates from German Economics Ministry (quoted in Financial Times (4 May 1994)) and all other data from Heinze and Klempin (1994).

Whilst the data shown refers to the entire East German economy the trends which can be identified are indicative of performance in manufacturing. For example, investment rates have increased and levels of comparative productivity have improved. Nevertheless, the growth in relative labour costs since 1989 in East Germany has outstripped the increase in comparative productivity. By implication the comparative cost competitiveness of companies in East Germany has declined markedly notwithstanding the improvement in performance shown between 1991 and 1993.

2. Methods and Design of the Inquiry

The method adopted is one of a matched plant comparison of a cross-section of manufacturing companies relative to their West German counterparts. Companies are matched in terms of product type, process type and post-unification establishment size category.[1]

Companies sampled were selected on the basis of two criteria: (1) that they provided a cross-section of East German industry and, (2) that they could be matched with a data bank of international firm comparisons made between Northern Ireland and West Germany. This data bank consisted of 42 pairs of matched companies in Northern Ireland and West Germany which were originally surveyed in 1988 (Hitchens, Wagner and Birnie, 1990).

The productivity and other data on the characteristics of the West German plants, such as machine age, technology levels and skills, relate to the situation at the time of the initial interviews in 1988. Since the differences between the

---

[1]   For more details see Hitchens, Wagner and Birnie (1993).

East and West German samples were almost always large and the profile of West German sample firms in 1991 in terms of machinery and skills was reported essentially similar to that in 1988 the conclusions drawn are robust.

The Sample

Table 2 shows the number of factories sampled by sector in East Germany and West Germany. Firms and sectors (with the exception of clothing and miscellaneous trades) were sampled across all Eastern *Länder*, including Berlin. Plants were sampled across a wide size range as represented both before and after unification. When these are compared as in table 3 a similar spread is shown for each area.

TABLE 2
Total Number of Plants Visited by Sector

	East Germany	West Germany
Engineering	10	10
Food, Drink & Tobacco	7	4
Clothing	3	12
Furniture and miscellaneous[a]	12	8
Total	32	34

[a] Electronics, steel, optical, glass, gravel, brushes, packaging and disinfectants.

TABLE 3
Size Distribution of Factories Compared
(per cent of total sample plants)

Employees	East Germany	West Germany
Under 50	20	13
50 - under 100	7	29
100 - under 500	37	36
500 - under 1000	10	6
1000 - under 3000	23	13
3000 - under 5000	3	3
5000 and over	--	--
Total	100	100

Productivity: Levels

Firms visited were asked to supply data on the physical output (i.e. volume, weight or number of units) of the major products of the plant. This method of using physical indicators was also used in some of the early statistical comparisons of international productivity (Rostas, 1948) as well as previous matched plant studies (Daly, Hitchens and Wagner, 1985; Hitchens, Wagner and Birnie, 1990, 1991; Steedman and Wagner, 1987, 1989). The physical "units" being compared in East and West Germany were for similar product types but not counting the better quality of products made in West Germany, e.g. with regard to the finish of women's outerwear.[2] The results of the productivity measurements were in some cases supported by the results of consultants' studies shown to the interviewers by the East German firms. Further, in one-third of cases West German firms co-operating with East German plants provided assessments of East German productivity. Estimates derived from such managerial sources have been found to be especially reliable (Wagner, Hitchens and Birnie, 1991).

These physical productivity measures represent a partial indicator of comparative productivity given that they are a measure of only certain activities within the plants.[3] Moreover, the volume measures do not allow for the differing qualities of products. The importance of quality differences as an explanation of value added per head differences has been considered by Hitchens, Wagner and Birnie (1992).

Table 4 shows that physical productivity in 1991 averaged 59 percent that of West Germany and that there was little variability between sectors.

The productivity record of the firms was also measured using information supplied by the managers on sales, material inputs and hence value added per employee. These fall short of the physical productivity estimates because of: (1) relatively low capacity utilisation at the East German plants and, (2) lower product prices, which in itself is a reflection of low levels of demand as well as inferior product quality.

Table 4 shows that value added productivity levels achieved in mid 1991 lay between one-quarter and two-fifths of that of the West German counterparts. The better value added performance of plants sampled in food reflects new investment made at two plants post-unification. The estimate for clothing firms accords with

---

[2]   In a similar way the comparisons of UK firms with those in West Germany had often to involve matches of high quality West German products with lower quality UK products; Daly, Hitchens and Wagner (1985), and Hitchens, Wagner and Birnie (1990).

[3]   The assumption was that the comparative productivity of the principal activities is representative of all activities, with all of the activities operating at similar levels of utilisation.

an alternative estimate of 30 per cent and in some exceptional cases 50 per cent (*Handelsblatt* 1991, May 1). IFO (1991) reckon that East German manufacturing productivity was about one-third of the West German level in the fourth quarter of 1990. A detailed study based on the official statistics suggests that overall East German manufacturing output per head was 31 per cent of the West German level in 1987 (van Ark, 1994). Results for individual sectors were also similar to our own: 45 per cent in food, 37 per cent in basic metals and metal goods, 35 per cent in clothing and 27 per cent in miscellaneous manufacturing.

TABLE 4
Comparative Productivity by Sample Sector, mid 1991
(as per cent of level of matched West German counterparts,
EG/WG, WG = 100)

	Physical productivity	Value added per head
Food	60	40
Engineering	64	37
Clothing	50	27
Furniture	63	28[a]
Miscellaneous	58	33
Total sample	59	33

Note: In this table and, unless otherwise stated, in the following tables sectoral results are unweighed averages of the results for individual firms.

[a] Windfall benefit of orders from the Soviet Union (guaranteed by the German government under the Hermes programme) pushed the 1990-91 performance of some furniture firms in the short-term above this level.

Expected Improvements in Productivity Performance

Individual firms were asked how physical productivity levels could be raised to West German standards. All companies recognised the need to improve productivity and table 5 shows where these gains were expected to come from.

On average the East German firms anticipate that they can raise their physical productivity from 59 per cent to 84 per cent of the level in West Germany. In every sector except clothing investment in physical capital and technology was anticipated to yield larger productivity gains than those which would be realised from training and reorganisation of work. The final closing of the gap however may require much greater improvements in human capital than can be foreseen at present by management in the East because of their lack of familiarity with technologies, work organisation networks, and product developments. This limited foresight is in itself perhaps indicative of a skills and experience problem.

TABLE 5
Sources of Expected Productivity Gains by the East German Firms

| | 1991 physical productivity (EG/WG, WG=100) | Sources of expected gains | | 1994 physical productivity* (EG/WG, WG=100) |
| | | Machinery etc.[a] | Training etc.[b] | |
		(percentage point gains)		
Food	60	24	12	96
Engineering	64	13	6	82
Clothing	50	9	9	68
Furniture	63	18	14	95
Miscellaneous	58	10	8	76
Total sample	59	16	9	84

[a] New machinery, technology, machine add ons and application of data processing.
[b] Training and work organisation. * As forecasted in 1991.

3. Explanations of Comparative Performance

Product Quality

The main competitive disadvantage of the East German firms related to their products given that these were of generally poorer quality and were characterised by inferior market positions. Pre-unification production runs were very long compared to Western counterparts and firms were vertically integrated to a high degree. Many firms post-unification adjusted their product ranges, batch sizes and product quality. They also discontinued the type of consumer products which formerly they were obliged to produce in addition to their main lines. Products were improved through a reduction in vertical integration and the purchase of a wide range of material inputs from Western suppliers. The difficulties which will be entailed in raising the standard of products to Western levels range from very serious in the engineering sector to relatively simple at the food companies sampled.

It was much more difficult to develop new products as the managers and researchers were unfamiliar with Western markets and new technologies. The problem was exacerbated where firms sought to economise on R and D personnel. Overall the number of R and D employees in industry fell from 74,000 to 22,000 between 1989 and the end of 1991 (DIW, 1993).

Capacity Utilisation

Between 1989 and 1991 exports to Eastern countries fell by 60 per cent and while there has been some switch in export markets to Western countries the net effect, together with a depression in demand at home, is reflected in comparatively low levels of capacity utilisation and shiftworking.

Table 6 shows the level of capacity utilisation recorded in 1990-91 by sample plants across the sectors. It is highest in food and lowest in engineering. Shiftworking has on average fallen by two-fifths over the period, though this has held up in furniture where a number of orders made by the former Soviet Union were guaranteed for delivery by end 1991.

TABLE 6
East German Capacity Utilisation and Shiftworking by Sector

	Capacity utilisation (%, average of 1990-1991)	Shiftworking (no.) mid 1990	mid 1991
Food	69	2.5	1.4
Engineering	34	2.4	1.2
Clothing	50	1.0	1.0
Furniture	47	2.7	2.0
Miscellaneous	56	3.2	1.2

Age of Machinery

Comparisons of the capital stock of different Western economies have often concentrated on the age of machinery (Rostas, 1948; Anglo-American Council on Productivity, 1950; Bacon and Eltis, 1974; Daly, Hitchens and Wagner, 1985; Prais, 1986). A negative association between machinery age and industrial competitiveness performance might be anticipated.

Machine age by sector for East Germany is shown in Table 7 together with comparative figures for matched plants in West Germany. The table shows that capital stock is on average older than that in comparable firms in West Germany. Görzig and Gornig (1991) noted that average depreciation for machinery in East Germany was 26 years compared to 18 years in West Germany. Forty-seven per cent of East German firms sampled used at least some Western equipment. In general, companies were allowed to purchase Western machinery where Eastern bloc machines were unavailable or there was a requirement to work to finer tolerances as for example for exports to Western countries.

Eastern machines were not only subject to more frequent breakdowns but in the past had been forced to manufacture their own spare parts. As a result maintenance work forces were large and even post-unification the percentage of maintenance workers required to maintain equipment was found to be double that of their West German counterparts.

In contrast, those East German firms which were already exporting to the West prior to unification. These firms have on average more modern factories with a much higher proportion of younger machines (62 per cent were under 5 years old i.e. a younger machinery stock than that of West German counterparts) with consequent gains in terms of product quality and lower reject rates.

TABLE 7
Comparative Age of Machinery (%)

	Under 5 years		Over 10 years	
	EG	WG	EG	WG
Engineering	22	39	36	39
Clothing	44	57	5	8
Food	25	54	8	13
Other	37	57	36	24
Sample total	32	52	31	21
OECD estimates	27	40	50	28

Note: Sectoral results for the matched comparisons are unweighed averages of the results for individual firms.
Source: Sample results and OECD (1991).

Level of Technology

The relative age of machinery also indicates the level of technology used by companies. In eighty-five per cent of cases the technology was out of date by comparison with their West German counterparts. In some cases CNC machinery was purchased to produce specialist products, but post-unification many of these products have become redundant and the machines were standing idle.

The West German firms had the advantage of specialist machines, more computerisation, better electronic controls, machines capable of working on modern materials, more machine-linking and the ability to work to fine tolerances, for example in engineering.

Required Investment

Individual companies were asked to estimate their investment needs to attain environmental standards and to upgrade plant, machinery and buildings. In total it was estimated 128,000 DM (at 1991 prices) would be required for each job saved (assuming wages do reach parity with West Germany). This overall figure is above that estimated by the *Treuhand* after excluding the energy and car manufacturing sectors from their calculations (*Die Lage der Weltwirtschaft und der deutschen Wirtschaft Herbstgutachten*, 1991). Predicted investment was lowest in the clothing sector and high and variable in all other sectors sampled. Required investment will rise as wages rise towards parity with West Germany.

Stock of Pre-unification Machinery which Remained Viable under New Market Conditions

Table 8 (a.) shows that just over one-half of pre-unification machine stock is estimated by managers to be viable at the 1991 wage levels and that only 28 per cent would be viable when wage parity is achieved assuming similar products are made. This analysis excludes machinery purchased since mid 1990. For example two surviving food companies replaced most machinery with new Western machines and clothing companies bought second hand on the Western market.

TABLE 8

**(a.) Per cent of Pre-unification Machine Stock
still Usable under 1991 Market Conditions and with Wage Parity**

	At 1991 wage levels	At wage parity
Food	46	22
Engineering	56	41[a]
Clothing	38	18
Furniture	53	22
Miscellaneous	56	28
Total sample	52	28

[a] Engineering estimates are high in cases where a large proportion of CNC machines are considered usable.

**(b.) Distribution of Companies According to
Per cent of Machine Stock still Usable**

	More than 50 %	26-50 %	Under 25 %
	(per cent of total sample companies)		
with 1991 wage levels	48	14	38
with wage parity	23	13	64

Note: Total sample consisted of 29 plants.

Table 8 (b.) shows the distribution of viable machine stock by company sampled. While about half of the companies at the time of the interview could use 50 per cent or more of their machine stock profitably, 38 per cent of companies could only utilise 25 per cent. The viability of machines declines steeply as firms move towards wage parity when two-thirds of firms forecast that they will use less than one-quarter of their pre-unification machine stock. These figures are broad estimates and they are based on the optimistic assumption that firms will continue to manufacture a range of products similar to the present.

4. Management and Labour Force Quality

Shop-floor skills

On average twice the number of skilled persons are engaged at the East German plants relative to their West German counterparts reflecting the compulsory nature of apprenticeships in East Germany. These were generally two year apprenticeships compared with 3 to 3.5 years in West Germany. And as a consequence of the shorter training period and the technological lag in machinery and a much higher degree of work specialisation the East German skilled worker was more limited in his/her range of competences and less mobile between sectors.

TABLE 9
Percentage of Shopfloor Labour Force with Formal
Vocational Qualifications

	East Germany	West Germany
Engineering	88	68
Clothing	97	48
Food	76	23
Miscellaneous	90	22
Total sample	88	42

Note: All sectoral averages are the unweighted averages of the results for the individual plants.

Whilst the percentage of formally skilled workers exceeds that of West German counterparts the comparison exaggerates the relative skills base in East Germany. Many of the semi-skilled workers at the West German plants have undertaken an apprenticeship in another trade and moved into the industry where they are designated semi-skilled. Such job mobility was not characteristic of firms in East Germany which affected the comparisons of skill levels. There were also problems reported by 38 per cent of firms of difficulties experienced by workers in adjusting to Western style work habits. This poor worker motivation arose despite low absenteeism rates, which have fallen from 10 per cent pre-unification to 2 per cent in 1991 (compared with a West German rate of 6 per cent).

The lower level of skills has given rise to skilled workers being demoted to realign with the West German hierarchy of skills. For example at one engineering firm 90 per cent of employees were recorded as skilled before unification but this proportion shrank to 65 per cent following demotions giving rise to a similar proportion of skills as observed in the West German counterpart.

At the same time a number of strengths were noted. First, the best skills were retained where possible in the slimmed down labour forces. The remainder were placed on short-term working. Second, the apprenticeships undertaken covered the classic skills, e.g. in engineering drilling, milling, rotating and welding. In maintenance an ability to build, rebuild and improve machines and spare parts etc. was required to a greater extent than in the West which increased flexibility in terms of mechanical skills. These East German strengths provide a base upon which to build up to date skills and techniques.

Nevertheless, East German workers were not well trained in hydraulics, new materials or electronics. In addition their experience has been very specialised and low grade which is a reflection of the fact that most companies produced long runs of relatively simple products; there had been less "learning by doing". They were not trained up to the required DIN standards nor in appropriate work organisation or in data processing. In addition, they were more dependent on much detailed supervision. There was an absence of commercial skills. Only a quarter of the content of commercial training given to office staff in East Germany has been judged as useful under Western market conditions.

Meister were not as well technically qualified as their West German counterparts many having been demoted post-unification to the skilled worker level. They were also untrained in management techniques, new technology and were unused to exerting leadership over the shop-floor labour force. Their positions have often been filled by East German graduates.

Higher Qualifications of Management and Labour

We examined the number of higher level qualifications at the matched plants. Expressed as the percentage of employees with a university level qualification and the percentage having a technical qualification, i.e. a *Fachschule Ingenieur* (equivalent to an HND in Britain) the proportions of higher skills were found to be similar in the East and West German plants.[4]

However, the functional distribution of higher qualifications differs between East and West Germany. In West Germany a higher proportion of those with degrees are engaged in production, R and D and management and similarly West German companies would engage more technical qualifications in production.

---

[4]   This conclusion is supported by the data for the whole labour force; Sinn and Sinn (1991).

In contrast more than half those with degrees and or technical qualifications in East Germany were engaged in administration reflecting the need to handle the bureaucratic requirements of the central planning regime (Görzig and Gornig, 1991).

Despite the favourable proportion of formal qualifications the ability of East German managers to operate in the new market environment will depend upon commercial knowledge which has been deficient. Many managers gave examples where they experienced difficulties estimating costs for incoming orders, building up relations with suppliers, negotiating discounts and with product marketing. In general they lacked flexibility, were slow to take the initiative and had limited knowledge of Western technology and management techniques. In 76 per cent of cases managers had taken initial steps to improve their knowledge and understanding through co-operation with Western counterparts and by attending management courses (Wagner, Hitchens and Birnie, 1991). Other studies confirm that many East German managers underestimate their skill deficits and a great deal of further education is needed at this level (Icks, 1992).

5. Conclusions

Unification of East and West Germany presented an opportunity to investigate to what extent and by what means surviving East German companies will be able to raise their productivity (or output per head) to West German standards by 1996, when parity of wage levels is likely to occur.

The available indicators suggest that the main mechanism for competitive adjustment in the manufacturing sector has been very substantial contraction. For example, prior to unification East German manufacturing employed 3.265 million persons but by the first half of 1994 this figure had dropped to only 1.1 million. During 1989-1991 the volume index of output fell to only 30 per cent of its November 1989 level, that is annual output fell from 46 billion DM to only 15 billion DM in constant 1991 prices (Commission of the European Communities, 1994). There are, however, some indications of recovery. The index of output (second half of 1990 = 100) reached a low of 62 in the second quarter of 1992 and has since climbed to 68 in the second quarter of 1993, 78 in the fourth quarter and 82 in April 1994 (IWD, 1994). By the second half of 1993 annual output had risen to 23 billion DM also in 1991 constant prices.

Our own comparisons indicate a substantial productivity gap in manufacturing relative to West Germany. Closing that gap will require new products, product improvements, training of management and labour and additions to the capital stock. The planned wage increase to parity with West German rates will decrease the viability of the capital stock to just 28 per cent of its 1989 level. The higher wage costs will not only require more fixed capital investment, it will also raise training costs. While machinery is indicated a principal factor required to close the productivity gap training is recognised as deficient despite the high levels of formally qualified persons engaged at the plants. This will require training at all levels. Particular attention will need to be given to training in use of modern technology, and to learn about work organisation and the relevant commercial and legal background to business.

The survival of plants will depend on many factors including any locational advantages in serving the East German market, links developed with West German manufacturers either by way of ownership, joint ventures or other co-operative arrangements and most importantly development of product positioning. Failures will result from a range of problems including inexperience with marketing, advertising, design, innovation and redundant products. It is intended to revisit this sample of firms in 1995 (i.e. 4 years on from the first visits) to identify the survivors, measure productivity growth and trace critical success factors.

In anticipation of further work with sample firms, telephone interviews were conducted in August 1993. All but two companies had survived, and two-thirds were by then privatised (compared with 40 percent in 1991). Employment levels had continued to fall and at a faster rate than forecasted by management in 1991.[5] Investment had been less than anticipated and focused on improving product quality and complying with German and EC product standards and legal requirements. Plant and machinery had been upgraded rather than replaced. On and off the job training had continued but large gaps in knowledge and experience remained though compared with 1991 management had a clearer understanding of training needs and deficits.

Much of the East German industrial base has now been lost. Given that human capital is slower to create than physical capital this provides a justification for policy intervention to slow down the rate of closures (Akerlof, Rose, Yellen and Hessenius, 1991) and allow the surviving work force time to evolve towards the Western skills level. This should remain a priority despite the fact as this article has shown that much of the physical capital in East Germany is now redundant as are many of the products. Employment in remaining *Treuhand* companies stood at 132,000 in the first half of 1994 (Commission of the European Communities, 1994), mostly in heavy industries. Whilst the *Treuhand* is to wind itself up by the end of 1994 new management companies are being created to gradually privatise these residual state owned enterprises.

Turning to the comparisons between East Germany and Eastern Europe it is notable that East Germany is experiencing the same process of transition to the market economy as Hungary, the Czech Republic, Poland etc. though at a much more rapid rate given the very rapid rate of market integration (Burda, 1991). Thus there is a sense in which what is happening in East Germany today shows

---

[5] In 1991 sample firms averaged half their pre-unification size, by mid 1993 this was reduced to one-third.

what is likely to happen in the other countries, such as the reductions in overmanning and the breakup of highly integrated companies. However, there are also significant differences. East Germany has privileged access to the West German consumer and capital markets, know-how, as well as to funds for industrial and regional policy. The other Eastern economies have the disadvantages and advantages of relying much more on privatisation with indigenous management teams.[6] The Eastern European economies start from an even lower base than East Germany with respect to their comparative productivity level (Hitchens, Birnie, Hamar, Wagner, and Zemplinerova, 1995) as in East Germany basic skills are usually good and performance during the period of the planned economy suggests that at least some of the Eastern European economies, especially Hungary and Czechoslovakia, have the potential to display innovation and inventiveness now that incentives are being provided for these activities (Ray, 1991).

References

Anglo-American Council on Productivity (1950), *Productivity Team Reports on Cotton Spinning*, Anglo-American Council on Productivity, London.
Akerlof, G.A., Rose, A.K., Yellen, J.L. and Hessenius, H. (1991), "East Germany in from the cold: The economic aftermath of currency union", *Brookings Papers on Economic Activity*, no. 1, pp. 1-87.
Alexander, L. (1992), "Comments and discussion", in Dornbusch R. and Wolf, H, "Economic transition in East Germany", *Brookings Papers on Economic Activity*, 1992, no. 1, pp. 262-68.
Ark, B. van (1994), "Reassessing growth and comparative levels of performance in Eastern Europe: The experience of Manufacturing in Czechoslovakia and East Germany", Paper for the third EACES Conference, Budapest, 8-10 September.
Bacon, R.W. and Eltis, W.A. (1974), "The age of US and UK machinery", *Monograph*, no. 3, National Economic Development Organisation, London.
Barro, R.J. and Sala-i-Martin, X. (1991), "Convergence across states and regions", *Brookings Papers on Economic Activity*, 1991, no. 1, pp. 107-58.
Burda, M. (1991), "Labor and product markets in Czechoslovakia and the ex-GDR: A twin study", *Discussion Paper*, no. 78, Centre for Economic Policy Research, London.

---

[6]   However, Carlin and Mayer (1992) suggest that in a situation where there is a paucity of high quality managerial talent the East German method of privatisation is an appropriate model: concentrate the best managers in a privatisation agency and banks and then place them on the supervisory boards of the companies which are to be privatized.

Carlin, W. and Mayer, T. (1992), "Restructuring enterprises in Eastern Europe", *Discussion Papers in Economics*, no. 92-15, University College London, London.

Commission of the European Communities (1994), *Employment Observatory Labour Market Developments and Policies in the New German Lander*, Brussels.

Daly, A., Hitchens, D.M.W.N. and Wagner, K. (1985), "Productivity, machinery and skills in a sample of British and German manufacturing plants", *National Institute Economic Review*, no. 111, pp. 48-62.

DIW (1993), *Zur Situation der ausseruniversitären und industriellen Forschung in den neuen Bundesländern*, *Wochenbericht*, no. 44.

Dornbusch, R. and Wolf, H. (1992), "Economic transition in Eastern Germany", *Brookings Papers on Economic Activity*, 1992, no. 1, pp. 235-72.

Financial Times (1994, May 4), "Restructuring of Eastern Germany: A Survey".

Görzig, B. and Gornig, M. (1991), *Produktivität und Wettbewerbsfähigkeit der Wirtschaft der DDR*, DIW, Heft 121, Berlin.

Heinze, A., and Klempin, B. (1994), *Die Wirtschaftsstruktur in den neuen Ländern und Berlin-Ost*, in, *Zur wirtschaftlichen und sozialen Lage in den neuen Bundesländern*, March.

Hitchens, D.M.W.N., Wagner, K., and Birnie, J.E. (1990), *Closing the Productivity Gap: A Comparison of Northern Ireland, The Republic of Ireland, Britain and West Germany*, Avebury, Aldershot.

Hitchens, D.M.W.N., Wagner, K. and Birnie, J.E. (1991), "Improving productivity through international exchange visits", *Omega International Journal of Management Science*, vol. 19, no. 5, pp. 361-8.

Hitchens, D.M.W.N., Wagner, K., and Birnie, J.E. (1992), "Measuring the contribution of product quality to competitiveness: A note on theory and policy", *Economic and Social Review*, vol. 23, no. 4, pp. 455-463.

Hitchens, D.M.W.N., Wagner, K., and Birnie, J.E. (1993), *East German Productivity and the Transition to the Market Economy*, Avebury, Aldershot.

Hitchens, D.M.W.N., Birnie, J.E., Hamar, J., Wagner, K., and Zemplinerova, A. (1995), *The competitiveness of industry in the Czech Republic and Hungary*, Avebury, Aldershot.

Hughes Hallet, A.J. and Ma, Y. (1993), "East Germany, West Germany, and their Mezzogiorno Problem: A Parable for European Economic Integration", *Economic Journal*, vol. 103, no. 417, pp. 416-428.

Icks, A. (1992), "*Mittelständische Unternehmen als Qualifizierungspaten*", *Schriften zur Mittelstandsforschung*, no. 49, Stuttgart.

IFO, (1991), "*Konjunkturtest in den neuen Bundesländern*", *Schnelldienst*, no. 16-17.

IWD (1994), *Konjunktur-Tendenz*, 21 July.

OECD (1991), *A Survey-Germany*, Organisation of Economic Co-operation and Development, Paris.

Prais, S.J. (1986), "Some international comparisons of the age of the machine stock", *Journal of Industrial Economics*, vol. XXXIV, pp. 261-87.

Ray, G. (1991), "Innovation and technology in Eastern Europe: An international comparison", *Report Series*, no. 2, National Institute of Economic and Social Research, London.

Rostas, L. (1948), *Industrial Production, Productivity and Comparative Productivity in British and American Industries*, Cambridge University Press, Cambridge.

Siebert, H. (1991), "The integration of Germany", *European Economic Review*, vol. 35, pp. 591-602.

Sinn, G. and Sinn H.-W. (1991), *Kaltstart*, Mohr, Tubingen; and (1993), *Jumpstart*, MIT Press, Cambridge MA.

UBS, (1989/90), "Eastern Europe: A long way to prosperity", *International Finance*, issue 2, Union Bank of Switzerland, pp. 1-8.

Wagner, K., Hitchens, D.M.W.N, and Birnie, J.E. (1991), "Manageraustausch Eine Überlebensstragie für Unternehmen in den neuen Ländern", *Zeitschrift für Betriebswirtschaft*, 61, no. 9, pp. 969-980.

International Productivity Differences
K. Wagner and B. van Ark (editors)
© 1996 Elsevier Science B.V. All rights reserved.

Estimating the Productivity of Research and Development in French and United States Manufacturing Firms: An Exploration of Simultaneity Issues with GMM Methods

J. Mairesse* and B.H. Hall**

*   *Centre de Recherche en Economie et Statistique and National Bureau of Economic Research*
** *University of California, Berkeley and National Bureau of Economic Research*

1. Introduction

Industrial firms in developed economies engage in increasing amounts of organized research and development activity aimed at producing new and improved products and reducing costs. Economists would like to know the answers to two questions concerning the success (or failure) of this R&D activity: First, what is the magnitude of the returns earned by the firms that undertake it? Do these returns justify the investment being undertaken? Second, to what extent do the benefits of the R&D spill over to other firms, thus lowering their innovation costs, or to the firm's customers, through lower prices and improved products? In brief, what are the private and social returns to the R&D being performed. The standard approach to answering these questions is grounded in the productivity residual methodology: we measure the contribution of R&D to a firm's revenue or quantity of output, controlling for the other inputs into production. The former measure (the marginal revenue elasticity) is the relevant concept for the computation of private returns: it is the sum of the contribution of R&D to the equilibrium price of quality-adjusted goods sold by the firm and the contribution of R&D to the equilibrium quantity of quality-adjusted goods sold. The latter measure (the output elasticity) is what matters more for society as a whole: how the gains in productivity get allocated between the firm and its customers is of secondary importance for growth, although the allocation does affect the firm's incentive to undertake R&D.

One way to enrich our understanding of the sources and causes of productivity levels and growth is by using cross-country, cross-industry, and cross-time comparisons in order to isolate those features that are robust to changes in time, place, and institutions. The differences or variations that emerge from studies of this kind are also informative, particularly when they are linked to other known differences in the economic environment. A large number of studies of the relationship between R&D investment and productivity growth at the firm level have been conducted in the past using data through 1980 (see Mairesse and Sassenou, 1991, for a survey), but little has been done with the increasing amount of data which became available during the 1980s in most of the "big seven" OECD countries. This paper uses new datasets available in both the U.S. (a dataset based on Compustat files that has been updated to 1990 and then merged with deflators at the two-digit industry level)[1] and France (an R&D survey at the firm level, also updated to 1990, merged with conventional enterprise data on production)[2] to investigate whether the small but well-documented relationship between R&D and productivity growth at the firm level persisted during the 1980s and whether it is similar in the USA and France. While so doing, we distinguish somewhat more carefully than past studies between revenue growth and productivity growth itself.

The style of analysis is based on the traditional growth framework and draws on our experience with analyzing the French data for 1980-1987, which is described in Hall and Mairesse (1992). Since the work described in that paper, we have obtained a larger French sample and somewhat improved our deflators (we are now using sales and value added deflators at the two-digit level).

The US data is of somewhat lower quality than the French data, particularly since we do not have a measure of value added, nor do we have a reliable measure of labour costs. In addition, we do not have the information necessary to correct the capital and labour measures for R&D double counting as we do in France. Here, comparison of results using the French data can help. From these data we are able to gauge the changes which result when better measures of both right-hand-side and left-hand-side variables are used. The evidence suggests that estimates using sales instead of value added are not too badly biased, but that attempting to correct for materials or including materials directly in the regression can give misleading results. Correcting for double counting of R&D employees tends to rais the R&D significantly, which is consistent with an earlier work.

The plan of the paper is as follows: we first describe the data samples which we are using, and characterise the overall similarities and differences of the manufacturing sectors in the two countries. This is followed by a detailed examination of the form of the productivity-R&D relationship using the French data, where we have better variables. Once we have chosen a specification which is feasible for the US data as well, we present comparative results for the two countries. Since we find that the dating of our capital stocks (physical and R&D)

---

[1]   See Hall (1990) for a description of a slightly earlier version of the US data used here.

[2]   The two sources are the *Enquête annuelle sur les moyens consacrés à la recherche et au développement dans les entreprises*, conducted by the French Ministry of Research and Technology, and the *Enquête annuelle des entreprises*, conducted by INSEE.

affects the within-firm estimates greatly (with end of period capitals having higher coefficients than beginning period), the final section of the paper explores the role of simultaneity in the relationship, and presents in details GMM estimates of the relationship that are more efficient than conventional first differenced estimators with lagged right-hand-side variables as instruments.

2. Samples, Framework, and Variables

Table 1 shows some of the characteristics of the samples with which we will be working. In each case, we began with an unbalanced panel from 1981 to 1989, with up to 3 years of lagged values for each variable (that is, the actual data set goes from 1978 to 1989, and no firm has less than 3 years of data). Later in the paper we use two fully balanced subsets of data for each country. These subsets contain data for shorter periods, 1978 to 1985, and 1982 to 1989.[3] The data have been cleaned so that there are no jumps in the stock variables of absolute value greater than 200 percent, or in the flow variables of absolute value greater than 300 percent. Both samples cover a large fraction of the relevant population: the US sample has 50 percent of manufacturing employment and about 67 percent of industrial R&D in 1985,[4] whereas the French sample has about 22 percent of manufacturing employment and 56 percent of industrial R&D.[5] In both cases, firms had to perform and report R&D during the period to be in the sample, so there is some selectivity at work.

The samples for the two countries are fairly similar in industrial distribution. The most striking differences are the large number of computing, electronics and instrument firms in the United States, and pharmaceutical, chemical, food and machinery firms in France. The balanced samples used in the latter half of the paper omit a large number of the Computing and Electronics firms in the USA, many of whom are small recent entrants, and are somewhat more heavily weighted toward the food and pharmaceutical industries in France.[6]

---

[3]   For the USA, the unbalanced panel has 1073 firms and the balanced subpanels 535 and 442 firms respectively, whereas for France, the numbers are 1232, 447, and 381. There is a substantial overlap between the two different subperiods in each country; this overlap is greater for France than for the USA.

[4]   According to the National Science Foundation, domestic R&D expenditure in 1985 was 58 billion dollars, while our sample had total R&D spending of 39 billion dollars.

[5]   According to the OECD, total R&D performed by business enterprises in France in 1985 was $6.04 billion dollars (using a purchasing power parity rate of 7.27 francs per dollar to convert from francs to dollars), while our sample has $3.37 billion dollars of R&D.

[6]   In both countries the aircraft and other transportation sector has an extremely high R&D-to-sales ratio, and it has about 50 percent of the private enterprise-performed, government-funded R&D. Because we believe that estimating the productivity of R&D in this sector may be problematic due to fact that a primary customer is the go-

TABLE 1
Unbalanced Sample Characteristics: French and US Manufacturing, 1981-1989

Industry	Number of Firms	Number of Observations	Employment (000s)	R&D-Sales Ratio
United States				
Electronics, Computers, & Inst.	382	2254	2209	7.06
Pharmaceuticals	100	623	761	5.56
Chemicals	34	263	730	3.73
Autos	43	266	1668	3.23
Electrical Machinery	66	377	565	3.32
Machinery	135	899	832	2.59
Rubber & Plastics	36	204	279	2.16
Paper & Printing	41	264	395	2.02
Fabricated Metals	62	380	260	1.54
Wood, SCG, & Misc.	71	426	314	1.17
Primary Metals	27	162	195	1.12
Textiles & Leather	39	190	167	0.90
Food	37	213	879	0.95
Total	1073	6521	9254	2.93
Aircraft & other trans.	26	165	1074	3.60
France				
Electronics, Computers, & Inst.	186	910	188.6	6.04
Pharmaceuticals	191	1081	83.4	2.92
Chemicals	119	540	65.0	1.54
Autos	62	312	247.8	1.48
Electrical Machinery	109	538	94.6	2.24
Machinery	192	933	73.6	1.17
Rubber & Plastics	62	322	63.9	2.69
Paper & Printing	32	123	10.2	0.49
Fabricated Metals	78	378	29.3	0.78
Wood, SCG, & Misc.	38	240	44.5	0.82
Primary Metals	39	201	41.9	0.50
Textiles & Leather	38	202	13.6	0.82
Food	86	502	65.1	0.29
Total	1232	6282	1021.7	2.26
Aircraft & other trans.	32	195	93.7	9.41

Employment and R&D to sales are for the middle year of the sample, 1985. The R&D to sales ratio shown is a *sales-weighted* average, which is the *industry* R&D to sales ratio.

The framework in which we measure the contribution of R&D to productivity growth is a standard growth accounting one, based on the Cobb-Douglas production function.[7] The basic equation is the following:

$$y_{it} = a_i + \lambda_t + \alpha c_{it} + \beta l_{it} + \gamma k_{it} + \varepsilon_{it} \qquad (1)$$

where i and t index firms and years respectively, y is output, c is capital, l is labour, k is knowledge or R&D capital, and the lower case letters denote logarithms. The equation allows for both additive firm and year effects. In this formulation, y denotes a value added output concept, since materials are not included in the model. Although we have a measure of value added for the French data, we do not have one for the US data. Therefore we present estimates using both sales and value added, and also including materials for the French data, so that we can calibrate the results using sales for comparison to the US results.

Our measure of capital stock is a constructed estimate of plant and equipment adjusted for inflation in both countries. Our measure of R&D capital is that described as K71 in Hall and Mairesse (1995) for France and in Hall (1990) for the USA. In both cases it is constructed from the past history of R&D investment, with a depreciation rate of 15 percent per year and a pre-sample growth rate of 5 percent per year. Our measure of labour is the number of workers in the firm. This is usually reported by the firms as the average number of workers during the year. In the United States, it may occasionally be the number of workers at the close of the fiscal year.

Conceptually, the value added, labour, and capital measures used to estimate equation (1) should be purged of the contribution of R&D materials, physical capital used in R&D laboratories, and R&D personnel, since these inputs do not produce current output, but are used to increase the stock of R&D capital. If this is not done, the cross section estimates (or estimates from firms in long run equilibrium where R&D spending does not change much from year to year) will not necessarily be incorrect, but the measured R&D coefficient will be some kind of "excess" elasticity of output to R&D rather than a total elasticity, i.e. the incremental productivity of R&D above and beyond the normal productivity of the capital and labour involved. In Hall and Mairesse (1992) we confirmed this interpretation, finding that estimates corrected for R&D inputs tended to give R&D elasticities which were 0.06-0.08 higher than uncorrected estimates (and that most of the effect could be achieved by correcting the labour variables).

---

vernment, we have omitted it in the regressions that follow. In fact, removing it changed the results very little.

[7]   For more details, see our earlier paper (Hall and Mairesse, 1995).

Here we correct only value added and labour for the French data, but we are unable to do so for the US data, since we do not have the appropriate measures.

3. Comparing the Conventional Estimates for France and the United States

Table 2 presents a series of estimates of equation (1) for the French data. The four horizontal panels have increasingly less restrictive assumptions on the error term. The first is a regression pooled across firms and time, with individual year dummies, while the second also allows for industry effects (at the sectoral level shown in table 1). The third and fourth allow for additive firm effects, first the estimator with overall firm means removed, and then estimates in growth rates. Except for simultaneity and measurement error bias in the right-hand-side variables, these last two panels should have the same estimates. On the whole, the two capital coefficients appear to be similarly insignificant, while the labour coefficient is somewhat lower for the growth rate estimates, suggesting the presence of measurement error.

The first column of the table shows the basic specification which we will also use for the US data. The second column displays the same sales regression with materials included on the right-hand-side, while the third uses value added instead of sales. The average materials share in these data is sixty percent, so the estimated coefficient is somewhat high, especially when permanent differences across firms are controlled for. This is typical of these kinds of data and can happen for two reasons: the measurement error bias can be less for materials than for other inputs[8], or there are shortrun increasing returns to materials.[9]

How do the estimates using sales in column (1) compare with those which either include materials, or use value added as a dependent variable? If we simply compare column (1) with column (3), we can see that the labour coefficient is typically somewhat lower for sales, while the capital coefficient is somewhat higher in the cross section dimension, but about the same and insignificant in the within dimension. The estimates using sales and excluding materials seem to give results for R&D capital that are quite similar to those using value added. Unfortunately, they are also insignificant in the within-firm dimension. Adding materials to the equation merely reduces the coefficients by the estimated materials share, but their magnitudes are more or less what one would predict from the value added equation. The conclusion is that the regression of sales on labour, capital, and knowledge capital is likely to give results which are quite similar to those obtained using value added as a dependent va-

---

[8] Griliches and Hausman (1986).

[9] Shortrun increasing returns can occur for any of a number of reasons, most, but not all, of them involving a failure of perfectly competitive conditions. See R. E. Hall (1988) for further discussion of this point.

TABLE 2
Productivity Regressions 1981-1989, France (6282 observations)

Capital Dating		Beginning of Year			End of Year
Dep. Variable	Log Sales	Log Sales	Log VA	Log VAC	Log VAC
Total					
Log L	.591(.017)	.193(.005)	.699(.012)	.630(.012)	.597(.012)
Log C	.295(.012)	.043(.002)	.193(.008)	.183(.008)	.210(.009)
Log K	.090(.006)	.024(.001)	.092(.004)	.165(.004)	.172(.004)
Log M		.735(.004)			
R^2(s.e.)	.868(.489)	.993(.115)	.926(.349)	.923(.357)	.927(.347)
Within Ind.					
Log L	.681(.011)	.201(.003)	.749(.008)	.679(.008)	.645(.008)
Log C	.204(.009)	.038(.002)	.153(.007)	.141(.007)	.168(.007)
Log K	.109(.006)	.023(.002)	.093(.004)	.167(.004)	.176(.004)
Log M		.734(.003)			
R^2(s.e.)	.899(.429)	.993(.112)	.933(.333)	.930(.340)	.933(.332)
Within Firm					
Log L	.819(.013)	.199(.006)	.900(.017)	.841(.016)	.790(.017)
Log C	-.045(.013)	.001(.005)	-.036(.016)	-.007(.015)	.050(.016)
Log K	.008(.011)	-.010(.004)	-.016(.013)	.013(.013)	.069(.014)
Log M		.791(.005)			
R^2(s.e.)	.713(.143)	.956(.056)	.597(.178)	.602(.176)	.606(.175)
First Diff.					
Log L	.645(.032)	.154(.012)	.715(.035)	.666(.032)	.606(.032)
Log C	-.001(.007)	-.002(.002)	-.006(.008)	-.003(.008)	.130(.025)
Log K	-.003(.003)	.000(.001)	-.005(.003)	-.004(.003)	.080(.021)
Log M		.793(.011)			
R^2(s.e.)	.256(.146)	.878(.059)	.192(.185)	.182(.187)	.190(.186)

All equations contain year dummies. The industry dummies used in the second panel
are at the level given in table 1. Variables:

Log L   Logarithm of average employment during the year.
Log C   Logarithm of gross plant and equipment at the beginning or end of the
           year, adjusted for inflation.
Log K   Logarithm of the R&D capital stock at the beginning or end of the year,
           as computed in Hall and Mairesse (1995).
Log M   Logarithm of materials expenditures during the year.
Log Sales Logarithm of sales during the year deflated by an overall manufacturing
           deflator.
Log VA   Logarithm of value added during the year.
Log VAC   Logarithm of value added during the year, corrected for R&D material
           cost. In this column, Log L has also been corrected for the number of
           R&D employees.

riable (possibly with a slightly lower labour coefficient in all dimensions and a slightly higher physical capital coefficient in the totals).

The final two columns of table 2 investigate two questions: first, what is the effect of correcting labour and value added for R&D inputs, and second, what are the differences in the estimates when we use end of year capitals rather than beginning of year? The answer to the first question is that the double counting corrections raise the R&D capital elasticity by about .07 in the cross section dimension, .03 in the within dimension, and not at all in first differences. This is entirely consistent with our earlier results (which use a smaller sample for 1980 to 1987) and those of Cuneo and Mairesse (1984) (which use data from 1972 to 1977), as well as those of Schankerman (1981) (which use US data in the cross section dimension only).

Using end of year capital stocks rather than beginning of year raises the capital coefficients slightly in the cross section, but it changes the results dramatically in the time series dimension. The within-firm physical and R&D capital coefficients both triple, and the first difference estimates go from essentially zero to quite plausible numbers which are closer to the shares of both capitals in value added. Why does this happen? Because the capital used in production during the year is likely to be some weighted average of beginning and end of year capital, it is difficult to know precisely which dating to use, but either one ought to work about as well (or as badly) unless something other than a simple production relationship is driving the regression. Unfortunately, the most likely explanation is simultaneity between changes in value added (or sales) and investment of both types, driven either by demand shocks or liquidity shocks. This is why we explore the use of instrumental variables to correct for simultaneity bias and reexamine this question later in the paper.[10]

Our explorations with the French data give us confidence that there is information in the simple sales regression without materials inputs, which is all we can estimate using US data. We therefore present estimates of the sales productivity regression for the United States in table 3, together with estimates of the identical model for France (the first column repeated from table 2). We use two different measures of sales as the dependent variable: sales deflated by a single manufacturing sector deflator, and sales deflated by a two-digit level deflator. The French cross section estimates are more or less comparable with those of earlier periods, but the estimates within firm are lower: Cuneo and Mairesse (1984) obtain .11 for these estimates on a sample of 182 firms from 1972 to 1977 (where the data are corrected for double counting, but they also show that these corrections do not make much difference in within-firm estimates). When we use a single common sales deflator for all industries, the results for the

---

[10]   For general discussion of simultaneity issues in estimating production functions, see Griliches and Mairesse (1995).

United States are slightly weaker: where Griliches and Mairesse (1984) obtained .05 in cross section and .09 within using 133 firms from 1966 to 1977, the results here are about .04 both in the cross section and within firms. They also agree with those of Hall (1993b), which were obtained using a superset of these firms.

In contrast to these fairly weak results, using sales deflators at the two-digit level (the columns labelled Log S (2-D)), raises the estimated R&D capital coefficient in the United States substantially, from about 0.04 to 0.25 in totals, from 0.04 to 0.17 in within firms, and from 0.01 to 0.09 in growth rates. For

TABLE 3
Productivity Regressions 1981-1989

Observations	United States (6521)		France (6282)	
Dependent Variable	Log Sales	Log S (2-D)	Log Sales	Log S (2-D)
Totals				
Log L	.666(.010)	.779(.021)	.591(.017)	.578(.017)
Log C	.289(.008)	-.021(.018)	.295(.013)	.303(.012)
Log K	.035(.005)	.246(.012)	.090(.006)	.093(.006)
R^2(s.e.)	.936(.360)	.816(.849)	.868(.489)	.862(.499)
Within Ind.				
Log L	.712(.009)	.707(.021)	.681(.011)	.681(.011)
Log C	.204(.008)	.128(.019)	.204(.009)	.204(.009)
Log K	.063(.005)	.173(.013)	.109(.006)	.110(.006)
R^2(s.e.)	.967(.339)	.837(.800)	.899(.429)	.898(.430)
Within Firm				
Log L	.742(.010)	.702(.013)	.819(.013)	.828(.014)
Log C	.126(.011)	.142(.014)	-.046(.013)	-.052(.013)
Log K	.041(.011)	.170(.014)	.008(.011)	.013(.011)
R^2(s.e.)	.720(.145)	.673(.193)	.713(.143)	.530(.145)
First Diff.				
Log L	.585(.019)	.592(.020)	.645(.032)	.648(.032)
Log C	.148(.020)	.171(.021)	-.001(.007)	.001(.007)
Log K	.010(.024)	.092(.026)	-.003(.003)	-.003(.003)
R^2(s.e.)	.416(.156)	.402(.167)	.256(.146)	.249(.146)

The variables are the same as those in table 2 with capital stocks at the beginning of the year. All equations contain year dummies. The industry dummies are at the level given in table 1. The standard error estimates for the total and first differenced estimates are heteroscedastic-consistent, those for the within industry and within firm estimates are conventional estimates.

the French data there is no such increase. The reason for this is quite simple: the United States deflator for the computing sector is based on a hedonic price index for computers, and as a consequence it declines by about 80 percent during the 1980s as computer hardware becomes much more powerful and much less expensive. Because this industry also has a growing R&D budget, this price decline and the attendant growth in real output means that the estimated contribution of R&D to the output productivity of this industry is very substantial.[11] However, in terms of sales undeflated or only deflated by our overall deflator, the firms in this industry have not seen the same kind of productivity gain, because consumers have captured most of the benefits in the form of cheaper computers. In France, on the other hand, the computing deflator is a more conventional measure that does not capture the tremendous decline in the price of raw computing power, so deflation at the industry level does not have the same effect on the estimated productivity of R&D.

A remaining mystery in our results is the within-firm physical capital coefficient for the French firms, which is negative, sometimes significantly so. It is unclear why this is so: it was true throughout table 2 also, except in the last column where we used end of year capital. This result contrasts with those of Cuneo and Mairesse (1984) for the seventies and our own earlier results for 1980-1987. Understanding this puzzle awaits future work with the French data.

4. Trying to Correct for Simultaneity Bias with GMM

The sensitivity of our estimates to the dating of capital stock suggests that the assumption of zero correlation between regressors and disturbances necessary for the consistency of estimates is unlikely to be justified. We have already indicated that this correlation can arise because of simultaneity between sales and both types of investment. The failure of the non-correlation assumption in panel data causes more problems than it does in conventional regression estimation, because it frequently invalidates estimates based on data where firm means have been removed, even when instrumental variable estimation is used to correct for simultaneity.[12] This is because the only instruments normally available are

---

[11] Some of this gain may be mismeasured or even overstated, because important inputs to the computer industry (semiconductors and computer components) have also suffered substantial price declines during the same period, but these have not been captured at all in our regression. These inputs are typically contained in the materials input to the firm's production at cost. When there are large price changes in these inputs, the assumption for the purpose of production function estimation that the cost of the omitted materials and intermediate goods is a constant fraction of sales within a firm, is more likely to fail.

[12] Firm means are removed by subtracting $\bar{y}_i = \beta \bar{x}_i + \alpha_i + \bar{\varepsilon}_i$ from the model in equation (2), leaving the equation to be estimated:

lagged values of the right hand side variables and in short panels the correlation of these variables with the disturbance remains after the firm-level means of the dependent variable have been removed. The usual solution to this problem is to use first differences (growth rates) for estimation rather than the within firm correction. In addition to simultaneity bias, another source of bias likely to be present is that arising from measurement error in all the variables; under a variety of assumptions, this error tends to bias the first differenced coefficients more towards zero than does the within-firm estimator (Griliches and Hausman, 1986). Thus it is desirable to develop within-firm estimators that remain consistent even when lagged instruments are used.

Since earlier work with these kinds of data (Griliches and Mairesse, 1984), a series of papers have been published which attempt to systematise the methods for estimating and testing the validity of instrumental variable estimates of panel data models where there may be simultaneity, measurement error, and effects correlated with the regressors (Griliches and Hausman, 1986; Arellano and Bond, 1991; Keene and Runkle, 1992; Schmidt, Ahn, and Wyhowski, 1992). With the exception of Griliches and Hausman, who take a some what different route, the approach followed in these papers is to set up a series of successively stronger (more numerous) orthogonality conditions which are valid under various versions of the panel data model and to use the results of Generalized Method of Moments (GMM) estimation on these conditions to choose among the specifications. The appeal of this method for panel data rests in the weakness of the distributional assumptions necessary to carry it out: it does not require the assumptions of zero covariance across years (except to the extent that this is necessary to validate the instruments), or homoscedasticity across firms for efficiency.[13] The standard error estimates which emerge from a GMM estimation are also robust to the presence of correlation across equations and heteroscedasticity. There is a cost to this flexibility of course, in the form of somewhat larger standard errors, but this may be of less concern when we are dealing with large panel datasets.

In this section of the paper, we use the GMM approach to panel data

---

$$y_{it} - \bar{y}_i = \beta \, (x_{it} - \bar{x}_i) + \varepsilon_{it} - \bar{\varepsilon}_i$$

This removes the firm effect α_i but contaminates the disturbance ε_{it} with the disturbances ε_{i1} , ..., ε_{iT} from the other years of data.

[13] Allowing for heteroskedasticity when estimating with heterogeneous groups of firms is essential, if only because we cannot sustain the assumption that the production function we are estimating is identical across firms. If instead of $y_{it} = \beta x_{it}$, the model is $y_{it} = \beta_i x_{it}$, estimating an average β across firms will perforce introduce a size-related heteroskedasticity into the disturbance, of the form $(\bar{\beta} - \beta_i)x_{it}$. If the variation in β is random across firms, no bias will ensue, but the standard errors will be wrong unless we allow for this heteroskedasticity. If the variability is related to the average level of x_{it}, it will be absorbed in the fixed effect, and cause no bias.

estimation in order to investigate the importance of correlated effects, simultaneity, and measurement error for our estimates. As instruments for labour, capital, and R&D capital, we use these same variables lagged 3 years and we test for the admissibility of more recent lags as instruments. Although this choice of instruments will be justified if simultaneity is of concern, when the source of bias is measurement error in the capitals, this measurement error is likely to be correlated over time, and lagged capital not a very good instrument. We investigated this possibility using investment and R&D expenditures as instruments for the capital stocks but found that using these alternative instruments made little difference and that we were able to accept the validity of the capital stocks as instruments in the presence of investment and R&D expenditures. To save space, the results of this investigation are not reported here.

To make our approach clear, consider the simple regression model with a single regressor, but with panel data:[14]

$$y_{it} = \beta x_{it} + u_{it} = \beta x_{it} + \alpha_i + \varepsilon_{it} \qquad i = 1,...,N; \quad t = \tau+1,...,T \qquad (2)$$

where there are τ periods of data available as instruments for the first year of estimation. β is the parameter of interest, and α_i is the firm effect, potentially correlated with x_{it}, $t = 1,...,T$. Our maintained model is that the effects are correlated (so we have to difference the equation) and that only lag 3 and higher x's are available as instruments for x_{it}, because later values are correlated with ε_{it}.[15] These assumptions imply the following set of orthogonality conditions:

$$E [x_{is} \Delta u_{it}] = 0 \qquad t = \tau+2,...,T; \quad s = 1,...,t-\tau-1 \qquad (3)$$

where $\Delta u_{it} = \Delta y_{it} - \beta \Delta x_{it}$. There are $(T-\tau-1)(T-\tau)/2$ orthogonality conditions in (3).

Estimation of (3) is performed using the method described in the Appendix. Consistent estimates can be obtained simply by minimizing the sum of squares of the empirical moments $[f(\beta)]$ corresponding to (3) with respect to β, but efficiency requires that we also form an estimate of their covariance $\hat{\Omega}$ and

---

[14] Our presentation from now on will suppress the presence of λ_t, the time effect, in the model. In estimation, we remove the year means from the data at the very start to avoid complications. This procedure has no effect on either the consistency or efficiency of estimation in the case of a linear model with additive time dummies. In fact, GMM estimates with time dummies excluded and year means removed are numerically identical to those with time dummies included (and a vector of ones included in the instruments).

[15] This choice is based on prior experience with firm data (Hall, 1991; and Blundell, Bond, Devereux, and Schiantarelli, 1992). It errs on the side of caution and is, in fact, not strictly necessary in these data, as we shall see.

minimise in that metric. In large samples (asymptotically), the minimised statistic $f(\hat{\beta})\ \hat{\Omega}^{-1}\ f'\ (\hat{\beta})$ is distributed as a chi-squared random variable with degrees of freedom equal to the number of orthogonality conditions in (3) less the number of estimated parameters β. As an example, suppose T is 8 and τ is 3, as in our data; then the number of orthogonality conditions (3) is $(8\text{-}3\text{-}1)(8\text{-}3)/2 = 10$. In our equation (2) example there is one β, so that the degrees of freedom will be 9. It can be shown that the set of moment conditions in (3) is equivalent to that used in the instrumental variable estimation of the within estimator of (2) where the firm-level means have been computed only over observations which postdate any disturbance that might be correlated with the instruments. Both use all the available information in the data.[16]

We use (3) as our basic specification, with sales as the dependent variable and labour, capital and R&D capital as the independent variables, and then test for the additional moment restrictions implied by the validity of lag 2 instruments, lag 1 instruments, lag 0 instruments (weak exogeneity), and then by using all years as instruments for all equations (strong exogeneity). We then compare each of these specifications individually with specifications of the following form:

$$E\ [x_{is}\ u_{it}] = 0 \qquad t = \tau+1,...,T;\ \ s = 1,...,t\text{-}\tau\text{-}1 \tag{4}$$

The moment conditions defined by equation (4) are appropriate if the firm-level effects are not correlated with the x's. In order for the procedure outlined above to be valid and in order to guarantee a non-negative chi-squared statistic for the tests, it is necessary to use an equivalent consistent estimate of $\hat{\Omega}$ for all the estimates; we ensure this by forming our estimate of the sample covariance of the $\{x_{is}\Delta u_{it}\}$ or $\{x_{is}u_{it}\}$ using estimates of u_{it} that are based on the βs estimated using the weakest specification (that of equation (3) with only lag 3 and higher instruments).

A drawback to GMM estimation for panel data under the current state of the art is that the results of asymptotic theory are somewhat incomplete when the datasets are unbalanced. Conceptually, if there are a small number of patterns of missing data, it would be possible to estimate the model separately for each subset of firms which had data in a particular set of years, and then combine these estimates optimally using their variance estimates as weights (see Bound, Griliches, and Hall, 1986, for a discussion and demonstration of a similar methodology applied to maximum likelihood estimation). Provided the number

---

16   Schmidt, Ahn, and Wyhowski show that there are additional moment restrictions involving second moments of the disturbances available for estimation when their variances do not change over time; we have not exploited these here because the assumption of constant variances does not appear to hold in our data.

298   *J. Mairesse and B.H. Hall*

of subsamples is fixed and the number of firms within each is allowed to grow, it would be possible to obtain asymptotic results for such a method. However, implementing this approach to estimation is extremely cumbersome, and we have chosen a simpler solution here. We created two subsets of the data that are balanced for subperiods within our overall period: the first is 1981-1985 (with the years 1978, 1979, and 1980 available as instruments) and the second is 1985-1989 (with 1982-1984 available as instruments).

The results of our sequence of specification tests using these balanced panels are shown in graphs 1 and 2 for France and graphs 3 and 4 for the United States as nested χ^2 graphs (see pages 19 to 22). Choosing the appropriate size for such a sequence of tests is of course somewhat arbitrary; we have selected the one per cent level of significance because of the fairly large number of tests conducted. In both periods (1981-1985 and 1985-1989), the absence of correlation between firm effects and the instruments is clearly rejected in all cases for the French and the US data, somewhat weakly for the United States in the first period. The US data reject weak exogeneity in both periods in favour of lag 1+ instruments. This can be due either to simultaneity bias or to measurement error in the right hand side variables. The picture for France is slightly more confused: in the first period, the data accept the strong exogeneity of the right hand side variables, while in the second strong exogeneity is rejected in favour of lag 0+ instruments (weak exogeneity). We chose to use the weaker set of instruments for both periods so that the results would be comparable.

In tables 4 and 5 we display the results of our preferred estimations using GMM with lag 0+ instruments for France and lag 1+ instruments for the United States (fifth column). For comparison, we also show the GMM estimates only using the lag 3+ instruments (fourth column), and the conventional total and first differenced estimates of the production function. The latter is estimated with both beginning and end of year capital stocks, and the former with beginning of year stocks (three first columns). Note that since we are trying to correct for simultaneity bias, our GMM estimates are performed on the specification with the end of year capital stocks. The pattern of the estimates are roughly similar across countries. Both countries have fairly large capital coefficients in the totals which are very substantially reduced in the differenced estimates, especially when beginning of year capital is used or capital is instrumented. As in the results for the whole period, the coefficient of R&D capital is somewhat larger in the totals for France than for the United States, but disappears or turns negative in the first differences in the two countries. One interpretation could be that firms which invest heavily in R&D have higher productivity growth on average in the long run, but there is weaker evidence of a short run effect. Note also that the physical capital coefficient in France has not been helped by obtaining estimates which correct for simultaneity; in the within-firm dimension, it is still implausibly low, even negative, albeit somewhat poorly measured. This is less true in the United States; correcting for simultaneity bias lowers the physical capital coefficient only slightly, while wiping out the R&D capital coefficient.

Despite the roughly similar pattern of our estimates, it is interesting to indicate a possibly substantial difference between the two countries which may help to explain why we were able to accept the weak exogeneity of the capital stocks for France, but not for the United States. As already said, the influence of current sales on investment, either because sales signals future demand or because of liquidity considerations, is a very likely source of simultaneity between end of year capital stocks and current year sales. In France, the correlations of the growth rate of sales with that of investment and R&D are 0.21 and 0.12 respectively, while for the United States these numbers are 0.30 and 0.32. Thus this particular source of simultaneity bias is potentially higher in the United States than in France. It is tempting to speculate whether this difference is due to a greater sensitivity to financial constraints in the US firms, especially because the sample is drawn entirely from publicly traded enterprises that may find it difficult (or expensive) to finance any investment, and particularly investment in intangibles such as R&D, in the public equity or debt markets. The French firms, on the other hand, may face somewhat softer budget constraints, and the heavier involvement of the government in industrial R&D may mitigate the effects of sales or earnings fluctuations. At the moment, however, this is just speculation.

Finally, the substantive result emerging from tables 4 and 5 is that the "excess" productivity of R&D is essentially zero in both periods in the United States and France (and even possibly slightly negative in France). The former result agrees with the finding in Hall (1993b) that, during the 1980s, the market value of the R&D investment undertaken by this sample of firms indicated that no excess returns were expected from such investment.

Looking now at our GMM estimates from an efficiency technical point of view, the bad news is that adding more moment conditions by using all the available instruments leaves us with standard errors of our estimated coefficients which are much larger than the (heteroskedastic consistent) standard errors of the usual first differenced estimates (reported in column 3 or column 2). This is particularly striking for the labour and ordinary capital coefficients, but much less for the R-D capital coefficient. The first stage R-squares suggest why: the growth of R&D capital is much more predictable from the past levels of capital and labour than is the growth of ordinary capital and the coefficient of this variable is therefore somewhat better measured than the others when we instrument it.[17]

---

[17]   These R-squares are the following: for France, .073, .295, and .531 for the growth

TABLE 4
Estimates for the Balanced French Panels, Dependent Variable: Log Sales

Independent Variable	Totals	First Diff.	First Diff.	GMM FE, 3+ Inst.	GMM FE, 0+ Inst.	GMM (IV) FE, 0+ Inst.	IV FE, 0+ Inst.
1981-1985: 447 Firms							
Log L	.548(.026)	.630(.061)	.573(.064)	1.213(.177)	1.049(.108)	.995(.125)	1.095(.204)
Log C	.307(.018)	-.028(.036)	.152(.048)	-.124(.086)	-.081(.061)	-.044(.067)	-.087(.090)
Log K	.103(.009)	.018(.036)	.075(.035)	-.085(.080)	-.063(.041)	-.056(.045)	-.092(.062)
std err	.487	.129	.127				
χ^2(d.f.)				35.5 (27)	67.8 (63)	48.0 (45)	17.6 (9)
1985-1989: 381 Firms							
Log L	.543(.026)	.752(.050)	.700(.055)	.425(.118)	.467(.084)	.445(.096)	.126(.160)
Log C	.356(.018)	-.066(.039)	.063(.042)	.015(.112)	.039(.066)	-.010(.082)	-.183(.118)
Log K	.078(.011)	-.132(.052)	.034(.055)	-.162(.102)	-.138(.044)	-.105(.054)	-.193(.077)
std err	.475	.148	.149				
χ^2(d.f.)				27.5 (27)	72.1 (63)	51.3 (45)	5.7 (9)

The variables are the same as in table 2, with capital stocks at the beginning of year for the first two columns, and at the end of year for the five last ones. All equations contain year dummies and industry dummies at the level given in table 1. Heteroscedastic-consistent estimates of the standard errors are shown in parentheses.

The method of estimation in the first 3 columns is ordinary least squares. In the last 4 columns two-step GMM is used. The column labelled IV uses only those moment conditions that are implied by the usual pooled IV estimator, while that labelled GMM(IV) uses the same moments, but imposes them for each year of data separately. See the text for a description of the instruments.

TABLE 5
Estimates for the Balanced US Panels, Dependent Variable: Log Sales

Independent Variable	Totals	First Diff.	First Diff.	GMM FE, 3+ Inst.	GMM FE, 1+ Inst.	GMM (IV) FE, 1+ Inst.	IV FE, 1+ Inst.
1981-1985: 535 Firms							
Log L	.576(.015)	.650(.028)	.555(.028)	.877(.130)	.897(.076)	.881(.093)	1.26 (.22)
Log C	.358(.012)	.088(.027)	.190(.029)	.218(.143)	.144(.090)	.126(.103)	.012(.156)
Log K	.035(.007)	.027(.032)	.120(.035)	.009(.102)	.033(.061)	.031(.067)	-.062(.083)
std err	.325	.129	.127				
χ^2(d.f.)				42.0 (27)	81.7 (51)	62.7 (33)	10.8 (6)
1985-1989: 442 Firms							
Log L	.639(.015)	.542(.030)	.423(.032)	.317(.116)	.384(.076)	.489(.104)	.552(.160)
Log C	.313(.015)	.138(.030)	.212(.035)	.336(.130)	.172(.085)	.099(.109)	-.057(.163)
Log K	.041(.008)	-.033(.040)	.147(.045)	-.139(.091)	-.039(.048)	.006(.059)	.069(.084)
std err	.343	.132	.130				
χ^2(d.f.)				32.8 (27)	61.2 (51)	49.7 (33)	21.1 (6)

See table 4 for precisions on the variables and methods of estimation.

Tables 4 and 5 also reveal an interesting fact about the efficiency gain from using GMM estimation for panel data rather than the conventional IV methods with stacked data. The column before last in the tables gives the GMM estimates (noted GMM (IV)) using as instruments only the lags 0 to 3 of the variables (for France) or the lags 1 to 3 (for the US), while the last column gives the standard IV estimates computed by using a GMM estimator only on the moment conditions corresponding to the stacked model.[18] All standard error estimates shown are robust, computed using the estimated variance of the orthogonality conditions from the model with lag 3+ instruments only, and so they can be directly compared. What is clear from the tables is that adding the longer lags as instruments where available produces little or no efficiency gain (because these additional lags are highly correlated with the instruments already present), but that switching from IV to GMM comes close to halving the standard errors. The reason is simple: GMM allows the projection on the instruments to be different for every year, whereas IV constrains it to be the same. In the traditional two stage least squares interpretation, GMM is using many more predictor variables, which implies a better predictor for the endogenous variables in finite samples, and hence smaller standard errors in general. Which estimator is preferred depends somewhat on what we are willing to assume about the process generating our right-hand-side variables. Because there is no reason to assume that it will be the same every year when we include longer and longer lags as instruments, it seems plausible to allow the projection coefficients to vary. We suspect that the case here is not atypical, and that the efficiency gain from GMM in panel data is coming primarily from the different year instruments and not simply from the additional lags.[19]

---

rates of labor, capital, and R&D capital in the first period, and .089, .221, and .543 in the second period. For the United States, the numbers are .031, .107, and .444 for the first period and .018, .058, and .451 for the second.

[18] It can be shown that the IV moment condition corresponding to the orthogonality conditions $\left[\sum_{i=1}^{N} (u_{it} \otimes z_i) = 0, \ t = 1,..,T \right]$ is $\sum_{t=1}^{T} \sum_{i=1}^{N} (u_{it} \otimes z_i) = 0$. That is, the equivalent IV conditions just sum the relevant moment conditions over all the years in the panel. In the French case for example, there are 48 OCs in the second to the last column (= 4 years times 3 instruments times 4 lags). IV reduces this to 12 (=3 instruments times 4 lags).

[19] Note, however, that the small sample biases may become severe with an increasing number of instruments. See Bound, Jaeger and Baker (1993).

GRAPH 1
Testing for Exogeneity and Correlated Firm Effects
447 French Manufacturing Firms 1981-1985

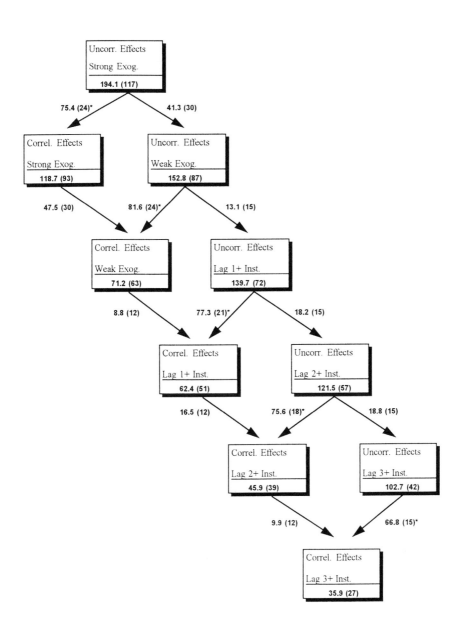

GRAPH 2
Testing for Exogeneity and Correlated Firm Effects
381 French Manufacturing Firms 1985-1989

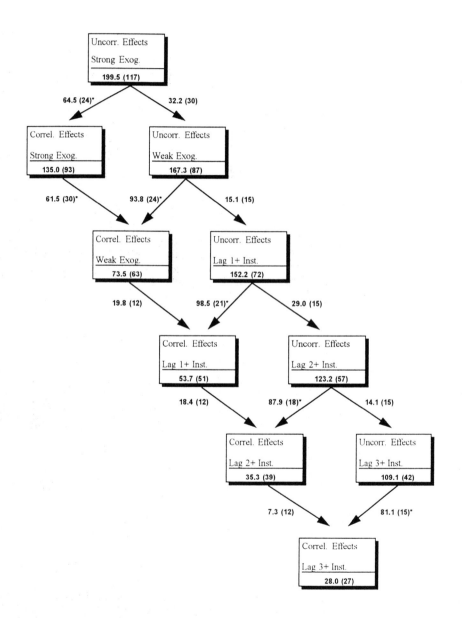

GRAPH 3
Testing for Exogeneity and Correlated Firm Effects
535 U.S. Manufacturing Firms 1981-1985

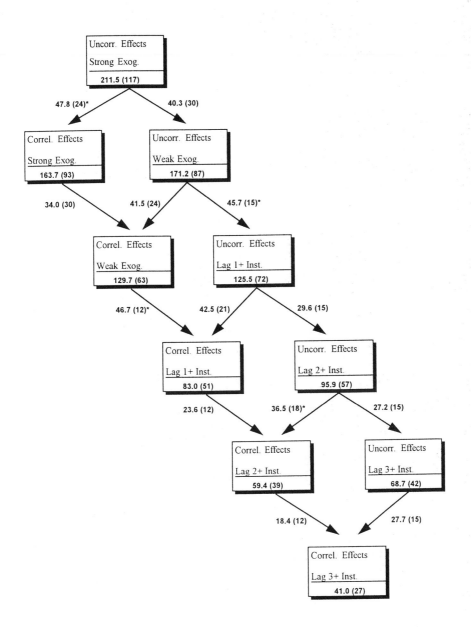

GRAPH 4
Testing for Exogeneity and Correlated Firm Effects
442 U.S. Manufacturing Firms 1985-1989

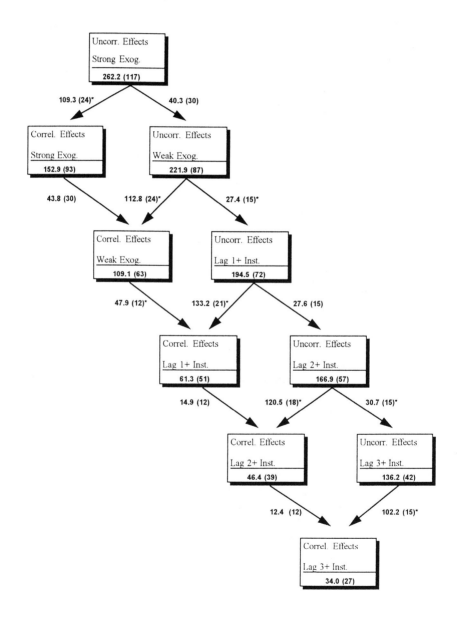

5. Conclusions

In analysing the regressions presented in tables 2 through 5 and their many variants, we have reached the following conclusions: 1) The R&D contribution to sales or productivity growth during the 1980s seems to be somewhat lower in the 1980s than it was in the 1970s in both countries. 2) Using sales instead of value added does not seriously bias the results, although attempting instead to correct for materials inputs may. 3) The dating of the capital stocks makes a huge difference to their estimated coefficients. All of the estimates shown in table 2 are based on beginning of period stocks, and the end of period estimates would be about half again as high. This suggested simultaneity between both kinds of investment and sales (due to demand or liquidity shocks). Although this explanation seems to hold for the United States, where we reject the exogeneity of capital in the production function equation, it is less persuasive for France, where contemporaneous instruments are accepted. We advanced the tentative hypothesis that the difference in behaviour across countries is due to the fact that liquidity constraints impact US R&D-doing firms more than French firms. 4) Finally, the capital stock coefficient in the within firm estimates in France is zero (or negative), which we regard as a puzzle, and possibly a warning about the data.

With respect to the main substantive finding of this paper, we want to stress the two following points. First, the measured R&D elasticity using data which is not corrected for double counting ought to be zero if R&D investment is earning a "normal" rate of return, comparable to that of other inputs. It is not unlikely that this is the situation in the United States during the 1980s, when total industrial R&D was not growing that quickly. Hall (1993a) finds that the stock market valuation of the same firms' R&D capital has fallen by a factor of 4 during the 1980s, which implies that the market has perhaps recognized the relatively low private productivity of such investment.

Second, the results for the United States that use a sales measure deflated by a two-digit level deflator and adjust to some extent for quality change are suggestive: here we find a very substantial excess contribution of R&D to productivity growth (0.10 within firm). The implication is that R&D investment has been very productive in increasing "true" output, but that most of the gains have gone to the consumer in the form of lower prices. Because the price indices for the United States are only partially corrected for quality change, and because those for France have essentially no such correction, we regard this last finding as an invitation for future research that attempts to focus on the quality as well as quantity of output.

Appendix - GMM Estimation for a Linear Panel Data Model with Fixed Effects

A - General Methodology

The general methodology described here is based on that of Arellano and Bond (1991), Arellano (1988), and Schmidt, Ahn and Wynkowski (1992). The authors of these papers categorise the moment conditions implied by the use of linear regression models with predetermined rather than exogenous right hand side variables in a panel data setting and suggest estimating this type of model by means of the generalized method of moments (GMM). GMM is appealing in this setting because it is robust to heteroskedasticity across firms and correlation of the disturbances within firms over time, and can be efficient under fairly weak assumptions on the disturbances.

The most general model being considered is a random coefficients model with correlated effects:

$$y_{it} = x_{it}\beta_i + \alpha_i + \varepsilon_{it} \qquad\qquad i = 1,...,N; \ t = 1,...,T$$

$$y_{it} = x_{it}\overline{\beta} + v_i x_{it} + \alpha_i + \varepsilon_{it} \qquad\qquad \text{where } v_i = \beta_i - \overline{\beta}$$

The overall means of the data have been removed, so that we can assume $E[\alpha_i] = 0$ without loss of generality. The maintained stochastic assumptions are the following:

$$
\begin{array}{ll}
E[\varepsilon_{it}] = 0 & E[\varepsilon_{it}^2] = \sigma^2 \\
E[v_i] = 0 & E[v_i^2] = \sigma_v^2 \\
E[\varepsilon_{it}\varepsilon_{js}] = 0 & \text{for } i \neq j \text{ and for all } t,s \\
E[v_i v_j] = 0 & \text{for } i \neq j \\
E[\alpha_i \alpha_j] = 0 & \text{for } i \neq j
\end{array}
$$

However, we do not necessarily wish to assume that $E[\alpha_i | x_{i1},..., x_{iT}] = 0$. If we define a new composite disturbance as

$$u_{it} = v_i x_{it} + \alpha_i + \varepsilon_{it}$$

and its first difference as

$$\Delta u_{it} = v_i \Delta x_{it} + \Delta \varepsilon_{it}$$

then the covariance matrix for $\Delta u_i' = (\Delta u_{i1}, \Delta u_{i2}, ..., \Delta u_{iT})$ is

$$E[\Delta u_i \, \Delta u_i' | x_i] = \sigma_v^2 \Delta x_i \, \Delta x_i' + E[\Delta \varepsilon_i \Delta \varepsilon_i']$$

where Δx_i and $\Delta \varepsilon_i$ have been defined analogously to Δu_i. Even without the presence of the α_i, this covariance matrix is intrinsically heteroskedastic as well as non-diagonal, once we allow for random coefficients. Thus we prefer GMM estimation on the moments of u_{it} or Δu_{it} with lagged and current values of the x's; which lags are chosen is a subject for exploration in the body of the paper.

Our general procedure is to begin with a fairly weak assumption about orthogonality between the disturbance and the lagged right hand side variables, such as orthogonality between x's lagged three times and contemporaneous disturbances, and then to add more recent lags until the additional restrictions are rejected by a chi-squared test on the orthogonality conditions. To be more precise, let all our moment conditions be defined as

$$E[u_i(\beta) \otimes z_i] = 0$$

where

$$u_i(\beta) = [u_{i1}(\beta), u_{i2}(\beta), ..., u_{iT}(\beta)] \quad \text{and} \quad u_{it}(\beta) = y_{it} - x_{it}\beta$$

$$z_i = [z_{i1}, ..., z_{im}] \text{ and } m = \text{number of instruments per year}$$

The sample equivalents of these moment conditions are

$$f(\beta) = \frac{1}{N}\sum_{i=1}^{N} f_i(\beta) = \frac{1}{N}\sum_{i=1}^{N} u_i(\beta) \otimes z_i$$

The GMM estimator of β minimises the quantity

$$\phi(\beta) = f'(\beta) A f(\beta)$$

with respect to β, where A is a positive definite symmetric matrix. If A can be chosen as a consistent estimate of the inverse of the covariance matrix Ω of $f(\beta)$, this estimator will be consistent and asymptotically efficient. Even if A is inconsistent, the estimates of β will be consistent under fairly general conditions (Amemiya, 1977; Chamberlain, 1984; Hansen, 1982).

To estimate Ω and A consistently, we obtain estimates of β by a consistent method for our maintained model (the one using the smallest number of orthogonality conditions), and compute the estimated residuals based on these β's:

$$\hat{u} = y_{it} - x_{it}\hat{\beta} \qquad i = 1,....,N; t = 1,....,T$$

The sample covariance of $\hat{u}_i \otimes z_i$ is then computed; note that it is necessary in computing this covariance that the sample means of $\hat{u}_i \otimes z_i$ be removed, because we do not assume that $E[u_i \otimes z_i] = 0$ for all moments of u and z under

J. Mairesse and B.H. Hall

the maintained model. Alternative methods for obtaining estimates of Ω and A are discussed below.

When we implement this GMM estimator for panel data, the z_i vector is the entire list of potential instruments $(x_{i1}, x_{i2}, ..., x_{iT})$ and the $u_i(\beta)$ are actually $\Delta u_i(\beta)$, the set of equations for the disturbances in the first differenced version of the maintained model. To test $E[\alpha_i \mid x_{i1}, ..., x_{iT}] = 0$, we add a set of moment conditions of the form $E[u_{it}(\beta) \otimes z_i] = 0$ to the set of differenced equations. This is equivalent to estimating the entire set of moment conditions in levels, but in this form the maintained model is clearly nested within the model which does not have correlated effects.

Until now, the Kronecker product notation, familiar from the work of Hansen (1982) and Hansen and Singleton (1982) has been used to simplify presentation. However, this notation is not generally suitable for panel data, because each time period t has a different number of instruments available with which to form orthogonality conditions. Our solution is to use a selection matrix on the original complete set of moment conditions, so that those which are not valid for a particular specification are not constrained to be zero. Define a kT by 1 vector S of zeroes and ones that selects the appropriate moments from $\dfrac{1}{N} \sum\limits_{i=1}^{N} u_i \otimes z_i$

Then the solution to the problem

$$\min_{\beta} \ f'(\beta) \ diag(S) \ \hat{A} \ diag(S) \ f(\beta)$$

is equivalent to the GMM estimator based only on the moment conditions which are valid under various exogeneity assumptions. Although these two estimators of β are equivalent (both are consistent), they do not necessarily coincide, since it is possible that the unused moment conditions will contribute covariance elements to the estimated covariance of $f(\beta)$, and these will appear in the computation of $\hat{A}$. One way around this particular problem is to use $diag(S)$ in the computation of the covariance matrix itself. This is what is done here.

B - Actual Implementation

Our implementation of the different GMM estimators for our specific model is very similar to that of Arellano and Bond (1991) and Blundell and Bond (1994), although we have been using TSP rather than Gauss.

After differencing to remove the fixed effects, the model is the following:

$$\Delta u_{it} = \Delta y_{it} - \Delta x_{it}\beta$$

The x's are not necessarily strictly or even weakly exogenous. Firms index by $i = 1,...,N$ and years by $t = 1,...,T$, with $T'-T$ years of presample data available. There are instruments available (including lagged x's) called z (m in each year, $t = T-T'+1,...,0,1,...,T$). Define the following row vectors:

$$\Delta u_i = (\Delta u_{i1}, \Delta u_{i2}, ..., \Delta u_{iT}) \text{ and } z_i = (z_i^{(1)}, z_i^{(2)},..., z_i^{(m)})$$

where

$$z_i^{(m)} = (z_{i,T-T'+1}^{(m)}, z_{i,T-T'+2}^{(m)},..., z_{i,0}^{(m)}, z_{i,1}^{(m)}, ..., z_{i,T}^{(m)}) \qquad \text{for all } m.$$

There are mT' elements in z_i and T elements in Δu_i. We begin by assuming that all the z's are valid instruments. Then the TmT' orthogonality conditions for the linear model specified above are the following:

$$f_i(\beta) = \Delta u_i \otimes z_i$$

The GMM estimator minimizes $\phi(\beta)$ with respect to β where

$$\phi(\beta) = \left[\frac{1}{N}\sum_{i=1}^{N}f_i(\beta)\right] A \left[\frac{1}{N}\sum_{i=1}^{N}f_i(\beta)\right]'$$

Asymptotically efficient estimates are obtained when $A = A_\infty$, the inverse of the true covariance of the moment conditions, or when A is replaced with a consistent estimator of A_∞. The GMM procedure in TSP uses the inverse of the sample covariance of the $f_i(\beta)$, evaluated at a consistent estimator of β (specifically, that from three stage least squares). Other consistent estimators of A can be computed if stronger assumptions are placed on the Δu's. We explore some of these possibilities here.

The sample covariance of the $\hat{f}_i = \Delta \hat{u}_i \otimes z_i$ is given by the following expression:[19]

$$A_N^{-1} = \frac{1}{N}\sum_{i=1}^{N}\left(\Delta \hat{u}_i \Delta \hat{u}_i' \otimes z_i z_i'\right)$$

---

[19] As noted above, because the time series structure of panel data means that the appropriate instruments are generally different for different time periods, in practice we will use a selection matrix to select the relevant moments from this Kronecker product.

The above equation suggests several ways to estimate the weighting matrix for GMM estimation:

(1) If the Δu_i are independently and identically distributed over time and across firms, then

$$plim \left[A_N^{-1} \right] = \sigma^2 I_T \otimes plim \left[\frac{Z'Z}{N} \right]$$

Therefore, use

$$A_N(1) = \left[\hat{\sigma}^2 I_T \otimes \frac{1}{N} \sum_{i=1}^{N} z_i z_i' \right]^{-1}$$

where $\hat{\sigma}^2$ is based on an initial consistent estimate of β (e.g, two or three stage least squares).

(2) If the Δu_i are serially correlated, but identically distributed across firms, then

$$plim \left[A_N^{-1} \right] = \Sigma \otimes plim \left[\frac{\acute{Z}Z}{N} \right] \qquad \text{where } \Sigma = plim \left[\Delta u \, \Delta \acute{u} \right]$$

$$A_N(2) = \left[\hat{\Sigma} \otimes \frac{1}{N} \sum_{i=1}^{N} z_i z_i' \right]^{-1}$$

where $\hat{\Sigma}$ is again based on an initial consistent estimate of β.

(3) If the Δu_i are independent across firms, but serially correlated and heteroskedastic, use the full GMM weighting matrix (as in Hansen and Singleton, 1982):

$$A_N(3) = \left[\frac{1}{N} \sum_{i=1}^{N} \Delta \hat{u}_i \Delta \hat{u}_i' \otimes z_i z_i' \right]^{-1}$$

Estimates of β computed using these three estimates of A_N plus an estimate simply equal to the identity matrix are shown in table A.1. Estimates of the standard errors that are consistent even if A_N is not equal to the covariance of the orthogonality conditions are also shown in this table. Except for the identity matrix case, there is little difference between either the estimated coefficients or the standard errors across different choices of A_N for these data. This contrasts with findings reported in Blundell and Bond (1995) and may reflect our relatively large sample size.

TABLE A.1
Different Estimates of A_N, Balanced US Panel: 1986-1989

	Lag 3+ Instruments	Lag 2+ Instruments	Lag 1+ Instruments	Lag 0+ (Weak Exog.)	Strong Exogeneity
$A_N = I$					
Log L	-.04 (.30)	0.27 (.10)	0.39 (.08)	0.46 (.07)	0.44 (.06)
Log C	0.78 (.38)	0.46 (.11)	0.32 (.09)	0.25 (.07)	0.39 (.06)
Log K	-.14 (.71)	-.09 (.08)	-.05 (.05)	-.04 (.05)	-.08 (.04)
Trace (DF)	35.4 (27)	51.6 (39)	67.2 (51)	103.2 (63)	166.9 (93)
P-value	0.128	0.085	0.064	0.001	0.000
Inst. Test (DF)	--	16.1 (12)	15.6 (12)	36.0 (12)**	63.8 (30)**

$$A_N(1) = \frac{\sigma^2}{N} [I_T \otimes Z' Z]$$

Log L	0.41 (.11)	0.30 (.10)	0.41 (.08)	0.46 (.07)	0.44 (.06)
Log C	0.53 (.15)	0.39 (.11)	0.29 (.08)	0.24 (.07)	0.33 (.06)
Log K	-.11 (.11)	-.06 (.08)	-.05 (.05)	-.04 (.05)	-.07 (.04)
Trace (DF)	36.2 (27)	51.2 (39)	66.8 (51)	103.5 (63)	166.8 (93)
P-value	0.11	0.09	0.068	0.001	0.000
Inst. Tes (DF)	--	15.0 (12)	15.6 (12)	36.8 (12)**	63.2 (30)**

$$A_N(2) = \Sigma \otimes \frac{1}{N} Z' Z$$

Log L	0.43 (.10)	0.32 (.10)	0.42 (.08)	0.47 (.07)	0.41 (.06)
Log C	0.42 (.12)	0.36 (.10)	0.28 (.08)	0.24 (.07)	0.33 (.06)
Log K	-.10 (.08)	-.05 (.08)	-.04 (.05)	-.04 (.05)	-.07 (.04)
Trace (DF)	39.6 (27)	51.1 (39)	66.6 (51)	103.7 (63)	166.7 (93)
P-value	0.056	0.092	0.070	0.001	0.000
Inst. Test (DF)	--	16.1 (12)	15.5 (12)	37.0 (12)**	63.1 (30)**

$$A_N(3) = \frac{1}{N} \sum_{i=1}^{N} [\Delta u_i \Delta u_i' \otimes z_i z_i']$$

Log L	0.33 (.10)	0.33 (.10)	0.42 (.08)	0.47 (.07)	0.44 (.06)
Log C	0.33 (.10)	0.34 (.10)	0.28 (.08)	0.24 (.07)	0.33 (.06)
Log K	0.00 (.08)	-.02 (.08)	-.04 (.05)	-.04 (.05)	-.07 (.04)
Trace (DF)	32.8 (27)	51.2 (39)	66.6 (51)	103.7 (63)	166.7 (93)
P-value	0.205	0.091	0.070	0.001	0.000
Inst. Tes (DF)	--	18.5 (12)	15.4 (12)	37.1 (12)**	63.0 (30)**

Notes: see next page

Notes:
All standard error estimates are robust to the presence of heteroskedasticity.
The row labelled "Inst. Test" is a chi-squared test for the validity of the additional instruments in the corresponding column, relative to the column on the left. This test statistic is distributed asymptotically as a chi-squared random variable with degrees of freedom equal to the number of additional moment restrictions under the null that all of the moment restrictions used hold. ** denotes values of the statistic for which the p-value is less then 0.01.

References

Amemiya, T. (1977), "The Maximum Likelihood and the Three Stage Least Squares Estimator in the Crest Nonlinear Simultaneous Equations Model", *Econometrica*, No. 45.

--- and T. MaCurdy (1986), "Instrumental Variable Estimation of an Error-Components Model", *Econometrica*, No. 54.

Arellano, M. (1988), "An Alternative Transformation for Fixed Effects Models with Predetermined Variables", Oxford University Applied Discussion Paper No. 57, Institute of Economics and Statistics, Oxford University.

--- and S. Bond (1991), "Some Tests of Specification for Panel Data: Monte Carlo Evidence and an Application to Employment Equations", *Review of Economic Studies*, No. 58.

Blundell, R.S., S. Bond, M. Devereux, and F. Schiantarelli (1992), "Investment and Tobin's Q", *Journal of Econometrics*, No. 51.

--- and S. Bond (1995), "Initial Conditions and Moment Restrictions in Dynamic Panel Data Models", University College (London)/Nuffield College (Oxford), mimeographed.

Bound, J., Z. Griliches, and B.H. Hall (1986), "Wages, Schooling, and IQ of Brothers and Sisters: Do the Family Factors Differ?", *International Economic Review*, No. 27.

---, D.A. Jaeger, and R. Baker (1993), "The Cure can be worse than the disease: A Cautionary Tale Regarding Instrumental Variables", National Bureau of Economic Research Technical Working Paper No. 137, Cambridge, Mass..

Chamberlain, G. (1984), "Panel Data", in Griliches, Z, and M. Intriligator (eds.), *The Handbook of Econometrics*, Volume II, Amsterdam, North Holland.

Cuneo, P. and J. Mairesse (1984), "Productivity and R&D at the Firm Level in French Manufacturing", in Griliches, Zvi, (ed.), *R&D, Patents, and Productivity*, Chicago, Ill., University of Chicago Press.

Gray, W. (1992), "TFP: The Productivity Database", Cambridge, Mass.: National Bureau of Economic Research, Diskette.

Griliches, Z. and J.A. Hausman (1986), "Errors in Variables in Panel Data", *Journal of Econometrics*, vol. 31.

--- and J. Mairesse (1983), "Comparing Productivity Growth: An Exploration of French and U.S. Industrial and Firm Data", *European Economic Review*, vol. 21.

--- and J. Mairesse (1990), "R&D and Productivity Growth: Comparing Japanese and U.S. Manufacturing Firms", in Hulten, Charles R. (ed.), *Productivity Growth in Japan and the United States*,, University of Chicago Press, Chicago, Illinois.

--- and J. Mairesse (1995), "Production Functions: The Search for Identification", National Bureau of Economic Research Working Paper No. 5067, Cambridge, Mass.

Hall, B.H. (1993a), "The Stock Market Valuation of Research and Development Investment During the 1980s", *American Economic Review*, vol. 83.

--- (1993b), "Industrial Research During the 1980s: Did the Rate of Return Fall?", *Brookings Papers on Economic Activity. Micro Economics* (2), Washington D.C.

--- (1991), "R&D Investment at the Firm Level: Does the Source of Financing Matter?", mimeographed.

--- (1990) "The Manufacturing Sector Master File: 1959-1987", National Bureau of Economic Research Working Paper No. 3366, Cambridge, Mass.

--- and J. Mairesse (1995), "Exploring the Relationship between R&D and Productivity in French Manufacturing Firms", *Journal of Econometrics*, vol. 65.

Hall, R.E. (1988) "The Relation between Price and Marginal Cost in U.S. Industry", *Journal of Political Economy*, vol. 96.

Hansen, L.P. (1982) "Large Sample Properties of Methods of Moments Estimators", *Econometrica*, vol. 50.

--- and K. Singleton (1982), "Generalized Instrumental Variables Estimation of Nonlinear Expectations Models, *Econometrica*, vol. 50.

Holtz-Eakin, D., W. Newey, and H. Rosen (1988), "Estimating Vector Autoregressions with Panel Data", *Econometrica*, vol. 56.

Keane, M.P. and D.E. Runkle (1992), "On the Estimation of Panel Data Models with Serial Correlation When Instruments are not Strictly Exogenous", *Journal of Business and Economic Statistics*, vol. 10.

Mairesse, J. and M. Sassenou (1991), "R&D and Productivity: A Survey of Econometric Studies at the Firm Level", *Science-Technology-Industry Review*, No. 8. Paris, OECD.

OECD (1991), *Basic Science and Technology Statistics*, OECD, Paris.

Schankerman, M. (1981), "The Effect of Double Counting and Expensing on the Measured Returns to R&D", *Review of Economics and Statistics*, vol. 63.

Schmidt, P., S.C. Ahn, and D. Wyhowski (1992), "Comment on Keane and Runkle", *Journal of Business and Economic Statistics*, vol. 10.

Subject Index

Author Index